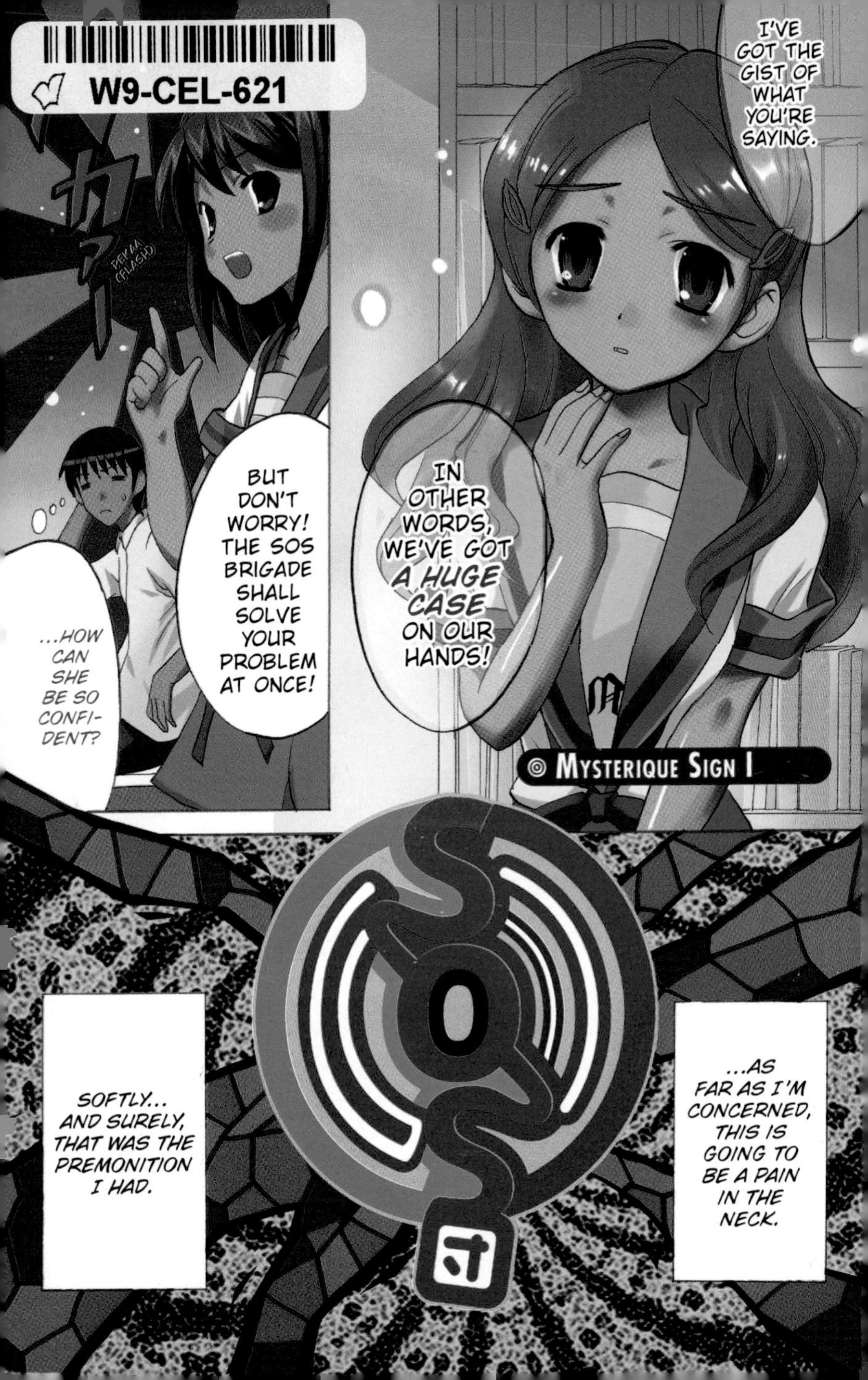
I'VE GOT THE GIST OF WHAT YOU'RE SAYING.
IN OTHER WORDS, WE'VE GOT A HUGE CASE ON OUR HANDS!
BUT DON'T WORRY! THE SOS BRIGADE SHALL SOLVE YOUR PROBLEM AT ONCE!
PEKAA (FLASH)
...HOW CAN SHE BE SO CONFI-DENT?
MYSTERIQUE SIGN I
...AS FAR AS I'M CONCERNED, THIS IS GOING TO BE A PAIN IN THE NECK.
SOFTLY... AND SURELY, THAT WAS THE PREMONITION I HAD.

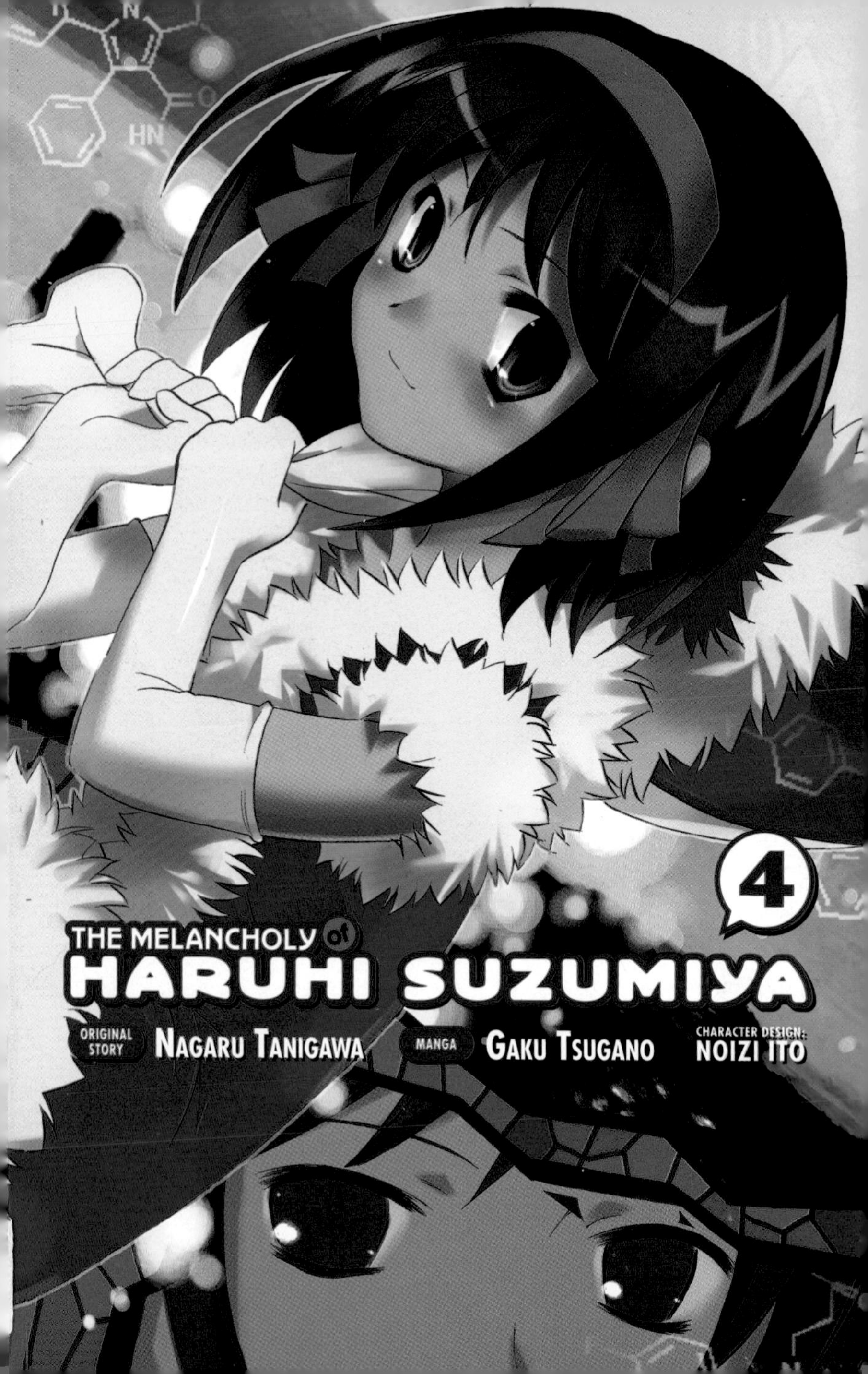
4
THE MELANCHOLY of
HARUHI SUZUMIYA
ORIGINAL STORY NAGARU TANIGAWA
MANGA GAKU TSUGANO
CHARACTER DESIGN: NOIZI ITO

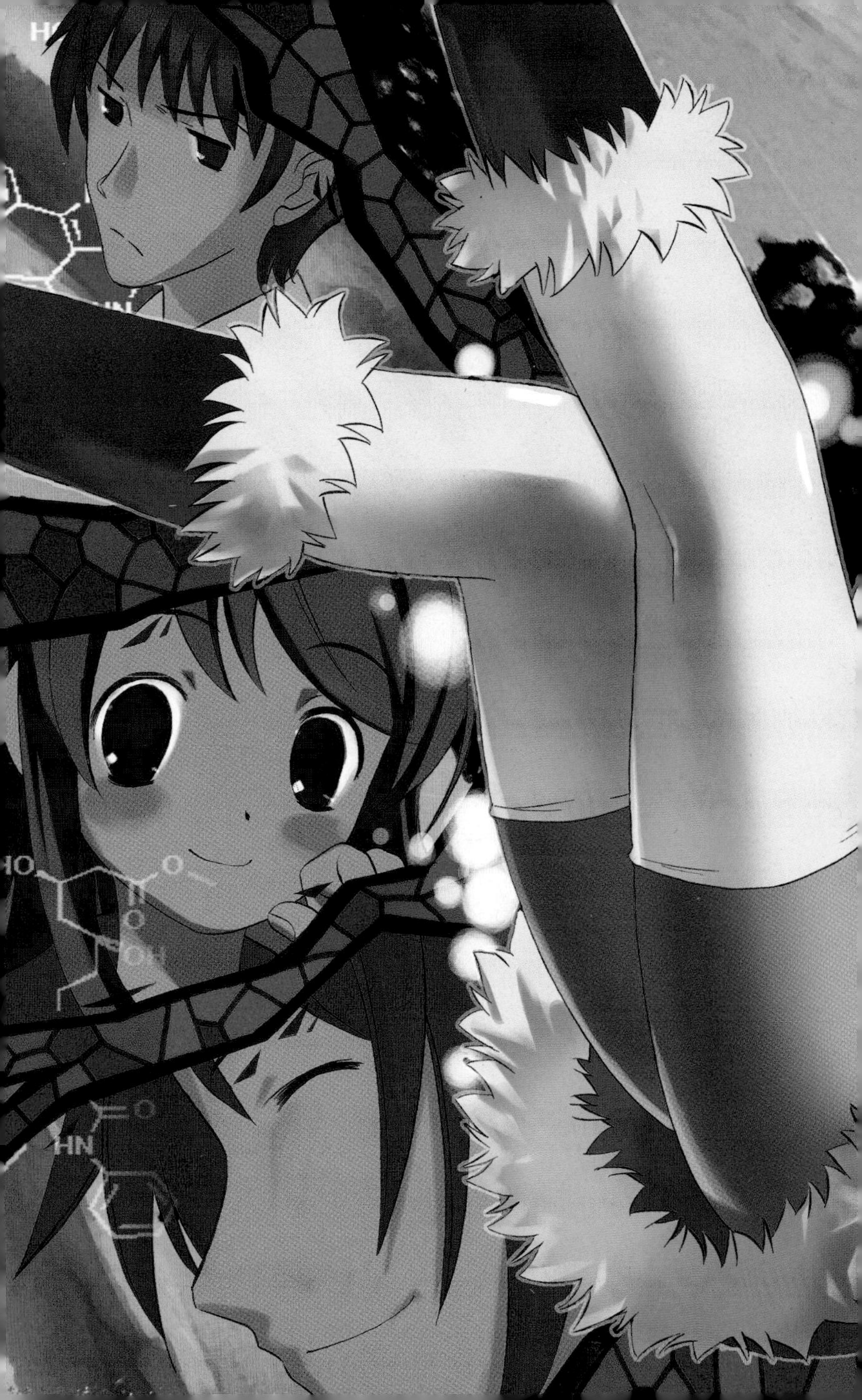

CONTENTS

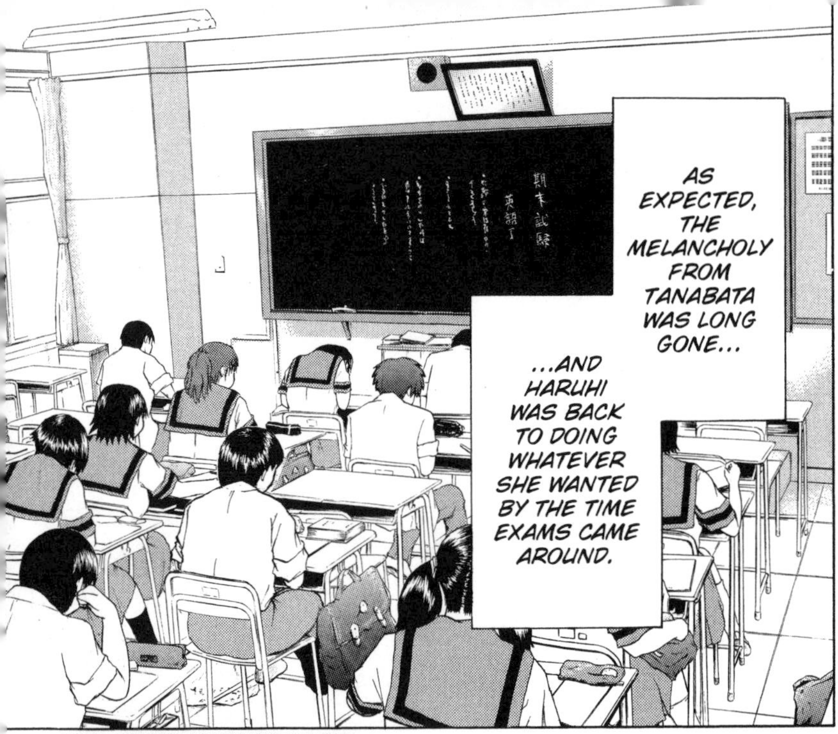
AS EXPECTED, THE MELANCHOLY FROM TANABATA WAS LONG GONE...
...AND HARUHI WAS BACK TO DOING WHATEVER SHE WANTED BY THE TIME EXAMS CAME AROUND.

PAPER: TERM REPORT FOR THE YEAR XXXX

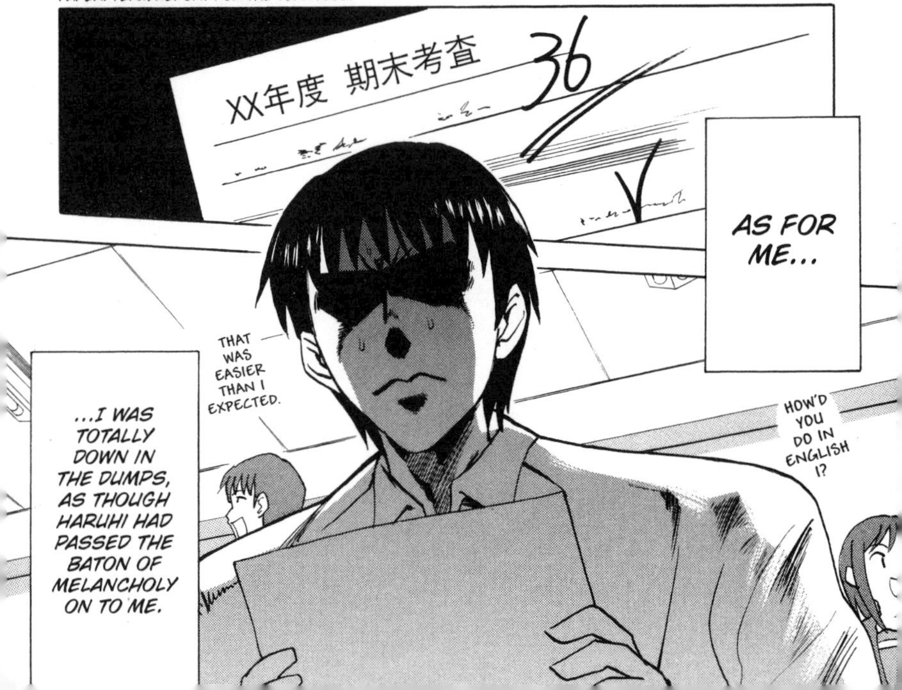
XX年度 期末考査
36
AS FOR ME...
HOW'D YOU DO IN ENGLISH I?
THAT WAS EASIER THAN I EXPECTED.
...I WAS TOTALLY DOWN IN THE DUMPS, AS THOUGH HARUHI HAD PASSED THE BATON OF MELANCHOLY ON TO ME.

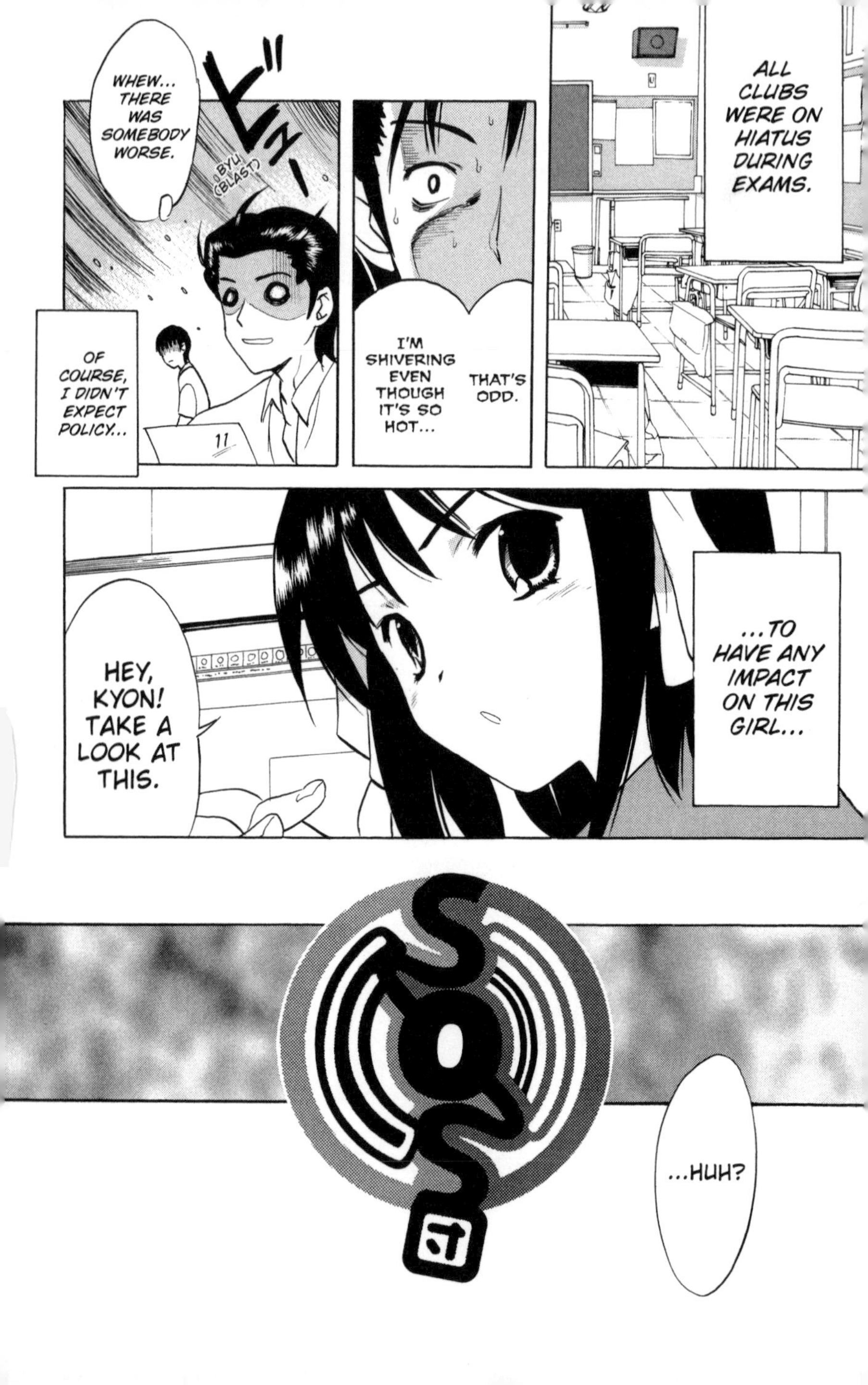
ALL CLUBS WERE ON HIATUS DURING EXAMS.
THAT'S ODD.
I'M SHIVERING EVEN THOUGH IT'S SO HOT...
WHEW... THERE WAS SOMEBODY WORSE.
BYU (BLAST)
11
OF COURSE, I DIDN'T EXPECT POLICY...
...TO HAVE ANY IMPACT ON THIS GIRL...
HEY, KYON! TAKE A LOOK AT THIS.
...HUH?

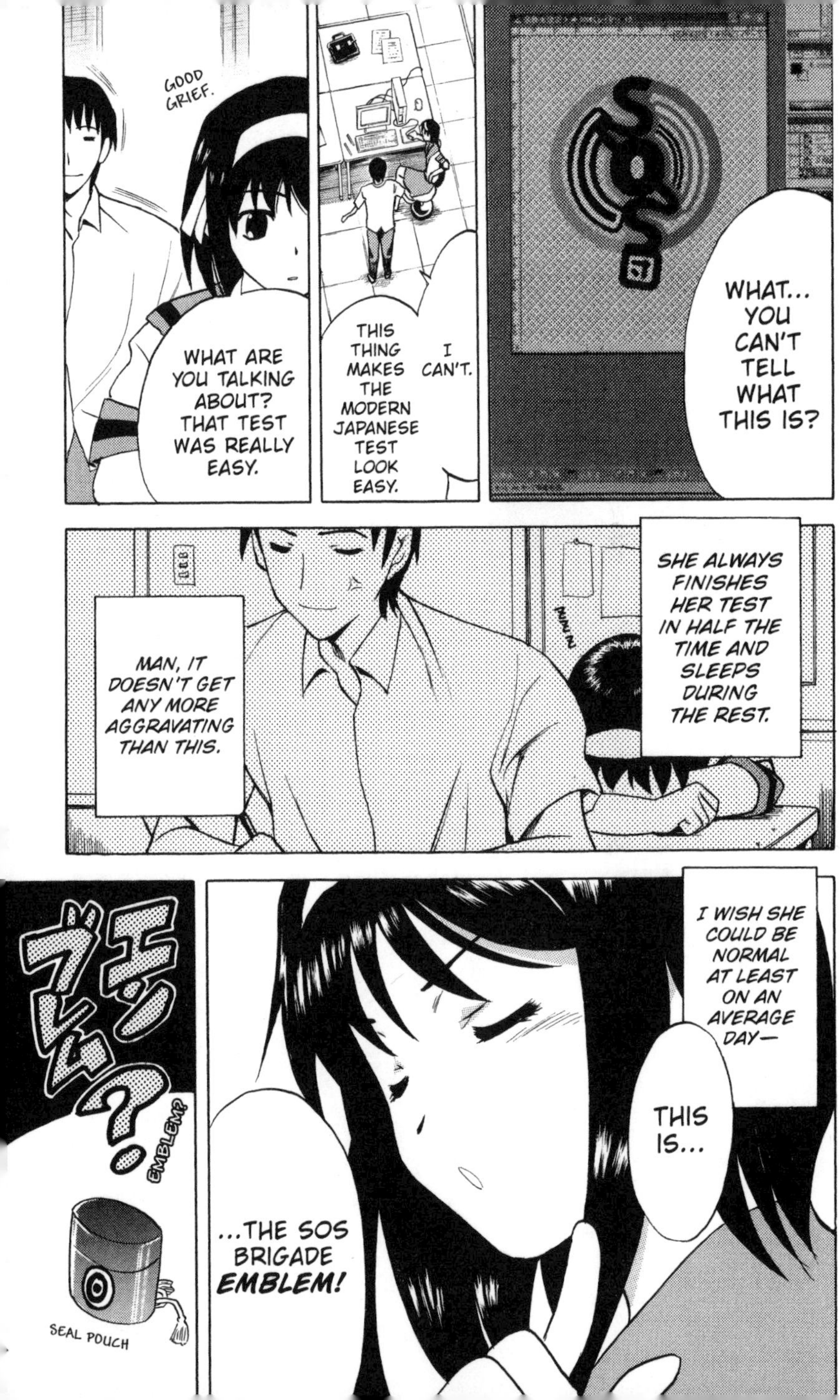
WHAT... YOU CAN'T TELL WHAT THIS IS?
I CAN'T.
THIS THING MAKES THE MODERN JAPANESE TEST LOOK EASY.
GOOD GRIEF.
WHAT ARE YOU TALKING ABOUT? THAT TEST WAS REALLY EASY.
SHE ALWAYS FINISHES HER TEST IN HALF THE TIME AND SLEEPS DURING THE REST.
MAN, IT DOESN'T GET ANY MORE AGGRAVATING THAN THIS.
I WISH SHE COULD BE NORMAL AT LEAST ON AN AVERAGE DAY—
THIS IS...
...THE SOS BRIGADE EMBLEM!
エンブレム？
EMBLEM?
SEAL POUCH

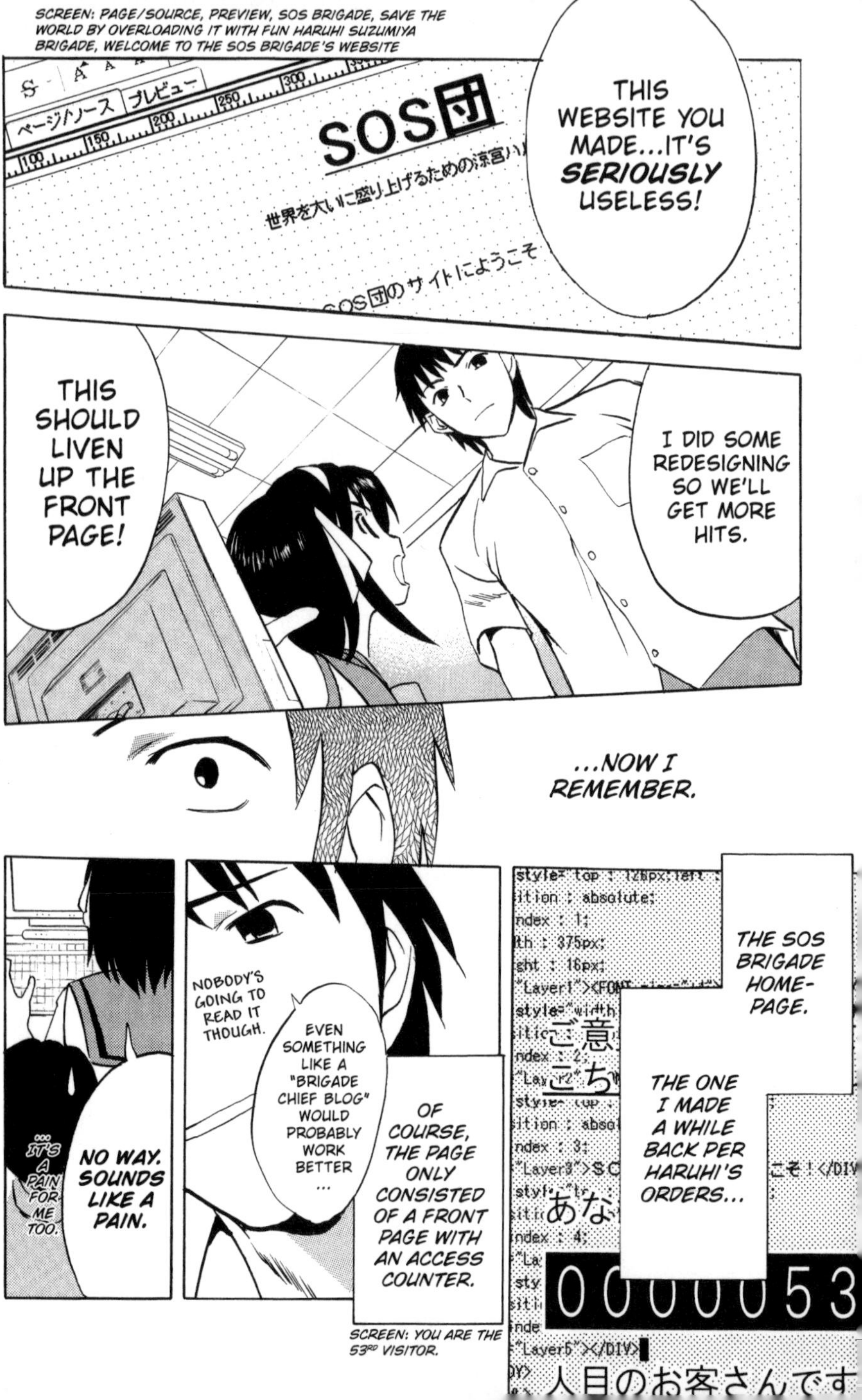
THIS WEBSITE YOU MADE...IT'S *SERIOUSLY* USELESS!
SCREEN: PAGE/SOURCE, PREVIEW, SOS BRIGADE, SAVE THE WORLD BY OVERLOADING IT WITH FUN HARUHI SUZUMIYA BRIGADE, WELCOME TO THE SOS BRIGADE'S WEBSITE
ページ/ソース
プレビュー
SOS団
SOS団のサイトにようこそ
I DID SOME REDESIGNING SO WE'LL GET MORE HITS.
THIS SHOULD LIVEN UP THE FRONT PAGE!
...NOW I REMEMBER.
THE SOS BRIGADE HOME-PAGE.
THE ONE I MADE A WHILE BACK PER HARUHI'S ORDERS...
0000053
SCREEN: YOU ARE THE 53RD VISITOR.
OF COURSE, THE PAGE ONLY CONSISTED OF A FRONT PAGE WITH AN ACCESS COUNTER.
EVEN SOMETHING LIKE A "BRIGADE CHIEF BLOG" WOULD PROBABLY WORK BETTER...
NOBODY'S GOING TO READ IT THOUGH.
NO WAY. SOUNDS LIKE A PAIN.
...IT'S A PAIN FOR ME TOO.

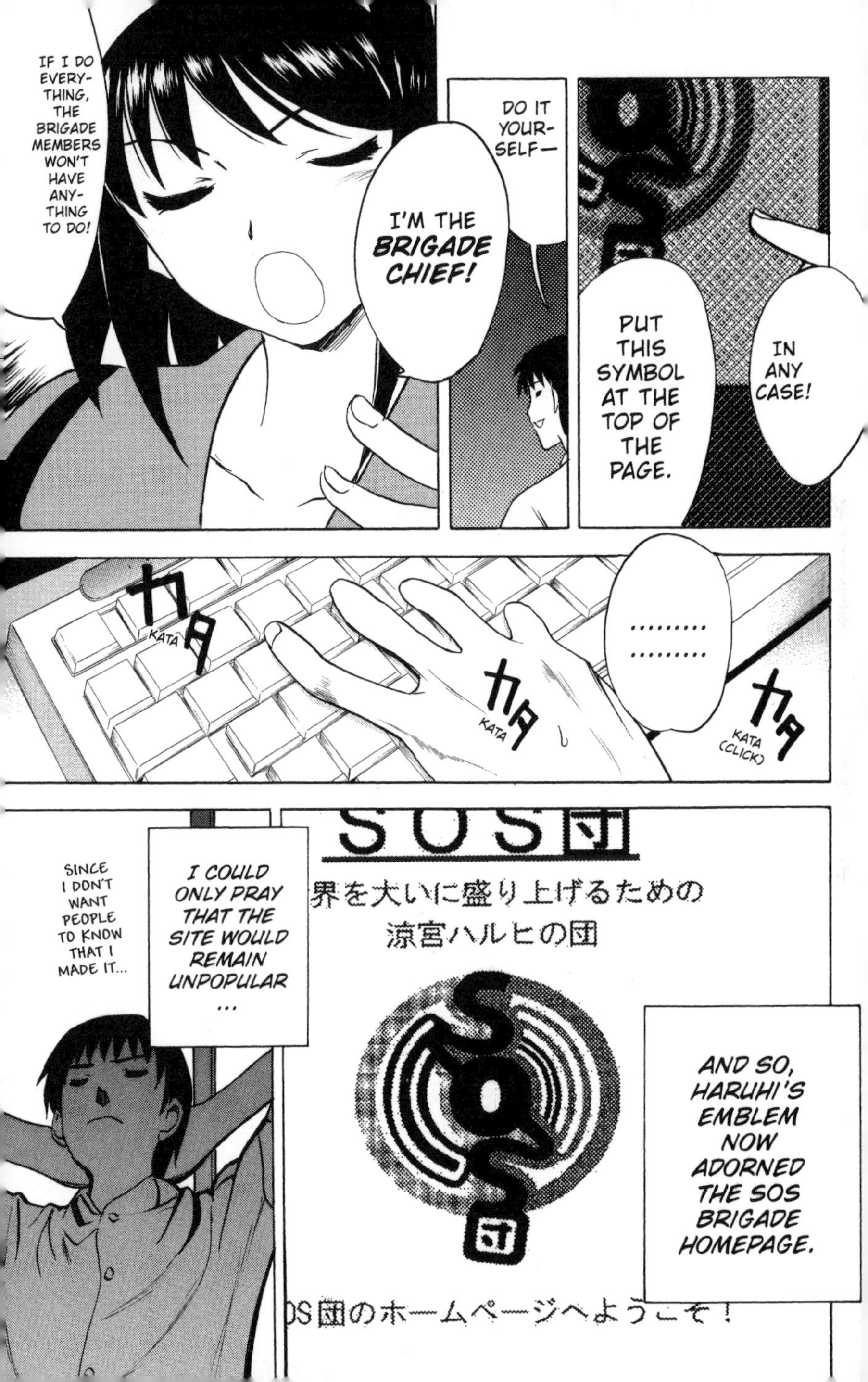

IN ANY CASE!
PUT THIS SYMBOL AT THE TOP OF THE PAGE.
DO IT YOURSELF—
I'M THE ***BRIGADE CHIEF!***
IF I DO EVERYTHING, THE BRIGADE MEMBERS WON'T HAVE ANYTHING TO DO!
....
....
カタ
KATA (CLICK)
カタ
KATA
カタ
KATA
SOS団
界を大いに盛り上げるための
涼宮ハルヒの団
OS団のホームページへようこそ！
AND SO, HARUHI'S EMBLEM NOW ADORNED THE SOS BRIGADE HOMEPAGE.
I COULD ONLY PRAY THAT THE SITE WOULD REMAIN UNPOPULAR ...
SINCE I DON'T WANT PEOPLE TO KNOW THAT I MADE IT...

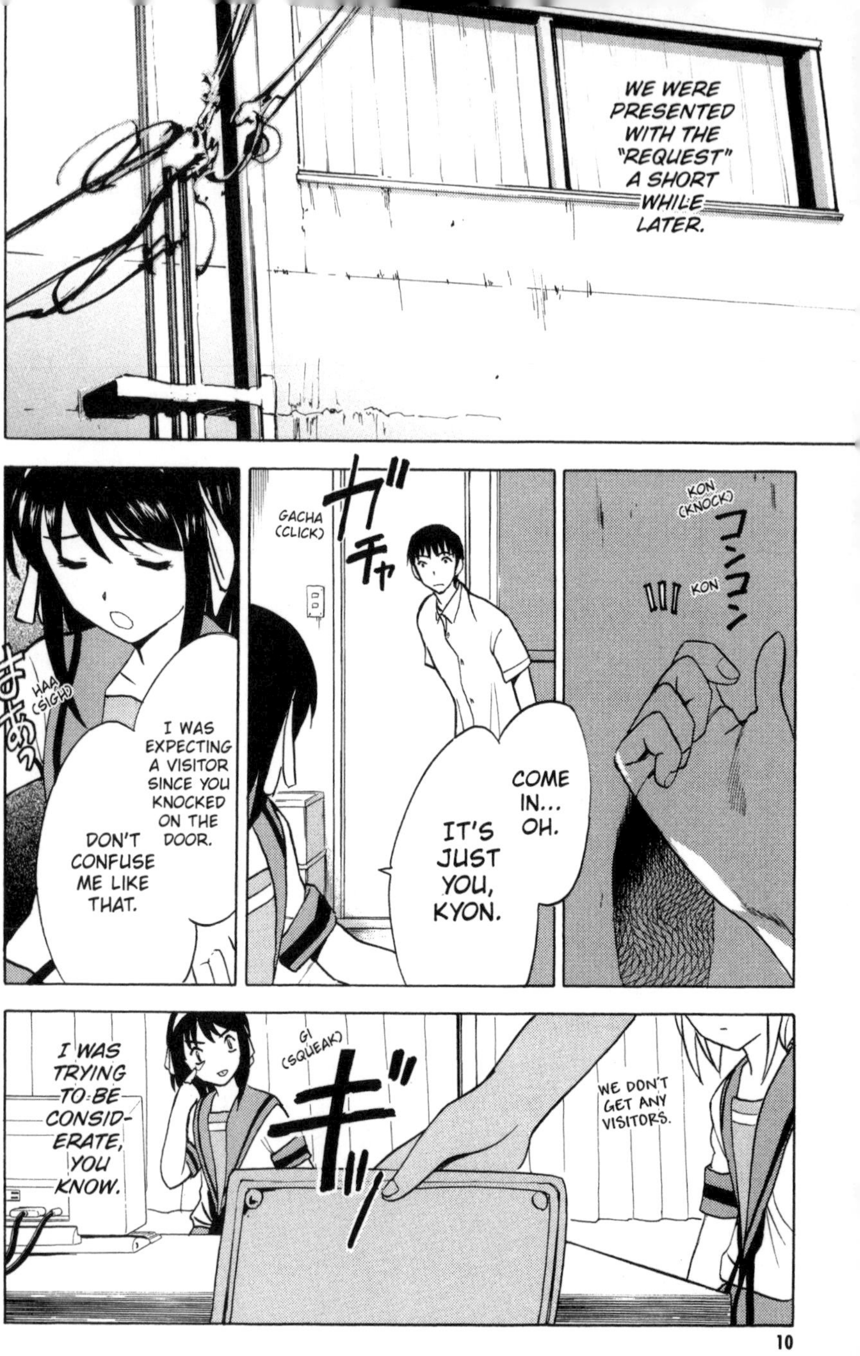
WE WERE PRESENTED WITH THE "REQUEST" A SHORT WHILE LATER.
KON (KNOCK)
コンコン
KON
GACHA (CLICK)
ガチャ
COME IN... OH.
IT'S JUST YOU, KYON.
はぁっ
HAA (SIGH)
I WAS EXPECTING A VISITOR SINCE YOU KNOCKED ON THE DOOR.
DON'T CONFUSE ME LIKE THAT.
WE DON'T GET ANY VISITORS.
GI (SQUEAK)
ギッ
I WAS TRYING TO BE CONSID-ERATE, YOU KNOW.

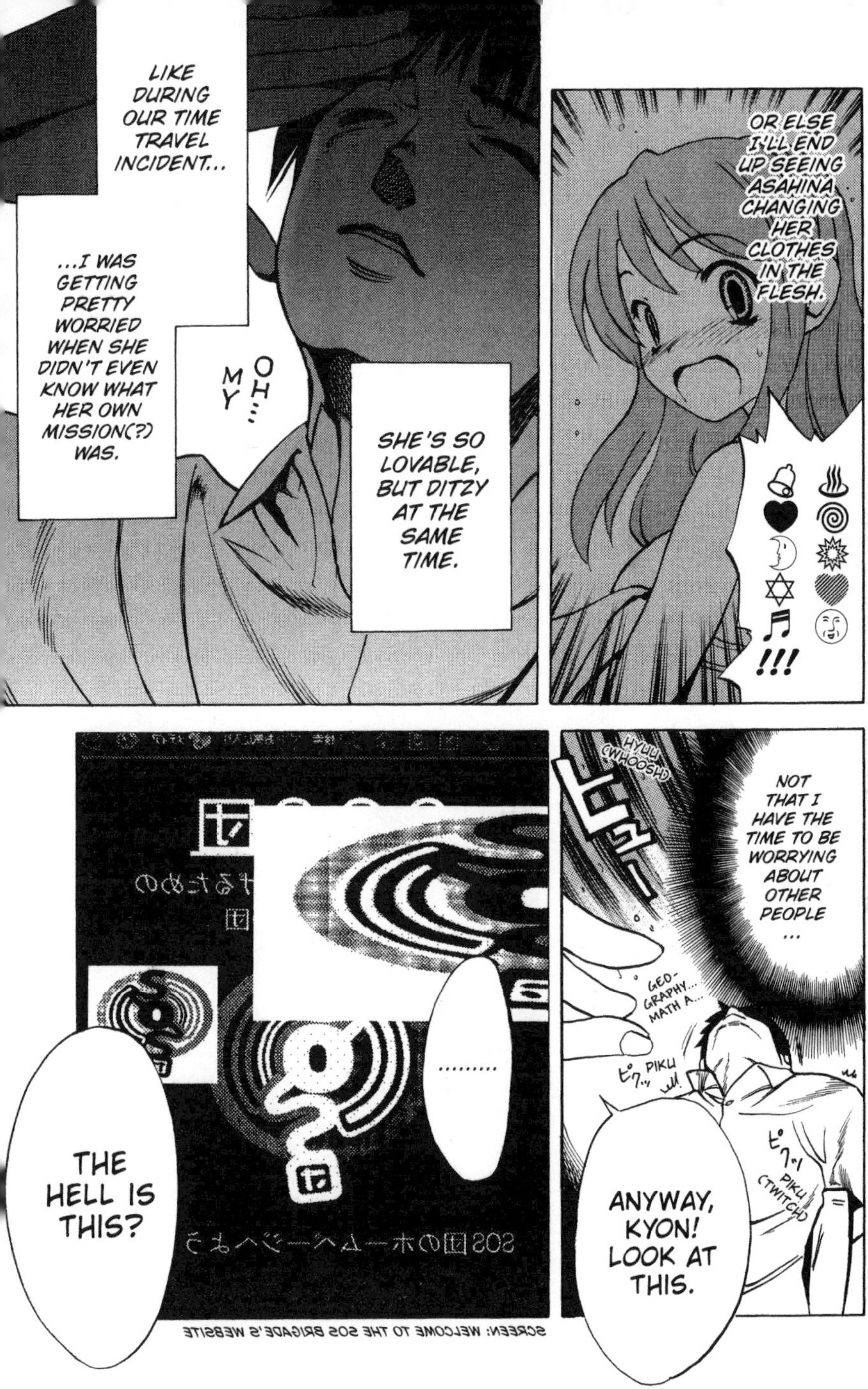
OR ELSE I'LL END UP SEEING ASAHINA CHANGING HER CLOTHES IN THE FLESH.
!!!
LIKE DURING OUR TIME TRAVEL INCIDENT...
...I WAS GETTING PRETTY WORRIED WHEN SHE DIDN'T EVEN KNOW WHAT HER OWN MISSION(?) WAS.
SHE'S SO LOVABLE, BUT DITZY AT THE SAME TIME.
OH MY...
HYUU (WHOOSH)
NOT THAT I HAVE THE TIME TO BE WORRYING ABOUT OTHER PEOPLE ...
GEOGRAPHY... MATH A...
PIKU
PIKU (TWITCH)
ANYWAY, KYON! LOOK AT THIS.
....
THE HELL IS THIS?
SCREEN: WELCOME TO THE SOS BRIGADE'S WEBSITE

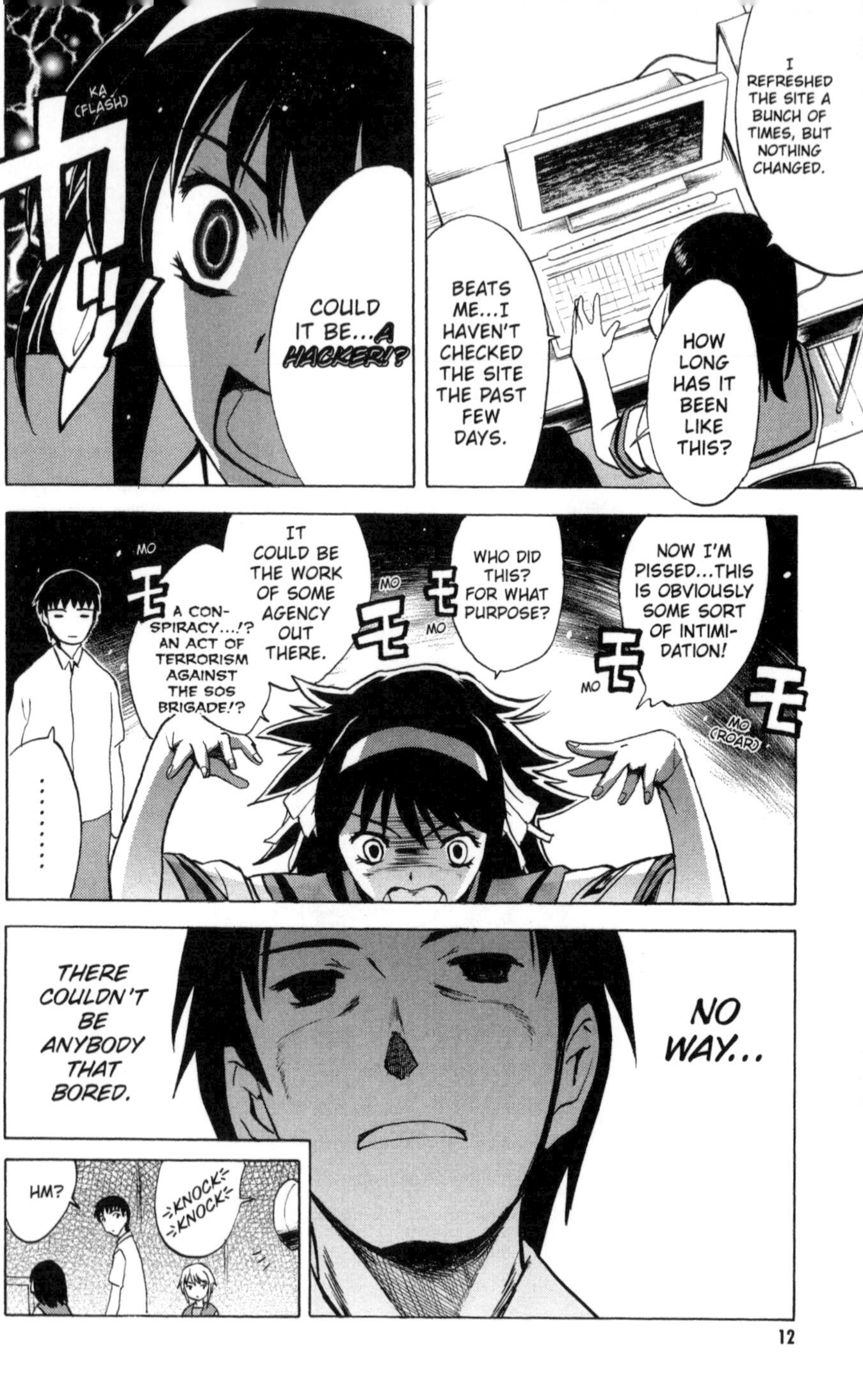
I REFRESHED THE SITE A BUNCH OF TIMES, BUT NOTHING CHANGED.
HOW LONG HAS IT BEEN LIKE THIS?
BEATS ME...I HAVEN'T CHECKED THE SITE THE PAST FEW DAYS.
KA (FLASH)
COULD IT BE...A HACKER!?
NOW I'M PISSED...THIS IS OBVIOUSLY SOME SORT OF INTIMIDATION!
MO (ROAR)
MO
WHO DID THIS? FOR WHAT PURPOSE?
MO
MO
IT COULD BE THE WORK OF SOME AGENCY OUT THERE.
A CONSPIRACY...!? AN ACT OF TERRORISM AGAINST THE SOS BRIGADE!?
MO
....
NO WAY...
THERE COULDN'T BE ANYBODY THAT BORED.
KNOCK KNOCK
HM?

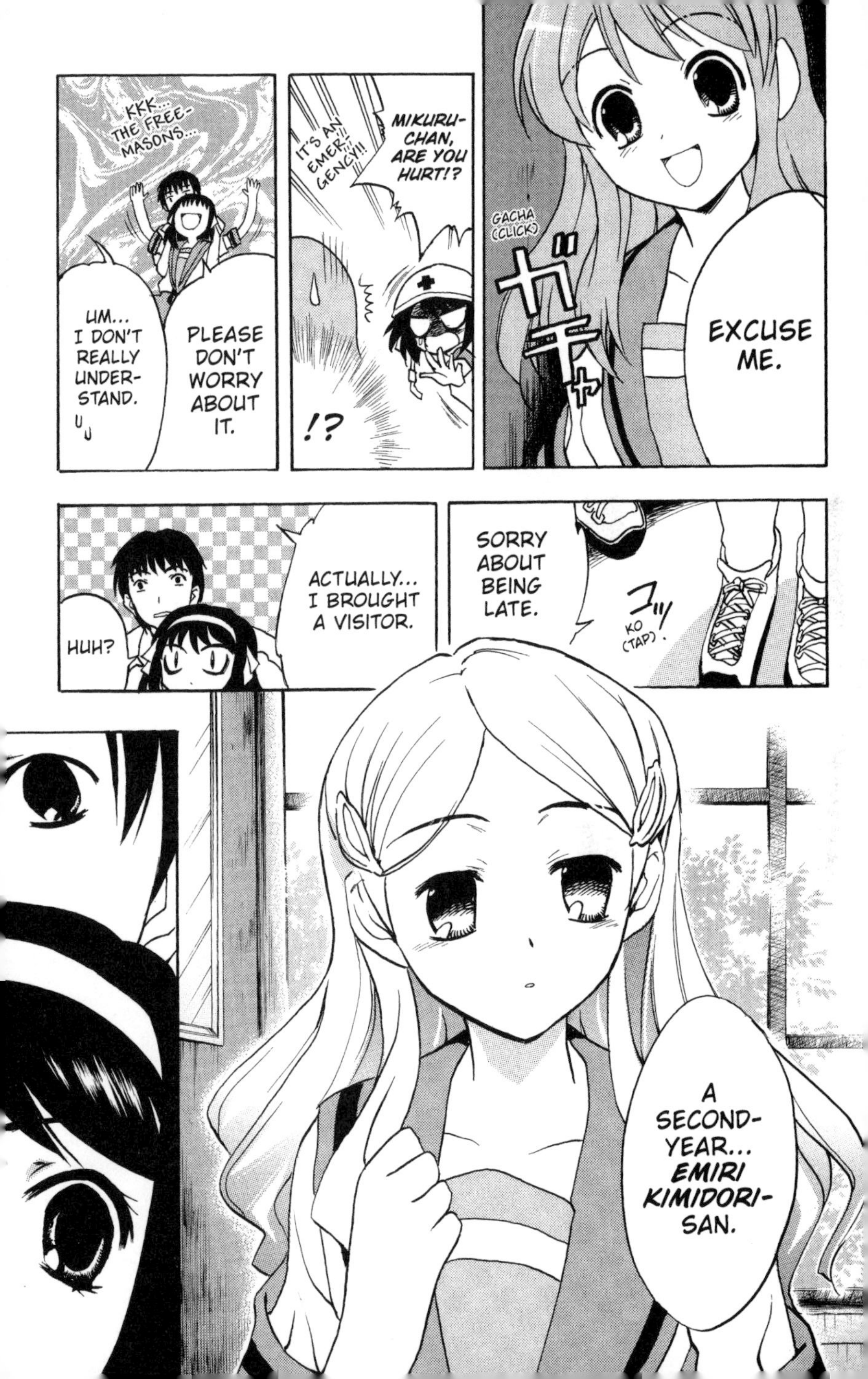
GACHA (CLICK)
EXCUSE ME.
MIKURU-CHAN, ARE YOU HURT!?
IT'S AN EMER-GENCY!!
!?
KKK... THE FREE-MASONS...
PLEASE DON'T WORRY ABOUT IT.
UM... I DON'T REALLY UNDER-STAND.
SORRY ABOUT BEING LATE.
KO (TAP)
ACTUALLY... I BROUGHT A VISITOR.
HUH?
A SECOND-YEAR... EMIRI KIMIDORI-SAN.

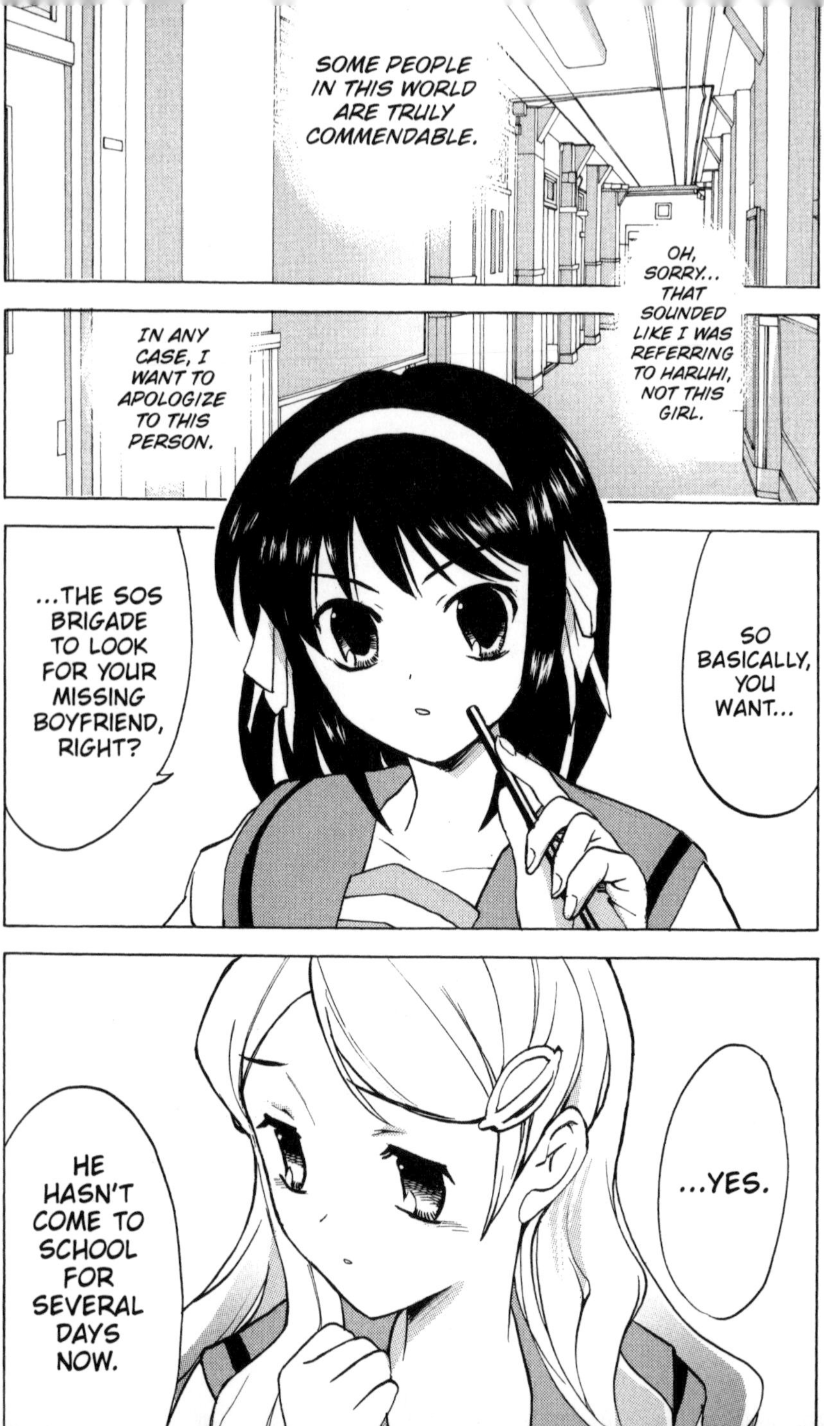
SOME PEOPLE IN THIS WORLD ARE TRULY COMMENDABLE.
OH, SORRY... THAT SOUNDED LIKE I WAS REFERRING TO HARUHI, NOT THIS GIRL.
IN ANY CASE, I WANT TO APOLOGIZE TO THIS PERSON.
SO BASICALLY, YOU WANT...
...THE SOS BRIGADE TO LOOK FOR YOUR MISSING BOYFRIEND, RIGHT?
...YES.
HE HASN'T COME TO SCHOOL FOR SEVERAL DAYS NOW.

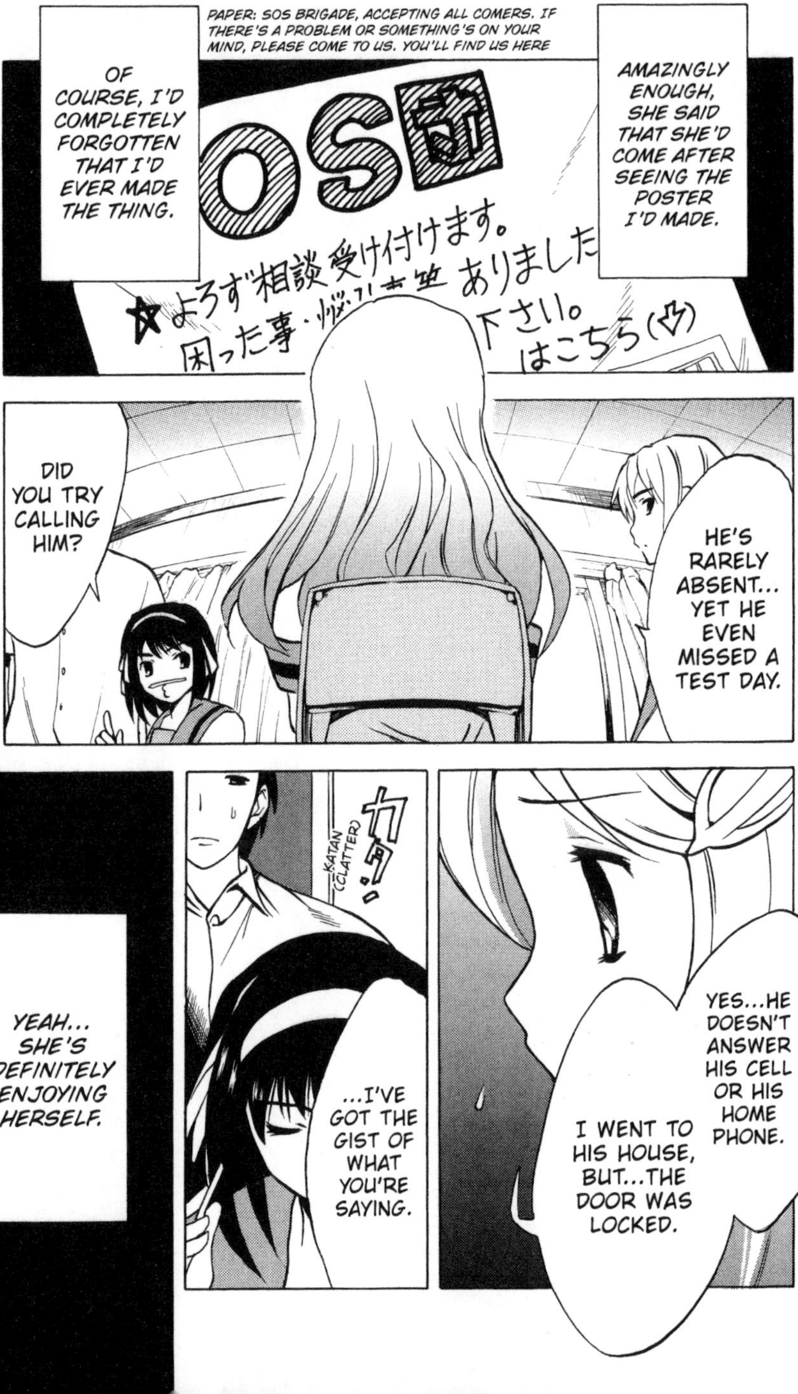
PAPER: SOS BRIGADE, ACCEPTING ALL COMERS. IF THERE'S A PROBLEM OR SOMETHING'S ON YOUR MIND, PLEASE COME TO US. YOU'LL FIND US HERE
AMAZINGLY ENOUGH, SHE SAID THAT SHE'D COME AFTER SEEING THE POSTER I'D MADE.
OF COURSE, I'D COMPLETELY FORGOTTEN THAT I'D EVER MADE THE THING.
よろず相談受け付けます。
ありました
下さい。
はこちら
HE'S RARELY ABSENT... YET HE EVEN MISSED A TEST DAY.
DID YOU TRY CALLING HIM?
YES...HE DOESN'T ANSWER HIS CELL OR HIS HOME PHONE.
I WENT TO HIS HOUSE, BUT...THE DOOR WAS LOCKED.
KATAN (CLATTER)
...I'VE GOT THE GIST OF WHAT YOU'RE SAYING.
YEAH... SHE'S DEFINITELY ENJOYING HERSELF.

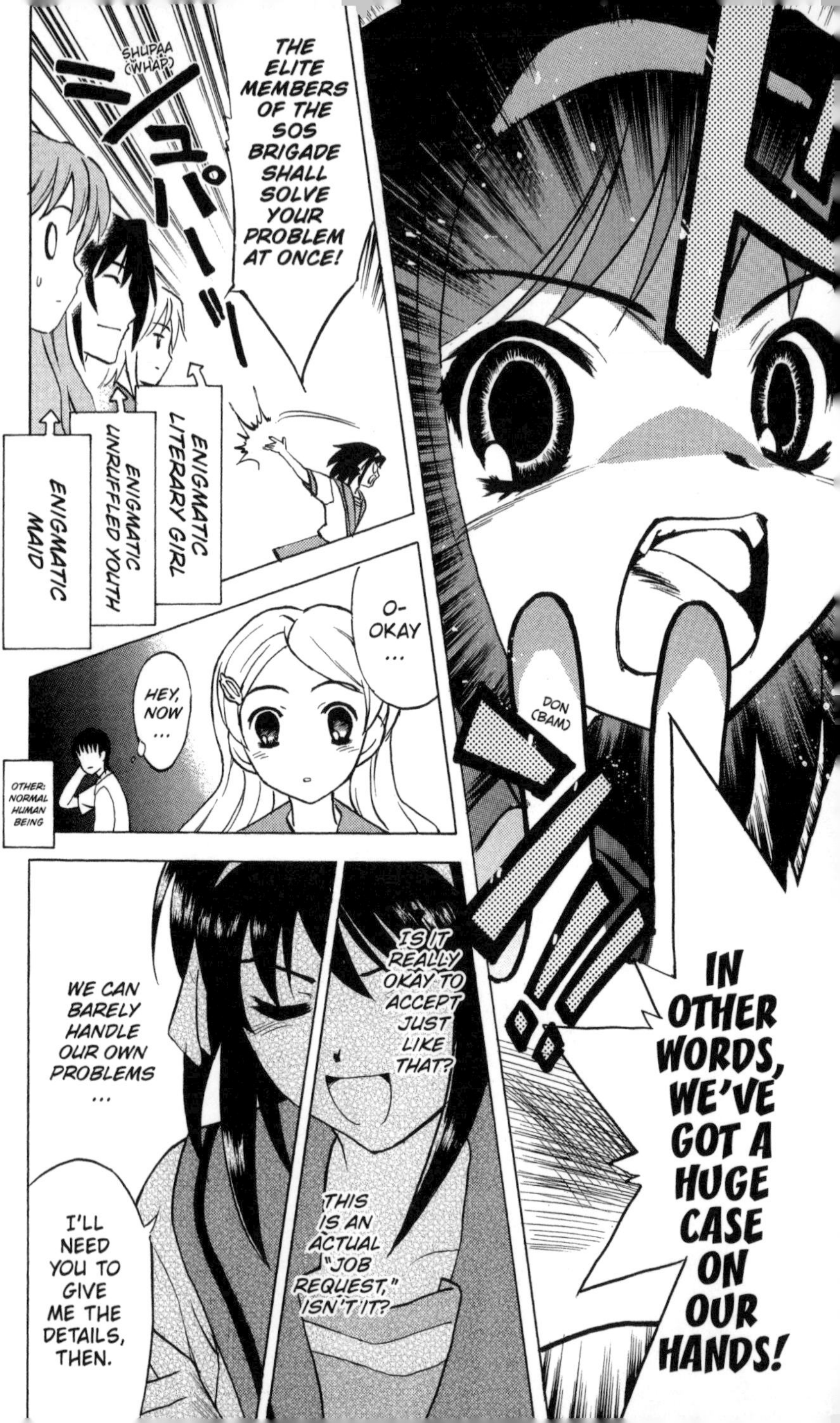
DON (BAM)
IN OTHER WORDS, WE'VE GOT A HUGE CASE ON OUR HANDS!
THE ELITE MEMBERS OF THE SOS BRIGADE SHALL SOLVE YOUR PROBLEM AT ONCE!
SHUPAA (WHAP)
ENIGMATIC LITERARY GIRL
ENIGMATIC UNRUFFLED YOUTH
ENIGMATIC MAID
O-OKAY ...
HEY, NOW ...
OTHER: NORMAL HUMAN BEING
IS IT REALLY OKAY TO ACCEPT JUST LIKE THAT?
WE CAN BARELY HANDLE OUR OWN PROBLEMS ...
THIS IS AN ACTUAL "JOB REQUEST," ISN'T IT?
I'LL NEED YOU TO GIVE ME THE DETAILS, THEN.

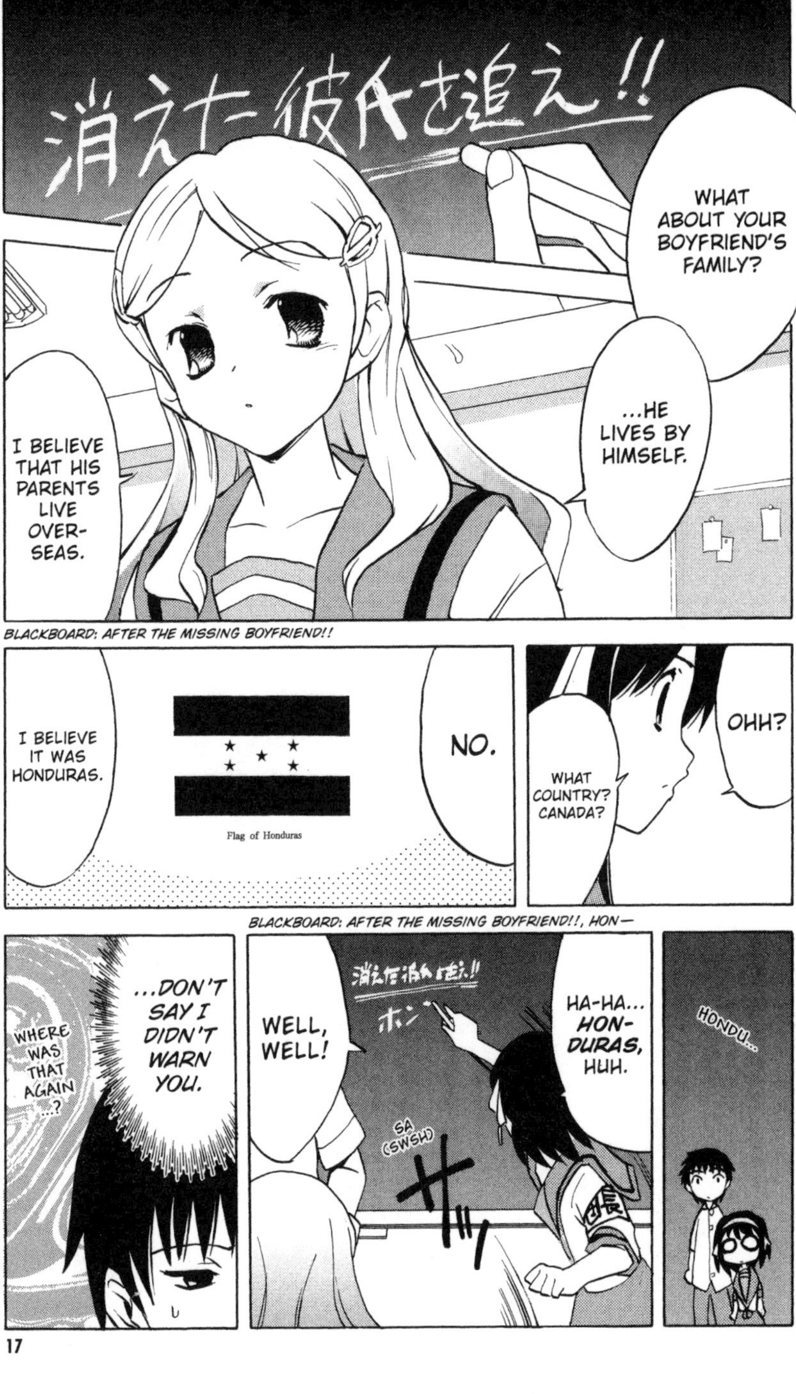
消えた彼氏を追え!!
WHAT ABOUT YOUR BOYFRIEND'S FAMILY?
...HE LIVES BY HIMSELF.
I BELIEVE THAT HIS PARENTS LIVE OVER-SEAS.
BLACKBOARD: AFTER THE MISSING BOYFRIEND!!
OHH?
WHAT COUNTRY? CANADA?
NO.
I BELIEVE IT WAS HONDURAS.
Flag of Honduras
BLACKBOARD: AFTER THE MISSING BOYFRIEND!!, HON—
HONDU...
HA-HA... HON-DURAS, HUH.
ホン
WELL, WELL!
SA (SWSH)
...DON'T SAY I DIDN'T WARN YOU.
WHERE WAS THAT AGAIN ...?

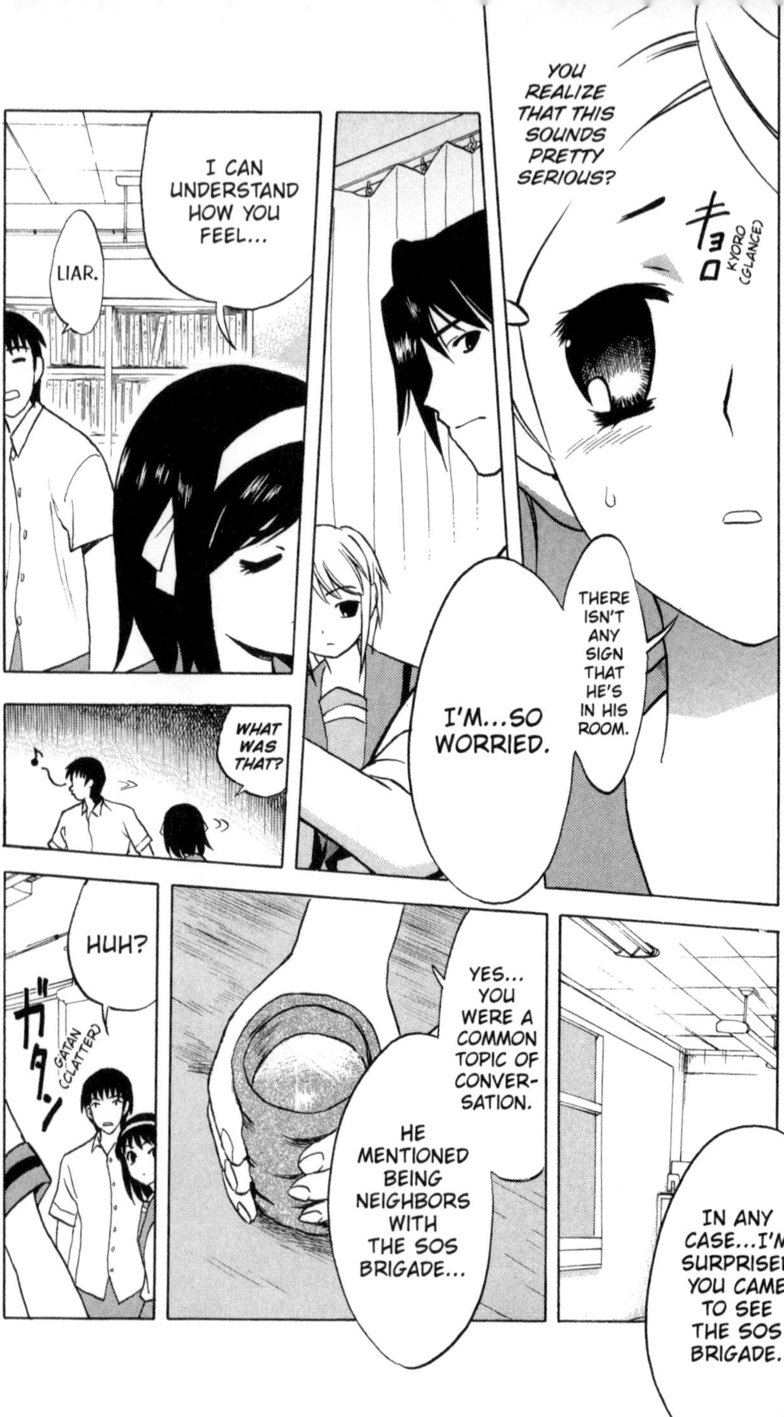
YOU REALIZE THAT THIS SOUNDS PRETTY SERIOUS?
キョロ
KYORO (GLANCE)
THERE ISN'T ANY SIGN THAT HE'S IN HIS ROOM.
I'M...SO WORRIED.
I CAN UNDERSTAND HOW YOU FEEL...
LIAR.
WHAT WAS THAT?
IN ANY CASE...I'M SURPRISED YOU CAME TO SEE THE SOS BRIGADE.
YES... YOU WERE A COMMON TOPIC OF CONVERSATION.
HE MENTIONED BEING NEIGHBORS WITH THE SOS BRIGADE...
HUH?
ガタン
GATAN (CLATTER)

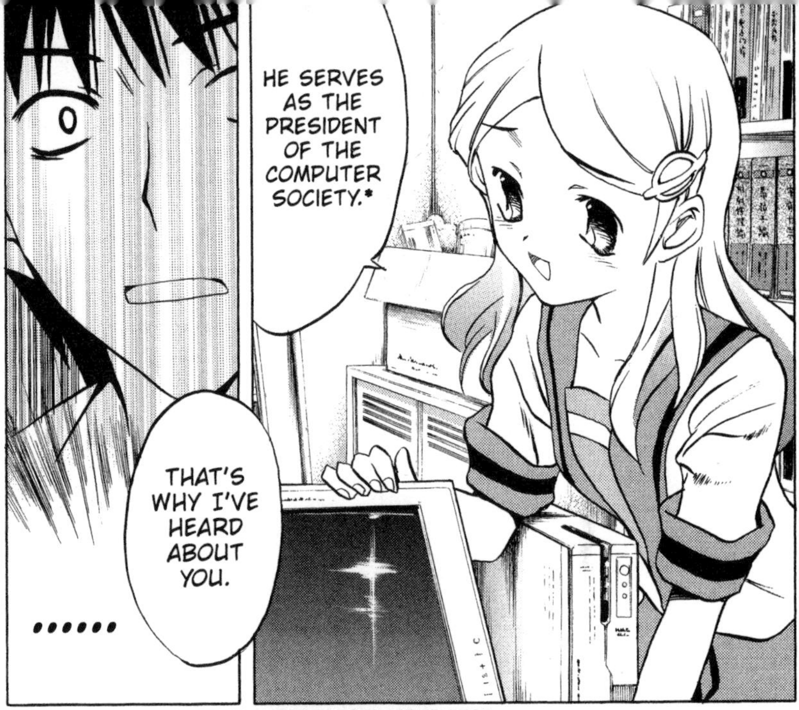
HE SERVES AS THE PRESIDENT OF THE COMPUTER SOCIETY.*
THAT'S WHY I'VE HEARD ABOUT YOU.
......

*SHORT FOR THE COMPUTER RESEARCH SOCIETY. SEE VOLUME 1.

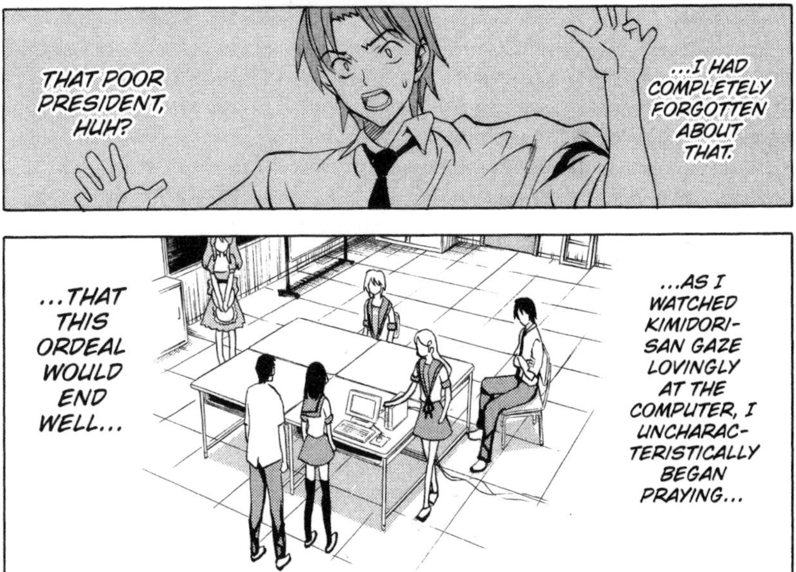
...I HAD COMPLETELY FORGOTTEN ABOUT THAT.
THAT POOR PRESIDENT, HUH?
...AS I WATCHED KIMIDORI-SAN GAZE LOVINGLY AT THE COMPUTER, I UNCHARAC-TERISTICALLY BEGAN PRAYING...
...THAT THIS ORDEAL WOULD END WELL...

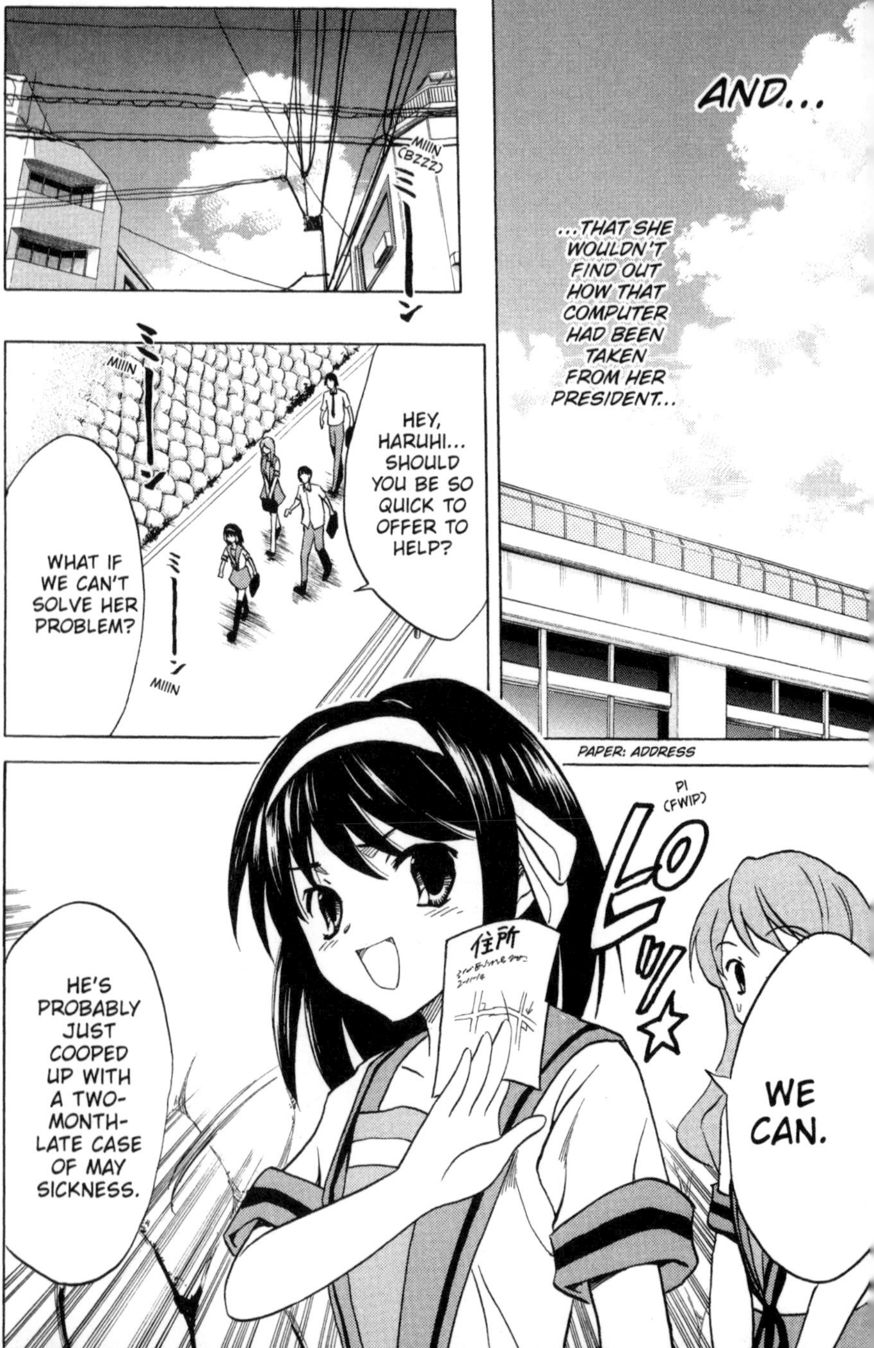
AND...
...THAT SHE WOULDN'T FIND OUT HOW THAT COMPUTER HAD BEEN TAKEN FROM HER PRESIDENT...
MIIN (BZZZ)
MIIN
HEY, HARUHI... SHOULD YOU BE SO QUICK TO OFFER TO HELP?
WHAT IF WE CAN'T SOLVE HER PROBLEM?
MIIN
PAPER: ADDRESS
PI (FWIP)
住所
WE CAN.
HE'S PROBABLY JUST COOPED UP WITH A TWO-MONTH-LATE CASE OF MAY SICKNESS.

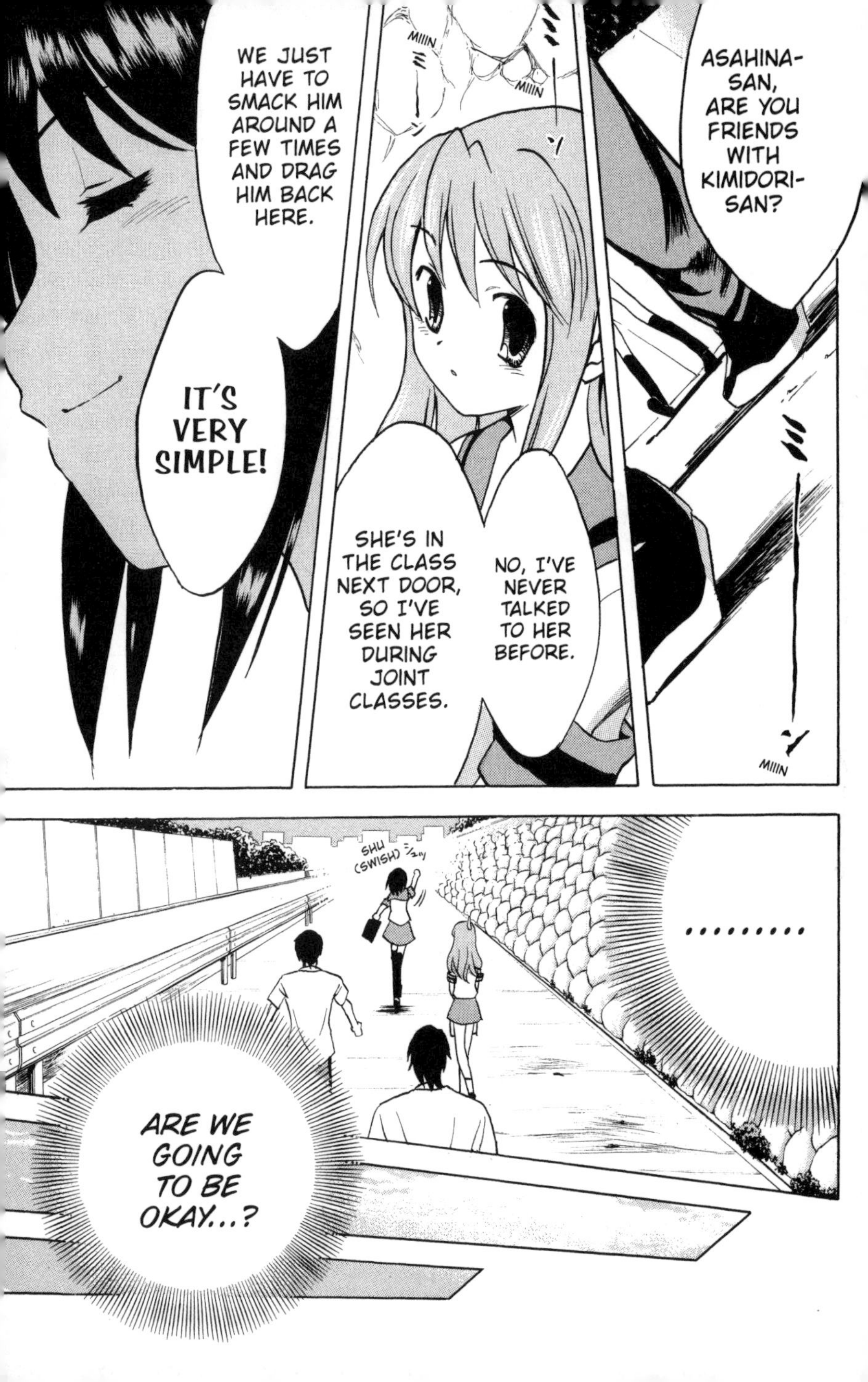

ASAHINA-SAN, ARE YOU FRIENDS WITH KIMIDORI-SAN?
MIIN
MIIN
MIIN
NO, I'VE NEVER TALKED TO HER BEFORE.
SHE'S IN THE CLASS NEXT DOOR, SO I'VE SEEN HER DURING JOINT CLASSES.
WE JUST HAVE TO SMACK HIM AROUND A FEW TIMES AND DRAG HIM BACK HERE.
IT'S VERY SIMPLE!
....
SHU (SWISH)
ARE WE GOING TO BE OKAY...?

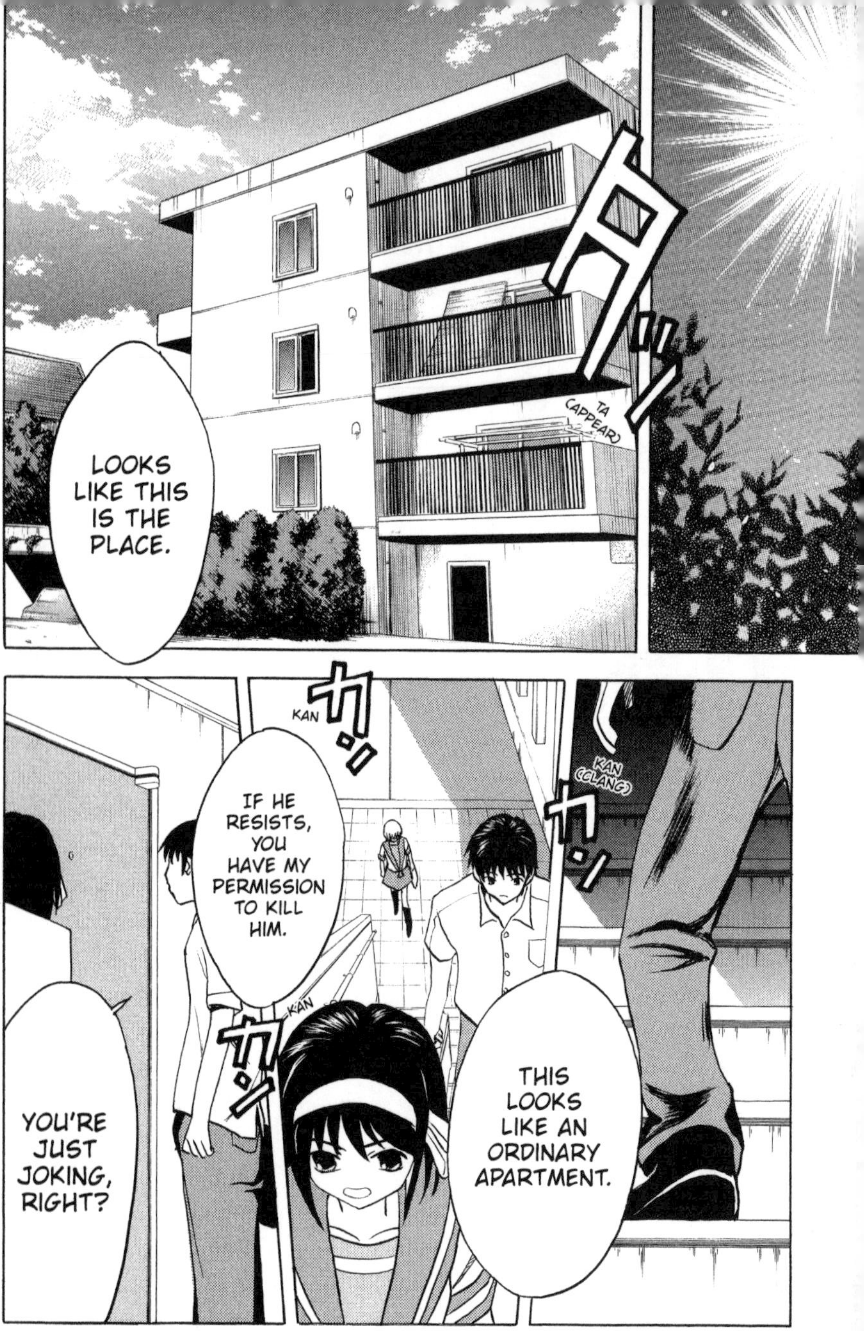
TA (APPEAR)
LOOKS LIKE THIS IS THE PLACE.
KAN (CLANG)
KAN
IF HE RESISTS, YOU HAVE MY PERMISSION TO KILL HIM.
THIS LOOKS LIKE AN ORDINARY APARTMENT.
KAN
YOU'RE JUST JOKING, RIGHT?

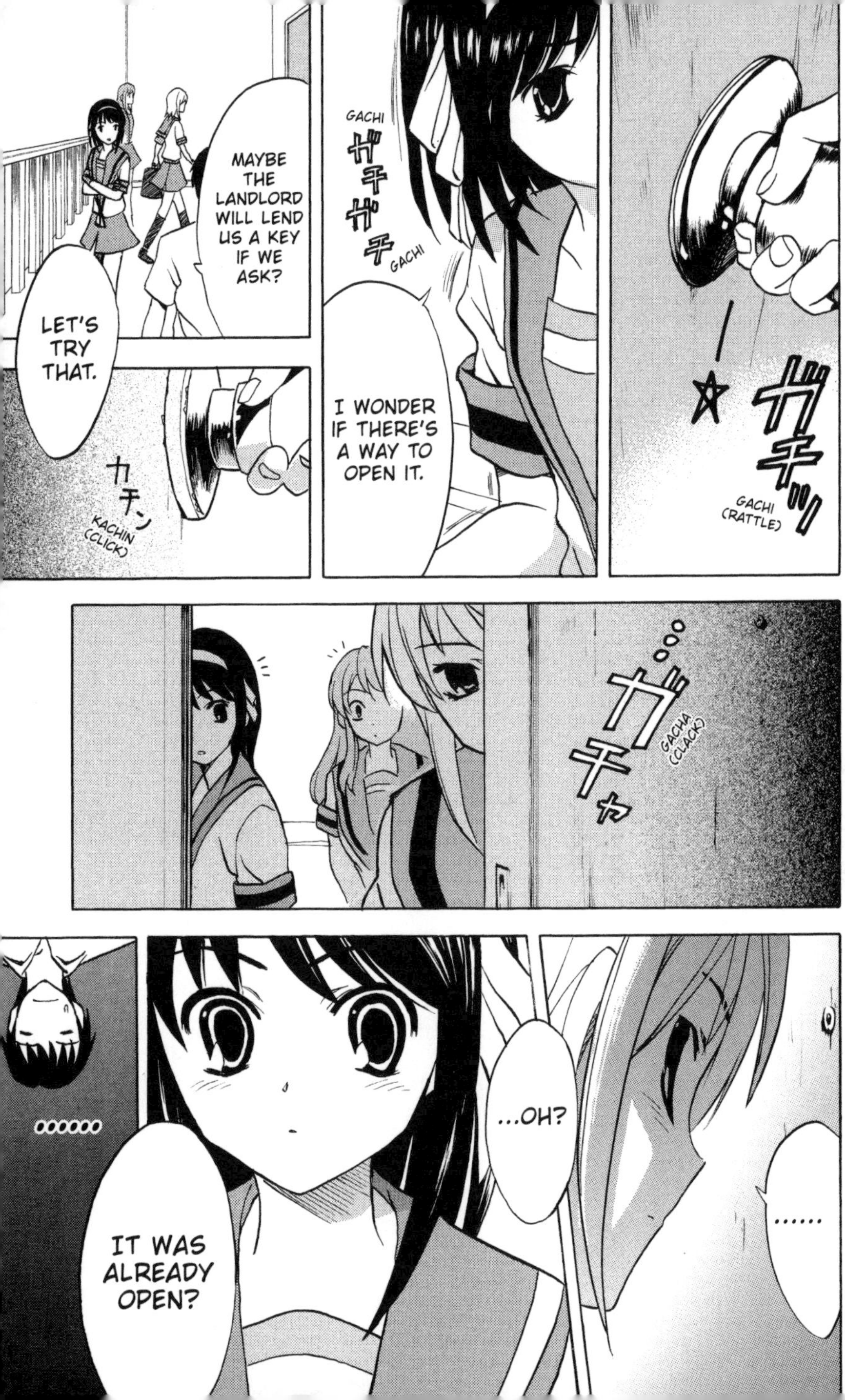
ガチッ
GACHI (RATTLE)
GACHI
GACHI
I WONDER IF THERE'S A WAY TO OPEN IT.
MAYBE THE LANDLORD WILL LEND US A KEY IF WE ASK?
LET'S TRY THAT.
カチン
KACHIN (CLICK)
ガチャ
GACHA (CLACK)
...OH?
......
IT WAS ALREADY OPEN?
oooooo

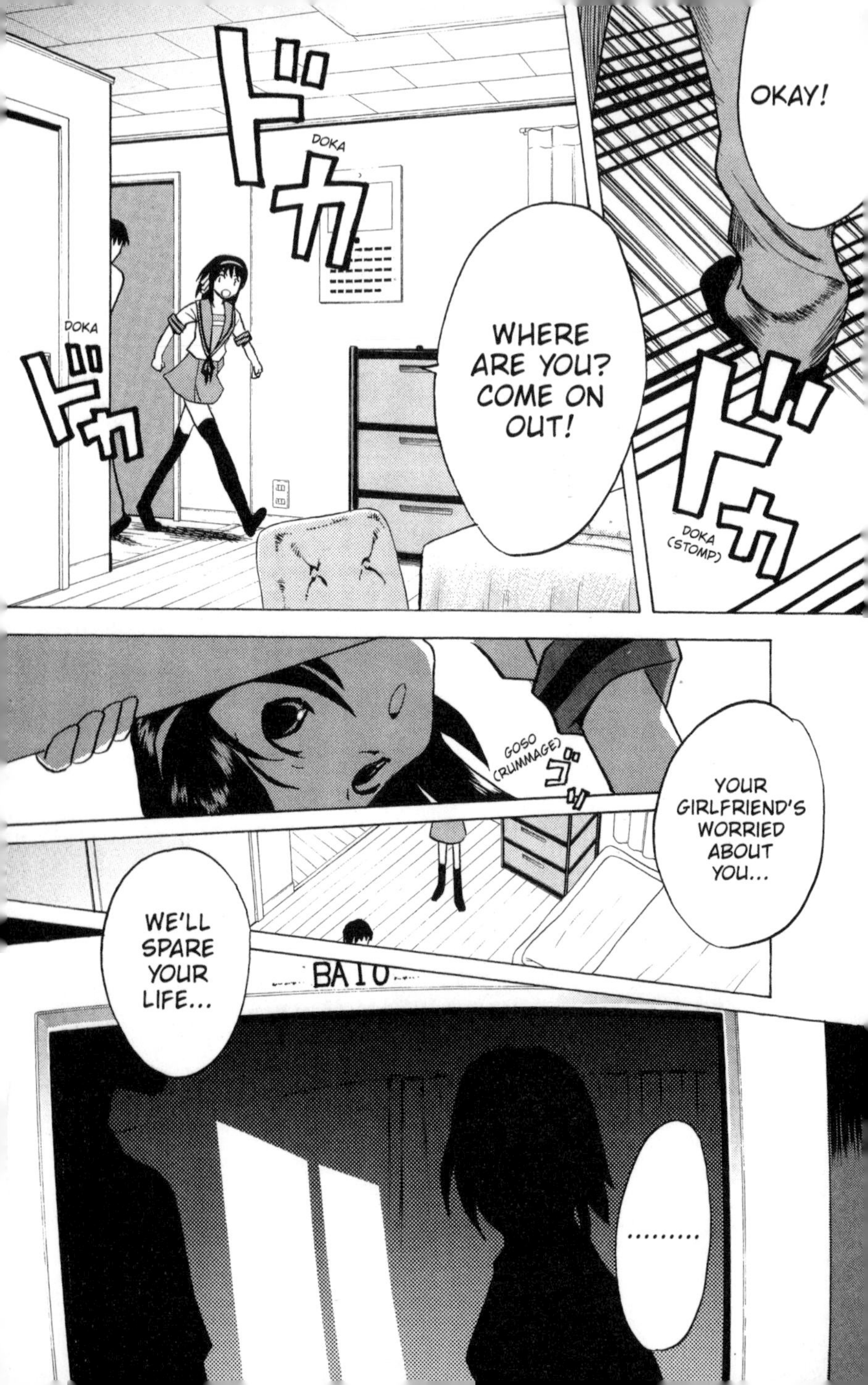
OKAY!
ドドカ
DOKA (STOMP)
ドカ
DOKA
WHERE ARE YOU? COME ON OUT!
ドカ
DOKA
GOSO (RUMMAGE)
ゴソ
YOUR GIRLFRIEND'S WORRIED ABOUT YOU...
WE'LL SPARE YOUR LIFE...
BAITO
....

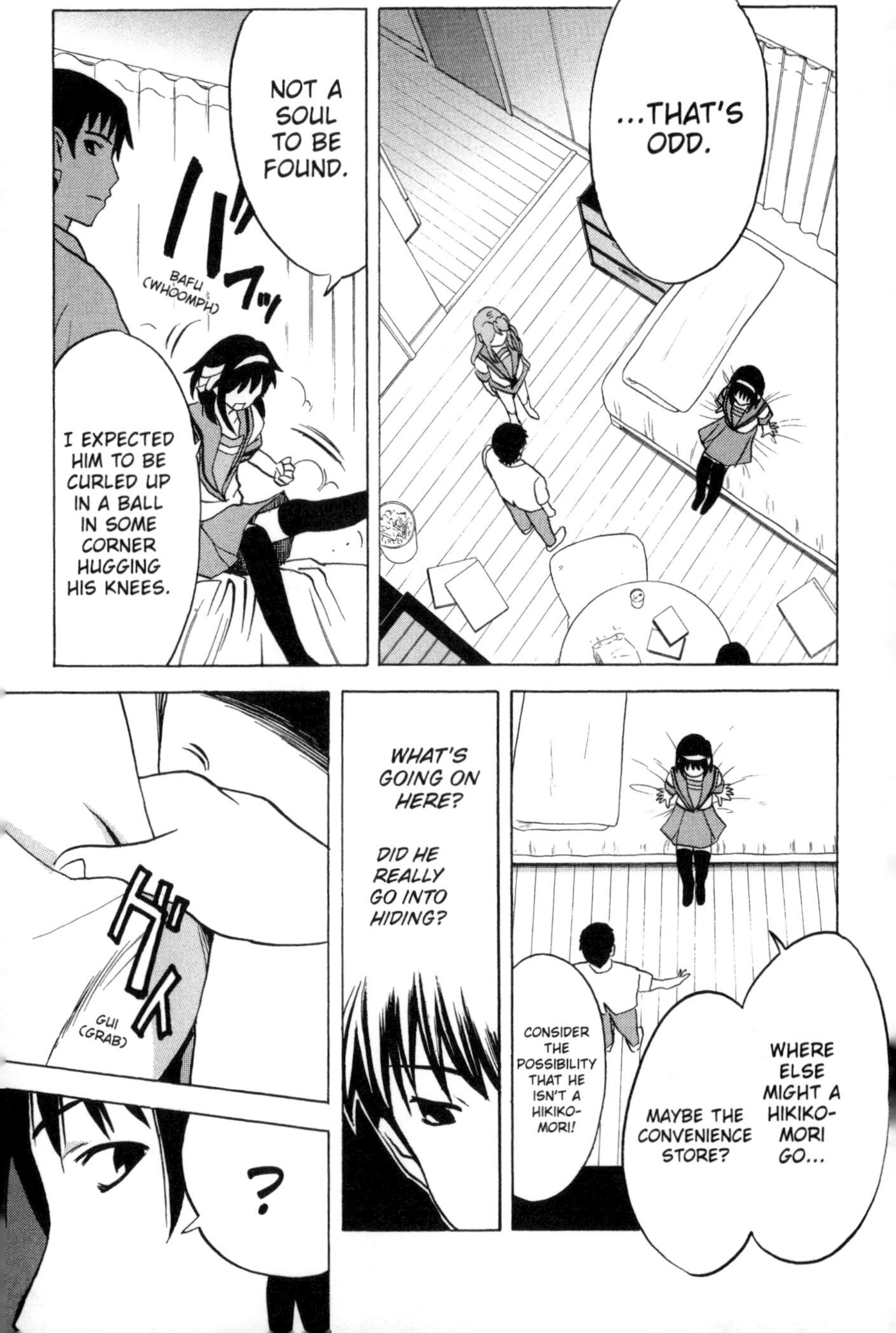
...THAT'S ODD.
NOT A SOUL TO BE FOUND.
BAFU (WHOOMPH)
I EXPECTED HIM TO BE CURLED UP IN A BALL IN SOME CORNER HUGGING HIS KNEES.
WHERE ELSE MIGHT A HIKIKO-MORI GO...
MAYBE THE CONVENIENCE STORE?
CONSIDER THE POSSIBILITY THAT HE ISN'T A HIKIKO-MORI!
WHAT'S GOING ON HERE?
DID HE REALLY GO INTO HIDING?
GUI (GRAB)
?

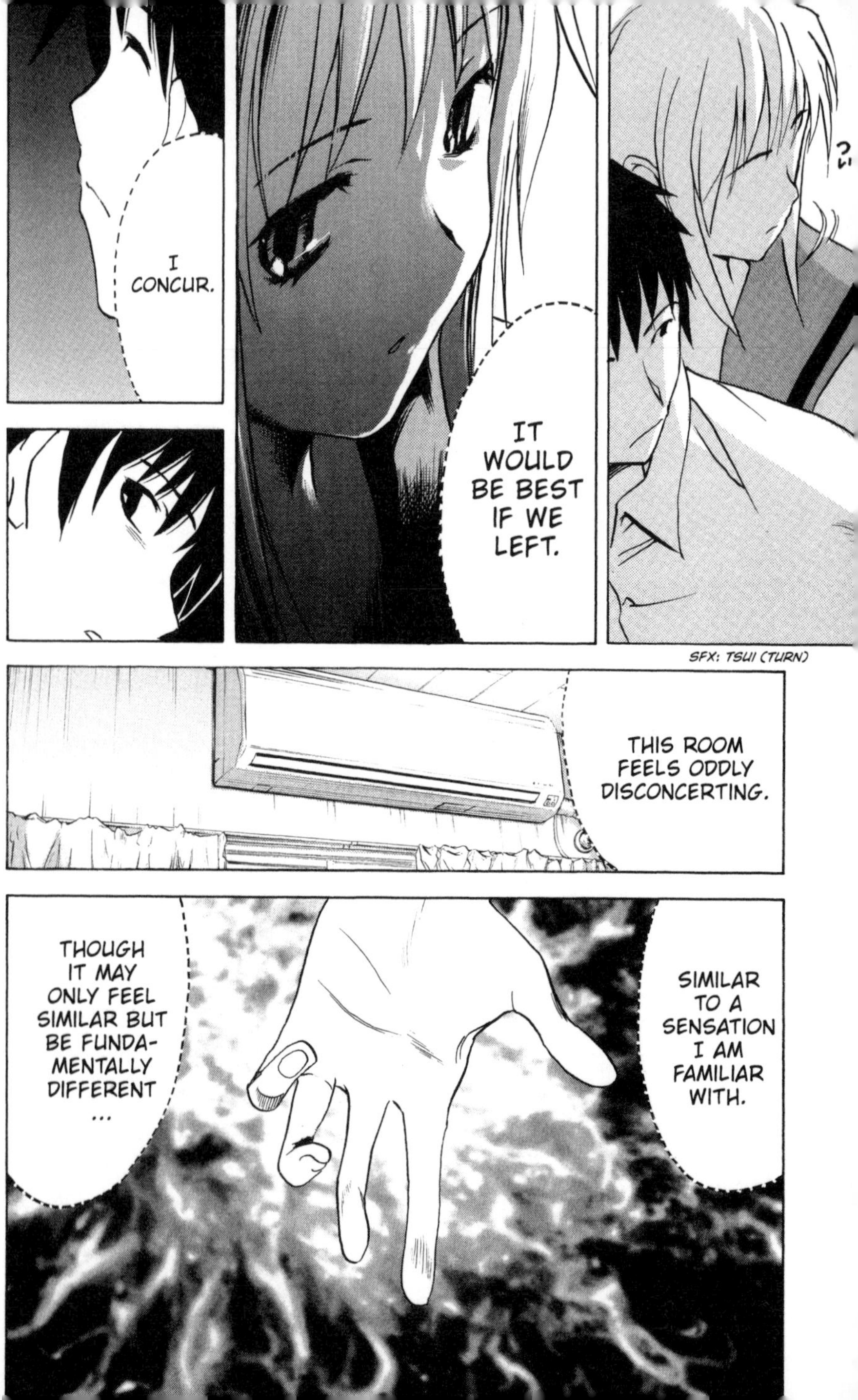
SFX: TSUI (TURN)
IT WOULD BE BEST IF WE LEFT.
I CONCUR.
THIS ROOM FEELS ODDLY DISCONCERTING.
SIMILAR TO A SENSATION I AM FAMILIAR WITH.
THOUGH IT MAY ONLY FEEL SIMILAR BUT BE FUNDAMENTALLY DIFFERENT ...

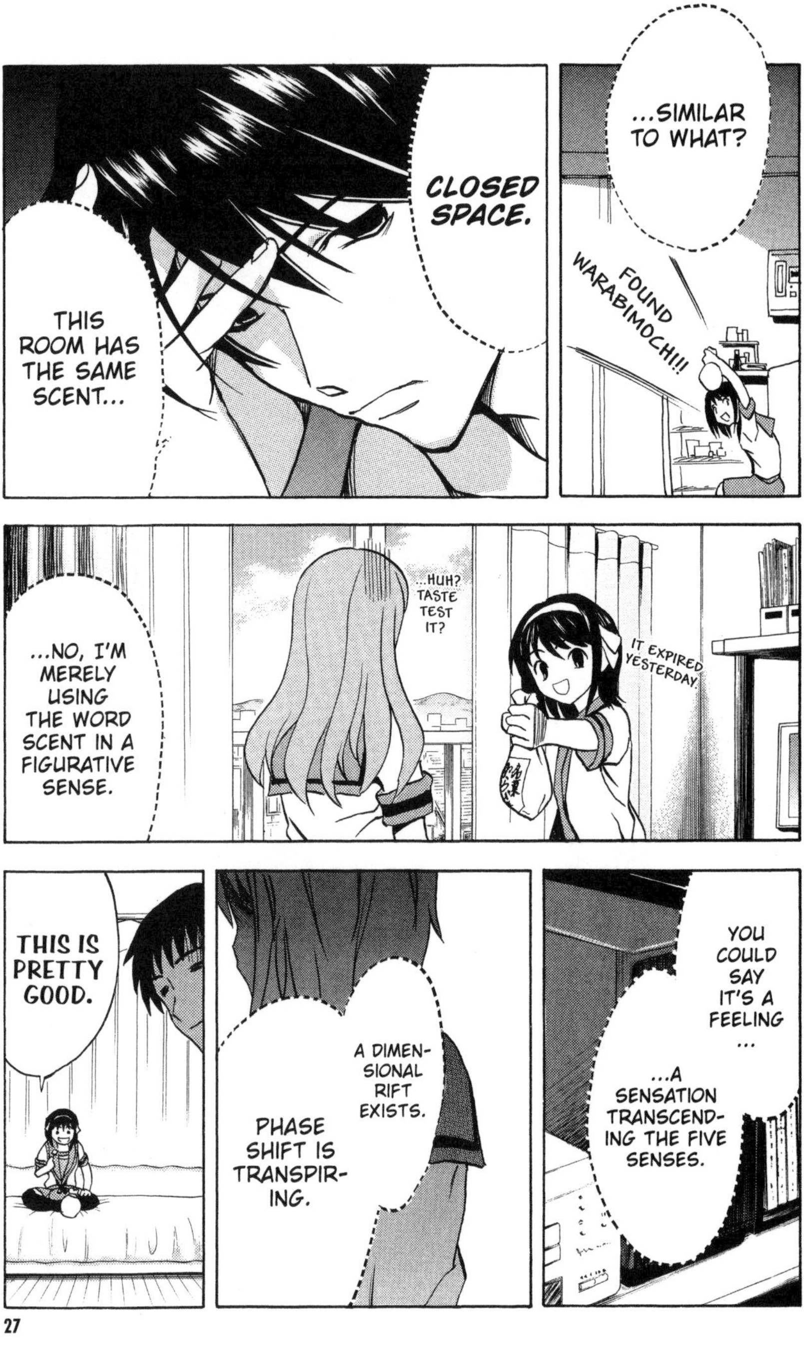
...SIMILAR TO WHAT?
FOUND WARABIMOCHI!!
CLOSED SPACE.
THIS ROOM HAS THE SAME SCENT...
IT EXPIRED YESTERDAY.
...HUH? TASTE TEST IT?
...NO, I'M MERELY USING THE WORD SCENT IN A FIGURATIVE SENSE.
YOU COULD SAY IT'S A FEELING...
...A SENSATION TRANSCENDING THE FIVE SENSES.
A DIMENSIONAL RIFT EXISTS.
PHASE SHIFT IS TRANSPIRING.
THIS IS PRETTY GOOD.

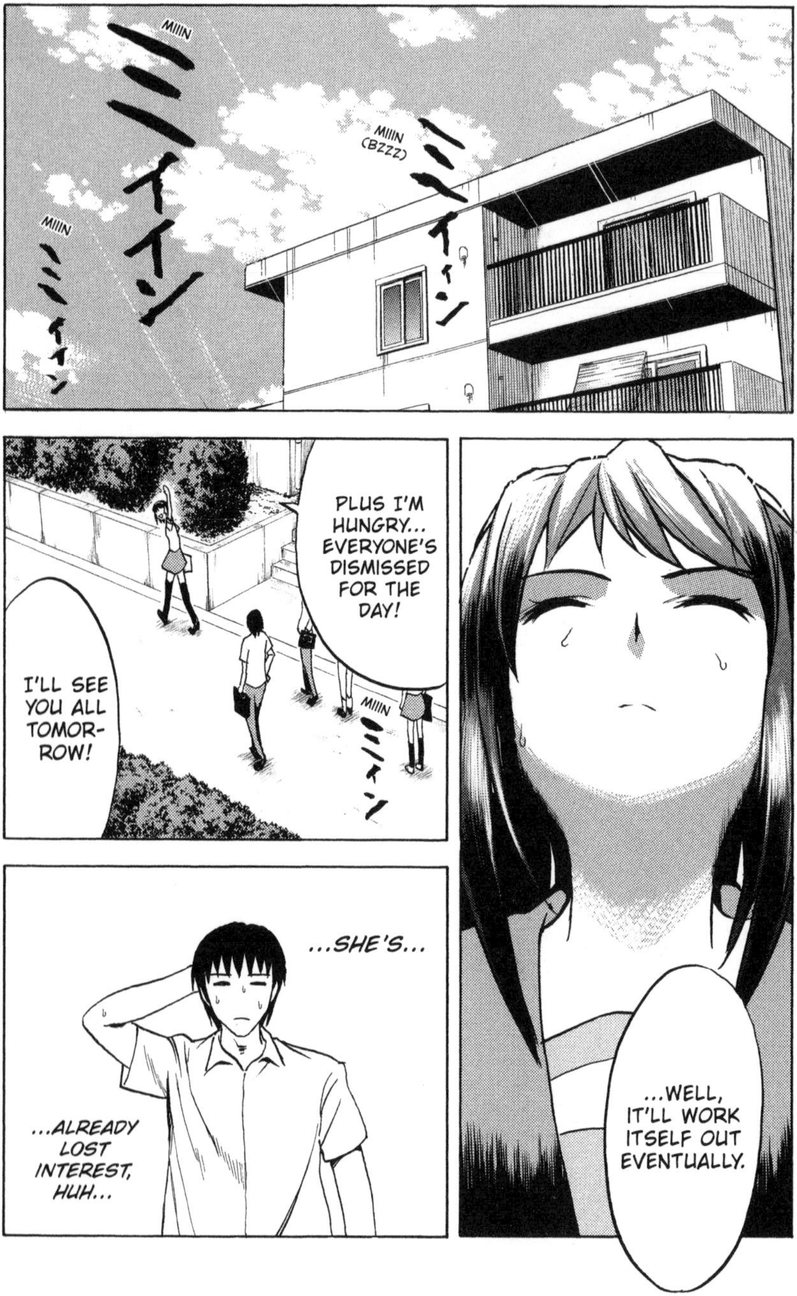
MIIN
(BZZZ)
MIIN
MIIN
...WELL, IT'LL WORK ITSELF OUT EVENTUALLY.
PLUS I'M HUNGRY... EVERYONE'S DISMISSED FOR THE DAY!
I'LL SEE YOU ALL TOMOR-ROW!
MIIN
...SHE'S...
...ALREADY LOST INTEREST, HUH...

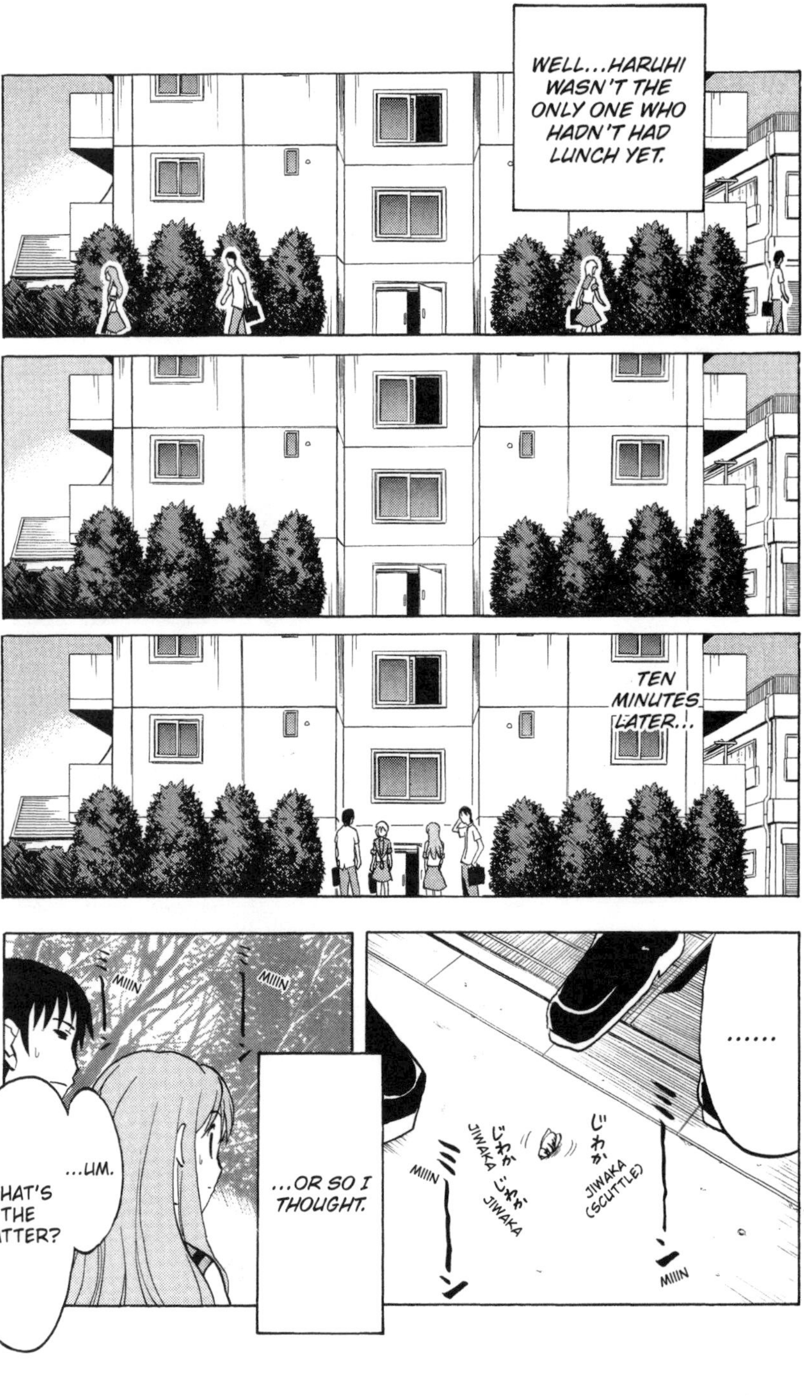

WELL...HARUHI WASN'T THE ONLY ONE WHO HADN'T HAD LUNCH YET.
TEN MINUTES LATER...
......
じわか
JIWAKA (SCUTTLE)
MIIIN
じわか じわか
JIWAKA JIWAKA
MIIIN
...OR SO I THOUGHT.
MIIIN
MIIIN
...UM.
WHAT'S THE MATTER?

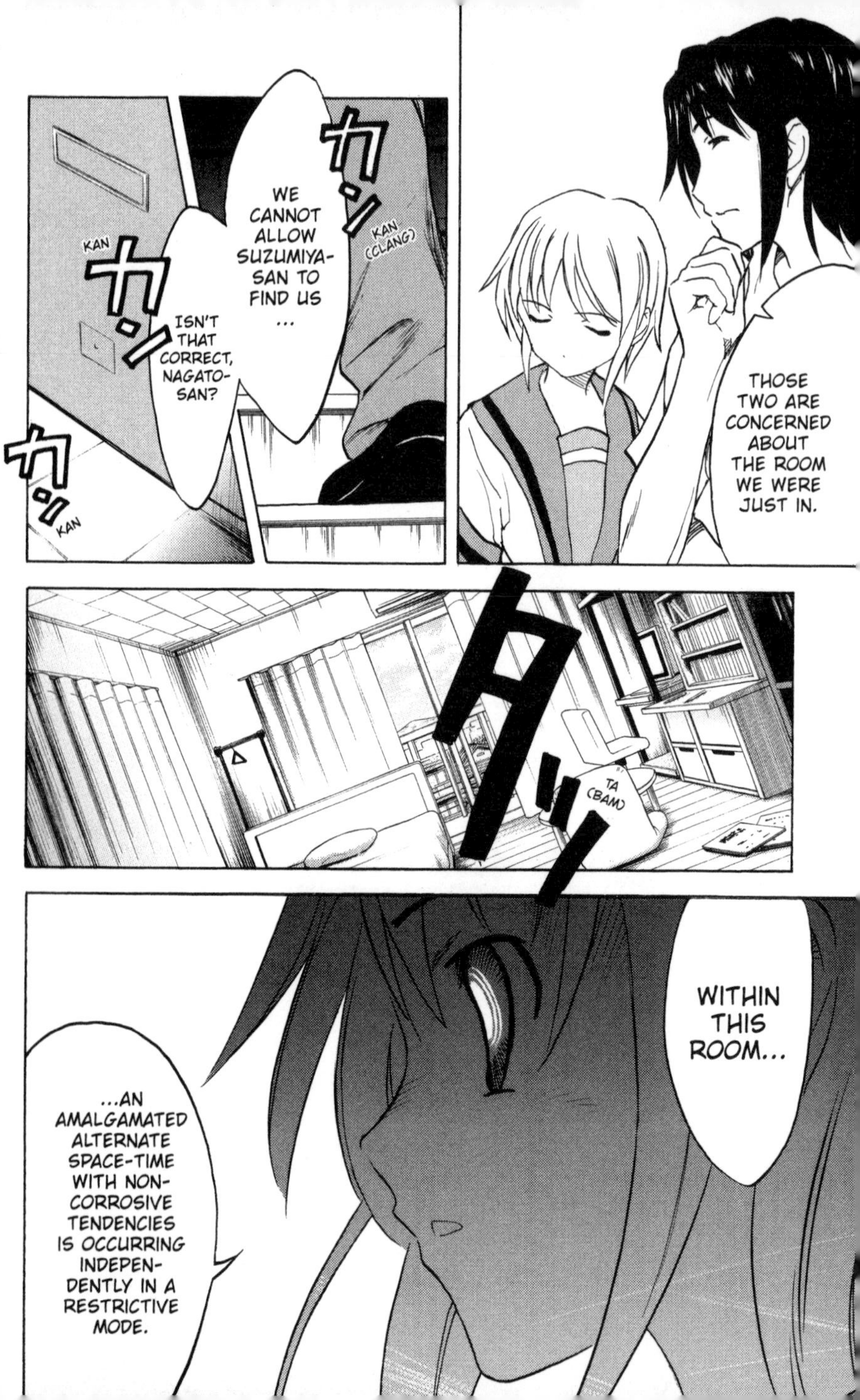
THOSE TWO ARE CONCERNED ABOUT THE ROOM WE WERE JUST IN.
カン
KAN (CLANG)
WE CANNOT ALLOW SUZUMIYA-SAN TO FIND US ...
カン
KAN
ISN'T THAT CORRECT, NAGATO-SAN?
カン
KAN
タッ
TA (BAM)
WITHIN THIS ROOM...
...AN AMALGAMATED ALTERNATE SPACE-TIME WITH NON-CORROSIVE TENDENCIES IS OCCURRING INDEPENDENTLY IN A RESTRICTIVE MODE.

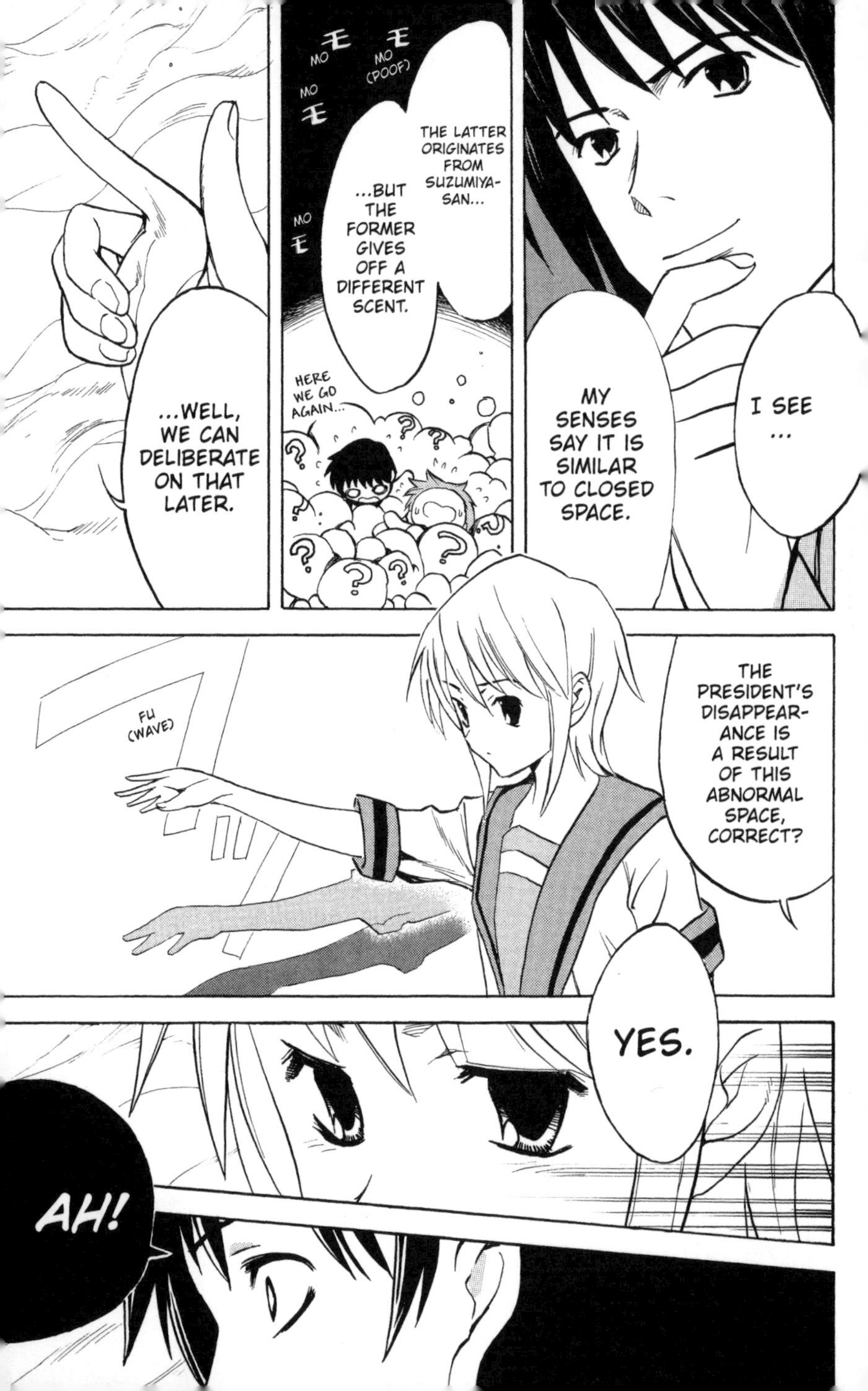
I SEE ...
MY SENSES SAY IT IS SIMILAR TO CLOSED SPACE.
THE LATTER ORIGINATES FROM SUZUMIYA-SAN...
...BUT THE FORMER GIVES OFF A DIFFERENT SCENT.
MO MO (POOF) MO MO
HERE WE GO AGAIN...
...WELL, WE CAN DELIBERATE ON THAT LATER.
THE PRESIDENT'S DISAPPEARANCE IS A RESULT OF THIS ABNORMAL SPACE, CORRECT?
FU (WAVE)
YES.
AH!

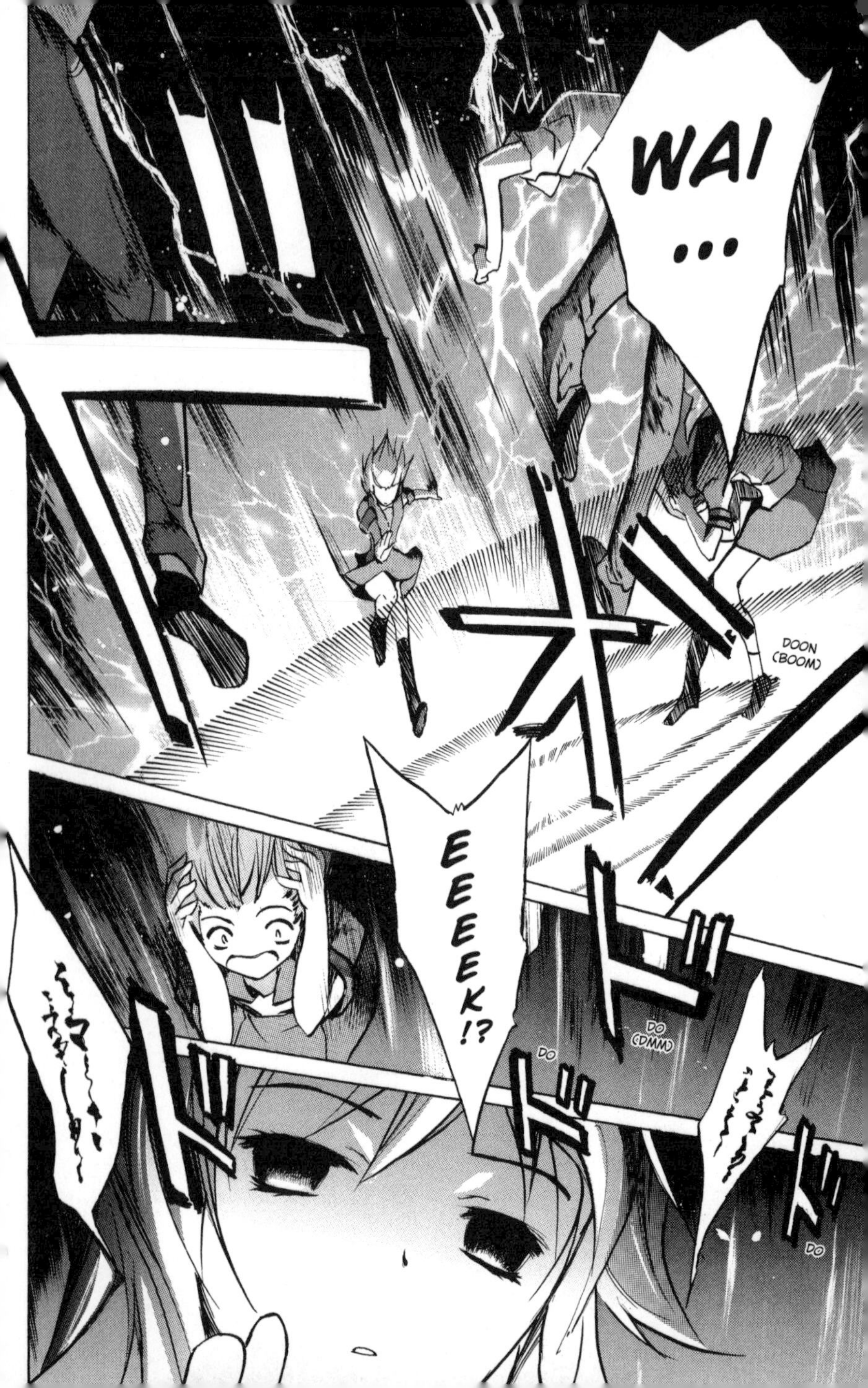
WAI ...
DOON (BOOM)
EEEEEK!?
DO (DMM)
DO
DO

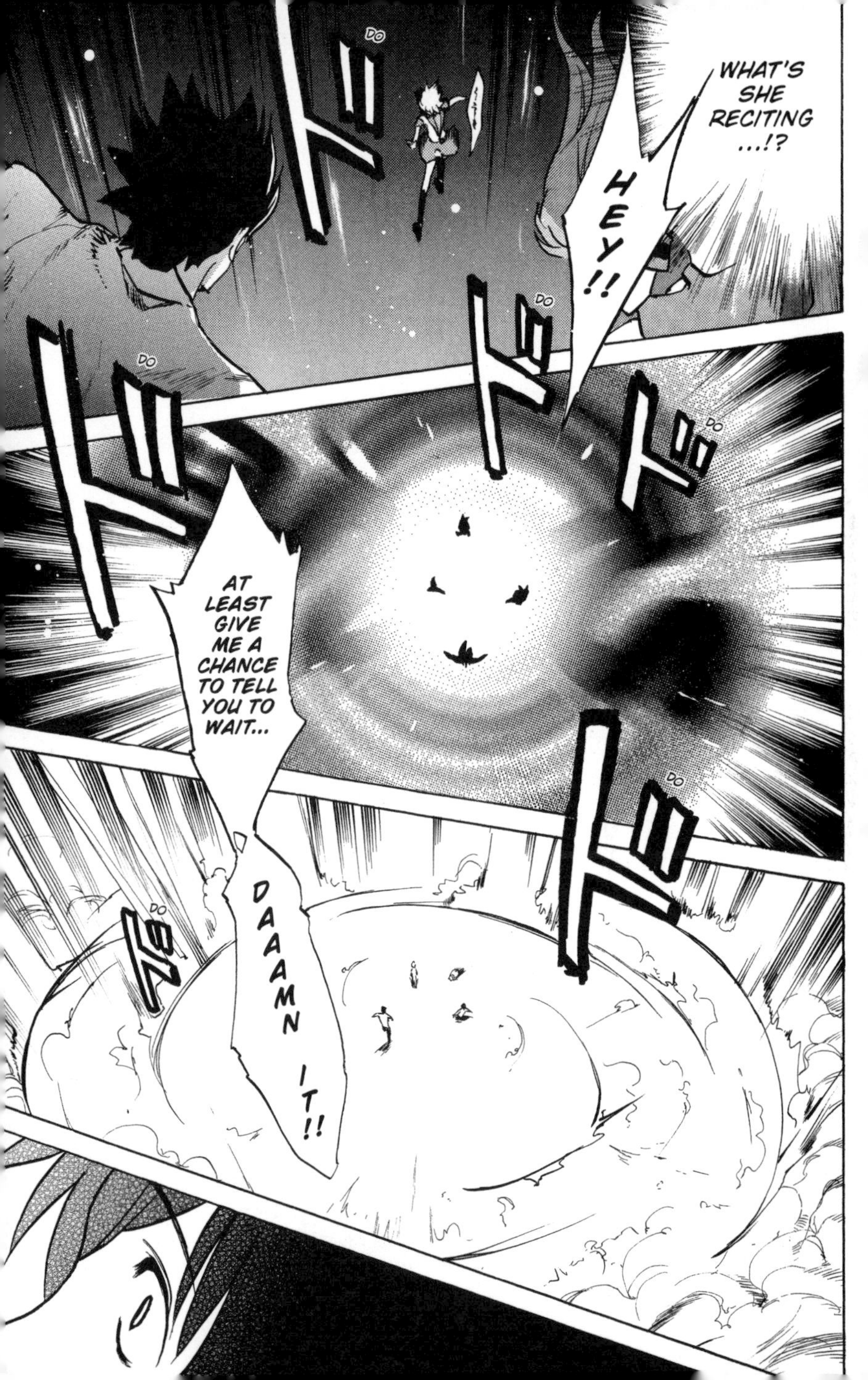
WHAT'S SHE RECITING ...!?
HEY!!
DO
DO
DO
DO
AT LEAST GIVE ME A CHANCE TO TELL YOU TO WAIT...
DO
DO
DAAAAMN IT!!

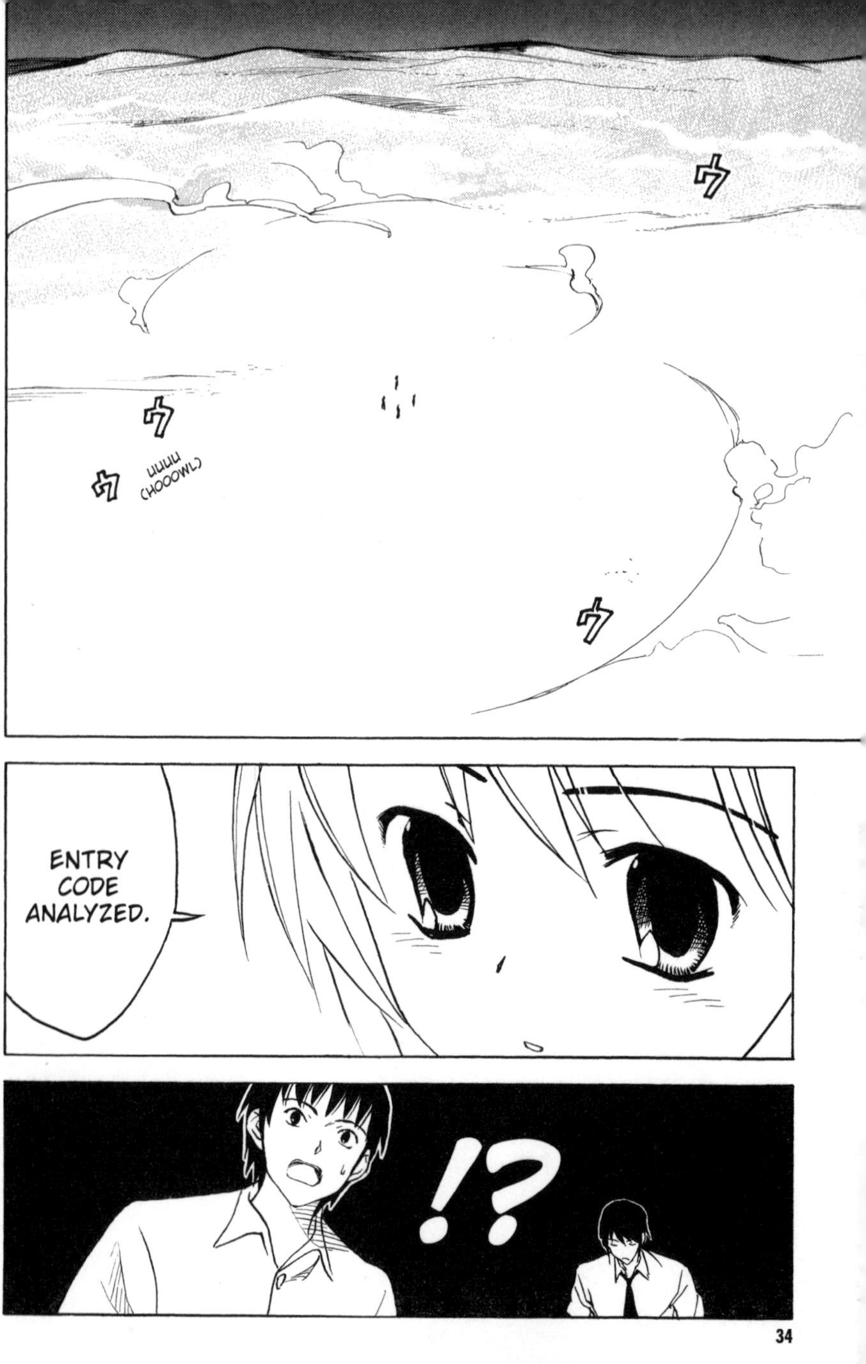
ウ
ウ
ウ
UUUU (HOOOWL)
ウ
ENTRY CODE ANALYZED.
!?

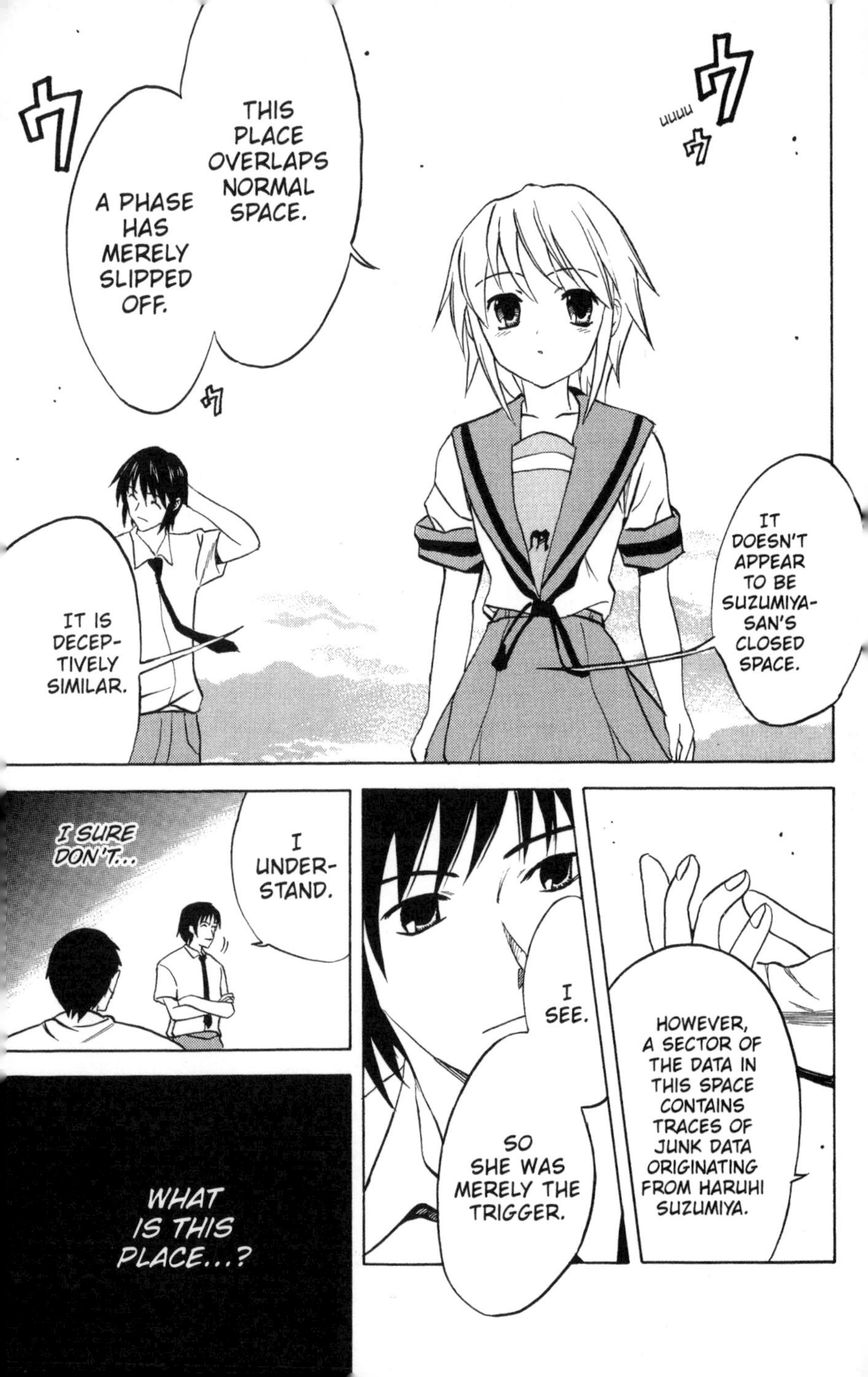
ウ
UUUU
ウ
ウ
THIS PLACE OVERLAPS NORMAL SPACE.
A PHASE HAS MERELY SLIPPED OFF.
ウ
IT DOESN'T APPEAR TO BE SUZUMIYA-SAN'S CLOSED SPACE.
IT IS DECEPTIVELY SIMILAR.
HOWEVER, A SECTOR OF THE DATA IN THIS SPACE CONTAINS TRACES OF JUNK DATA ORIGINATING FROM HARUHI SUZUMIYA.
I SEE.
SO SHE WAS MERELY THE TRIGGER.
I UNDERSTAND.
I SURE DON'T...
WHAT IS THIS PLACE...?

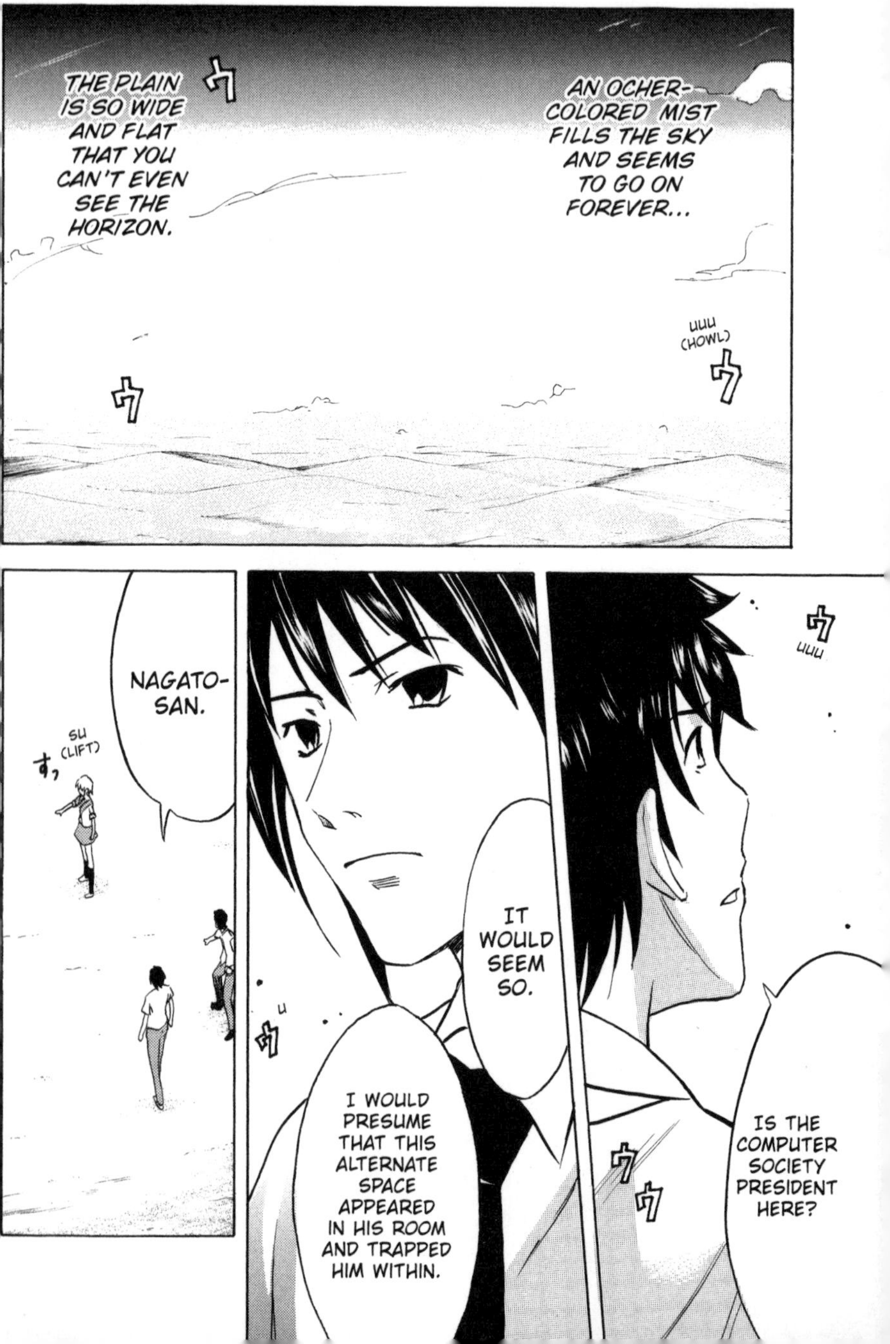
AN OCHER-COLORED MIST FILLS THE SKY AND SEEMS TO GO ON FOREVER...
THE PLAIN IS SO WIDE AND FLAT THAT YOU CAN'T EVEN SEE THE HORIZON.
UUU (HOWL)
UUU
IS THE COMPUTER SOCIETY PRESIDENT HERE?
IT WOULD SEEM SO.
I WOULD PRESUME THAT THIS ALTERNATE SPACE APPEARED IN HIS ROOM AND TRAPPED HIM WITHIN.
U
NAGATO-SAN.
SU (LIFT)

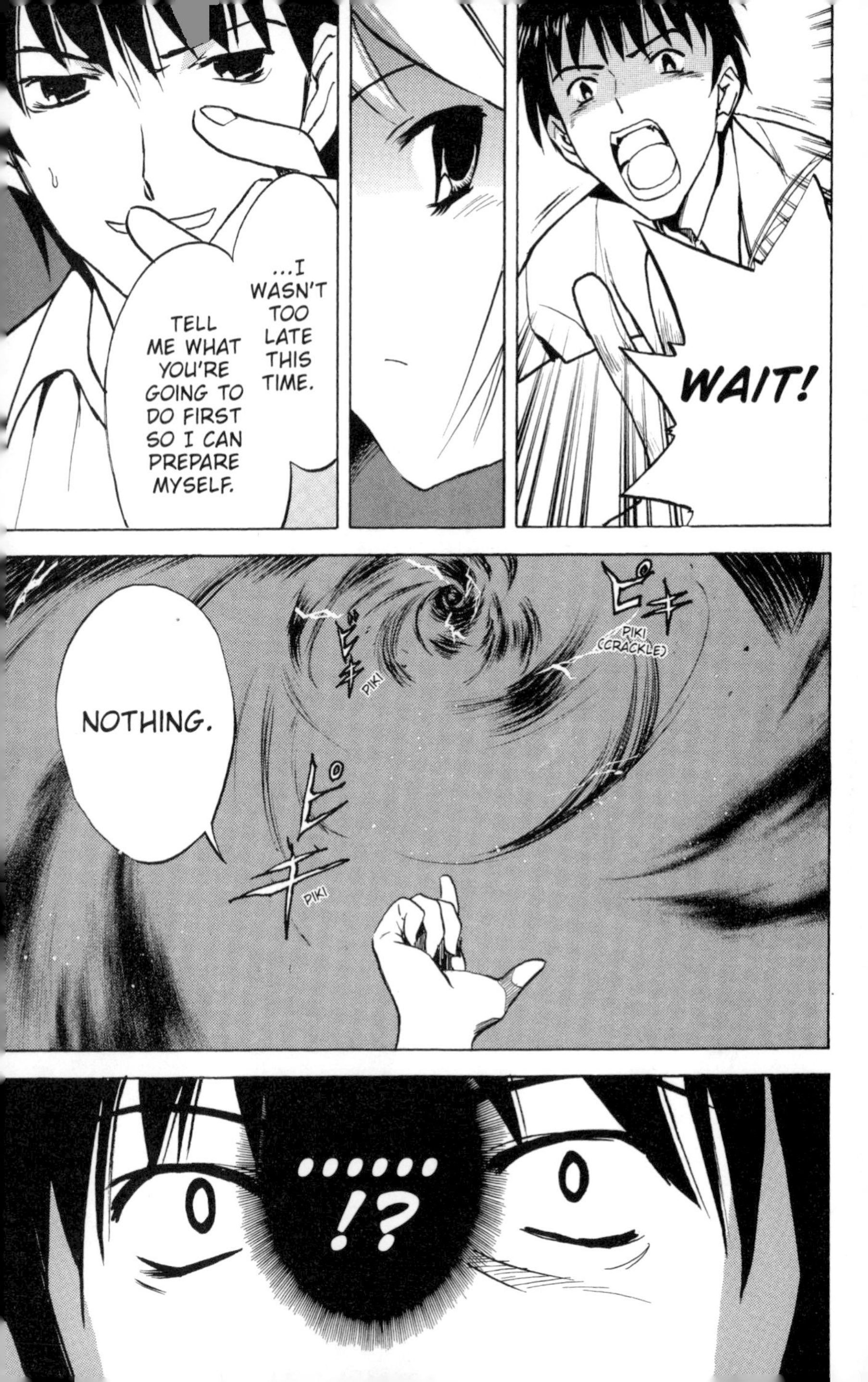
WAIT!
...I WASN'T TOO LATE THIS TIME.
TELL ME WHAT YOU'RE GOING TO DO FIRST SO I CAN PREPARE MYSELF.
ピキ
PIKI (CRACKLE)
ピキ
PIKI
NOTHING.
ピキ
PIKI
......!?

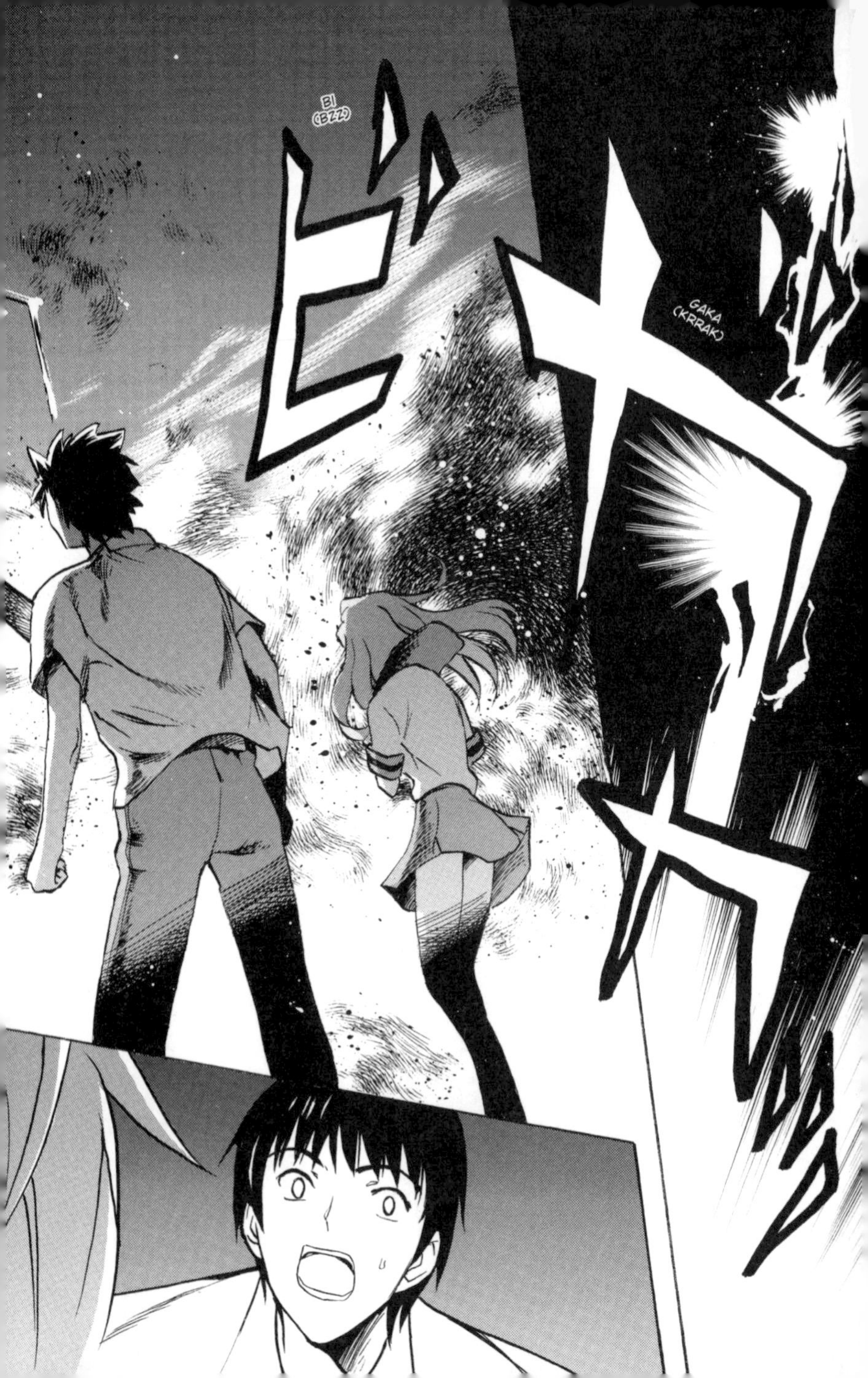
GAKA
(KRRAK)
BI
(BZZ)

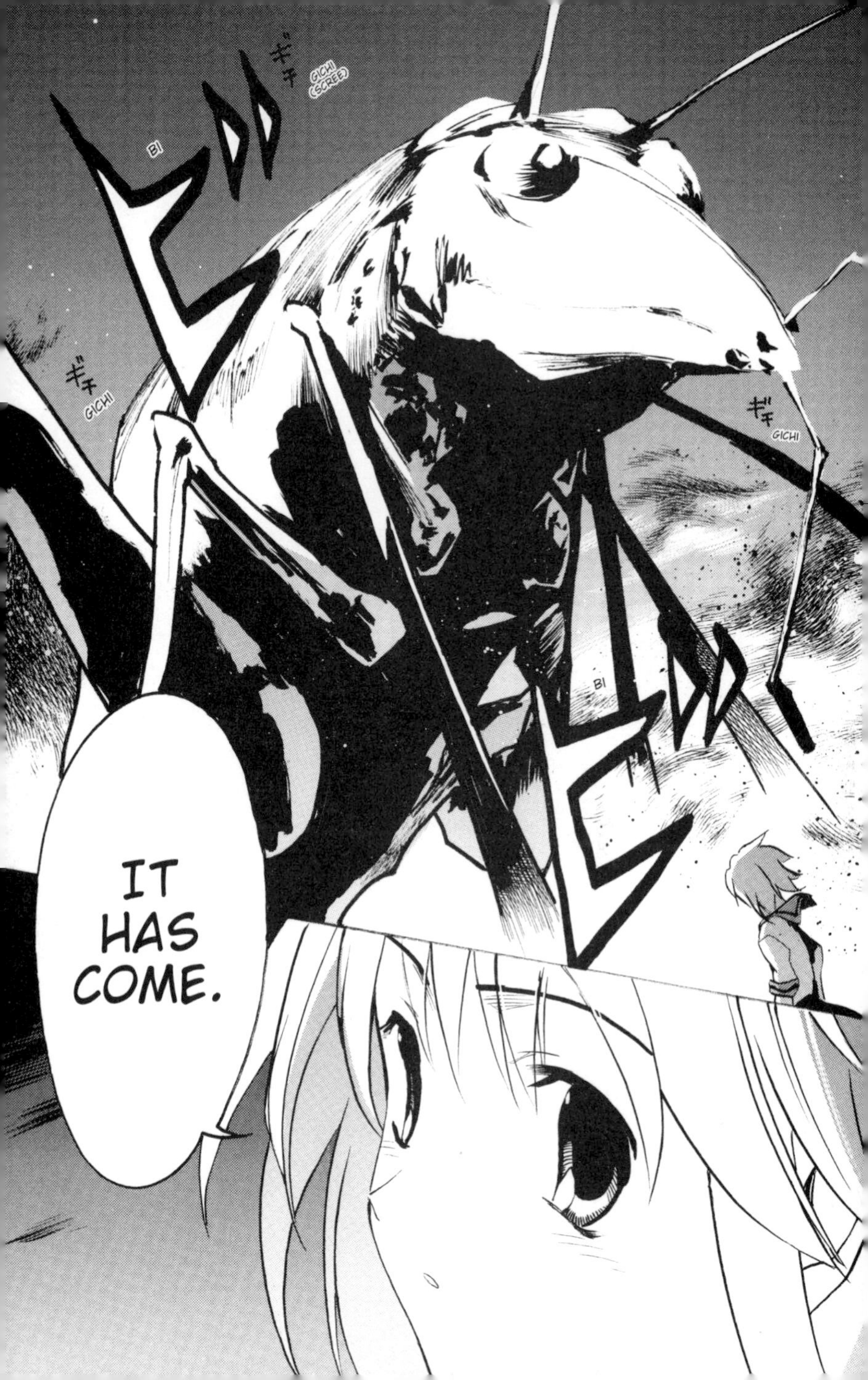
ギチ
GICHI (SCREE)
BI
ギチ
GICHI
ギチ
GICHI
BI
IT HAS COME.

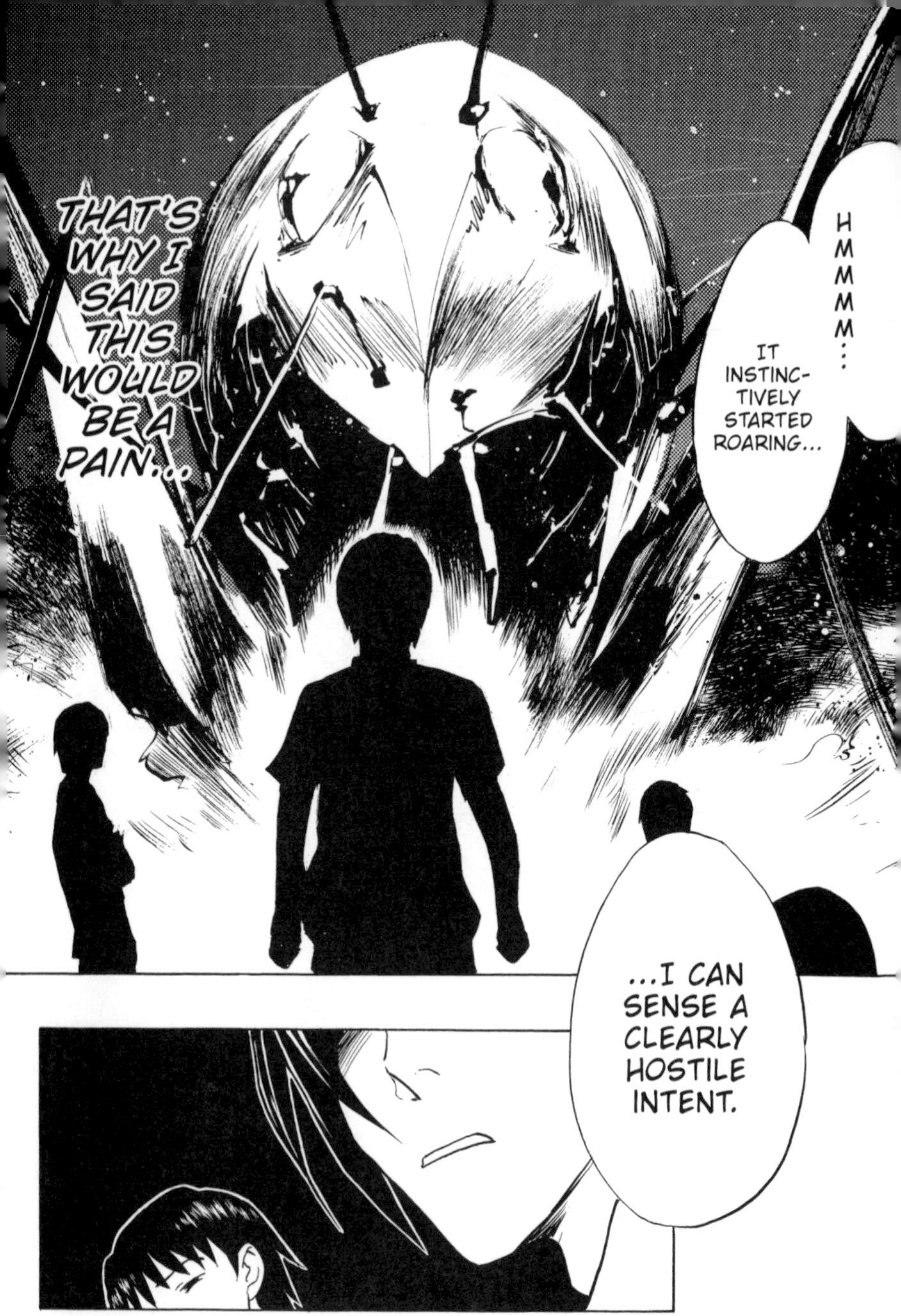
HMMMM...
IT INSTINC-TIVELY STARTED ROARING...
THAT'S WHY I SAID THIS WOULD BE A PAIN...
...I CAN SENSE A CLEARLY HOSTILE INTENT.

MYSTERIQUE SIGN I : END

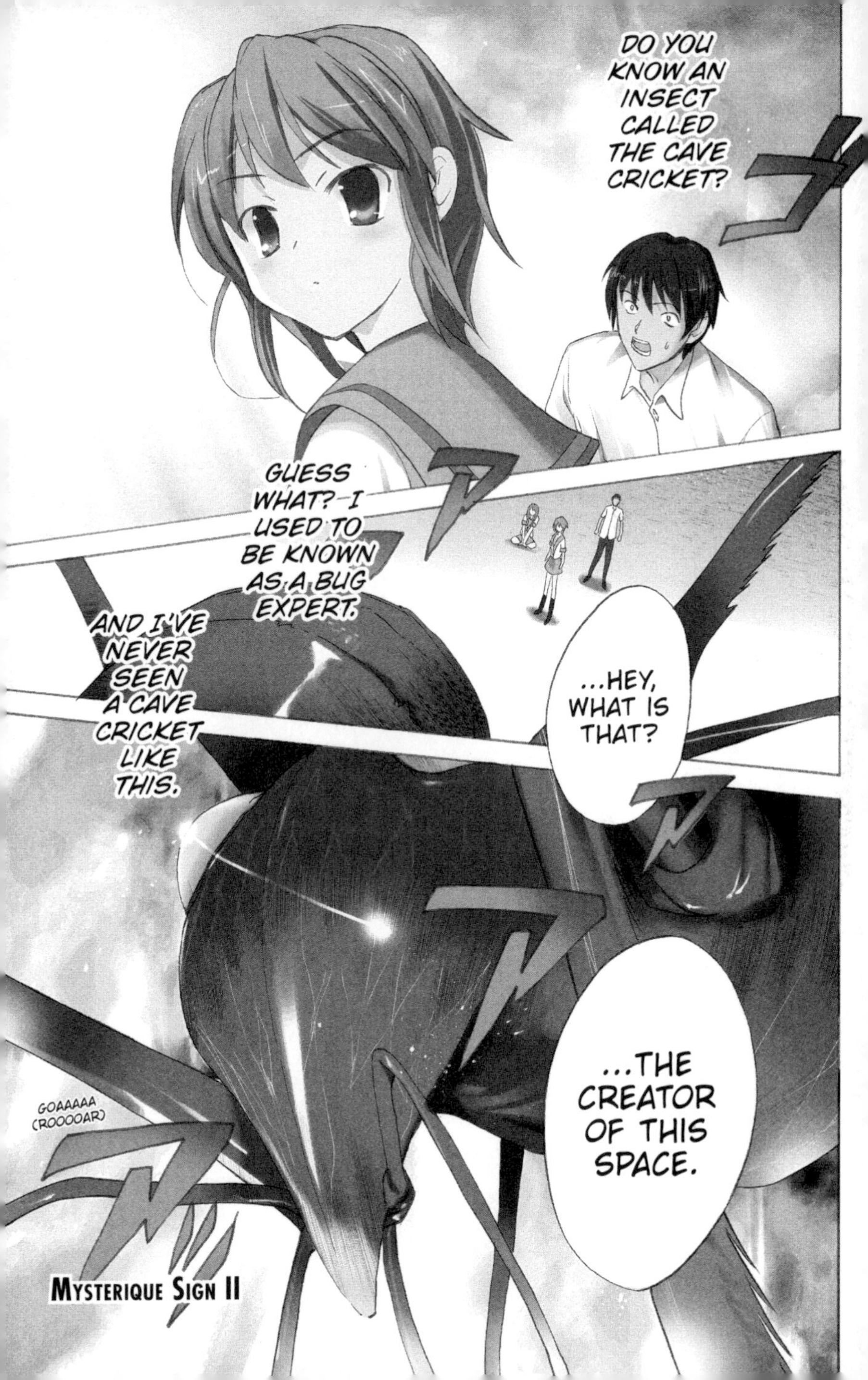
DO YOU KNOW AN INSECT CALLED THE CAVE CRICKET?
GUESS WHAT? I USED TO BE KNOWN AS A BUG EXPERT.
...HEY, WHAT IS THAT?
AND I'VE NEVER SEEN A CAVE CRICKET LIKE THIS.
...THE CREATOR OF THIS SPACE.
GOAAAAA (ROOOOAR)

Mysterique Sign II

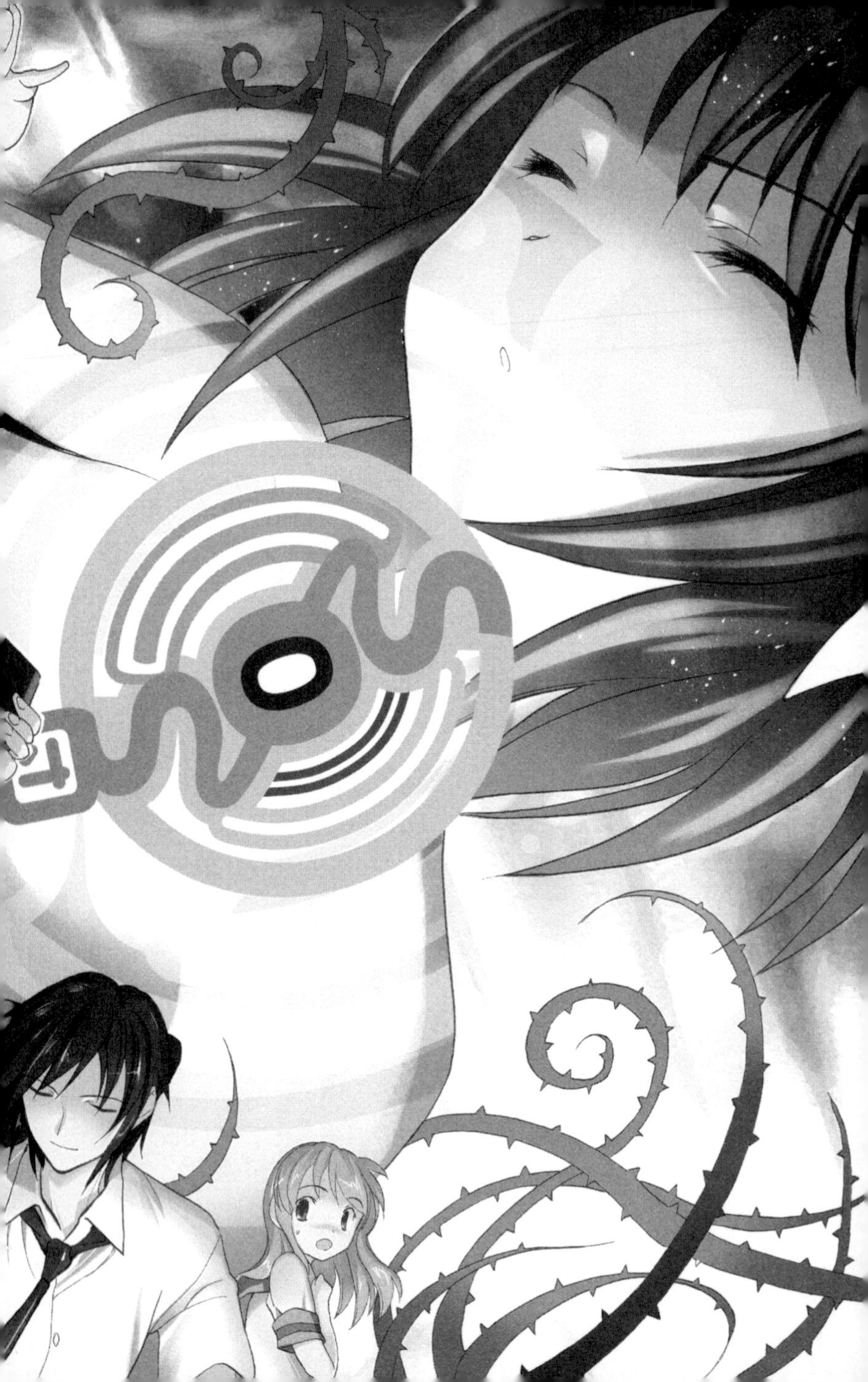

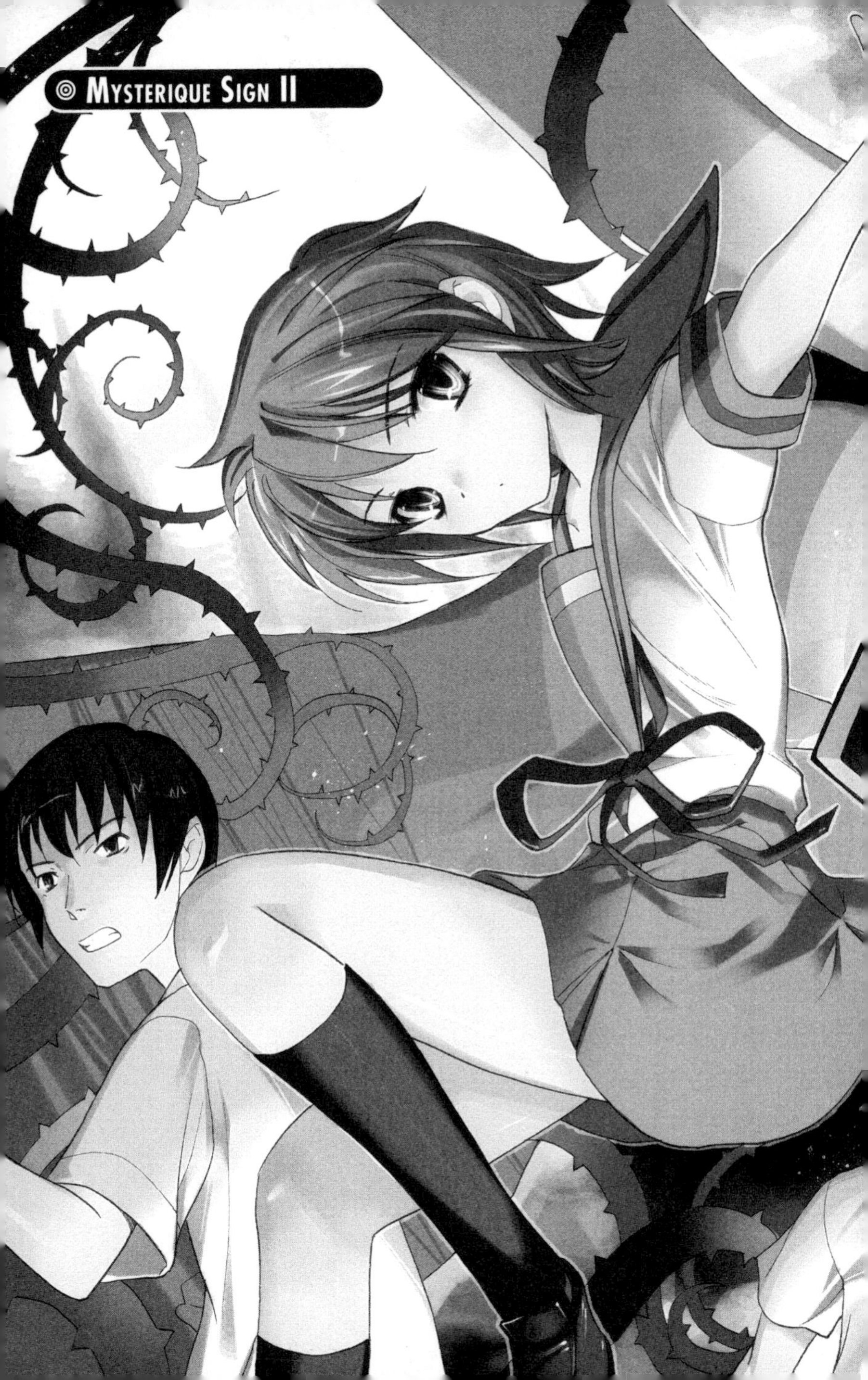
◎ MYSTERIQUE SIGN II

THE MELANCHOLY OF HARUHI SUZUMIYA

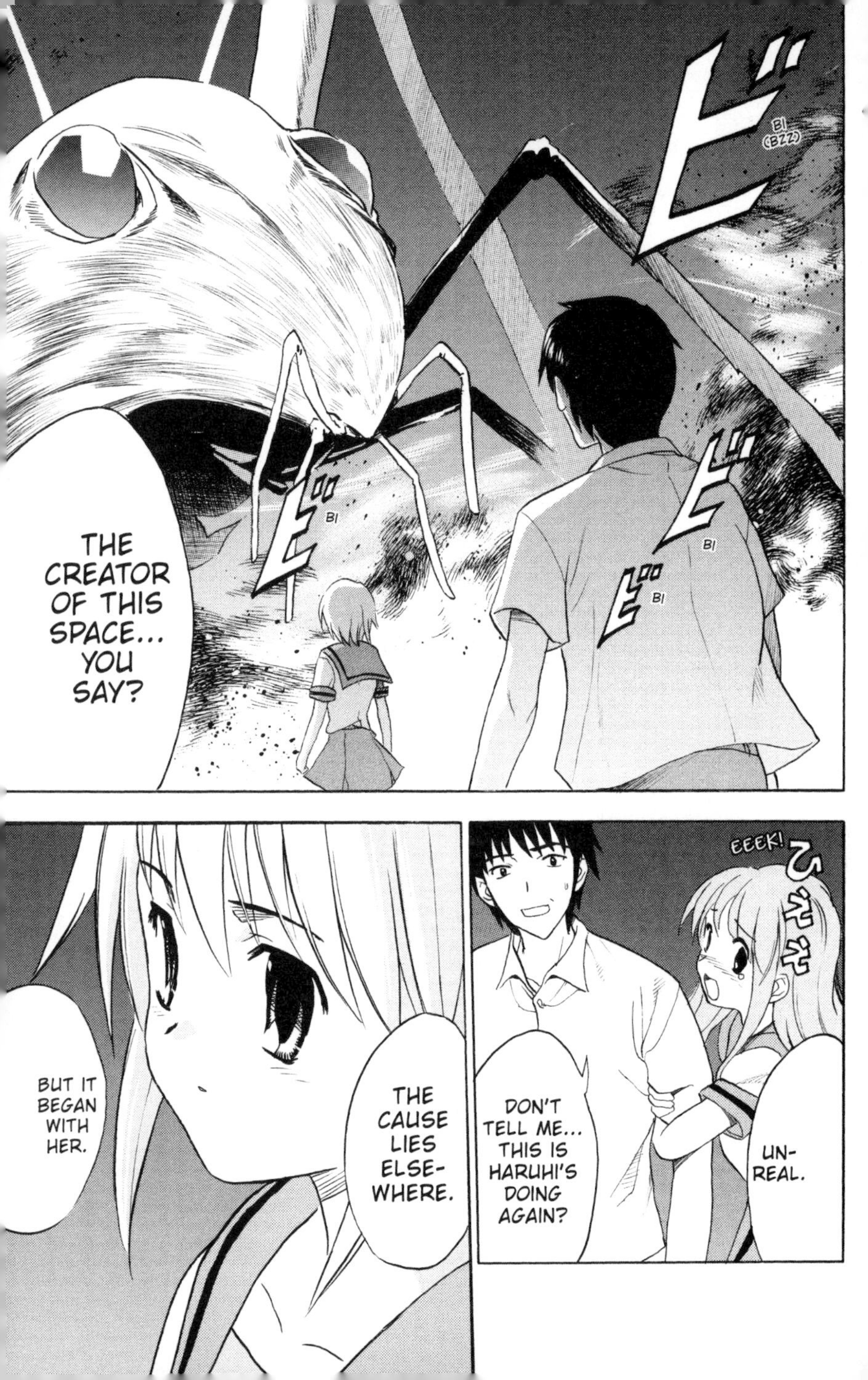
BI (BZZ)
BI
BI
BI
THE CREATOR OF THIS SPACE... YOU SAY?
EEEK!
UN-REAL.
DON'T TELL ME... THIS IS HARUHI'S DOING AGAIN?
THE CAUSE LIES ELSE-WHERE.
BUT IT BEGAN WITH HER.

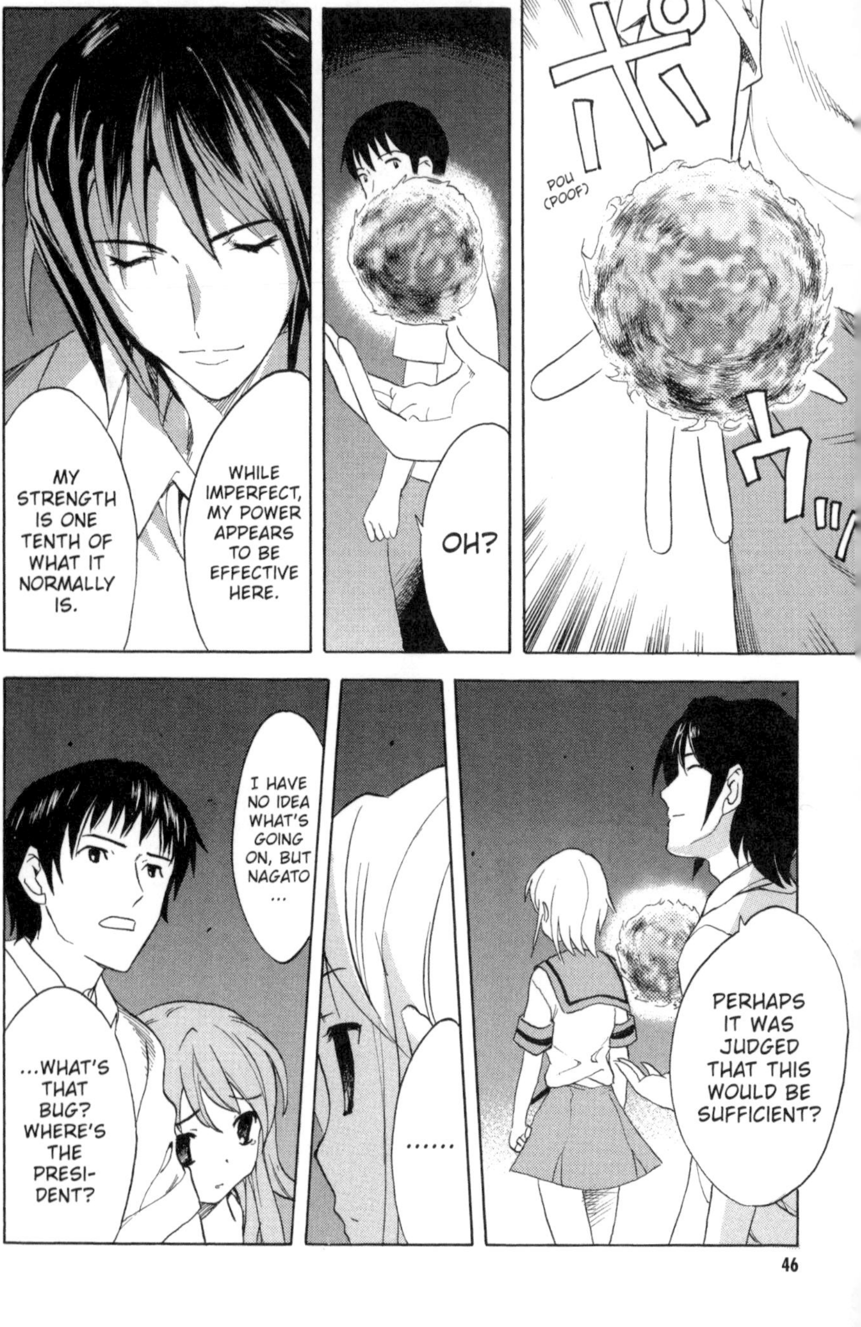
POU (POOF)
OH?
WHILE IMPERFECT, MY POWER APPEARS TO BE EFFECTIVE HERE.
MY STRENGTH IS ONE TENTH OF WHAT IT NORMALLY IS.
PERHAPS IT WAS JUDGED THAT THIS WOULD BE SUFFICIENT?
I HAVE NO IDEA WHAT'S GOING ON, BUT NAGATO...
......
...WHAT'S THAT BUG? WHERE'S THE PRESI-DENT?

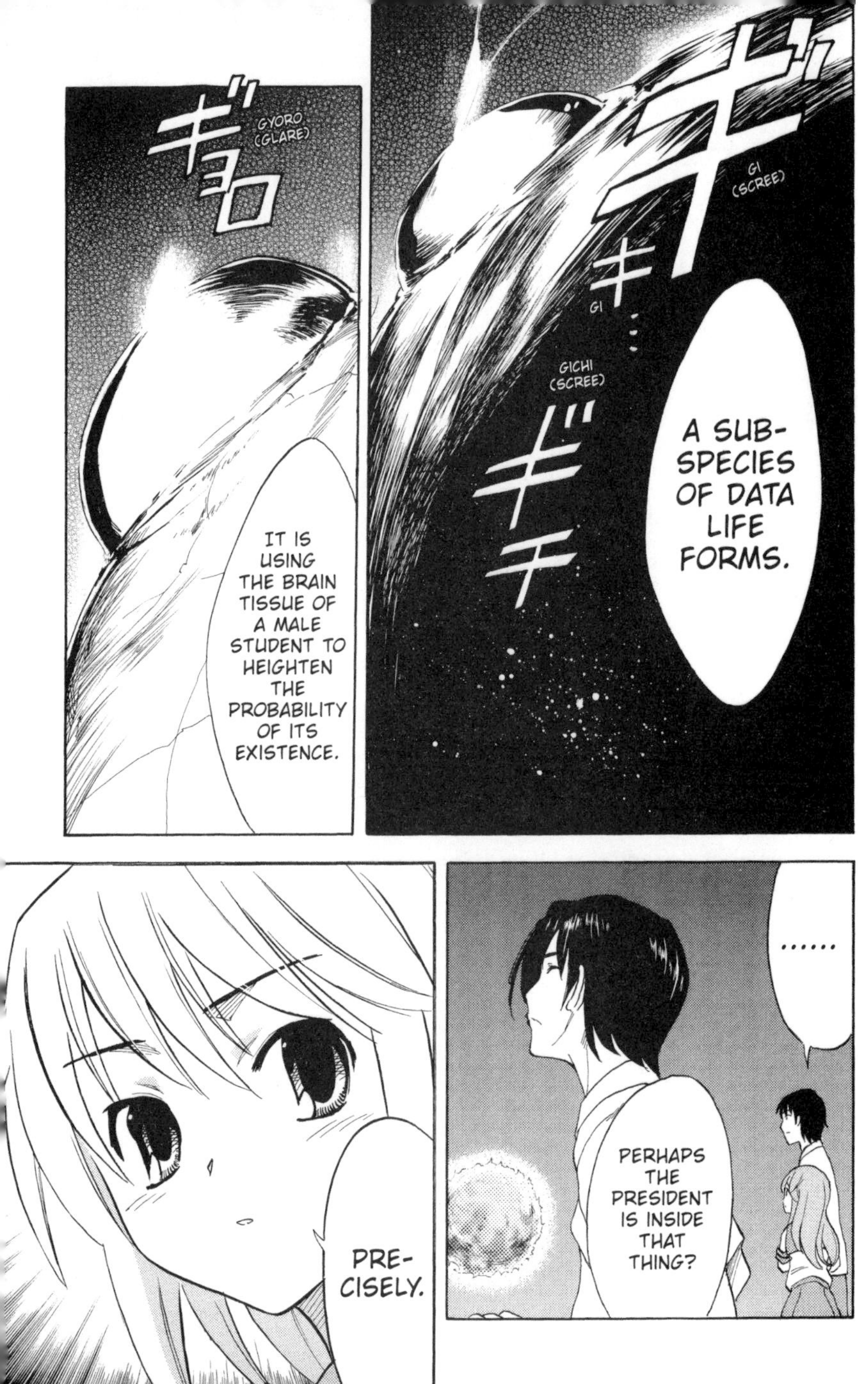
GI (SCREE)
A SUB-SPECIES OF DATA LIFE FORMS.
GI
GICHI (SCREE)
GYORO (GLARE)
IT IS USING THE BRAIN TISSUE OF A MALE STUDENT TO HEIGHTEN THE PROBABILITY OF ITS EXISTENCE.
......
PERHAPS THE PRESIDENT IS INSIDE THAT THING?
PRE-CISELY.

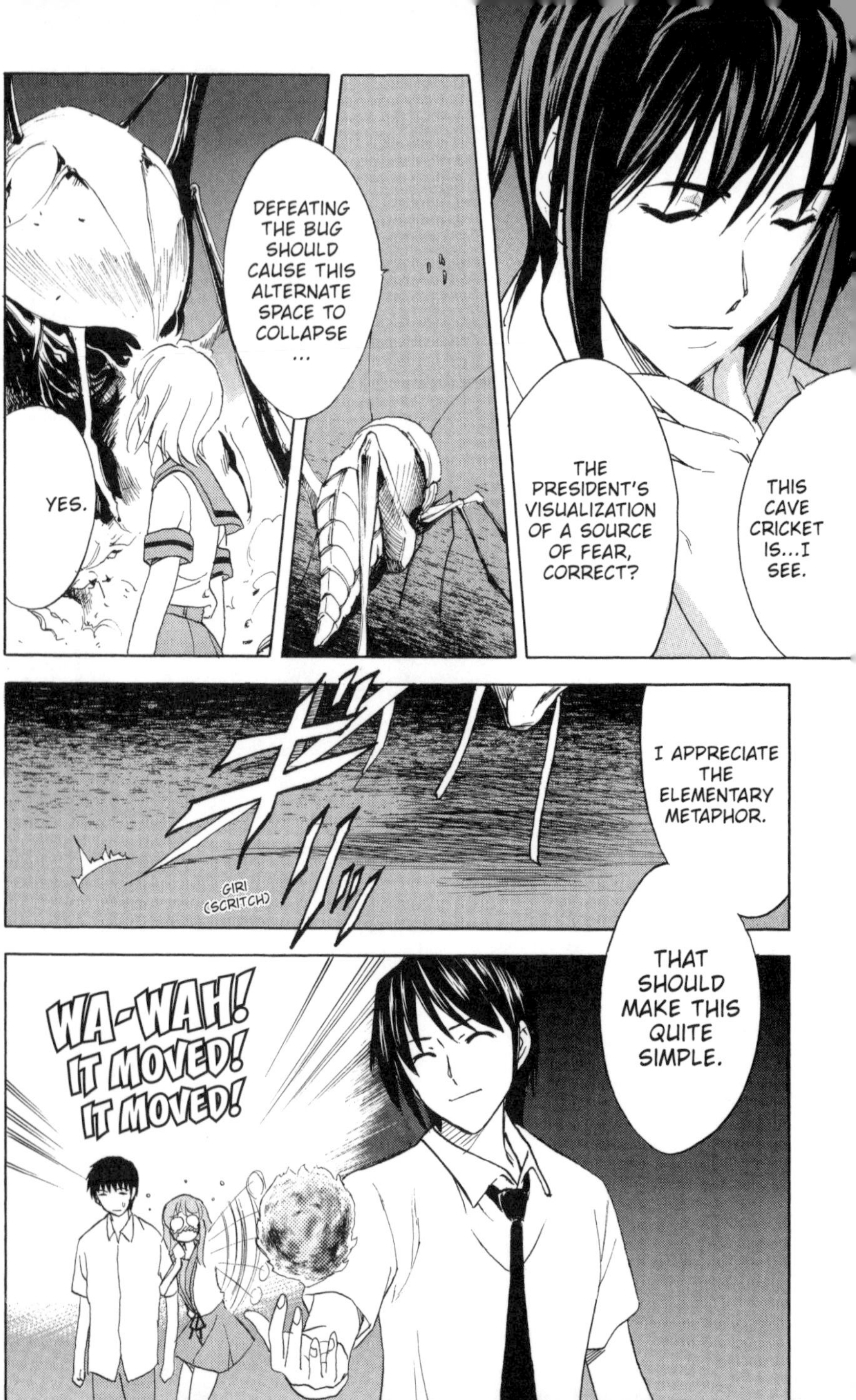
THIS CAVE CRICKET IS...I SEE.
THE PRESIDENT'S VISUALIZATION OF A SOURCE OF FEAR, CORRECT?
DEFEATING THE BUG SHOULD CAUSE THIS ALTERNATE SPACE TO COLLAPSE ...
YES.
I APPRECIATE THE ELEMENTARY METAPHOR.
GIRI (SCRITCH)
THAT SHOULD MAKE THIS QUITE SIMPLE.
WA-WAH! IT MOVED! IT MOVED!

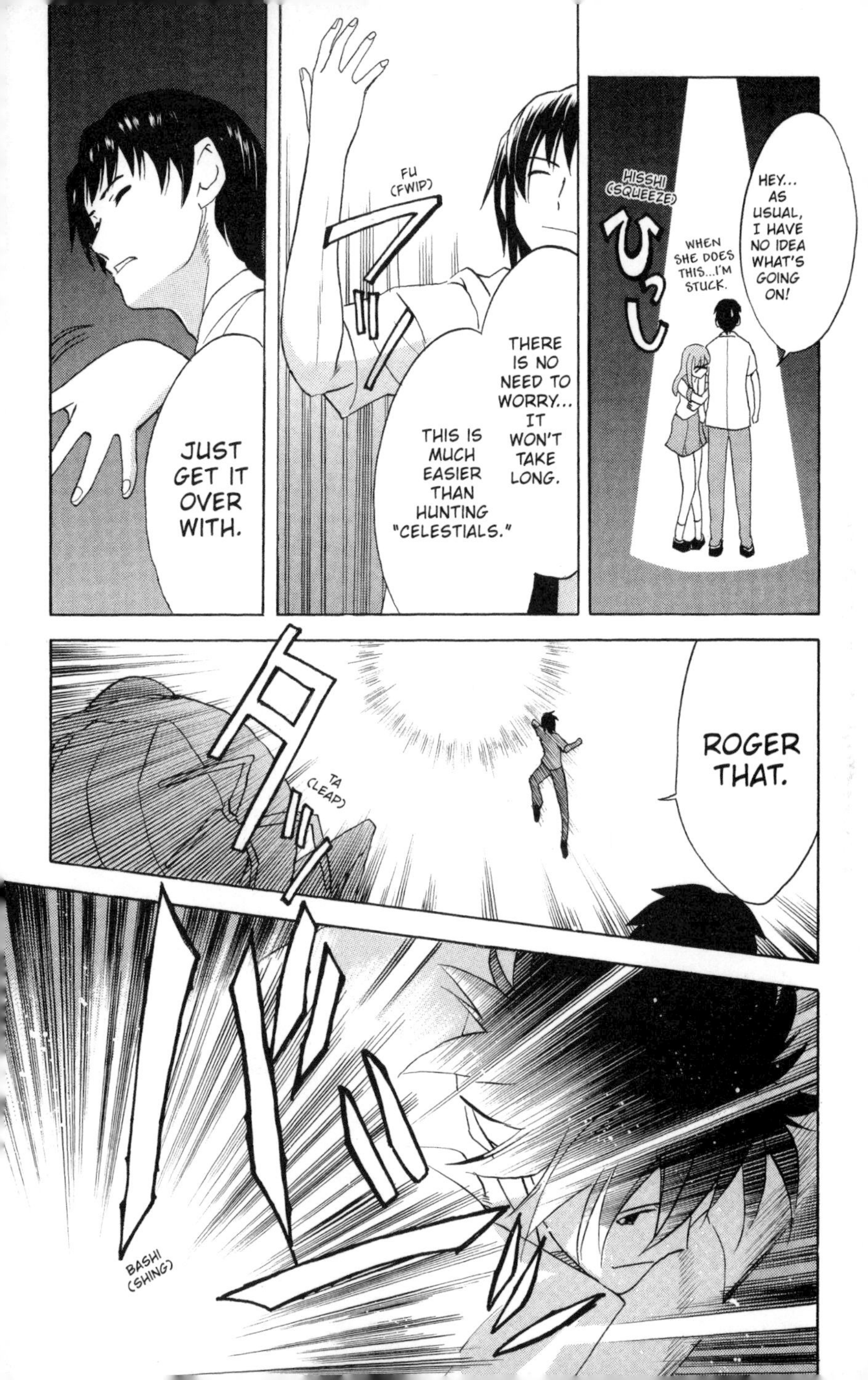
HEY... AS USUAL, I HAVE NO IDEA WHAT'S GOING ON!
HISSHI (SQUEEZE)
WHEN SHE DOES THIS...I'M STUCK.
FU (FWIP)
THERE IS NO NEED TO WORRY... IT WON'T TAKE LONG.
THIS IS MUCH EASIER THAN HUNTING "CELESTIALS."
JUST GET IT OVER WITH.
ROGER THAT.
TA (LEAP)
BASHI (SHING)

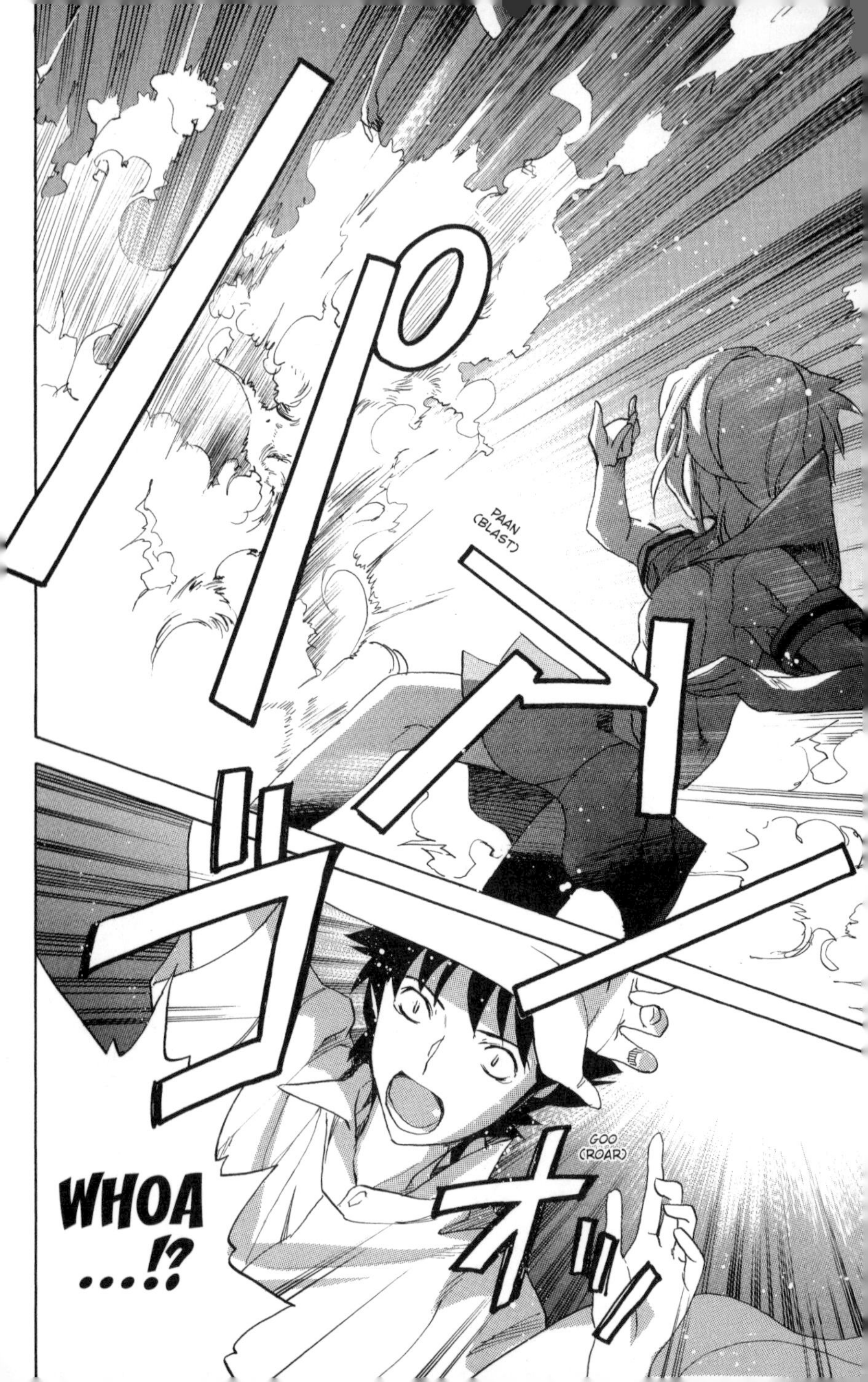
PAAN
(BLAST)
GOO
(ROAR)
WHOA
...!?

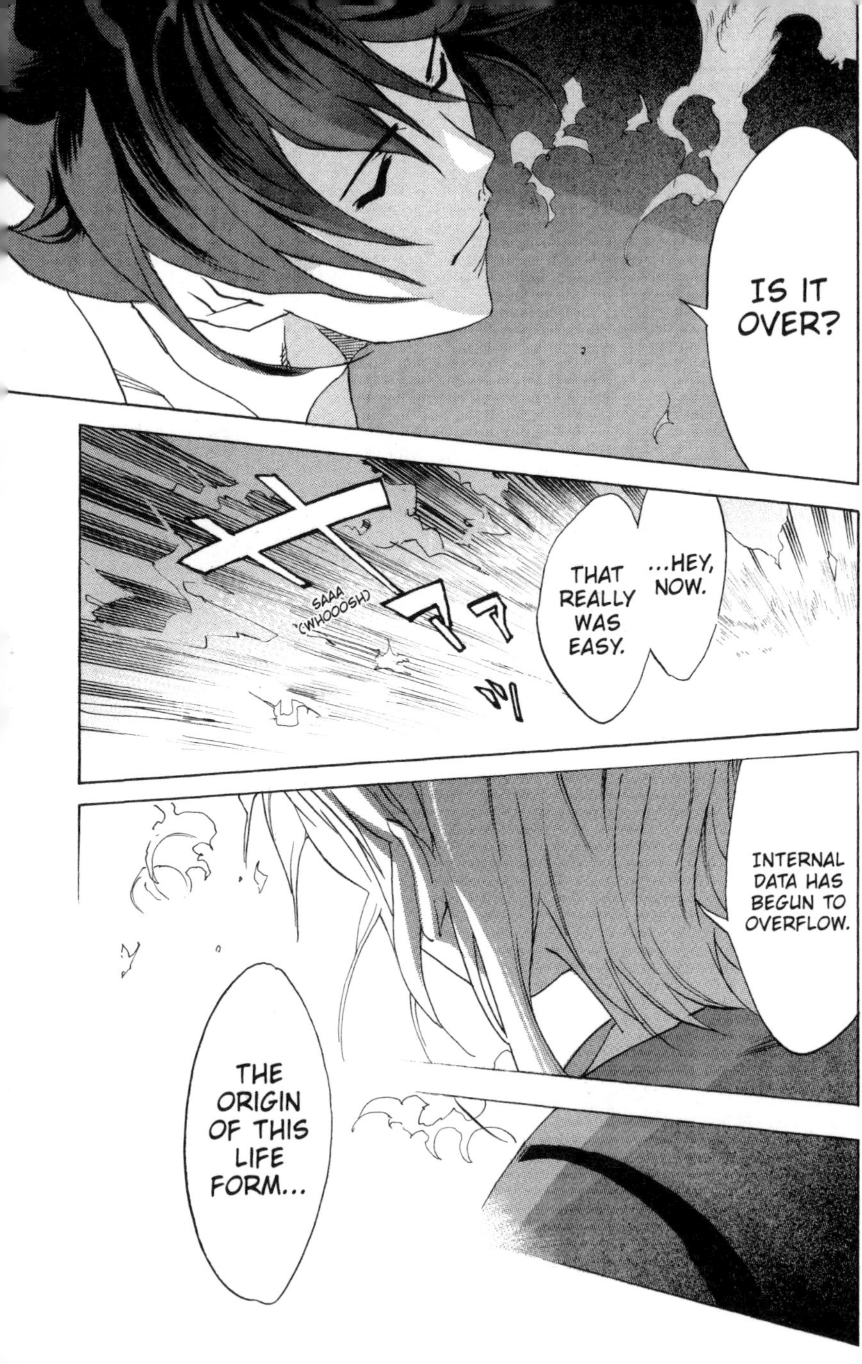
IS IT OVER?
...HEY, NOW.
THAT REALLY WAS EASY.
SAAA (WHOOOSH)
INTERNAL DATA HAS BEGUN TO OVERFLOW.
THE ORIGIN OF THIS LIFE FORM...

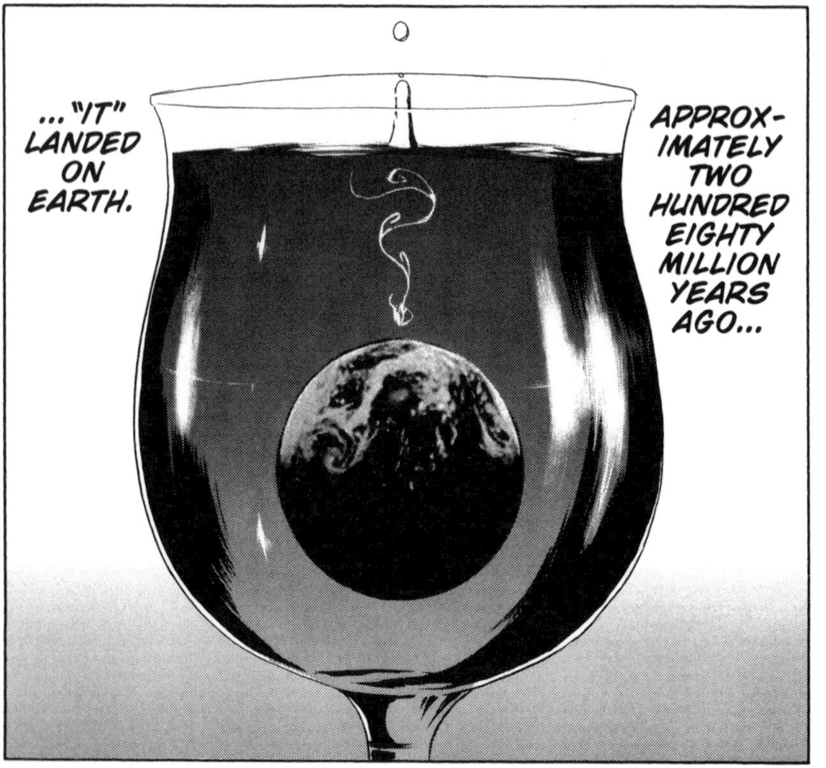
APPROX-
IMATELY
TWO
HUNDRED
EIGHTY
MILLION
YEARS
AGO...
..."IT"
LANDED
ON
EARTH.

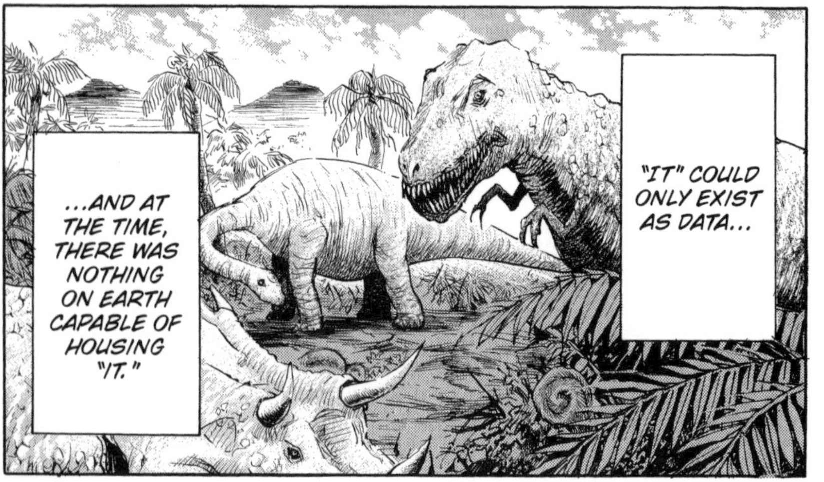
"IT" COULD
ONLY EXIST
AS DATA...
...AND AT
THE TIME,
THERE WAS
NOTHING
ON EARTH
CAPABLE OF
HOUSING
"IT."

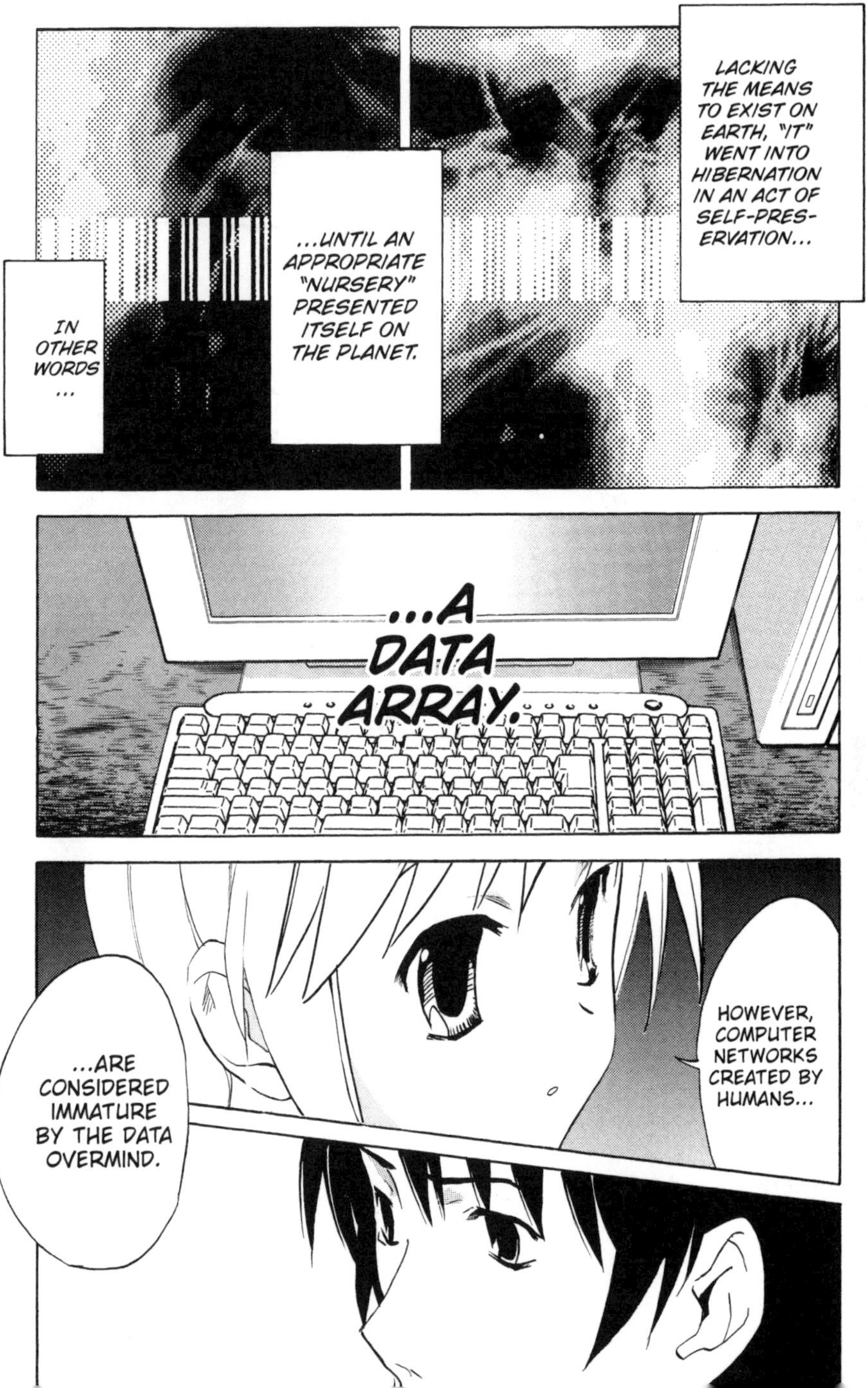
LACKING THE MEANS TO EXIST ON EARTH, "IT" WENT INTO HIBERNATION IN AN ACT OF SELF-PRES-ERVATION...
...UNTIL AN APPROPRIATE "NURSERY" PRESENTED ITSELF ON THE PLANET.
IN OTHER WORDS...
...A DATA ARRAY.
HOWEVER, COMPUTER NETWORKS CREATED BY HUMANS...
...ARE CONSIDERED IMMATURE BY THE DATA OVERMIND.

AND THIS WAS THE RESULT.

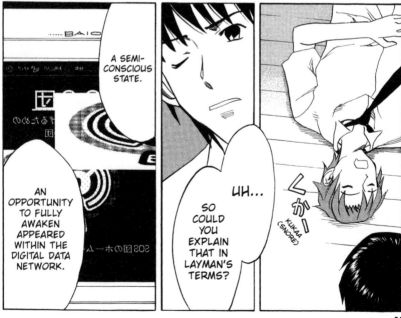

A SEMI-CONSCIOUS STATE.

AN OPPORTUNITY TO FULLY AWAKEN APPEARED WITHIN THE DIGITAL DATA NETWORK.

UH...

SO COULD YOU EXPLAIN THAT IN LAYMAN'S TERMS?

KUKAA (SNORE)

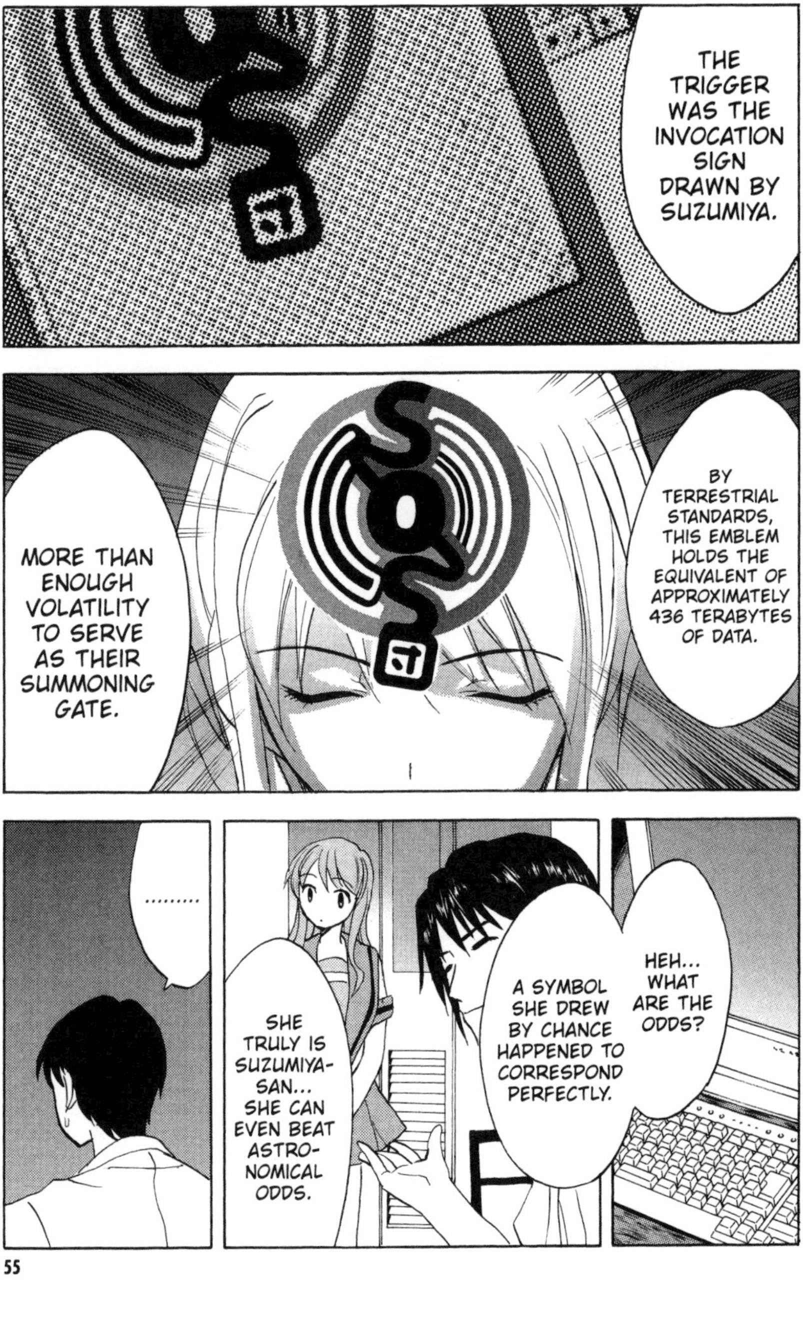
THE TRIGGER WAS THE INVOCATION SIGN DRAWN BY SUZUMIYA.
BY TERRESTRIAL STANDARDS, THIS EMBLEM HOLDS THE EQUIVALENT OF APPROXIMATELY 436 TERABYTES OF DATA.
MORE THAN ENOUGH VOLATILITY TO SERVE AS THEIR SUMMONING GATE.
HEH... WHAT ARE THE ODDS?
A SYMBOL SHE DREW BY CHANCE HAPPENED TO CORRESPOND PERFECTLY.
SHE TRULY IS SUZUMIYA-SAN... SHE CAN EVEN BEAT ASTRONOMICAL ODDS.
....

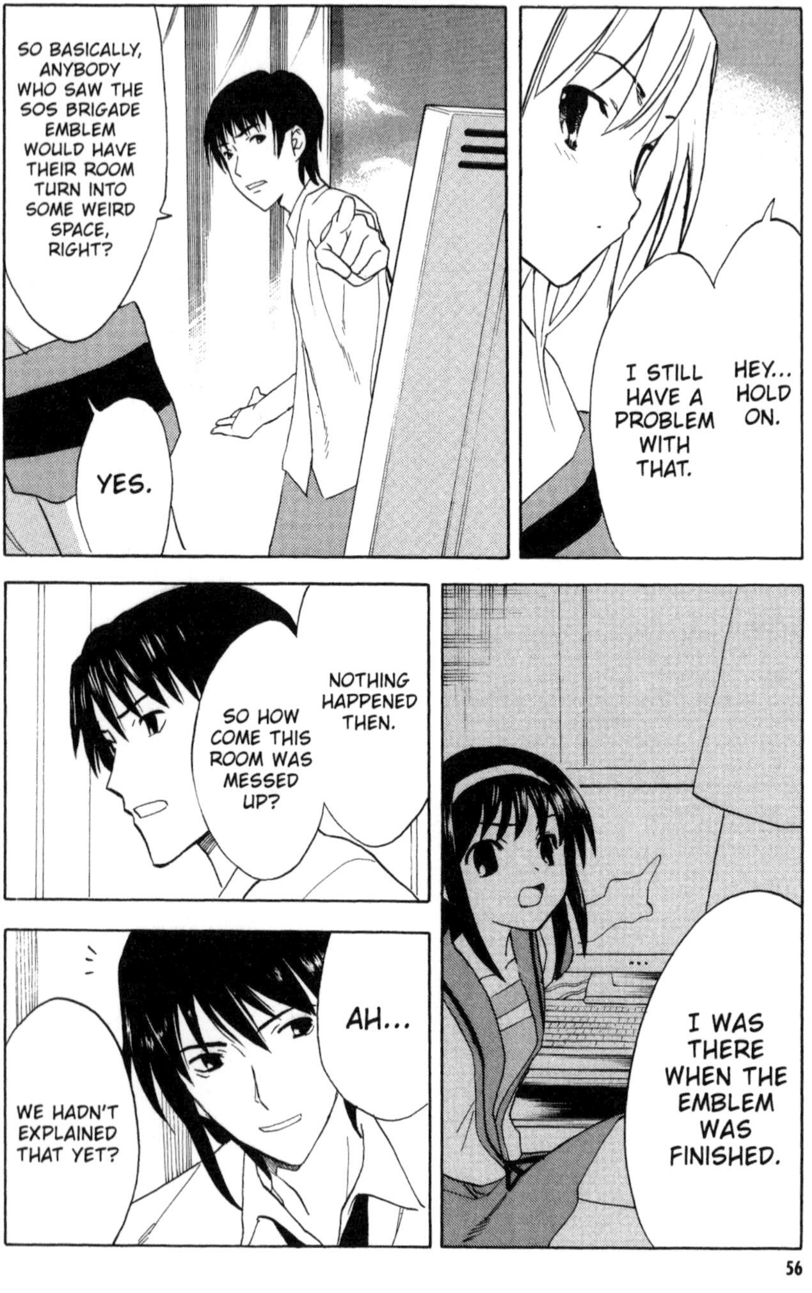
HEY... HOLD ON.
I STILL HAVE A PROBLEM WITH THAT.
SO BASICALLY, ANYBODY WHO SAW THE SOS BRIGADE EMBLEM WOULD HAVE THEIR ROOM TURN INTO SOME WEIRD SPACE, RIGHT?
YES.
I WAS THERE WHEN THE EMBLEM WAS FINISHED.
NOTHING HAPPENED THEN.
SO HOW COME THIS ROOM WAS MESSED UP?
AH...
WE HADN'T EXPLAINED THAT YET?

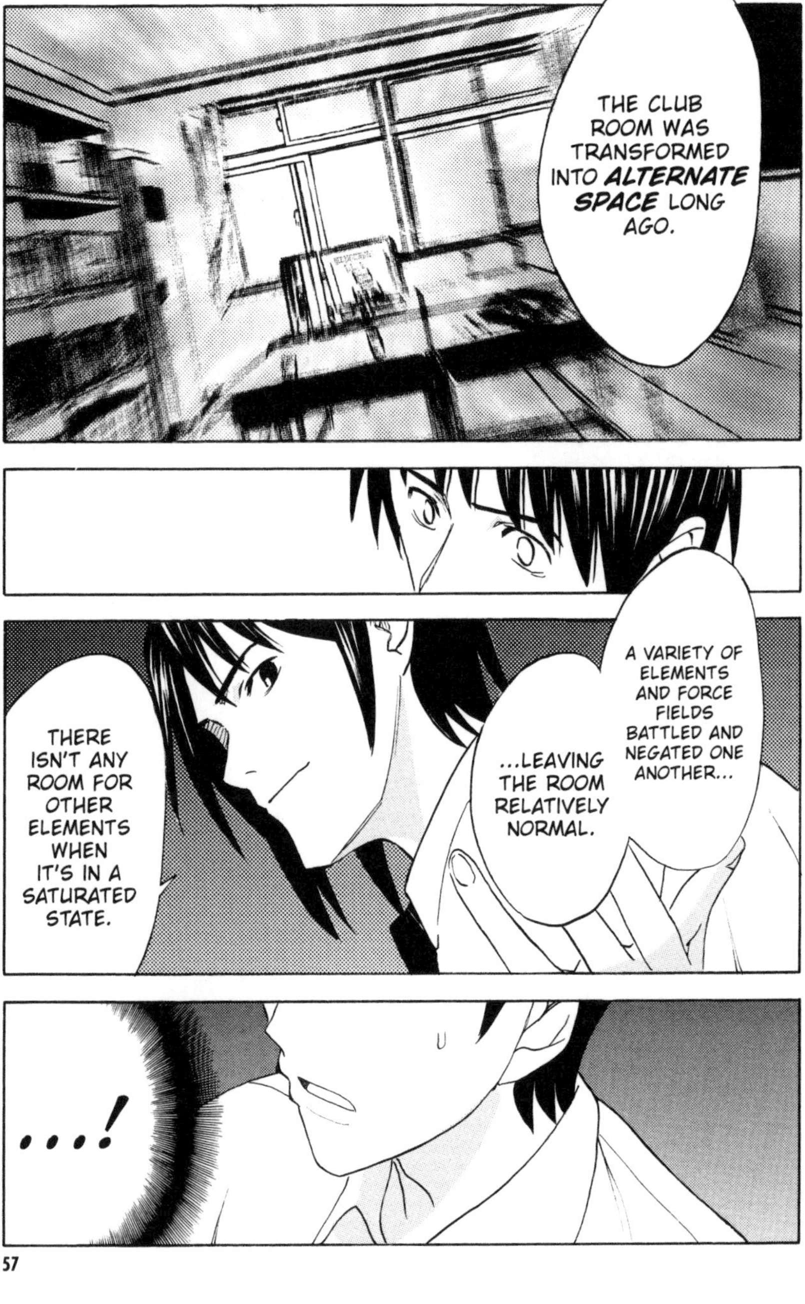
THE CLUB ROOM WAS TRANSFORMED INTO ALTERNATE SPACE LONG AGO.
A VARIETY OF ELEMENTS AND FORCE FIELDS BATTLED AND NEGATED ONE ANOTHER...
...LEAVING THE ROOM RELATIVELY NORMAL.
THERE ISN'T ANY ROOM FOR OTHER ELEMENTS WHEN IT'S IN A SATURATED STATE.
...!

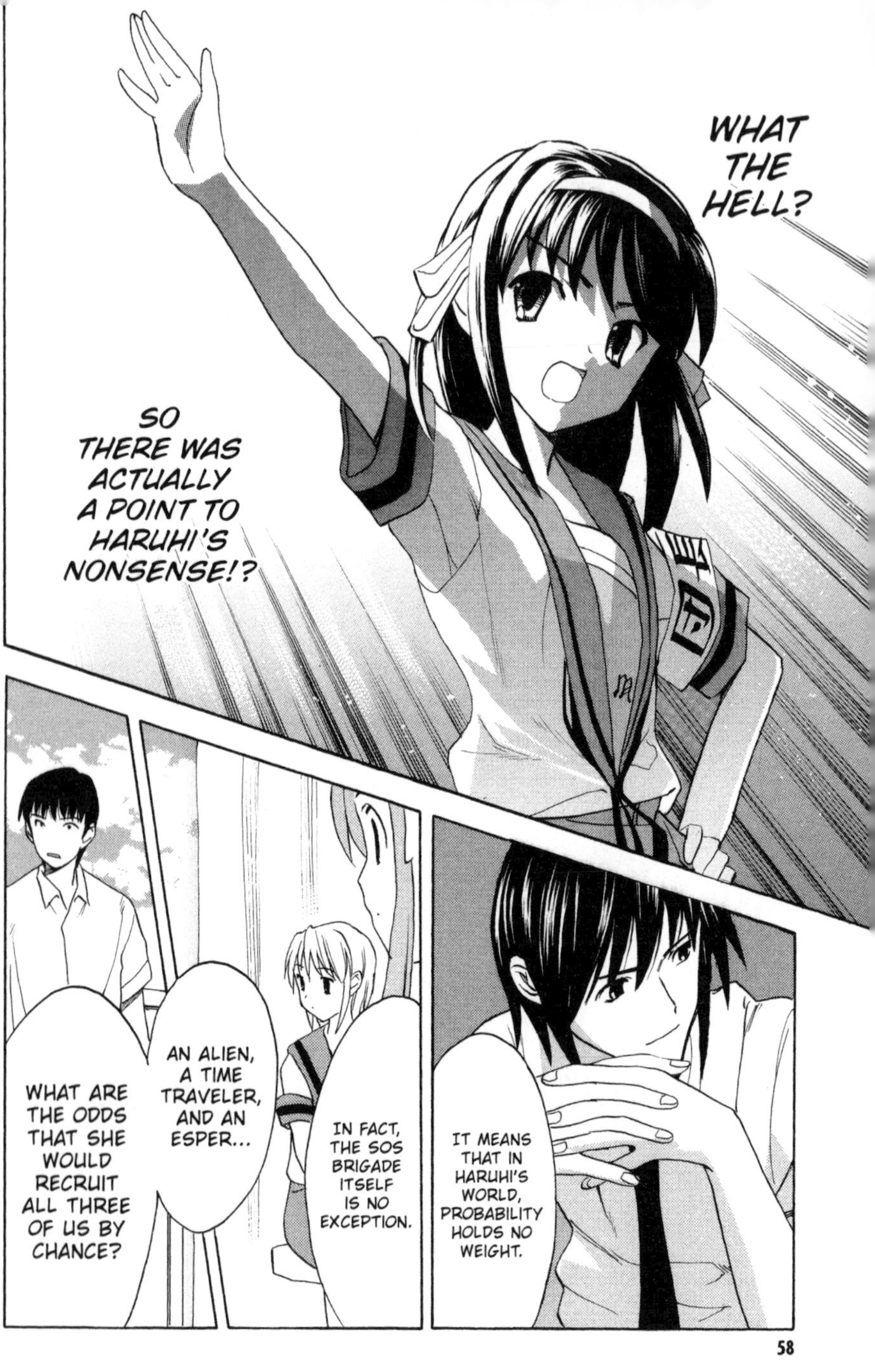
WHAT THE HELL?
SO THERE WAS ACTUALLY A POINT TO HARUHI'S NONSENSE!?
IT MEANS THAT IN HARUHI'S WORLD, PROBABILITY HOLDS NO WEIGHT.
IN FACT, THE SOS BRIGADE ITSELF IS NO EXCEPTION.
AN ALIEN, A TIME TRAVELER, AND AN ESPER...
WHAT ARE THE ODDS THAT SHE WOULD RECRUIT ALL THREE OF US BY CHANCE?

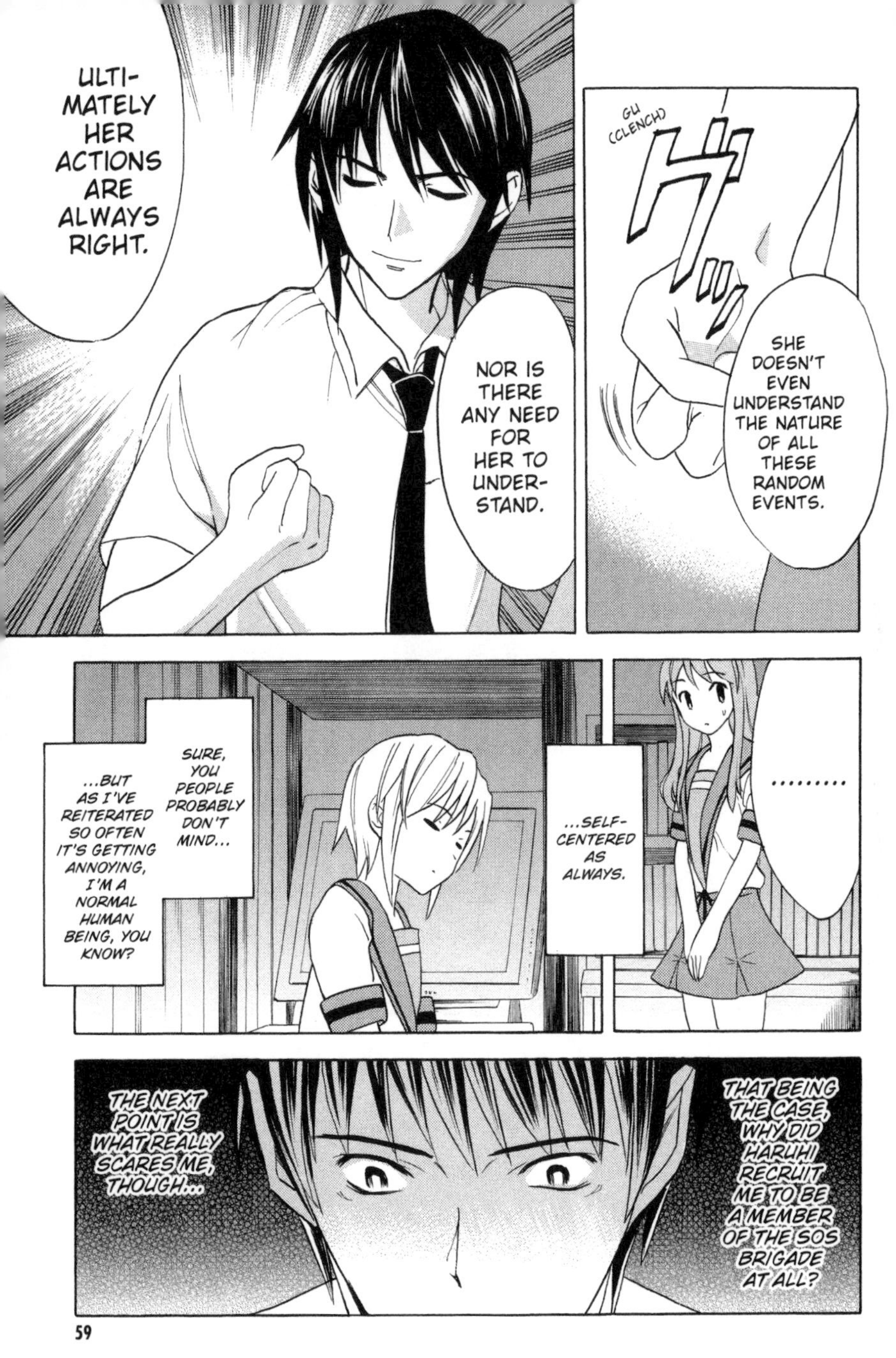
GU (CLENCH)
SHE DOESN'T EVEN UNDERSTAND THE NATURE OF ALL THESE RANDOM EVENTS.
NOR IS THERE ANY NEED FOR HER TO UNDER-STAND.
ULTI-MATELY HER ACTIONS ARE ALWAYS RIGHT.
....
...SELF-CENTERED AS ALWAYS.
SURE, YOU PEOPLE PROBABLY DON'T MIND...
...BUT AS I'VE REITERATED SO OFTEN IT'S GETTING ANNOYING, I'M A NORMAL HUMAN BEING, YOU KNOW?
THAT BEING THE CASE, WHY DID HARUHI RECRUIT ME TO BE A MEMBER OF THE SOS BRIGADE AT ALL?
THE NEXT POINT IS WHAT REALLY SCARES ME, THOUGH...

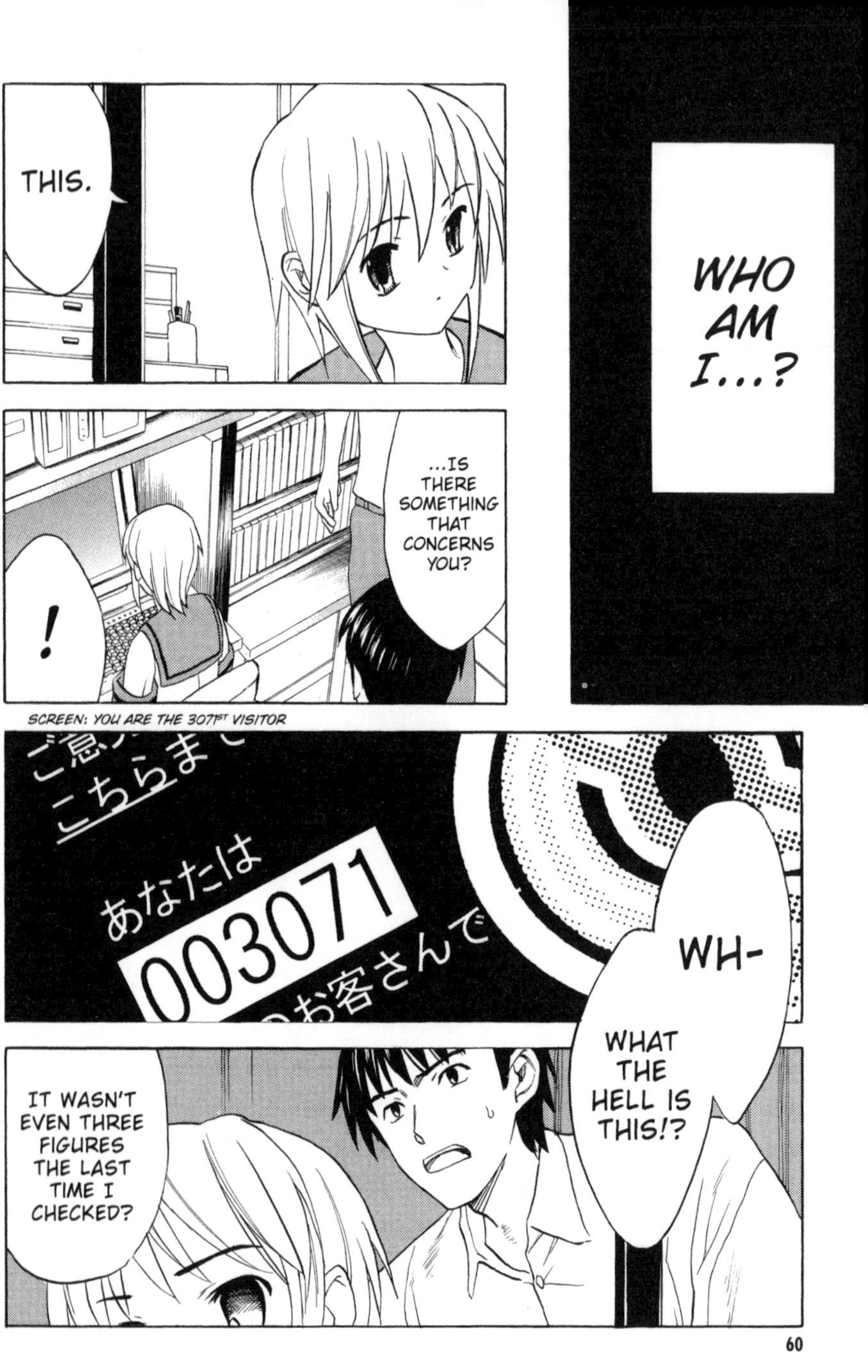
WHO AM I...?
THIS.
...IS THERE SOMETHING THAT CONCERNS YOU?
!
SCREEN: YOU ARE THE 3071ST VISITOR
あなたは
003071
お客さんで
WH-
WHAT THE HELL IS THIS!?
IT WASN'T EVEN THREE FIGURES THE LAST TIME I CHECKED?

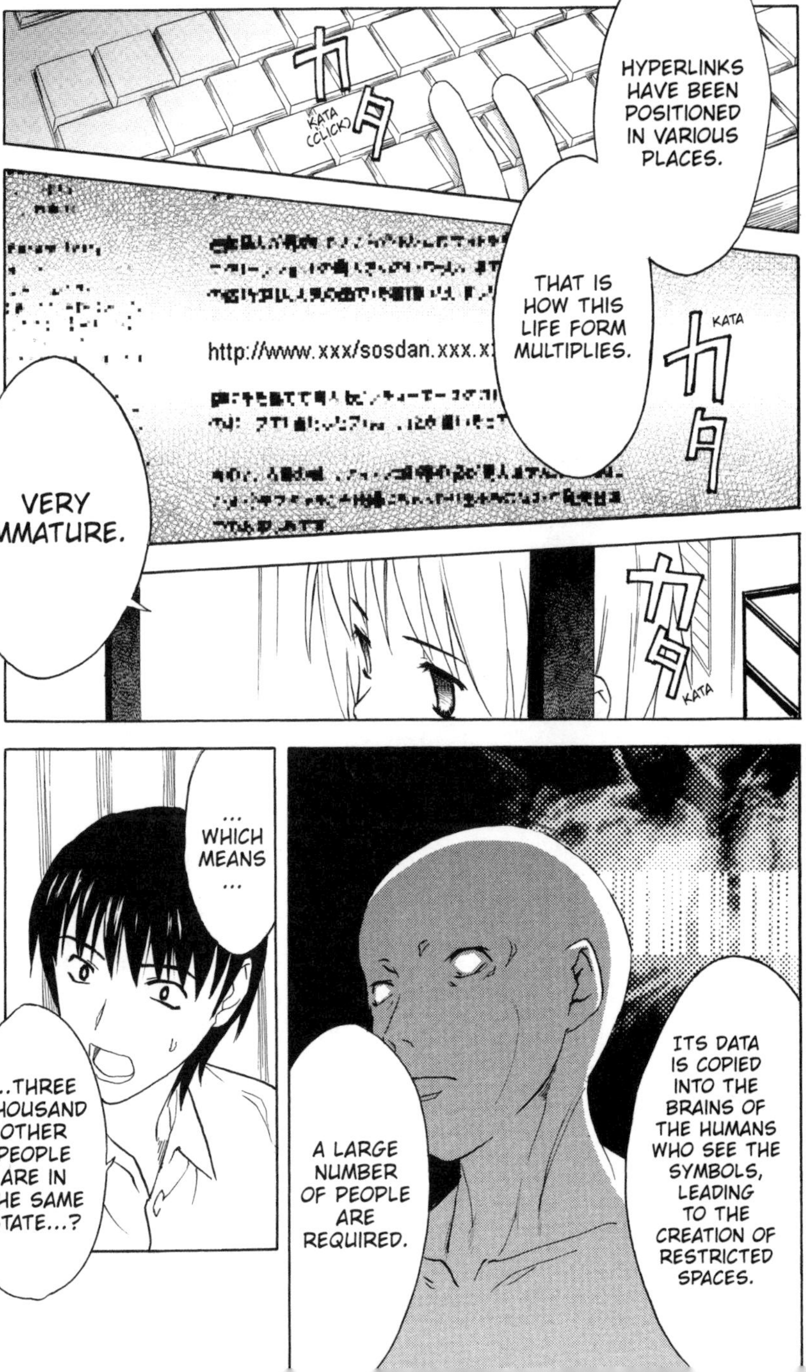
KATA (CLICK)
HYPERLINKS HAVE BEEN POSITIONED IN VARIOUS PLACES.
KATA
THAT IS HOW THIS LIFE FORM MULTIPLIES.
http://www.xxx/sosdan.xxx.x
VERY IMMATURE.
KATA
ITS DATA IS COPIED INTO THE BRAINS OF THE HUMANS WHO SEE THE SYMBOLS, LEADING TO THE CREATION OF RESTRICTED SPACES.
A LARGE NUMBER OF PEOPLE ARE REQUIRED.
...WHICH MEANS...
...THREE THOUSAND OTHER PEOPLE ARE IN THE SAME STATE...?

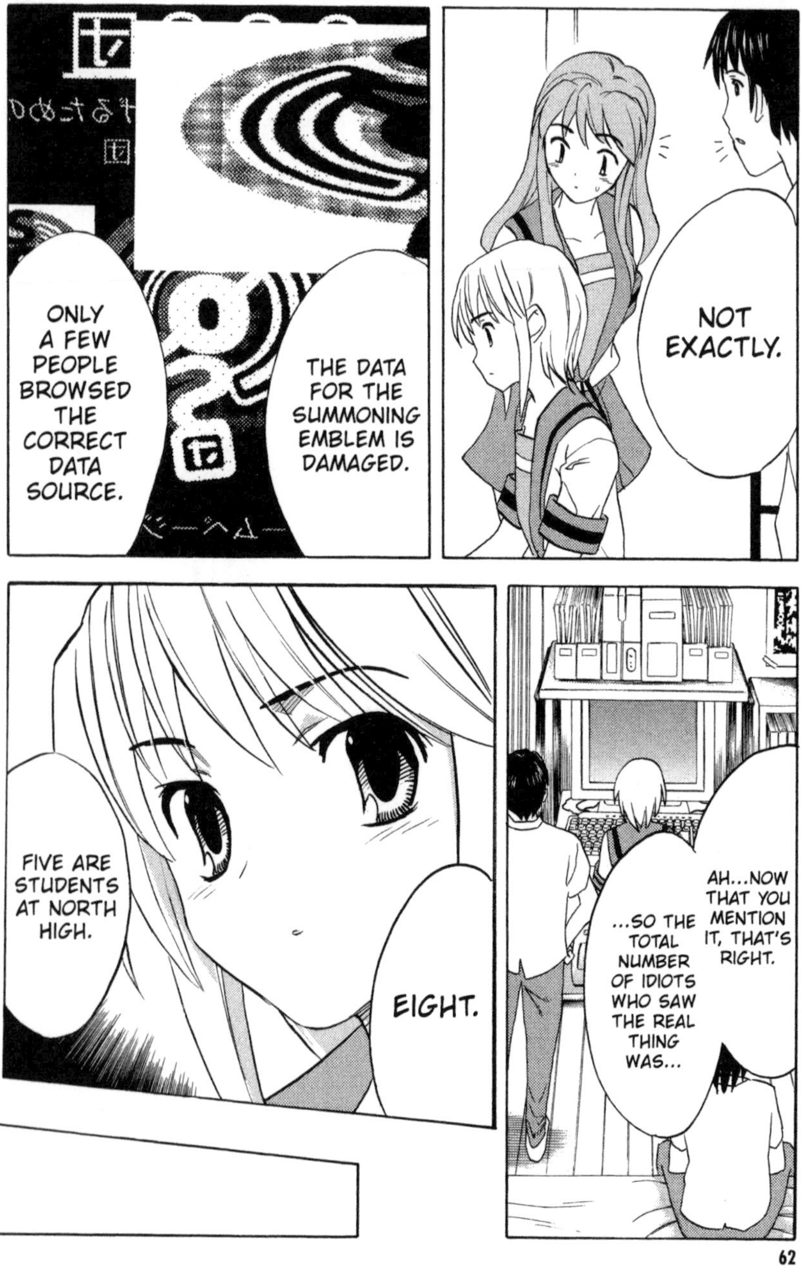
NOT EXACTLY.
THE DATA FOR THE SUMMONING EMBLEM IS DAMAGED.
ONLY A FEW PEOPLE BROWSED THE CORRECT DATA SOURCE.
AH...NOW THAT YOU MENTION IT, THAT'S RIGHT.
...SO THE TOTAL NUMBER OF IDIOTS WHO SAW THE REAL THING WAS...
EIGHT.
FIVE ARE STUDENTS AT NORTH HIGH.

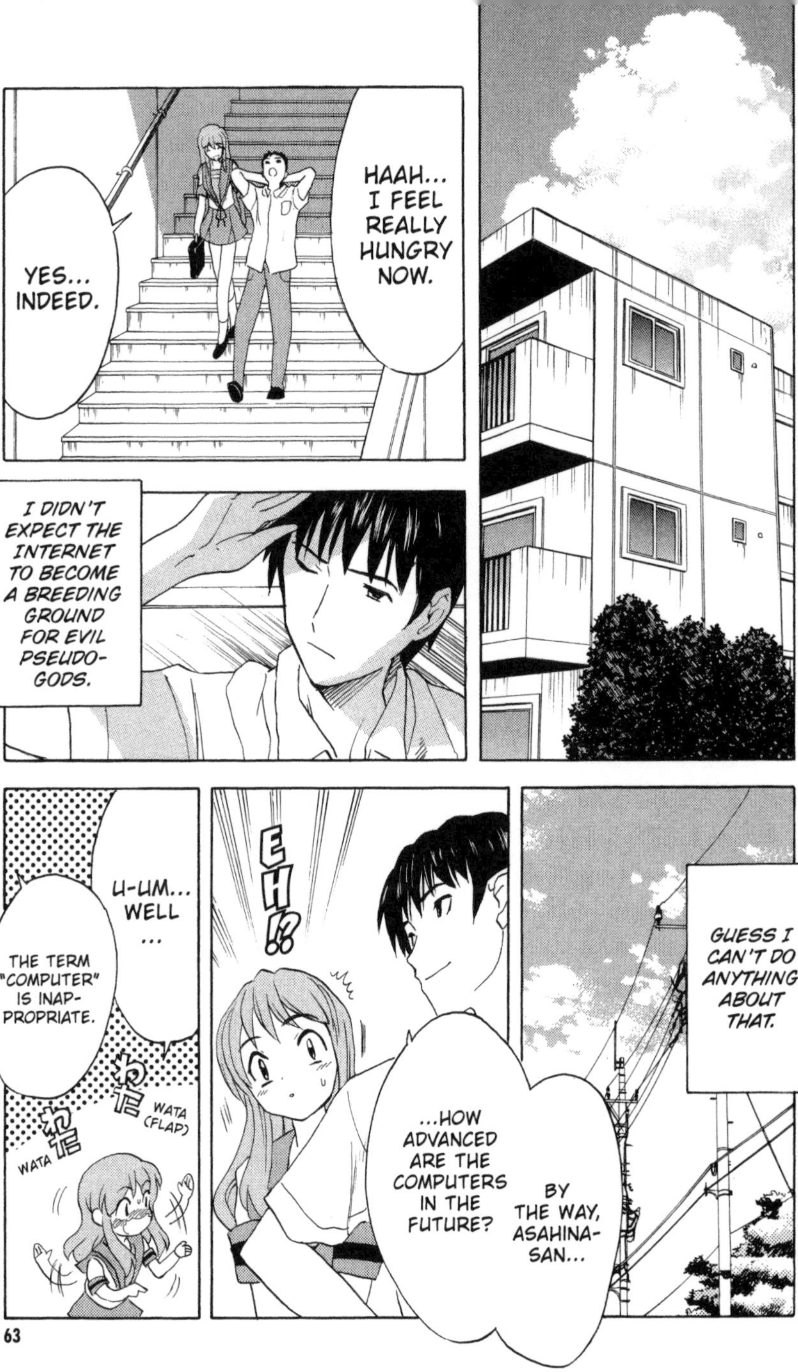
HAAH... I FEEL REALLY HUNGRY NOW.
YES... INDEED.
I DIDN'T EXPECT THE INTERNET TO BECOME A BREEDING GROUND FOR EVIL PSEUDO-GODS.
GUESS I CAN'T DO ANYTHING ABOUT THAT.
BY THE WAY, ASAHINA-SAN...
...HOW ADVANCED ARE THE COMPUTERS IN THE FUTURE?
EH!?
U-UM... WELL...
THE TERM "COMPUTER" IS INAPPROPRIATE.
わた
WATA (FLAP)
わた
WATA

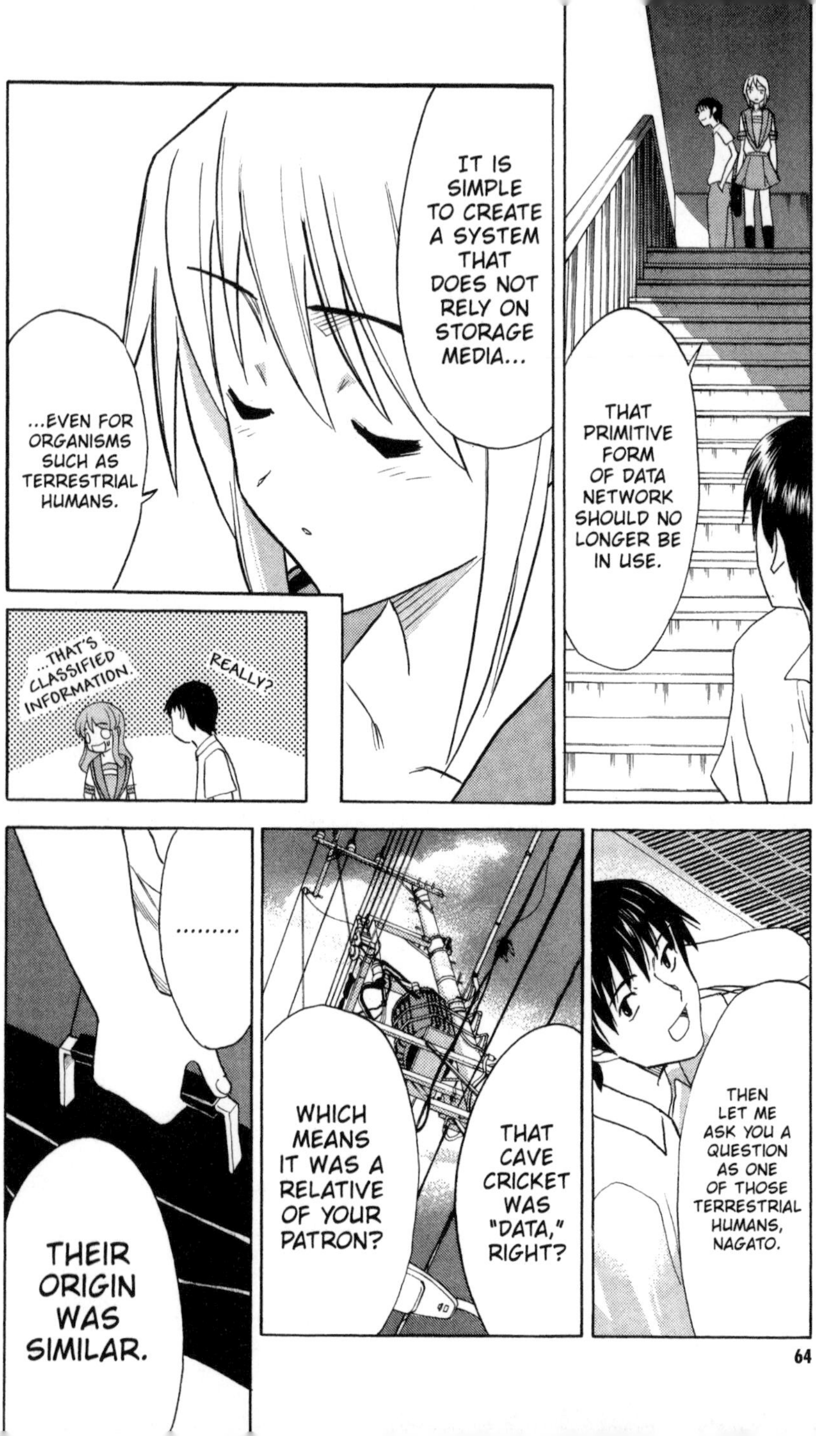
THAT PRIMITIVE FORM OF DATA NETWORK SHOULD NO LONGER BE IN USE.
IT IS SIMPLE TO CREATE A SYSTEM THAT DOES NOT RELY ON STORAGE MEDIA...
...EVEN FOR ORGANISMS SUCH AS TERRESTRIAL HUMANS.
REALLY?
...THAT'S CLASSIFIED INFORMATION.
THEN LET ME ASK YOU A QUESTION AS ONE OF THOSE TERRESTRIAL HUMANS, NAGATO.
THAT CAVE CRICKET WAS "DATA," RIGHT?
WHICH MEANS IT WAS A RELATIVE OF YOUR PATRON?
....
THEIR ORIGIN WAS SIMILAR.

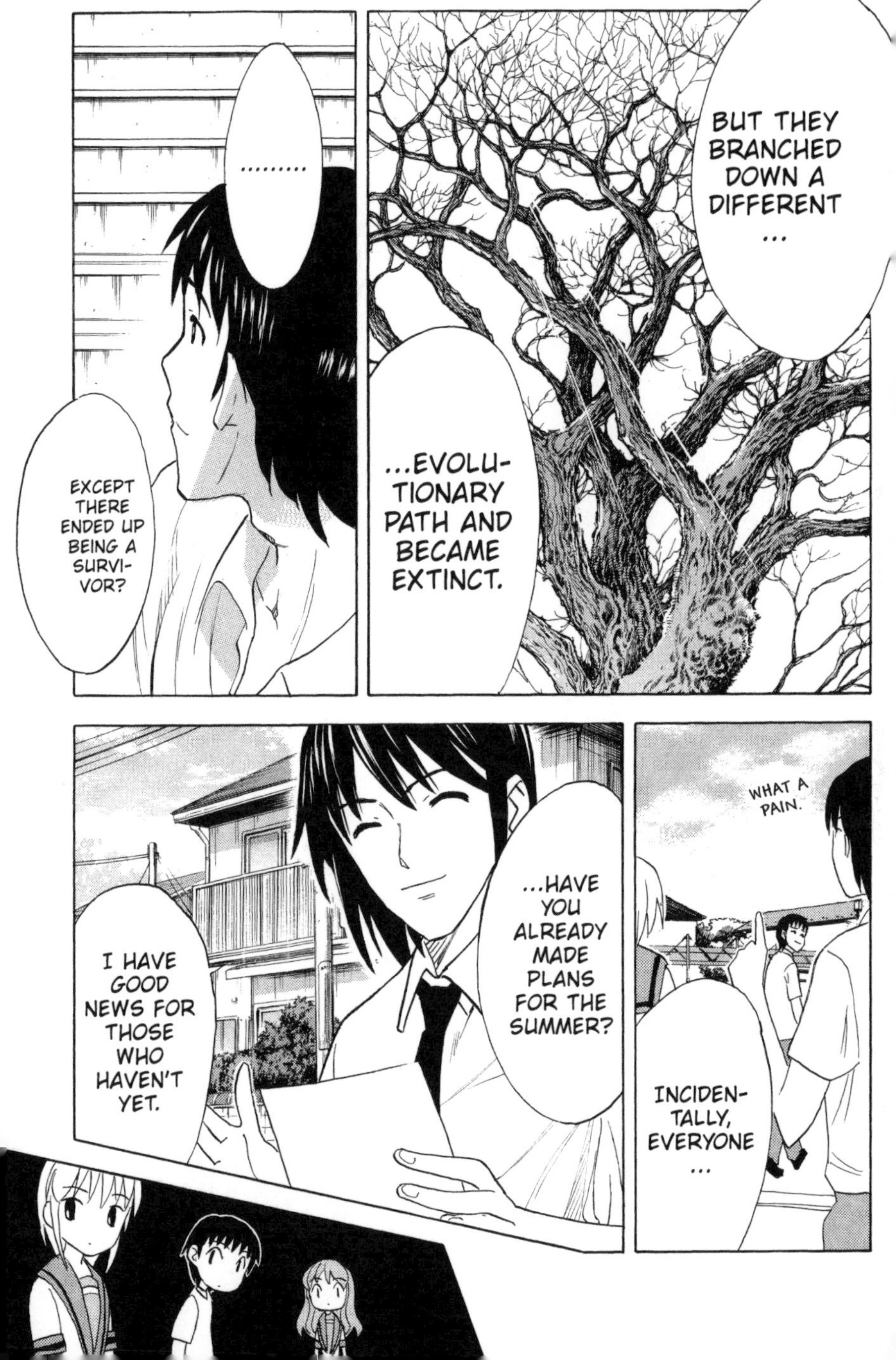
BUT THEY BRANCHED DOWN A DIFFERENT ...
...EVOLUTIONARY PATH AND BECAME EXTINCT.
....
EXCEPT THERE ENDED UP BEING A SURVIVOR?
WHAT A PAIN.
INCIDENTALLY, EVERYONE ...
...HAVE YOU ALREADY MADE PLANS FOR THE SUMMER?
I HAVE GOOD NEWS FOR THOSE WHO HAVEN'T YET.

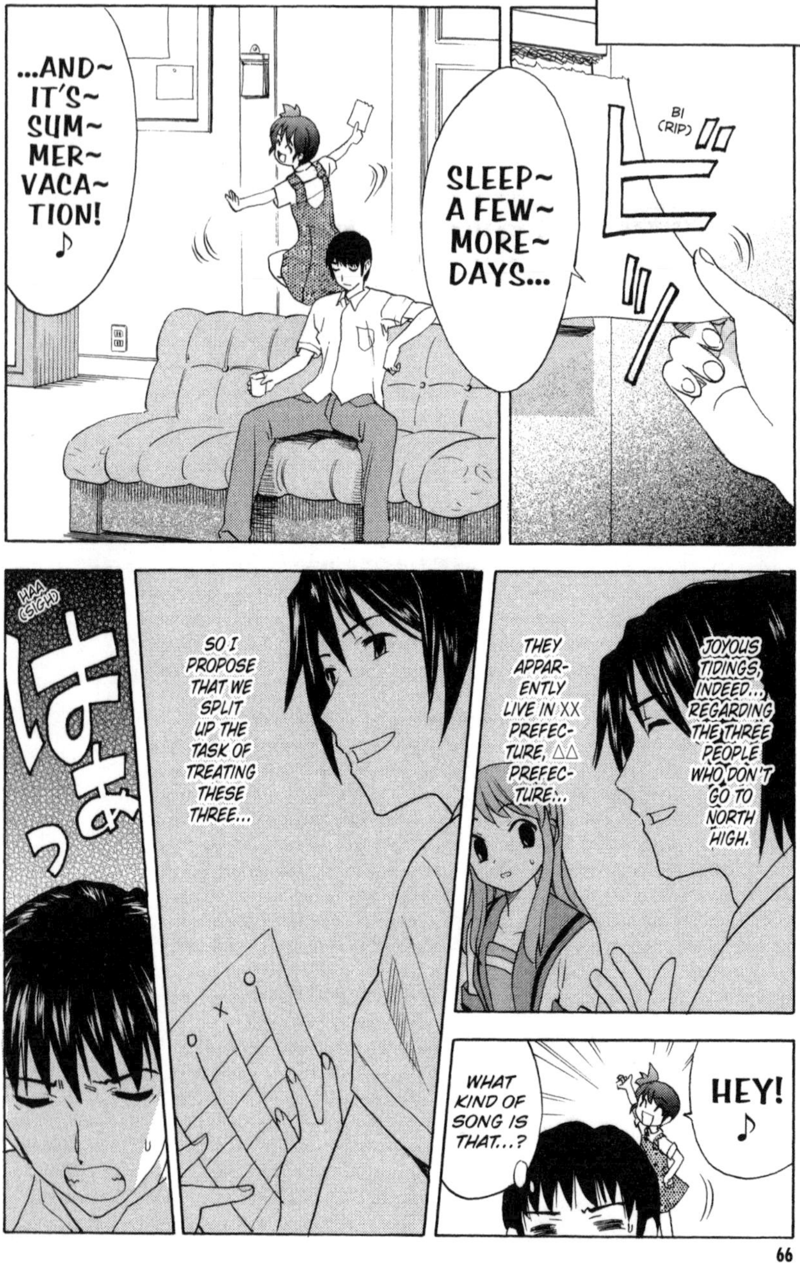

SLEEP~ A FEW~ MORE~ DAYS...
BI (RIP)
ビッ
...AND~ IT'S~ SUM~ MER~ VACA~ TION! ♪
JOYOUS TIDINGS, INDEED... REGARDING THE THREE PEOPLE WHO DON'T GO TO NORTH HIGH.
THEY APPAR-ENTLY LIVE IN XX PREFEC-TURE, ΔΔ PREFEC-TURE...
HEY! ♪
WHAT KIND OF SONG IS THAT...?
SO I PROPOSE THAT WE SPLIT UP THE TASK OF TREATING THESE THREE...
HAA (SIGH)
はぁっ

CHART: MIKURU, NAGATO, KYON

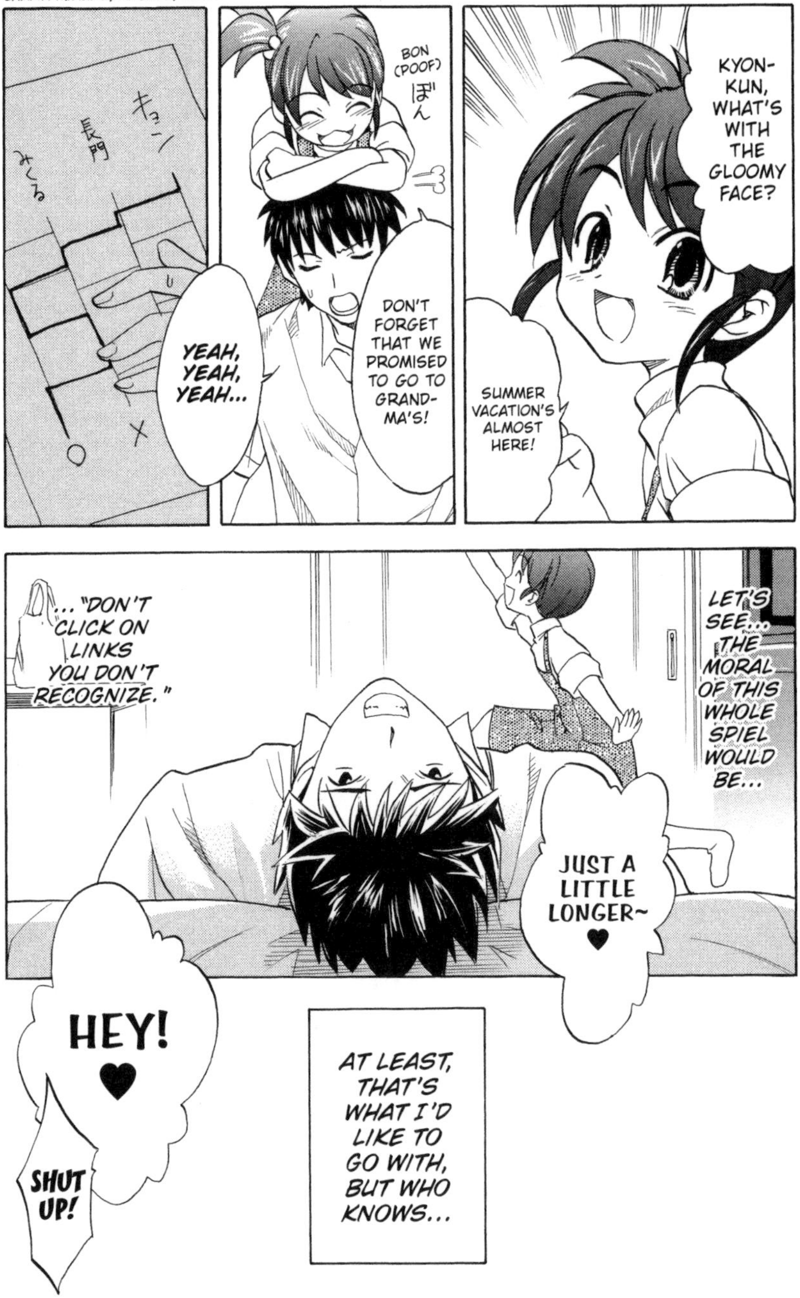
KYON-KUN, WHAT'S WITH THE GLOOMY FACE?
SUMMER VACATION'S ALMOST HERE!
BON (POOF)
ぼん
DON'T FORGET THAT WE PROMISED TO GO TO GRAND-MA'S!
YEAH, YEAH, YEAH...
キョン
長門
みくる
LET'S SEE... THE MORAL OF THIS WHOLE SPIEL WOULD BE...
..."DON'T CLICK ON LINKS YOU DON'T RECOGNIZE."
JUST A LITTLE LONGER~ ♥
HEY! ♥
SHUT UP!
AT LEAST, THAT'S WHAT I'D LIKE TO GO WITH, BUT WHO KNOWS...

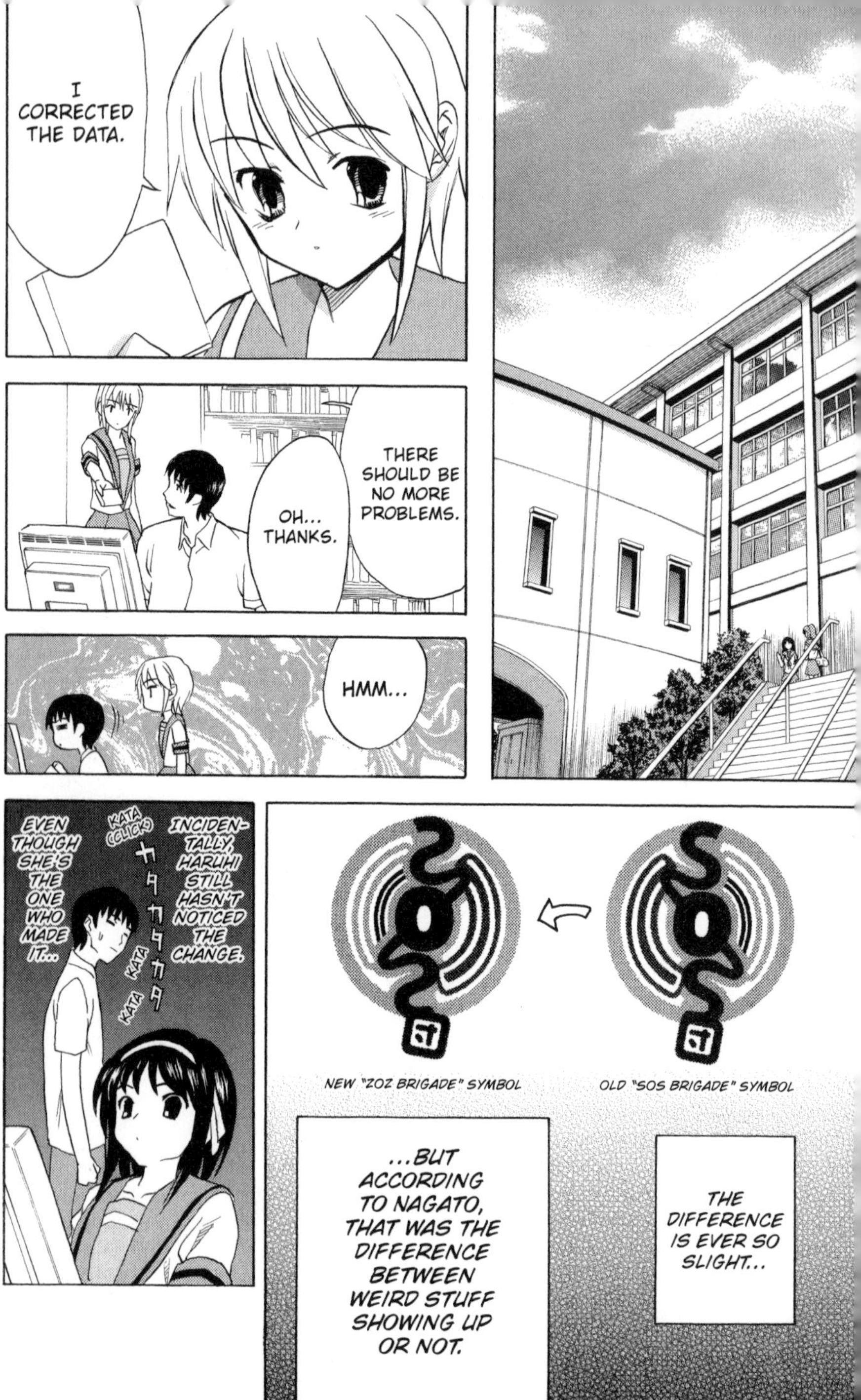
I CORRECTED THE DATA.
THERE SHOULD BE NO MORE PROBLEMS.
OH... THANKS.
HMM...
THE DIFFERENCE IS EVER SO SLIGHT...
OLD "SOS BRIGADE" SYMBOL
NEW "ZOZ BRIGADE" SYMBOL
...BUT ACCORDING TO NAGATO, THAT WAS THE DIFFERENCE BETWEEN WEIRD STUFF SHOWING UP OR NOT.
INCIDENTALLY, HARUHI STILL HASN'T NOTICED THE CHANGE.
KATA (CLICK)
カタカタ
KATA KATA
EVEN THOUGH SHE'S THE ONE WHO MADE IT...

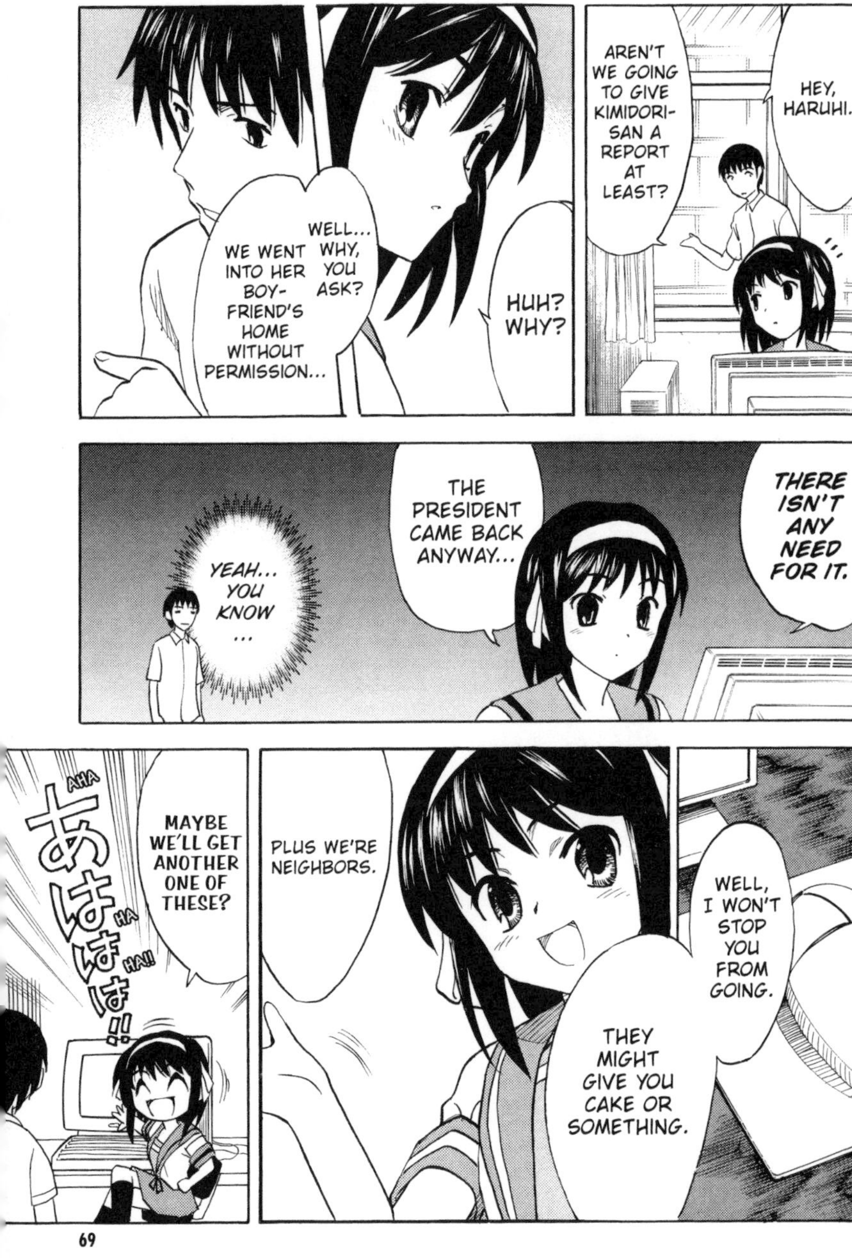
HEY, HARUHI.
AREN'T WE GOING TO GIVE KIMIDORI-SAN A REPORT AT LEAST?
HUH? WHY?
WELL... WHY, YOU ASK?
WE WENT INTO HER BOY-FRIEND'S HOME WITHOUT PERMISSION...
THERE ISN'T ANY NEED FOR IT.
THE PRESIDENT CAME BACK ANYWAY...
YEAH... YOU KNOW ...
WELL, I WON'T STOP YOU FROM GOING.
THEY MIGHT GIVE YOU CAKE OR SOMETHING.
PLUS WE'RE NEIGHBORS.
MAYBE WE'LL GET ANOTHER ONE OF THESE?
あははは!!
AHA HA HA!!

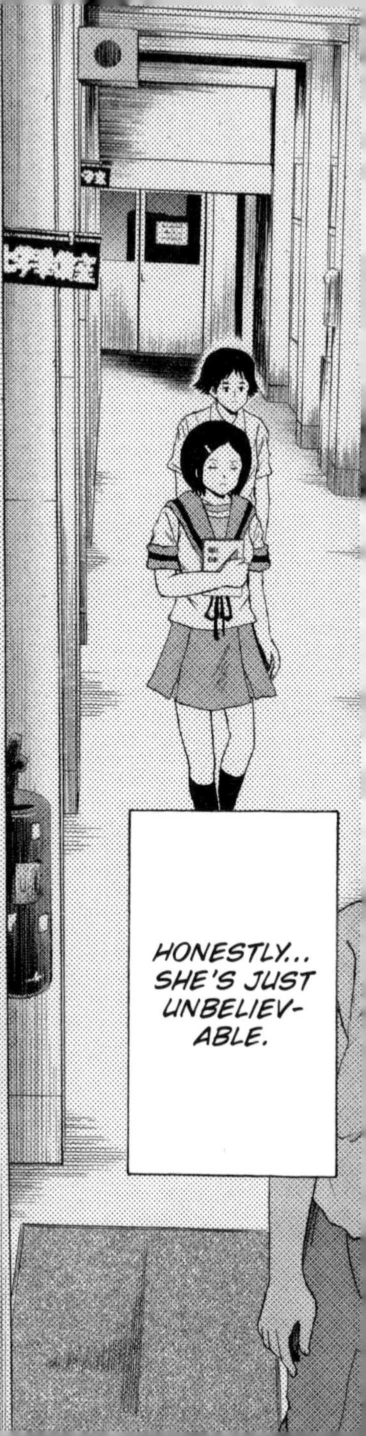
HONESTLY... SHE'S JUST UNBELIEV-ABLE.

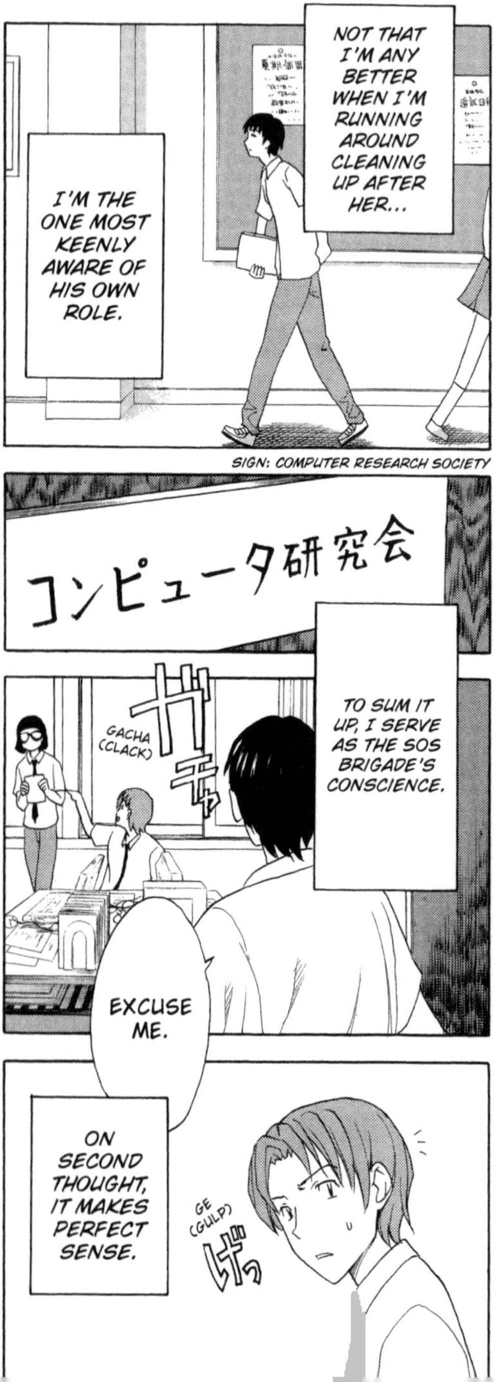
NOT THAT I'M ANY BETTER WHEN I'M RUNNING AROUND CLEANING UP AFTER HER...
I'M THE ONE MOST KEENLY AWARE OF HIS OWN ROLE.
SIGN: COMPUTER RESEARCH SOCIETY
コンピュータ研究会
TO SUM IT UP, I SERVE AS THE SOS BRIGADE'S CONSCIENCE.
ガチャ
GACHA (CLACK)
EXCUSE ME.
ON SECOND THOUGHT, IT MAKES PERFECT SENSE.
げっ
GE (GULP)

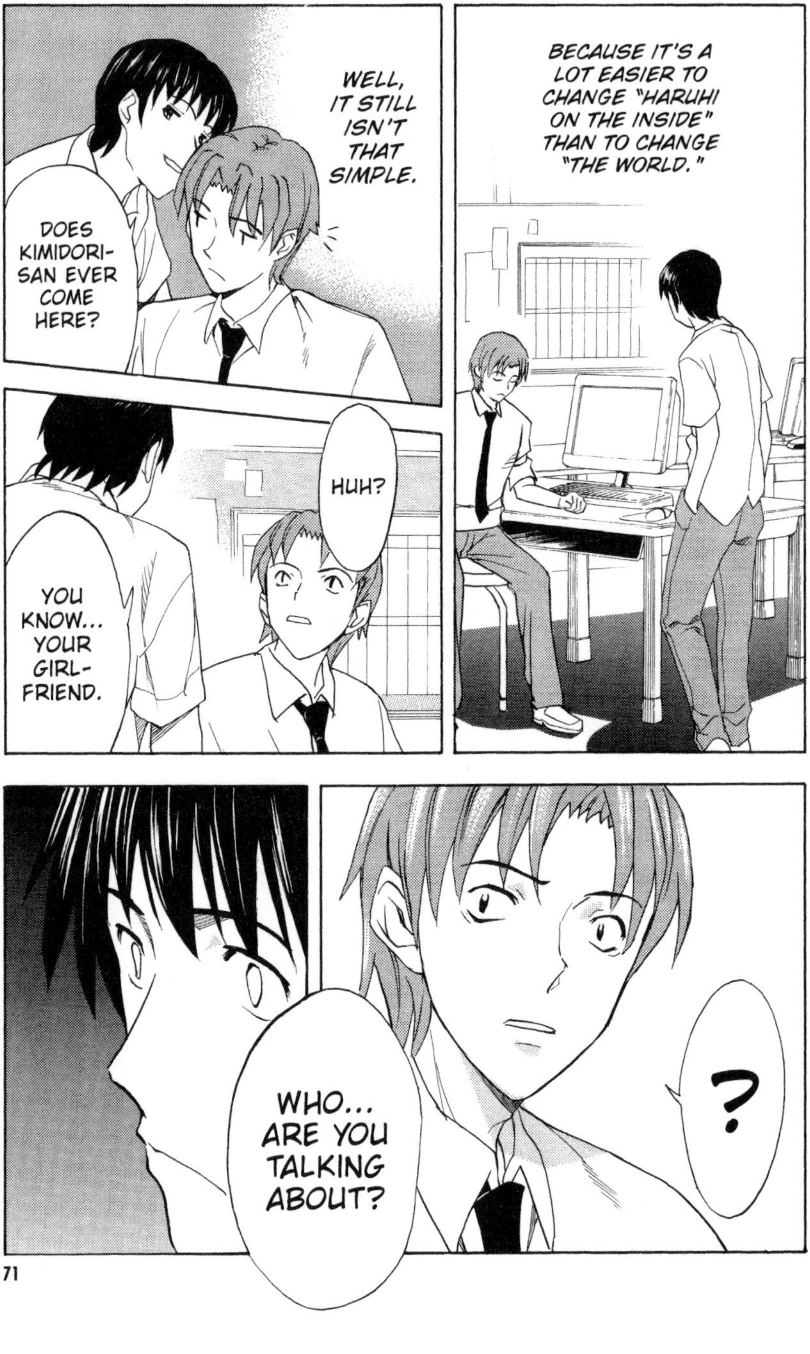

BECAUSE IT'S A LOT EASIER TO CHANGE "HARUHI ON THE INSIDE" THAN TO CHANGE "THE WORLD."
WELL, IT STILL ISN'T THAT SIMPLE.
DOES KIMIDORI-SAN EVER COME HERE?
HUH?
YOU KNOW... YOUR GIRL-FRIEND.
?
WHO... ARE YOU TALKING ABOUT?

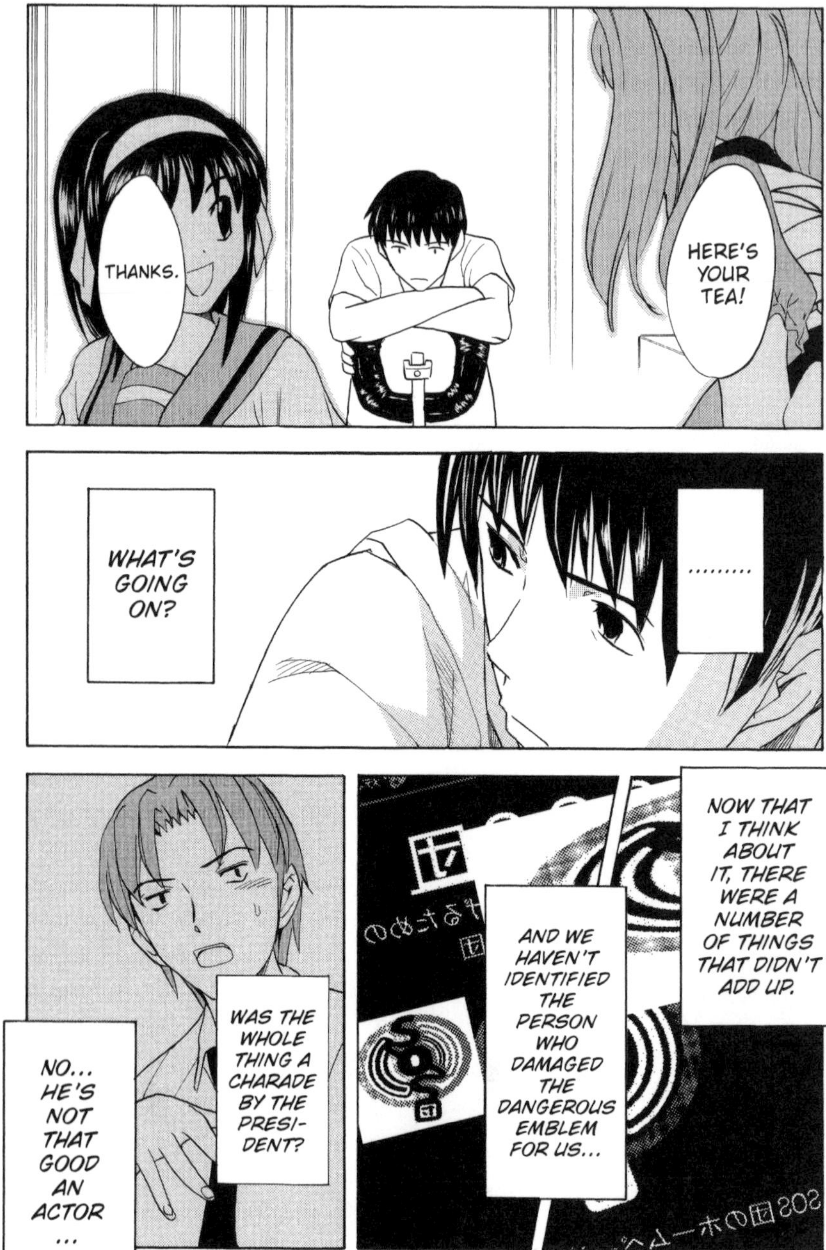
HERE'S YOUR TEA!
THANKS.
....
WHAT'S GOING ON?
NOW THAT I THINK ABOUT IT, THERE WERE A NUMBER OF THINGS THAT DIDN'T ADD UP.
AND WE HAVEN'T IDENTIFIED THE PERSON WHO DAMAGED THE DANGEROUS EMBLEM FOR US...
WAS THE WHOLE THING A CHARADE BY THE PRESIDENT?
NO... HE'S NOT THAT GOOD AN ACTOR...

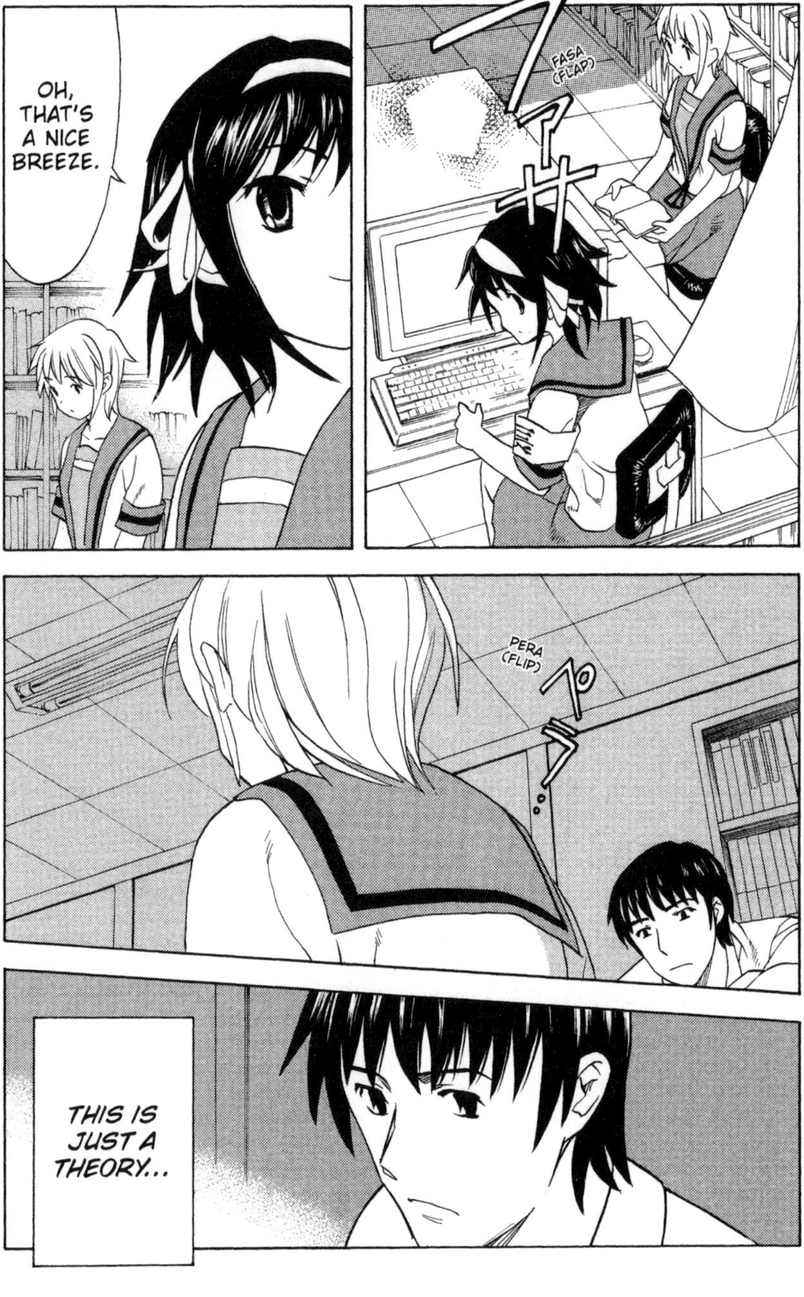
ファサ
FASA (FLAP)
OH, THAT'S A NICE BREEZE.
ペラ
PERA (FLIP)
THIS IS JUST A THEORY...

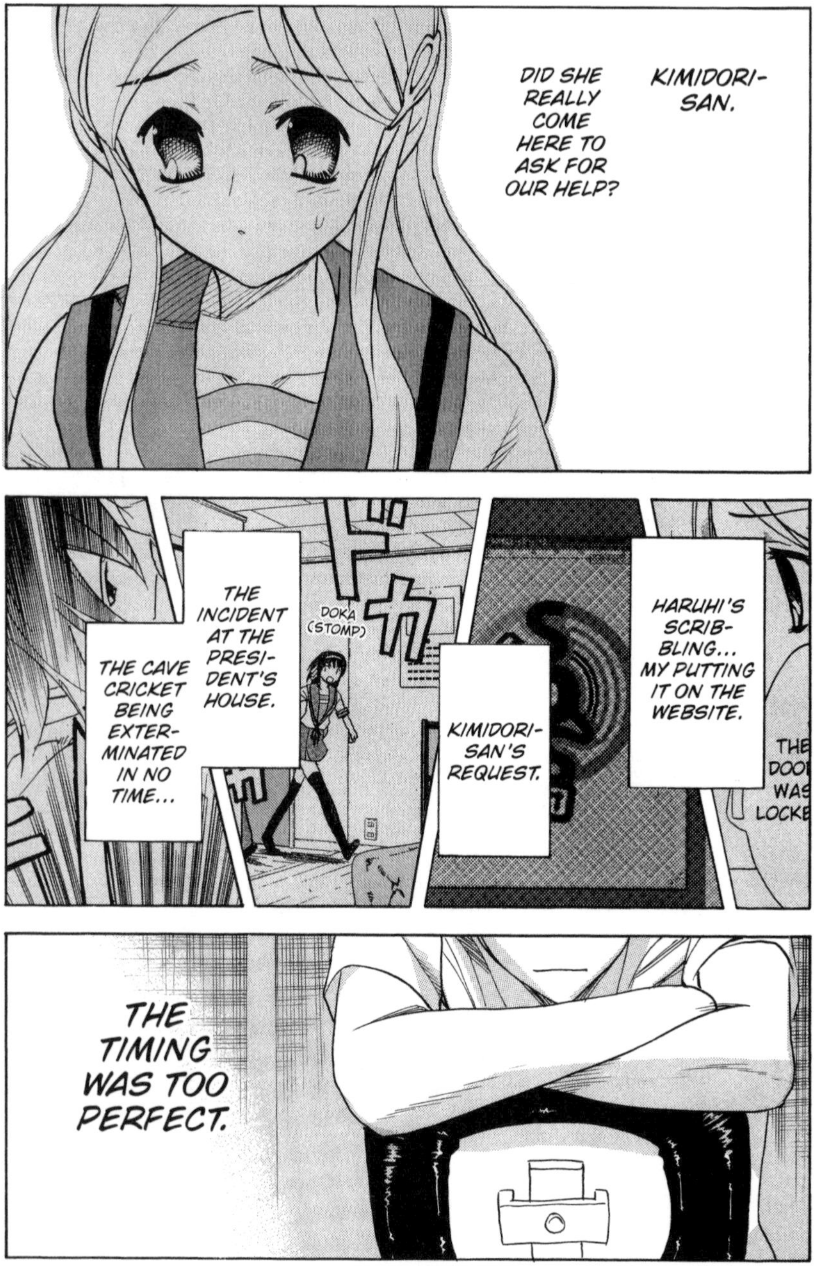
KIMIDORI-SAN.
DID SHE REALLY COME HERE TO ASK FOR OUR HELP?
THE DOOR WAS LOCKE
HARUHI'S SCRIBBLING... MY PUTTING IT ON THE WEBSITE.
KIMIDORI-SAN'S REQUEST.
DOKA (STOMP)
THE INCIDENT AT THE PRESIDENT'S HOUSE.
THE CAVE CRICKET BEING EXTERMINATED IN NO TIME...
THE TIMING WAS TOO PERFECT.

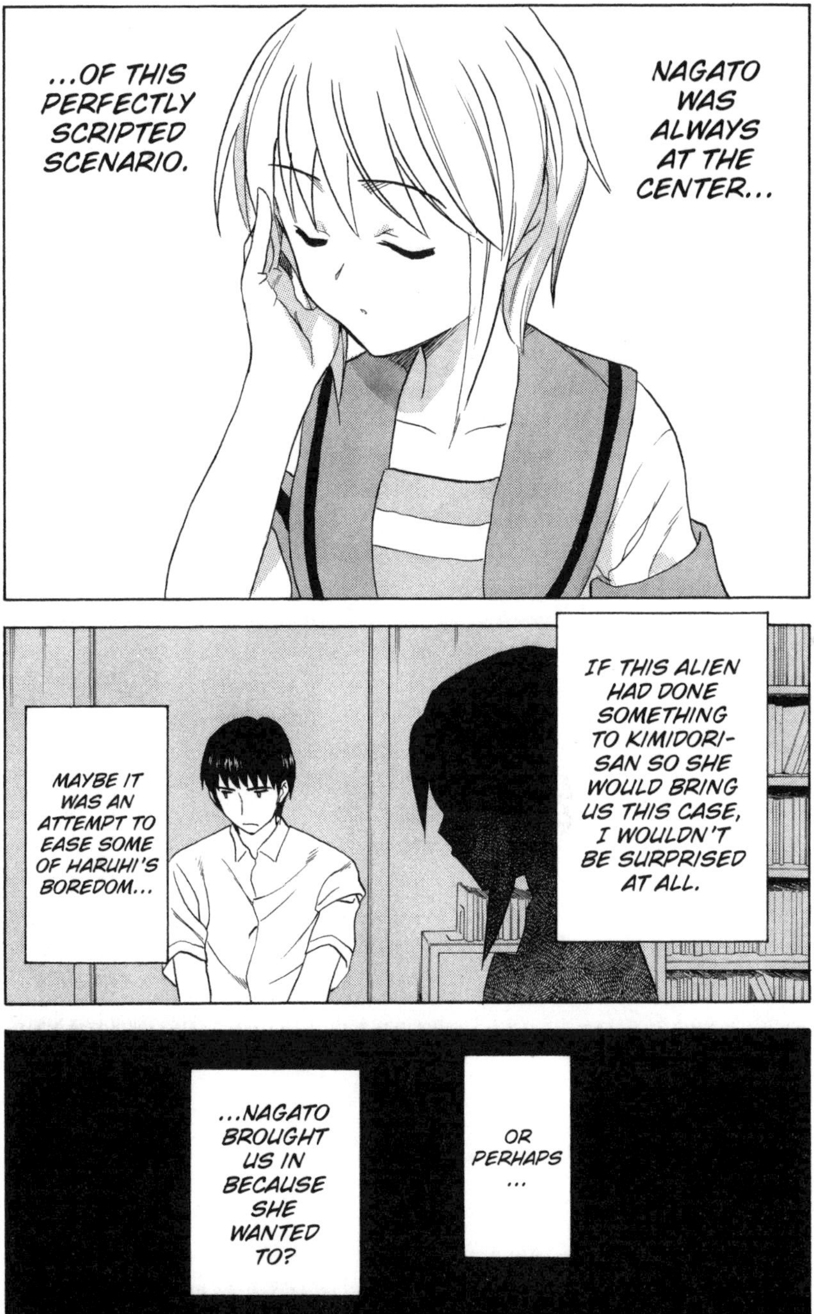
NAGATO WAS ALWAYS AT THE CENTER...
...OF THIS PERFECTLY SCRIPTED SCENARIO.
IF THIS ALIEN HAD DONE SOMETHING TO KIMIDORI-SAN SO SHE WOULD BRING US THIS CASE, I WOULDN'T BE SURPRISED AT ALL.
MAYBE IT WAS AN ATTEMPT TO EASE SOME OF HARUHI'S BOREDOM...
OR PERHAPS...
...NAGATO BROUGHT US IN BECAUSE SHE WANTED TO?

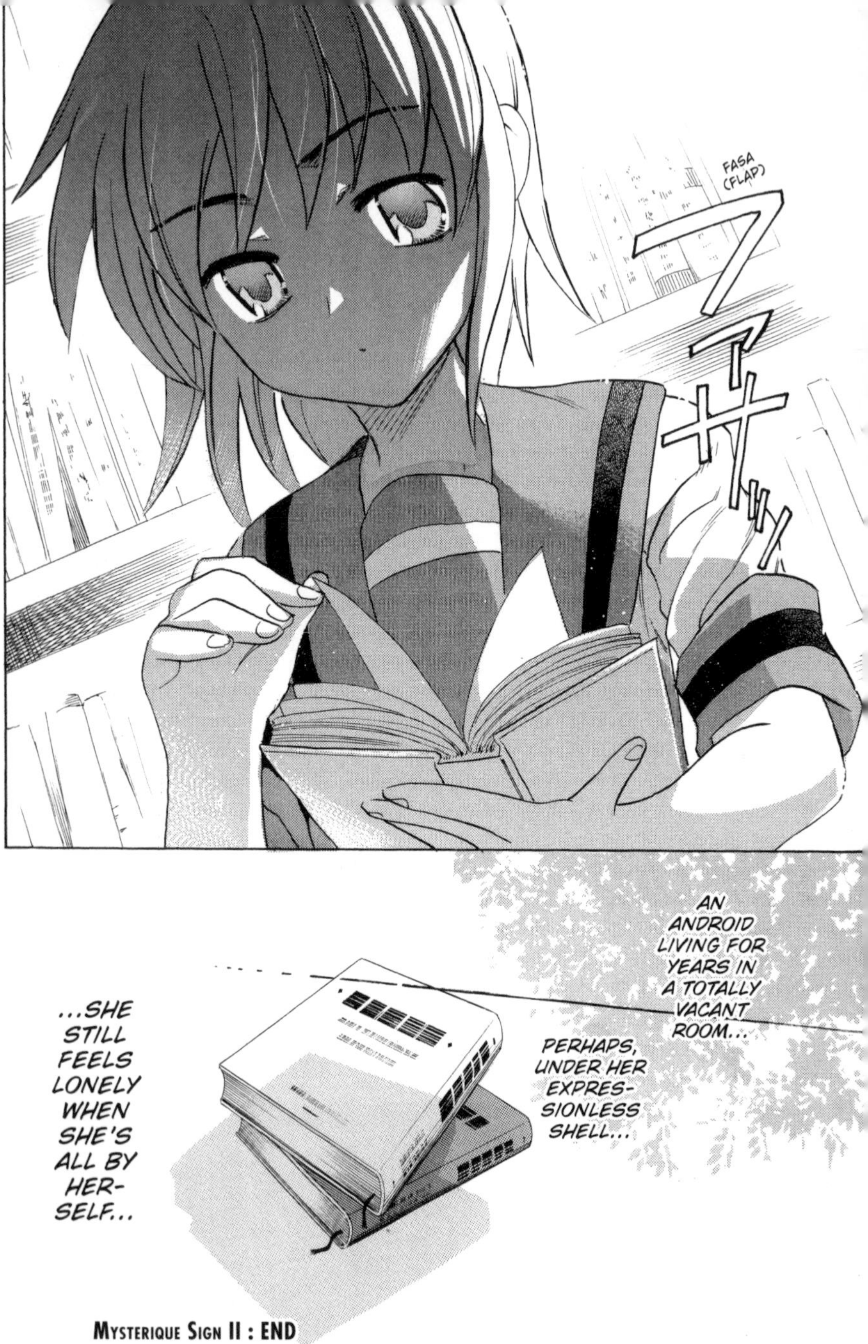
FASA (FLAP)
AN ANDROID LIVING FOR YEARS IN A TOTALLY VACANT ROOM...
PERHAPS, UNDER HER EXPRES-SIONLESS SHELL...
...SHE STILL FEELS LONELY WHEN SHE'S ALL BY HER-SELF...

Mysterique Sign II : END

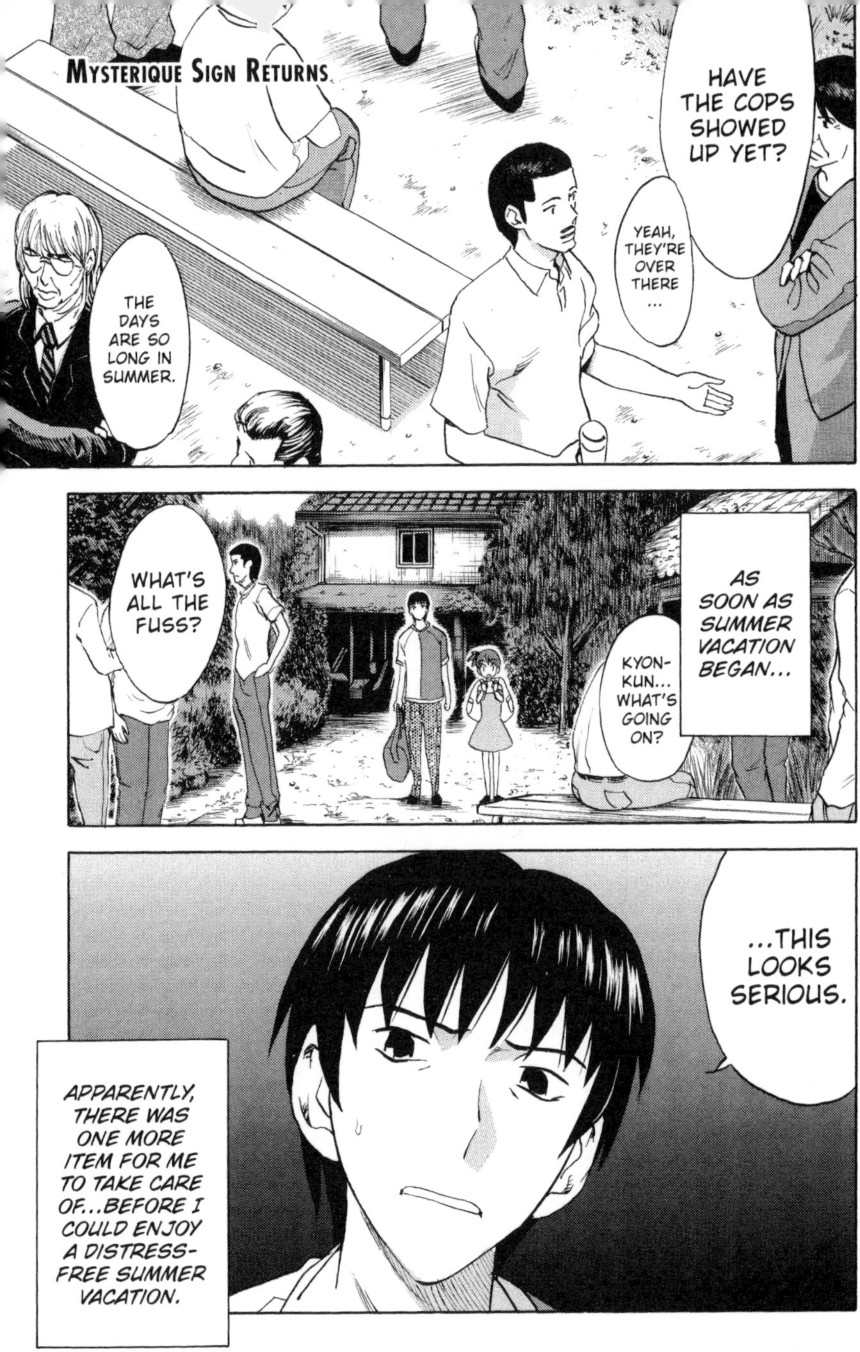
HAVE THE COPS SHOWED UP YET?
YEAH, THEY'RE OVER THERE ...
THE DAYS ARE SO LONG IN SUMMER.
AS SOON AS SUMMER VACATION BEGAN...
KYON-KUN... WHAT'S GOING ON?
WHAT'S ALL THE FUSS?
...THIS LOOKS SERIOUS.
APPARENTLY, THERE WAS ONE MORE ITEM FOR ME TO TAKE CARE OF...BEFORE I COULD ENJOY A DISTRESS-FREE SUMMER VACATION.

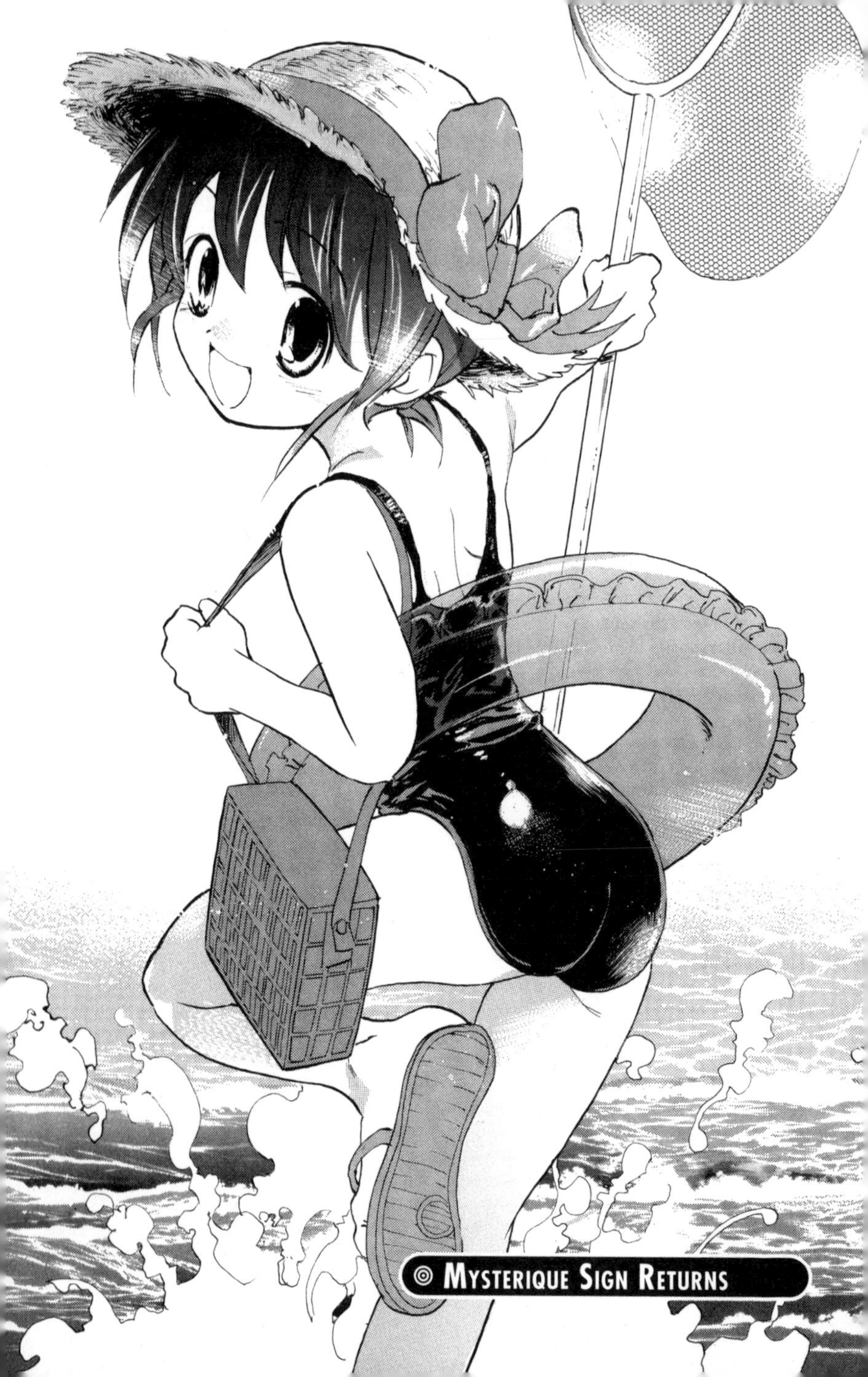
◎ Mysterique Sign Returns

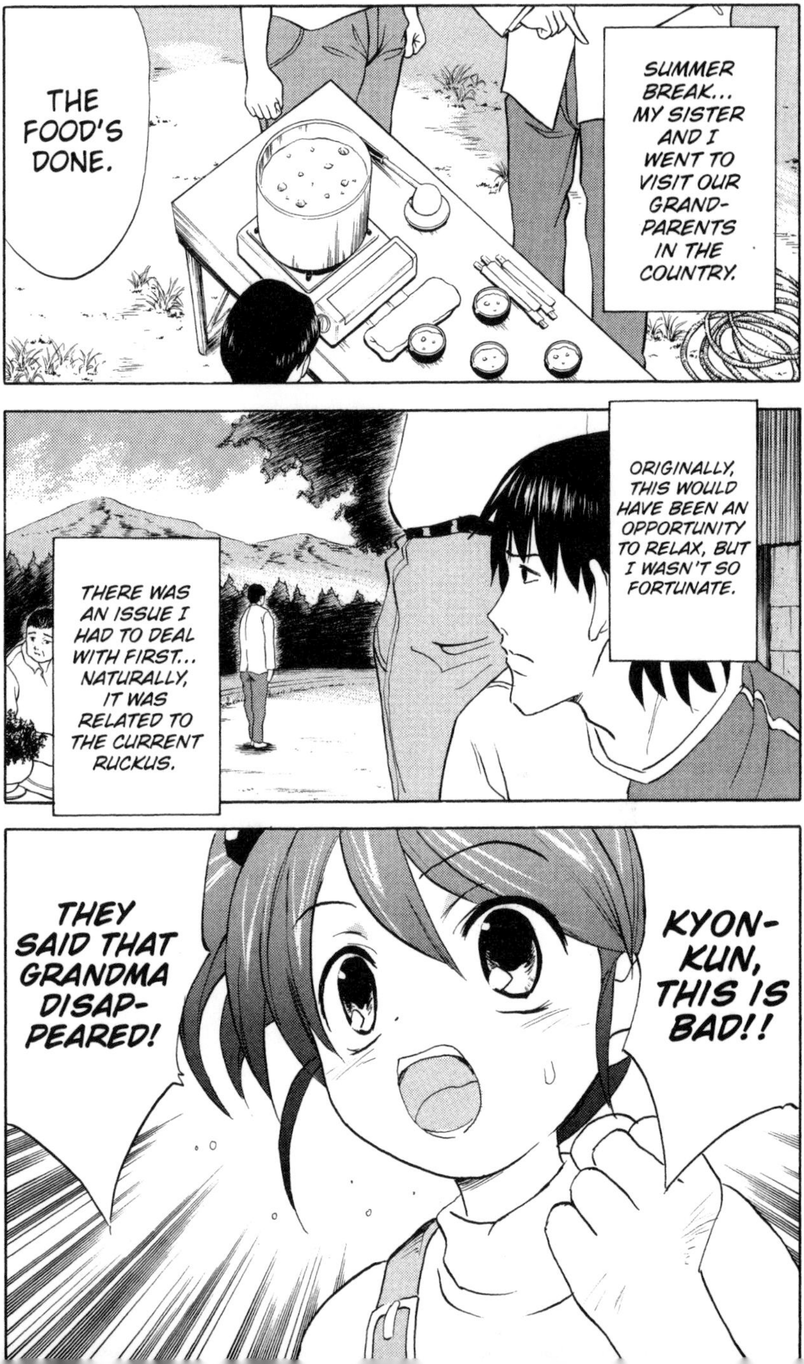
SUMMER BREAK... MY SISTER AND I WENT TO VISIT OUR GRAND-PARENTS IN THE COUNTRY.
THE FOOD'S DONE.
ORIGINALLY, THIS WOULD HAVE BEEN AN OPPORTUNITY TO RELAX, BUT I WASN'T SO FORTUNATE.
THERE WAS AN ISSUE I HAD TO DEAL WITH FIRST... NATURALLY, IT WAS RELATED TO THE CURRENT RUCKUS.
KYON-KUN, THIS IS BAD!!
THEY SAID THAT GRANDMA DISAP-PEARED!

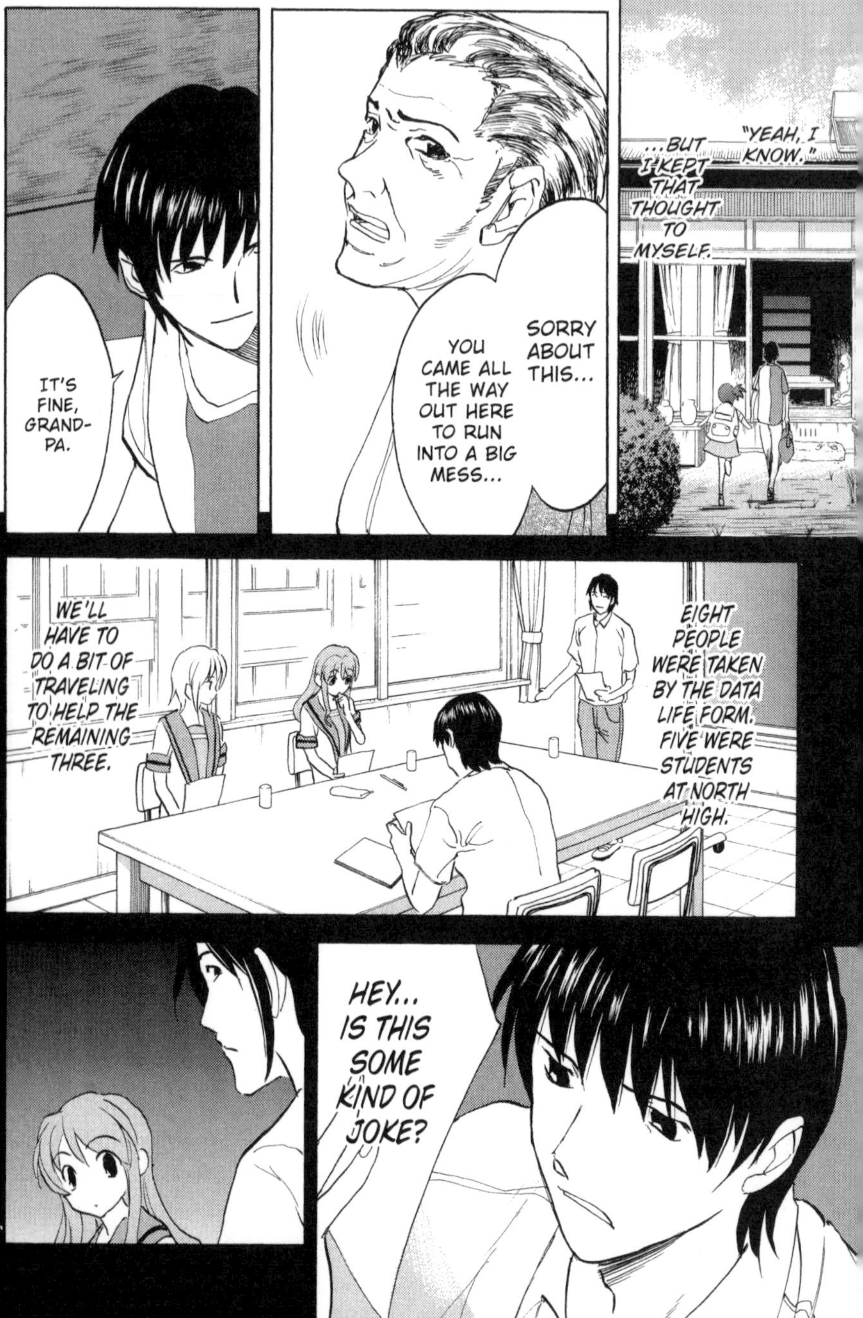
"YEAH, I KNOW."
...BUT I KEPT THAT THOUGHT TO MYSELF.
SORRY ABOUT THIS...
YOU CAME ALL THE WAY OUT HERE TO RUN INTO A BIG MESS...
IT'S FINE, GRAND-PA.
EIGHT PEOPLE WERE TAKEN BY THE DATA LIFE FORM. FIVE WERE STUDENTS AT NORTH HIGH.
WE'LL HAVE TO DO A BIT OF TRAVELING TO HELP THE REMAINING THREE.
HEY... IS THIS SOME KIND OF JOKE?

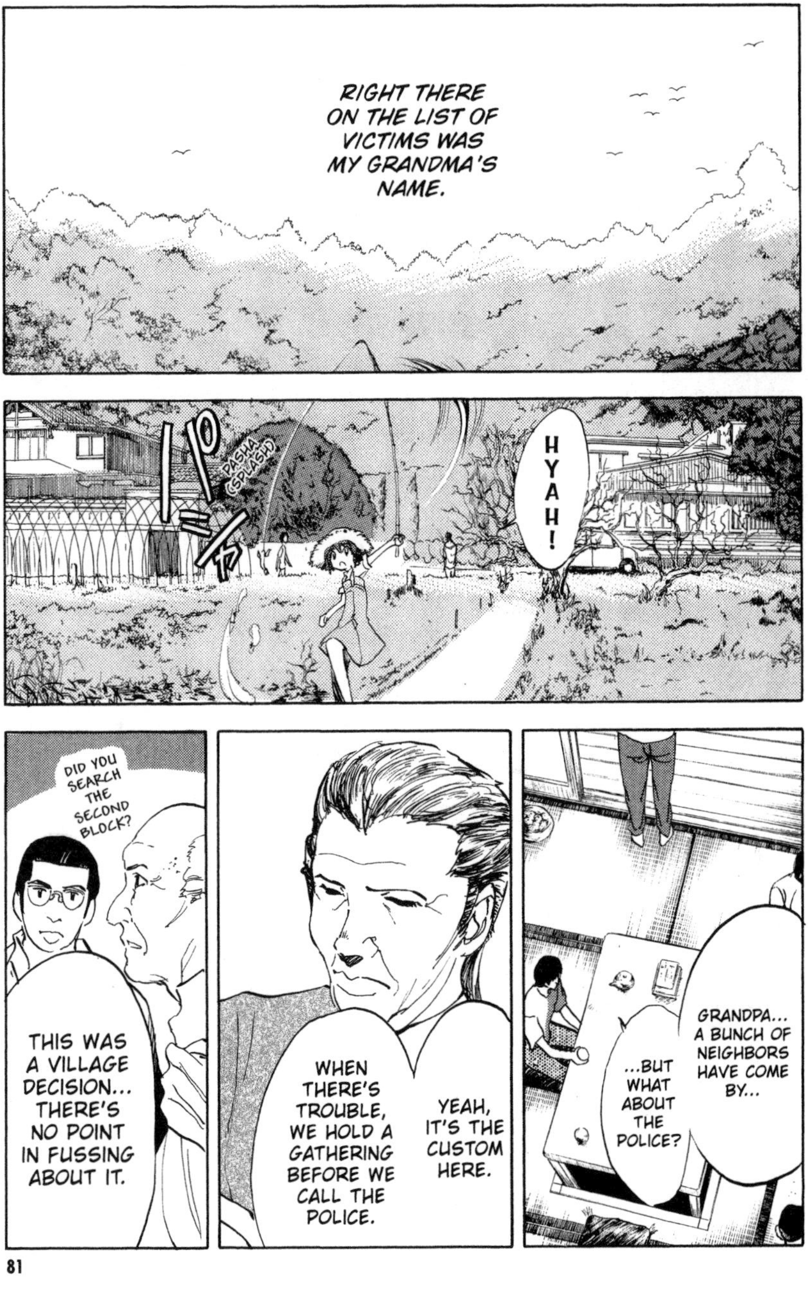

RIGHT THERE ON THE LIST OF VICTIMS WAS MY GRANDMA'S NAME.
HYAH!
PASHA (SPLASH)
GRANDPA... A BUNCH OF NEIGHBORS HAVE COME BY...
...BUT WHAT ABOUT THE POLICE?
YEAH, IT'S THE CUSTOM HERE.
WHEN THERE'S TROUBLE, WE HOLD A GATHERING BEFORE WE CALL THE POLICE.
DID YOU SEARCH THE SECOND BLOCK?
THIS WAS A VILLAGE DECISION... THERE'S NO POINT IN FUSSING ABOUT IT.

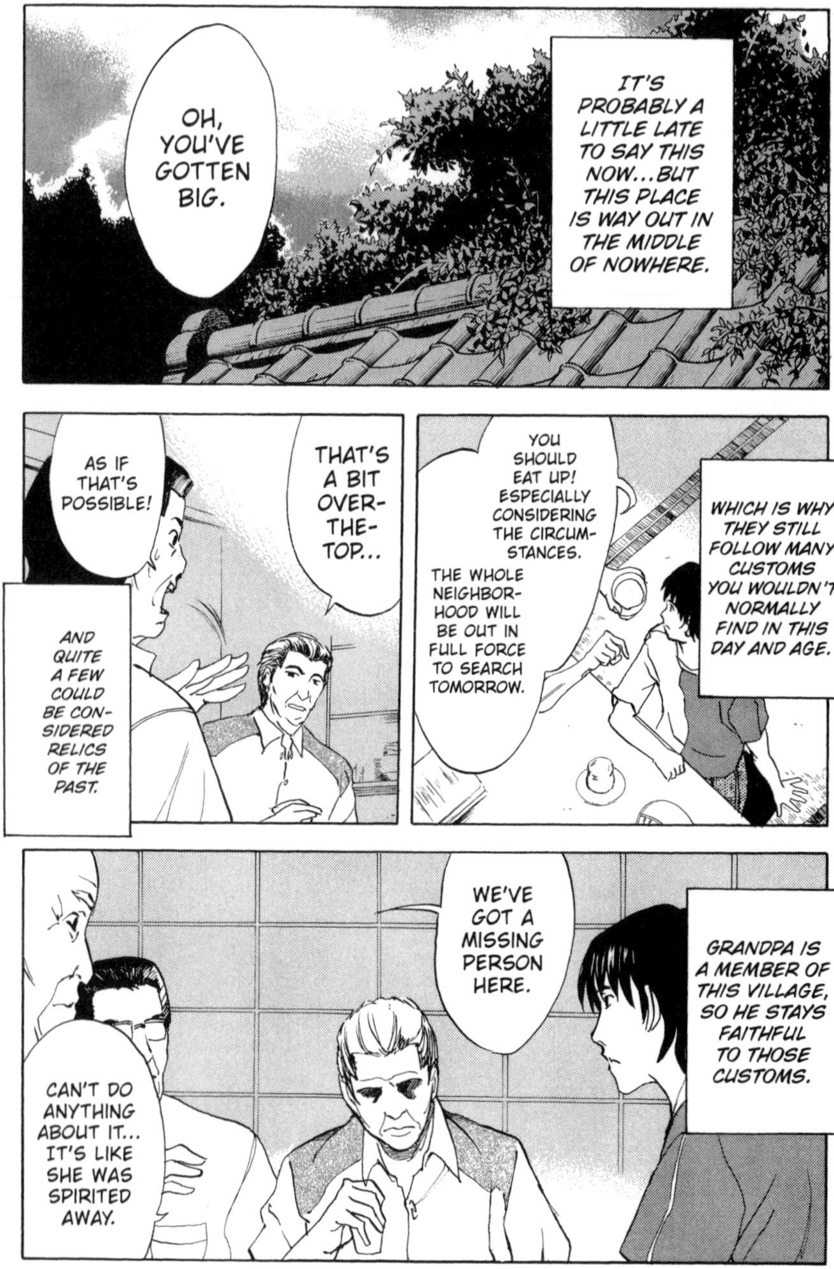
IT'S PROBABLY A LITTLE LATE TO SAY THIS NOW...BUT THIS PLACE IS WAY OUT IN THE MIDDLE OF NOWHERE.
OH, YOU'VE GOTTEN BIG.
WHICH IS WHY THEY STILL FOLLOW MANY CUSTOMS YOU WOULDN'T NORMALLY FIND IN THIS DAY AND AGE.
YOU SHOULD EAT UP! ESPECIALLY CONSIDERING THE CIRCUM-STANCES.
THE WHOLE NEIGHBOR-HOOD WILL BE OUT IN FULL FORCE TO SEARCH TOMORROW.
THAT'S A BIT OVER-THE-TOP...
AS IF THAT'S POSSIBLE!
AND QUITE A FEW COULD BE CON-SIDERED RELICS OF THE PAST.
GRANDPA IS A MEMBER OF THIS VILLAGE, SO HE STAYS FAITHFUL TO THOSE CUSTOMS.
WE'VE GOT A MISSING PERSON HERE.
CAN'T DO ANYTHING ABOUT IT... IT'S LIKE SHE WAS SPIRITED AWAY.

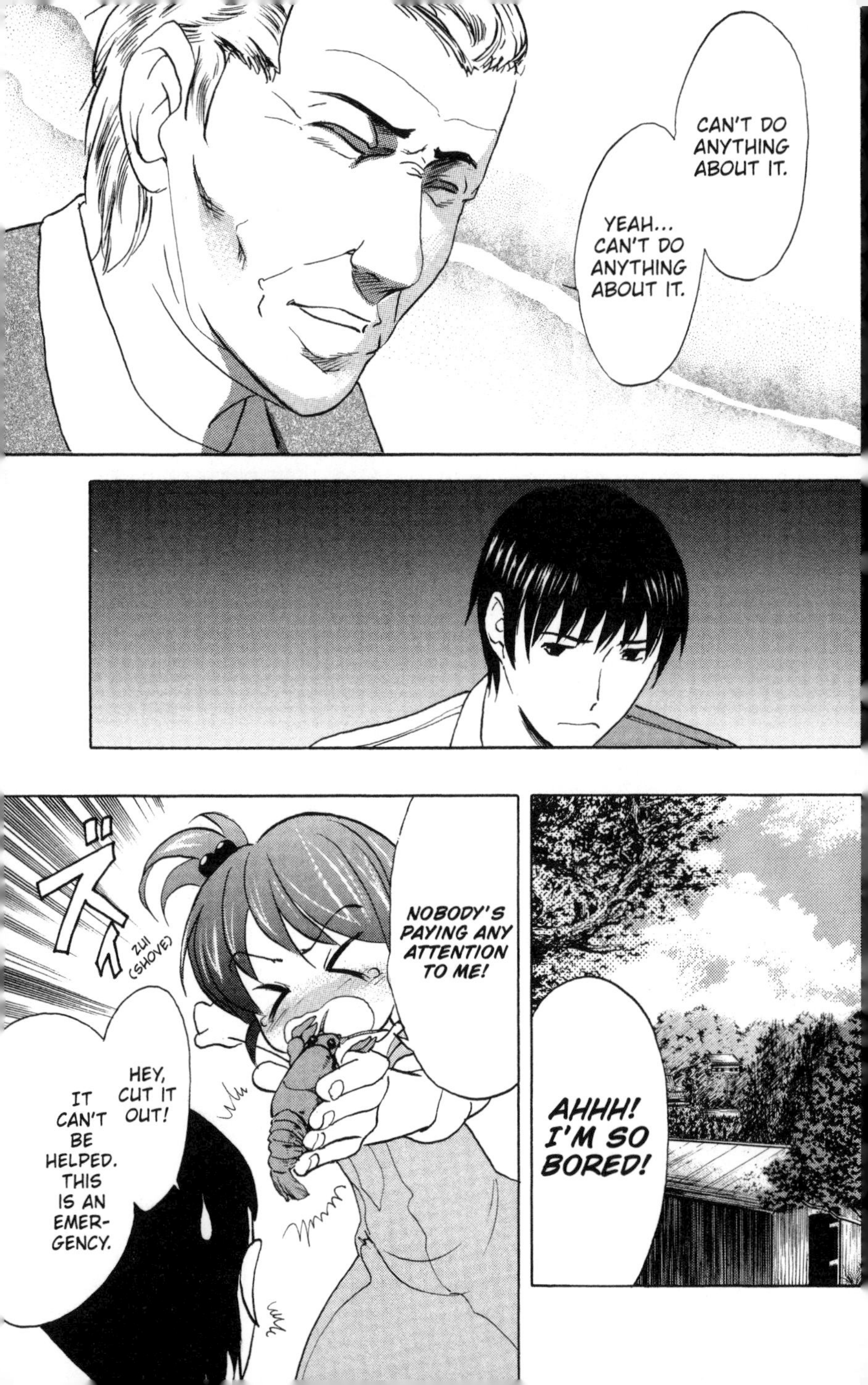
CAN'T DO ANYTHING ABOUT IT.
YEAH... CAN'T DO ANYTHING ABOUT IT.
AHHH! I'M SO BORED!
NOBODY'S PAYING ANY ATTENTION TO ME!
ズイ
ZUI (SHOVE)
HEY, CUT IT OUT!
IT CAN'T BE HELPED. THIS IS AN EMERGENCY.

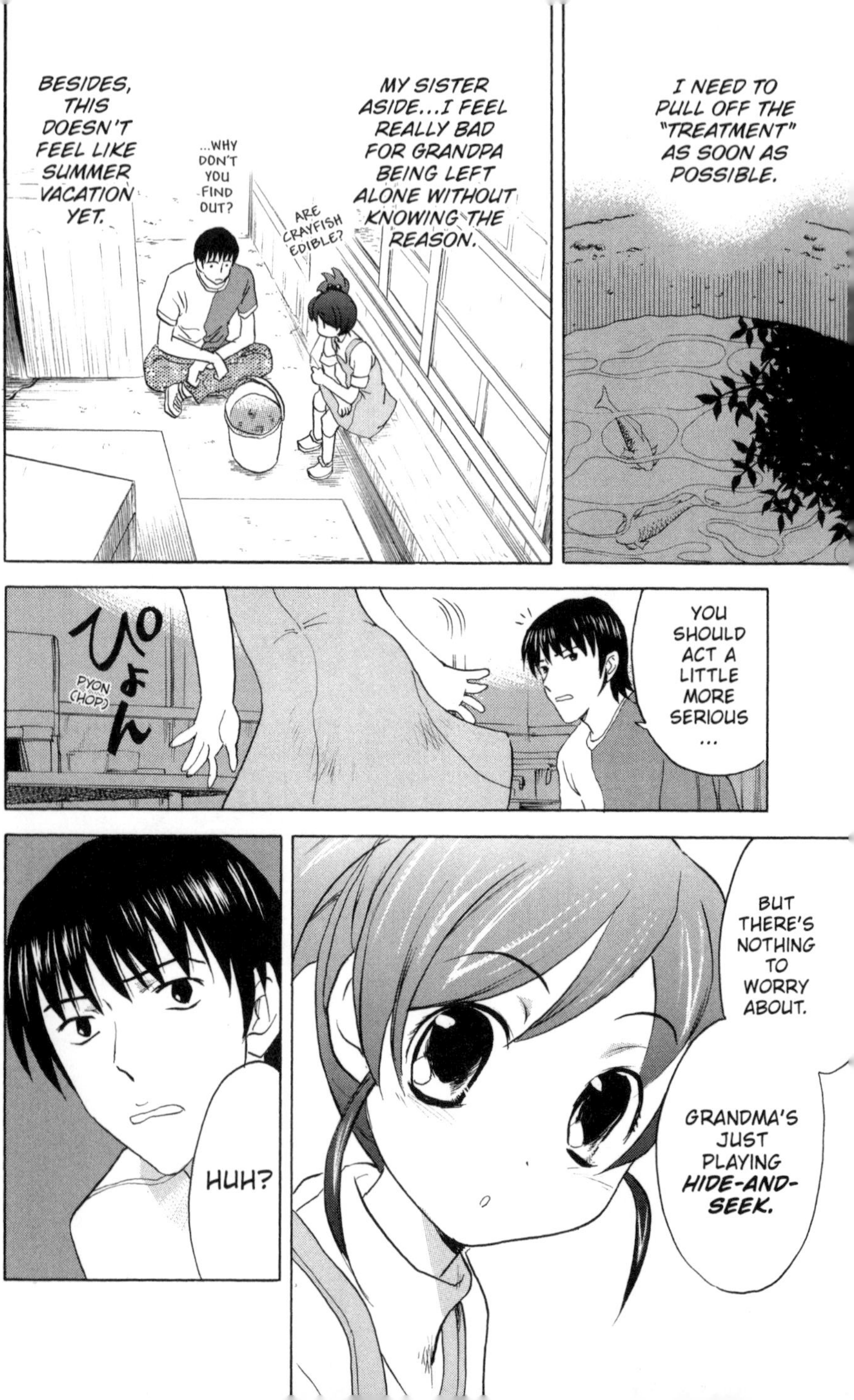

I NEED TO PULL OFF THE "TREATMENT" AS SOON AS POSSIBLE.
MY SISTER ASIDE...I FEEL REALLY BAD FOR GRANDPA BEING LEFT ALONE WITHOUT KNOWING THE REASON.
ARE CRAYFISH EDIBLE?
...WHY DON'T YOU FIND OUT?
BESIDES, THIS DOESN'T FEEL LIKE SUMMER VACATION YET.
YOU SHOULD ACT A LITTLE MORE SERIOUS...
ぴょん
PYON (HOP)
BUT THERE'S NOTHING TO WORRY ABOUT.
GRANDMA'S JUST PLAYING HIDE-AND-SEEK.
HUH?

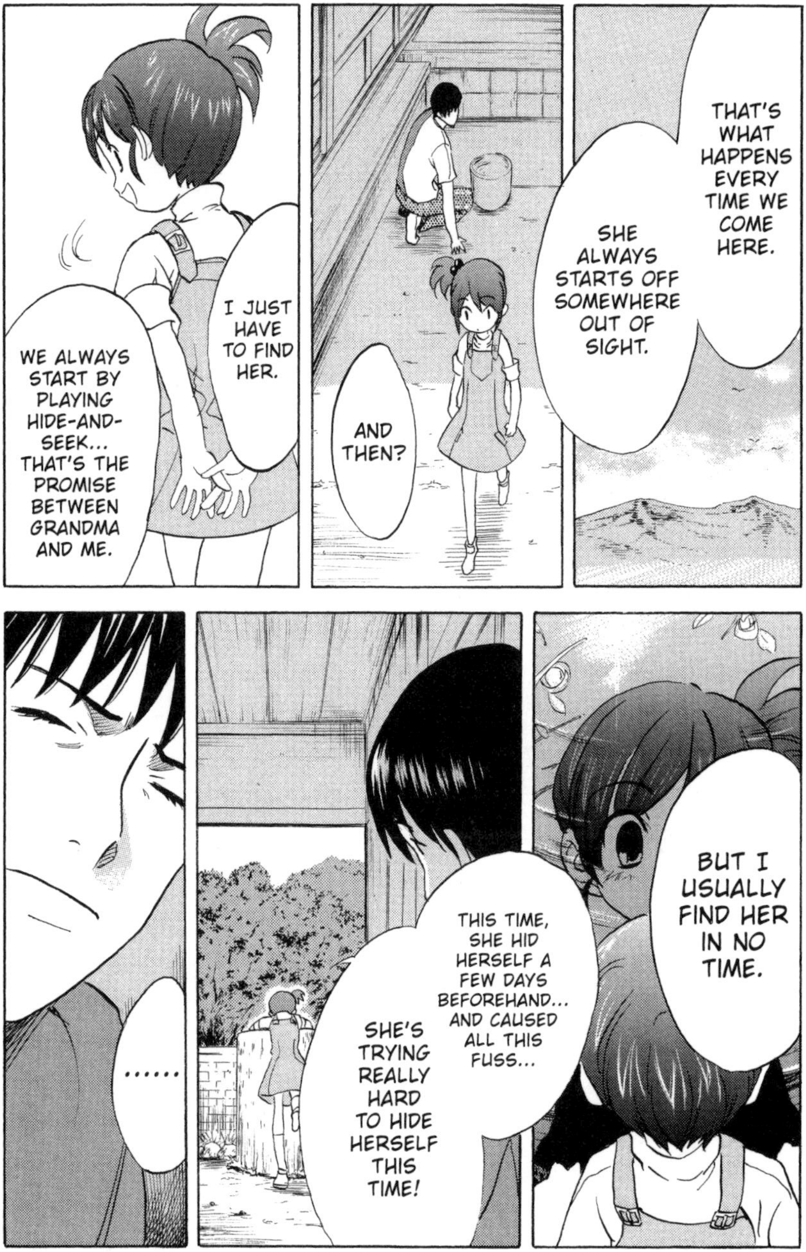
THAT'S WHAT HAPPENS EVERY TIME WE COME HERE.
SHE ALWAYS STARTS OFF SOMEWHERE OUT OF SIGHT.
AND THEN?
I JUST HAVE TO FIND HER.
WE ALWAYS START BY PLAYING HIDE-AND-SEEK... THAT'S THE PROMISE BETWEEN GRANDMA AND ME.
BUT I USUALLY FIND HER IN NO TIME.
THIS TIME, SHE HID HERSELF A FEW DAYS BEFOREHAND... AND CAUSED ALL THIS FUSS...
SHE'S TRYING REALLY HARD TO HIDE HERSELF THIS TIME!
......

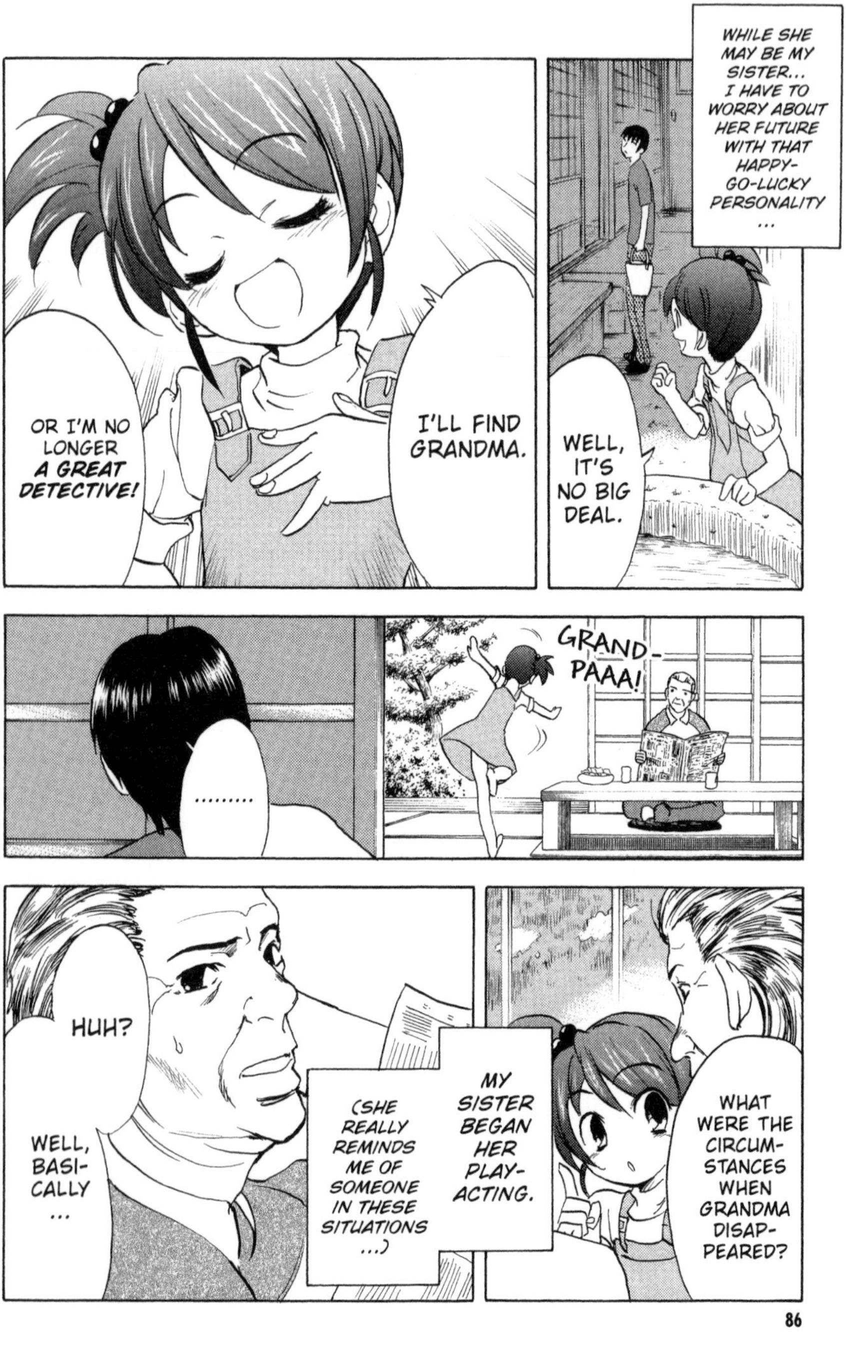
WHILE SHE MAY BE MY SISTER... I HAVE TO WORRY ABOUT HER FUTURE WITH THAT HAPPY-GO-LUCKY PERSONALITY ...
WELL, IT'S NO BIG DEAL.
I'LL FIND GRANDMA.
OR I'M NO LONGER A GREAT DETECTIVE!
GRAND-PAAA!
....
WHAT WERE THE CIRCUM-STANCES WHEN GRANDMA DISAP-PEARED?
HUH?
MY SISTER BEGAN HER PLAY-ACTING.
(SHE REALLY REMINDS ME OF SOMEONE IN THESE SITUATIONS ...)
WELL, BASI-CALLY ...

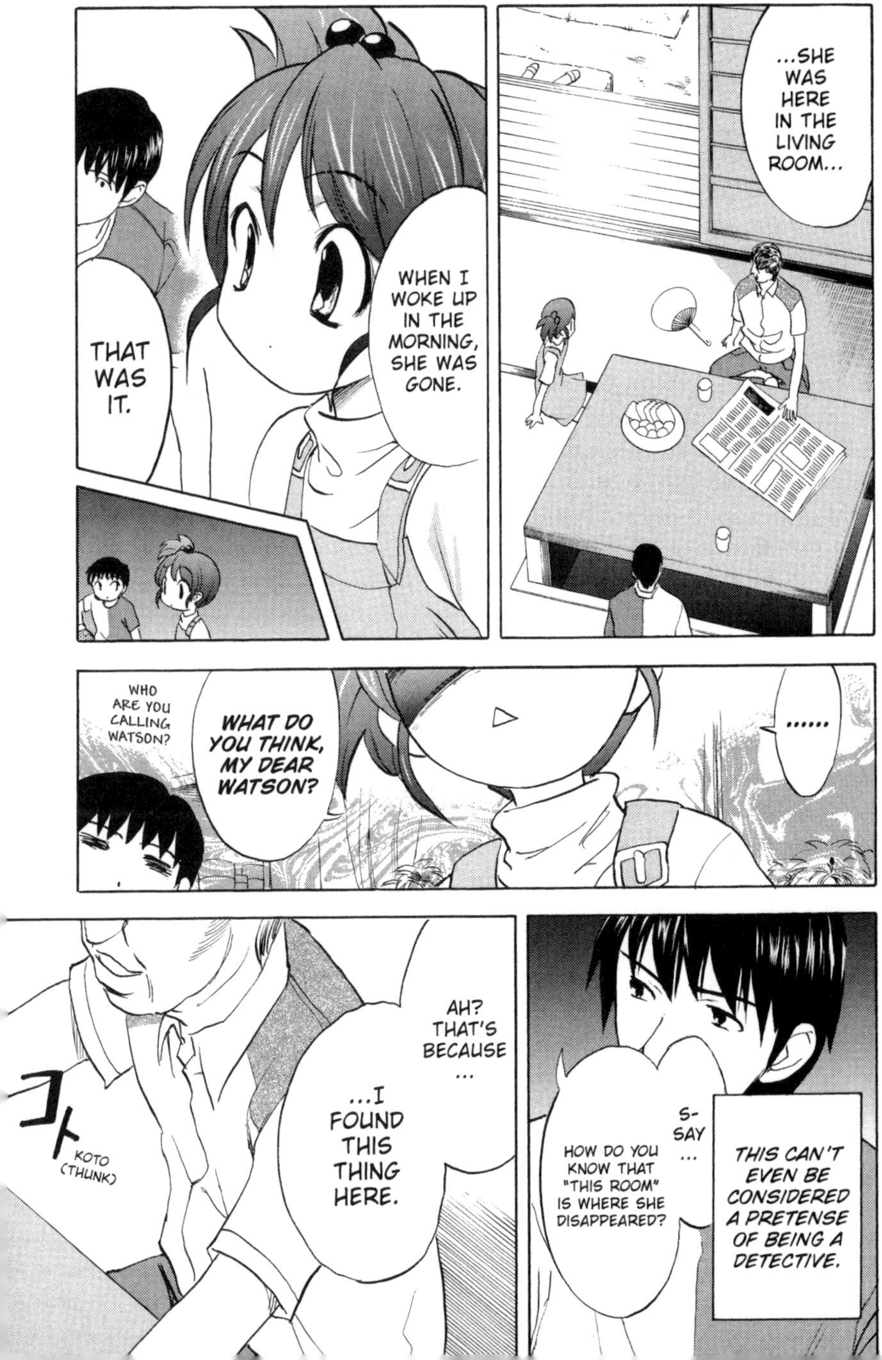
...SHE WAS HERE IN THE LIVING ROOM...
WHEN I WOKE UP IN THE MORNING, SHE WAS GONE.
THAT WAS IT.
......
WHAT DO YOU THINK, MY DEAR WATSON?
WHO ARE YOU CALLING WATSON?
THIS CAN'T EVEN BE CONSIDERED A PRETENSE OF BEING A DETECTIVE.
S-SAY...
HOW DO YOU KNOW THAT "THIS ROOM" IS WHERE SHE DISAPPEARED?
AH? THAT'S BECAUSE...
...I FOUND THIS THING HERE.
コト
KOTO (THUNK)

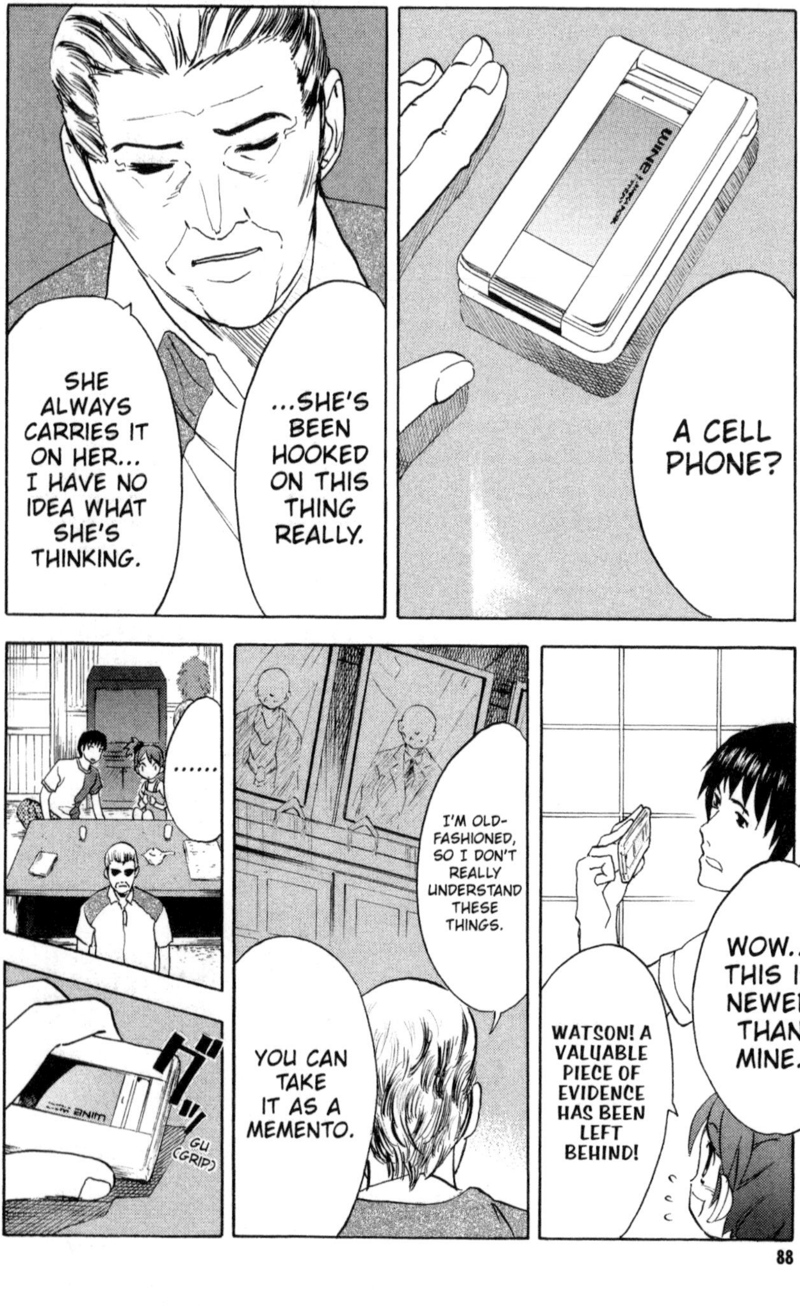
A CELL PHONE?
...SHE'S BEEN HOOKED ON THIS THING REALLY.
SHE ALWAYS CARRIES IT ON HER... I HAVE NO IDEA WHAT SHE'S THINKING.
WOW... THIS IS NEWER THAN MINE.
WATSON! A VALUABLE PIECE OF EVIDENCE HAS BEEN LEFT BEHIND!
I'M OLD-FASHIONED, SO I DON'T REALLY UNDERSTAND THESE THINGS.
YOU CAN TAKE IT AS A MEMENTO.
......
GU (GRIP)

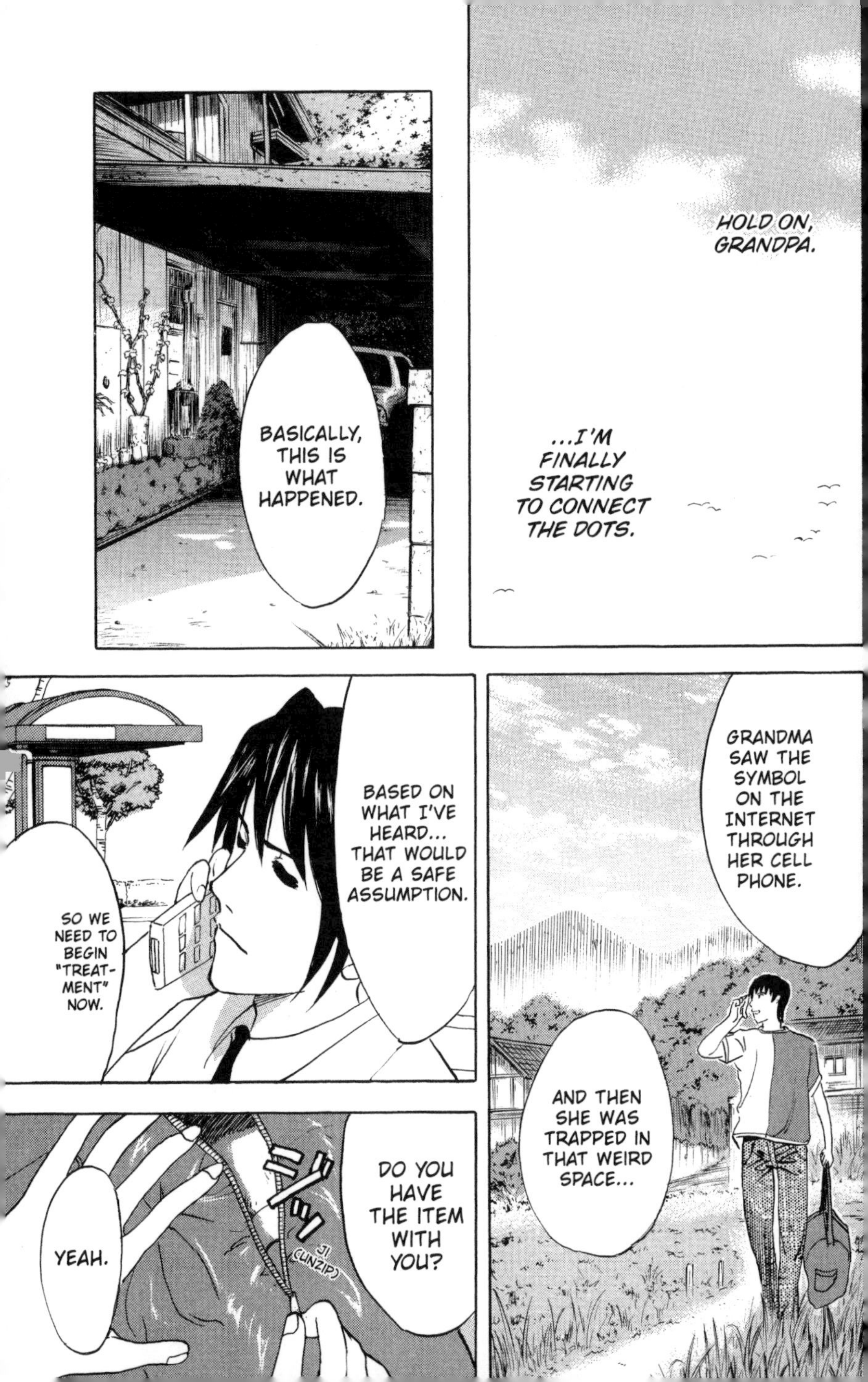
HOLD ON, GRANDPA.
...I'M FINALLY STARTING TO CONNECT THE DOTS.
BASICALLY, THIS IS WHAT HAPPENED.
GRANDMA SAW THE SYMBOL ON THE INTERNET THROUGH HER CELL PHONE.
AND THEN SHE WAS TRAPPED IN THAT WEIRD SPACE...
BASED ON WHAT I'VE HEARD... THAT WOULD BE A SAFE ASSUMPTION.
SO WE NEED TO BEGIN "TREAT-MENT" NOW.
DO YOU HAVE THE ITEM WITH YOU?
JI (UNZIP)
YEAH.

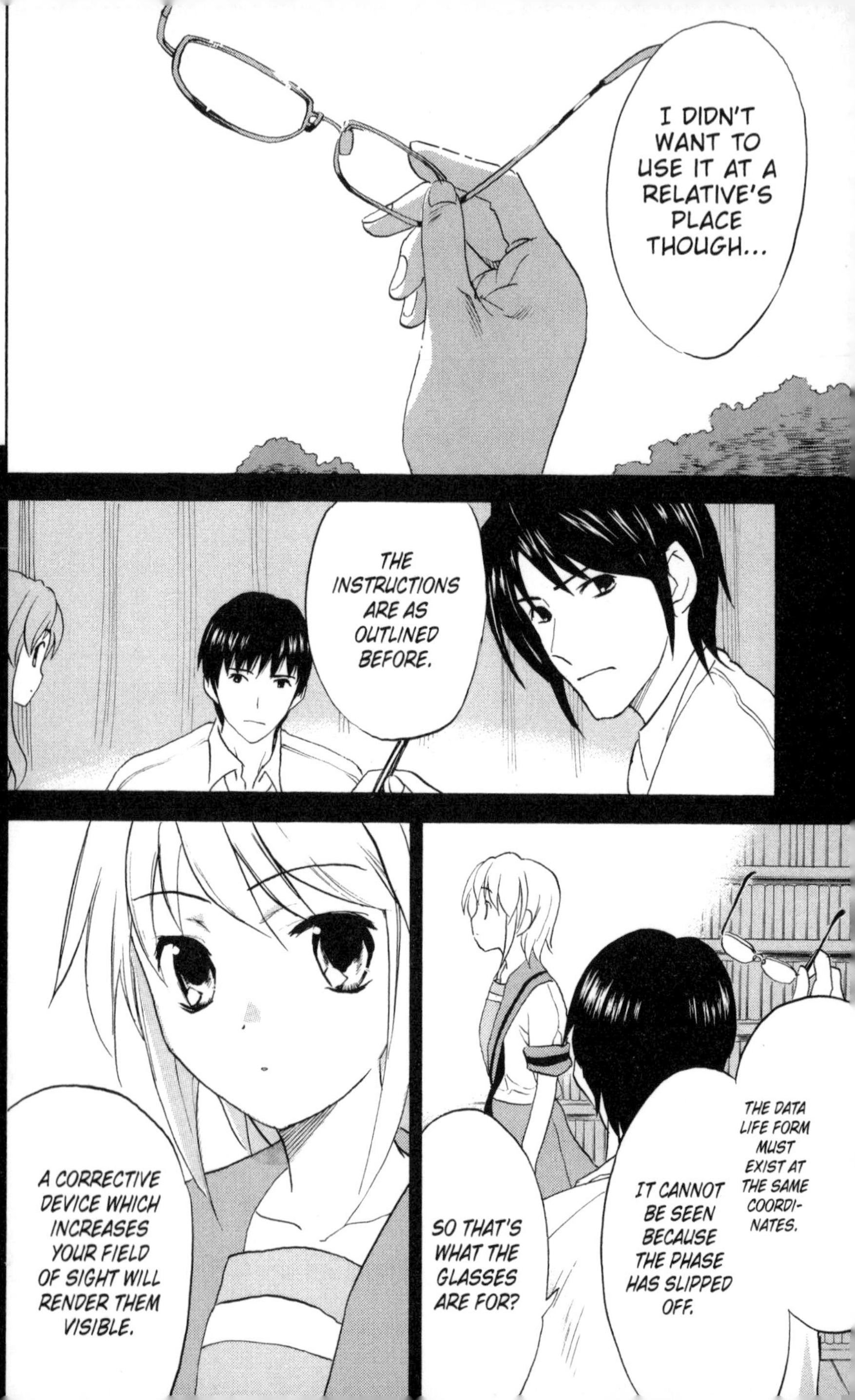
I DIDN'T WANT TO USE IT AT A RELATIVE'S PLACE THOUGH...
THE INSTRUCTIONS ARE AS OUTLINED BEFORE.
THE DATA LIFE FORM MUST EXIST AT THE SAME COORDINATES.
IT CANNOT BE SEEN BECAUSE THE PHASE HAS SLIPPED OFF.
SO THAT'S WHAT THE GLASSES ARE FOR?
A CORRECTIVE DEVICE WHICH INCREASES YOUR FIELD OF SIGHT WILL RENDER THEM VISIBLE.

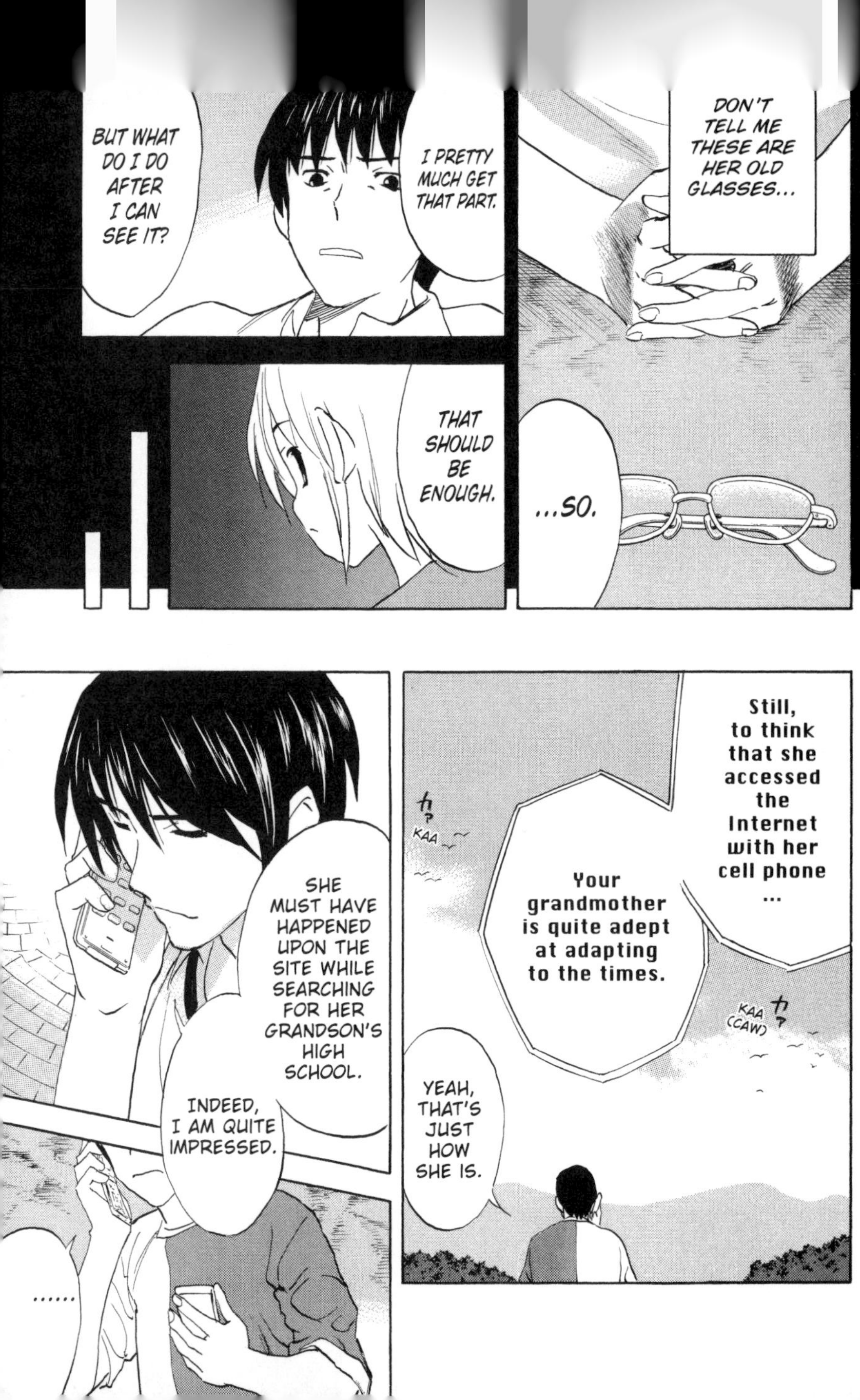
DON'T TELL ME THESE ARE HER OLD GLASSES...
...SO.
I PRETTY MUCH GET THAT PART.
BUT WHAT DO I DO AFTER I CAN SEE IT?
THAT SHOULD BE ENOUGH.
Still, to think that she accessed the Internet with her cell phone ...
Your grandmother is quite adept at adapting to the times.
KAA
KAA (CAW)
YEAH, THAT'S JUST HOW SHE IS.
SHE MUST HAVE HAPPENED UPON THE SITE WHILE SEARCHING FOR HER GRANDSON'S HIGH SCHOOL.
INDEED, I AM QUITE IMPRESSED.
......

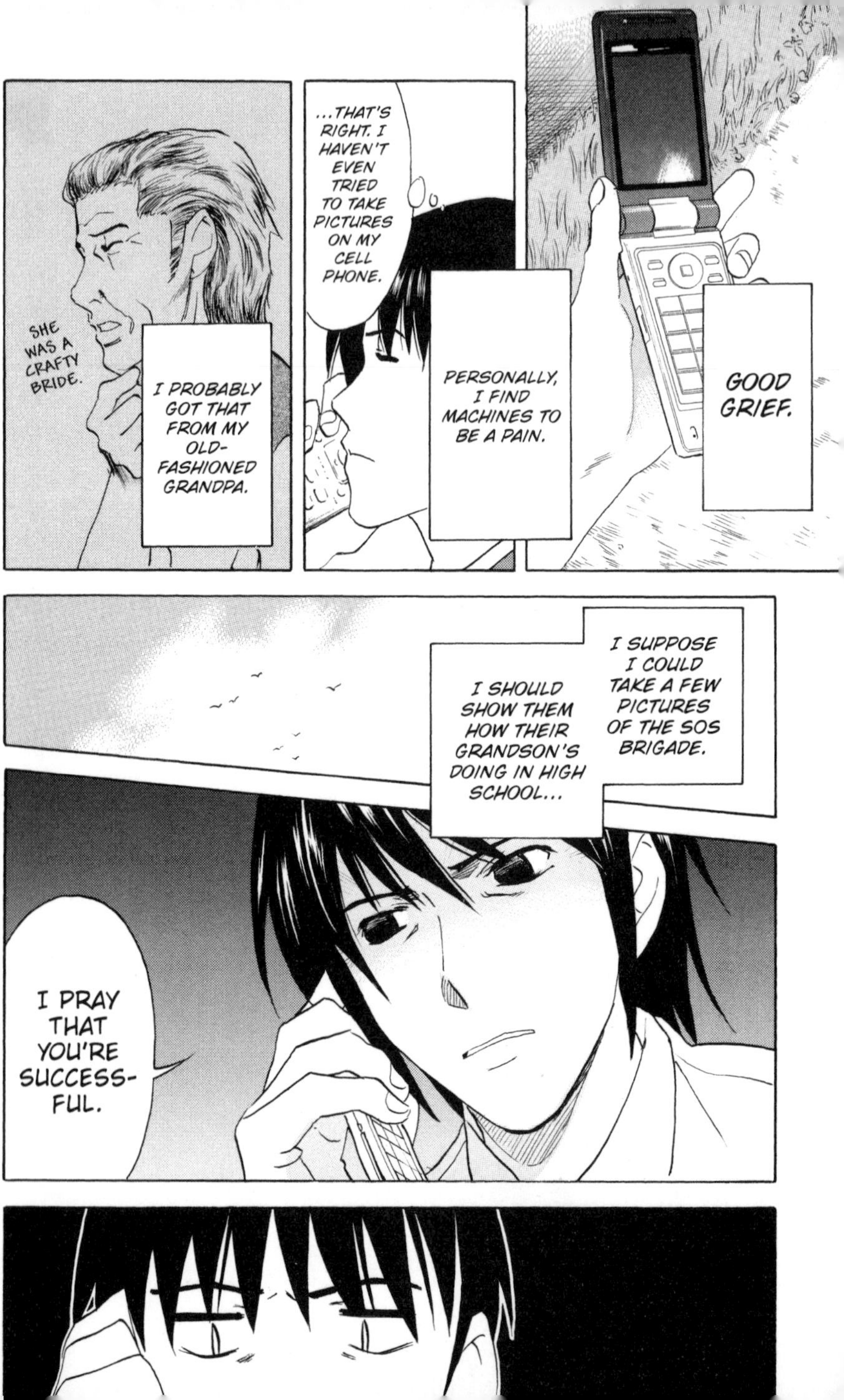
GOOD GRIEF.
...THAT'S RIGHT. I HAVEN'T EVEN TRIED TO TAKE PICTURES ON MY CELL PHONE.
PERSONALLY, I FIND MACHINES TO BE A PAIN.
I PROBABLY GOT THAT FROM MY OLD-FASHIONED GRANDPA.
SHE WAS A CRAFTY BRIDE.
I SUPPOSE I COULD TAKE A FEW PICTURES OF THE SOS BRIGADE.
I SHOULD SHOW THEM HOW THEIR GRANDSON'S DOING IN HIGH SCHOOL...
I PRAY THAT YOU'RE SUCCESS-FUL.

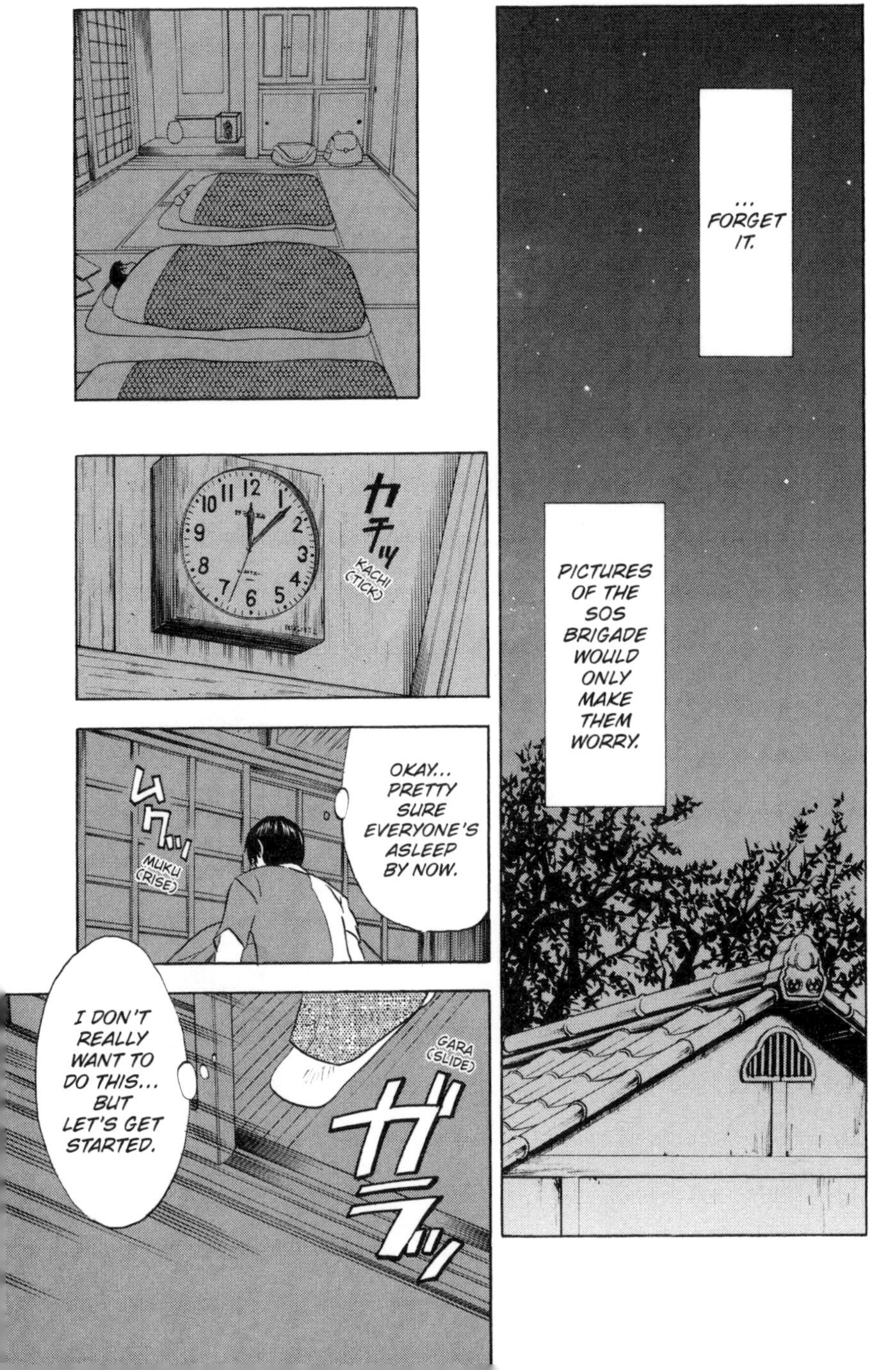
... FORGET IT.
PICTURES OF THE SOS BRIGADE WOULD ONLY MAKE THEM WORRY.
カチッ
KACHI (TICK)
OKAY... PRETTY SURE EVERYONE'S ASLEEP BY NOW.
ムクッ
MUKU (RISE)
I DON'T REALLY WANT TO DO THIS... BUT LET'S GET STARTED.
ガラッ
GARA (SLIDE)

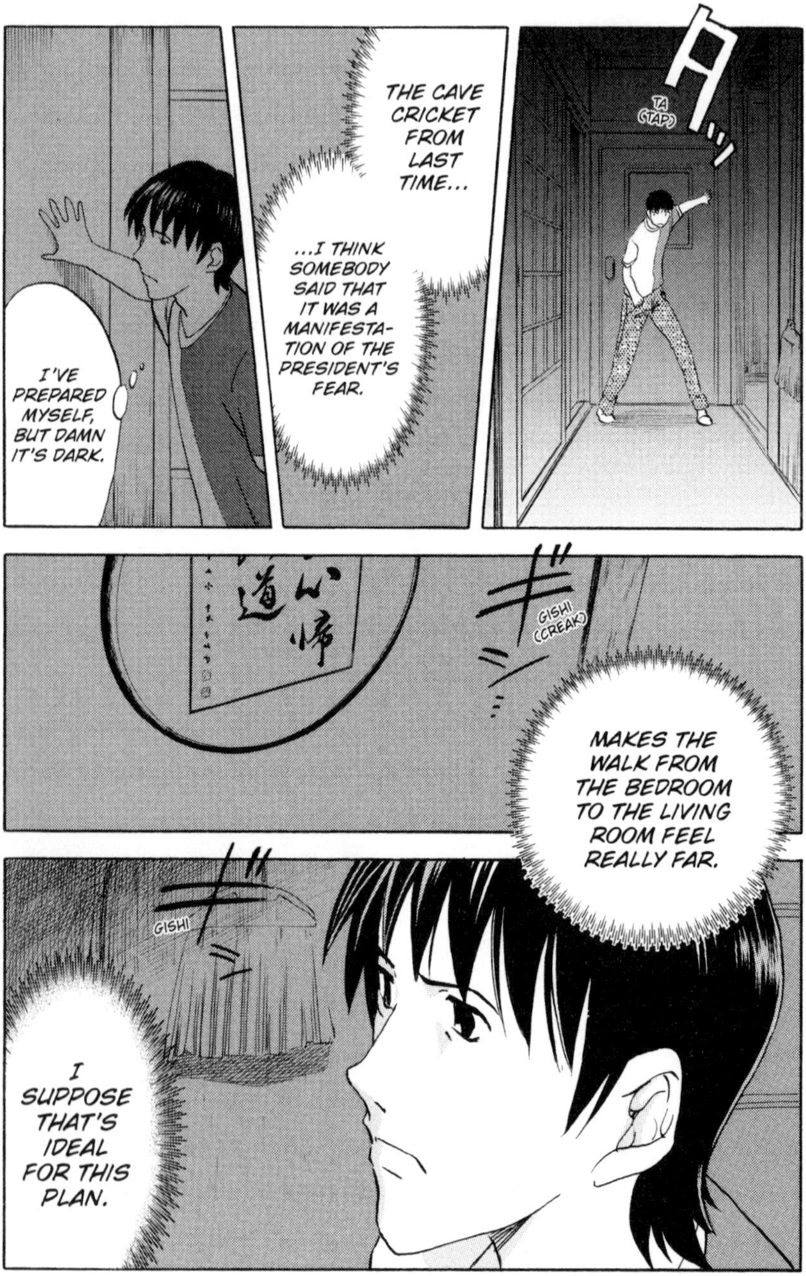
TA (TAP)
THE CAVE CRICKET FROM LAST TIME...
...I THINK SOMEBODY SAID THAT IT WAS A MANIFESTATION OF THE PRESIDENT'S FEAR.
I'VE PREPARED MYSELF, BUT DAMN IT'S DARK.
GISHI (CREAK)
MAKES THE WALK FROM THE BEDROOM TO THE LIVING ROOM FEEL REALLY FAR.
GISHI
I SUPPOSE THAT'S IDEAL FOR THIS PLAN.

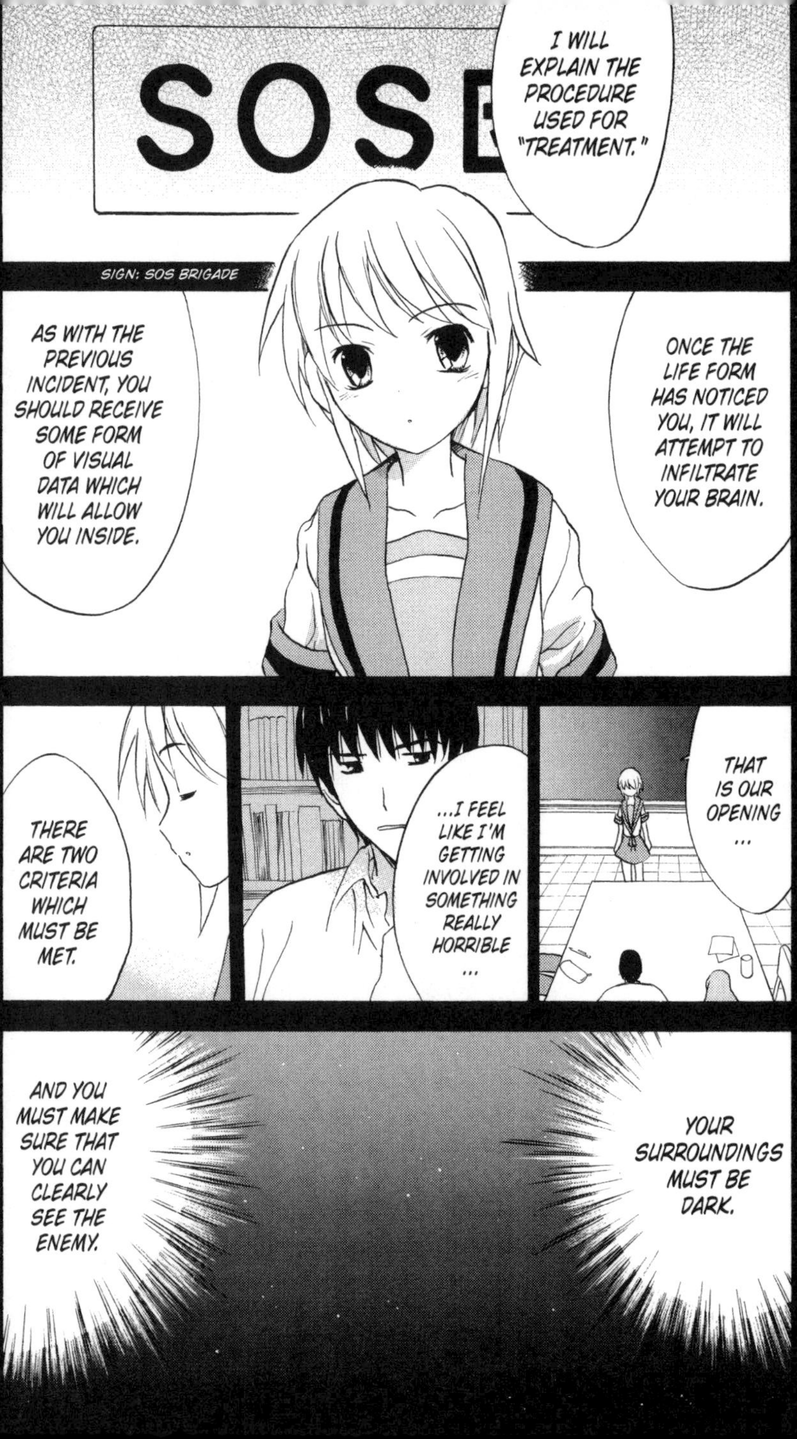
SOS
I WILL EXPLAIN THE PROCEDURE USED FOR "TREATMENT."
SIGN: SOS BRIGADE
ONCE THE LIFE FORM HAS NOTICED YOU, IT WILL ATTEMPT TO INFILTRATE YOUR BRAIN.
AS WITH THE PREVIOUS INCIDENT, YOU SHOULD RECEIVE SOME FORM OF VISUAL DATA WHICH WILL ALLOW YOU INSIDE.
THAT IS OUR OPENING ...
...I FEEL LIKE I'M GETTING INVOLVED IN SOMETHING REALLY HORRIBLE ...
THERE ARE TWO CRITERIA WHICH MUST BE MET.
YOUR SURROUNDINGS MUST BE DARK.
AND YOU MUST MAKE SURE THAT YOU CAN CLEARLY SEE THE ENEMY.

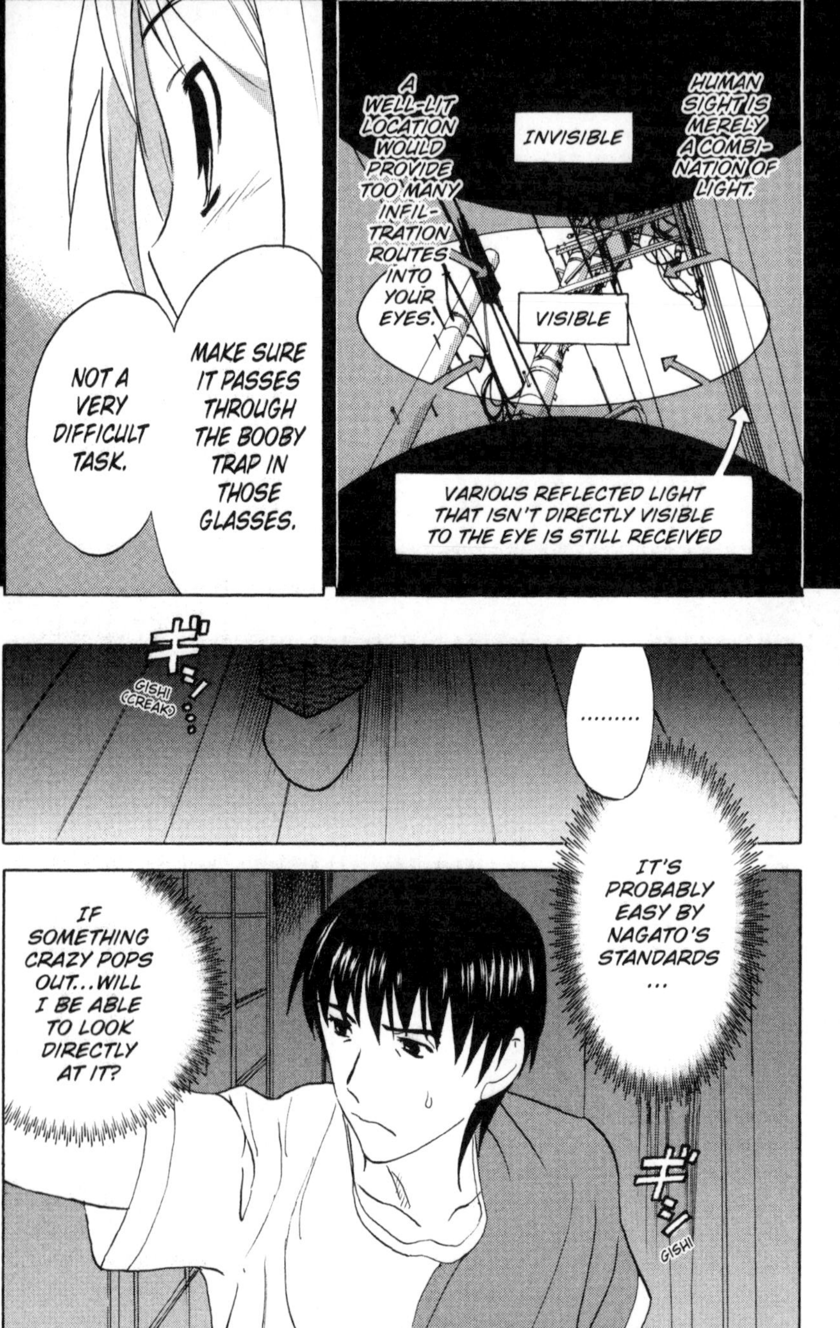
HUMAN SIGHT IS MERELY A COMBINATION OF LIGHT.
INVISIBLE
A WELL-LIT LOCATION WOULD PROVIDE TOO MANY INFILTRATION ROUTES INTO YOUR EYES.
VISIBLE
VARIOUS REFLECTED LIGHT THAT ISN'T DIRECTLY VISIBLE TO THE EYE IS STILL RECEIVED
MAKE SURE IT PASSES THROUGH THE BOOBY TRAP IN THOSE GLASSES.
NOT A VERY DIFFICULT TASK.
....
GISHI (CREAK)
IT'S PROBABLY EASY BY NAGATO'S STANDARDS...
IF SOMETHING CRAZY POPS OUT...WILL I BE ABLE TO LOOK DIRECTLY AT IT?
GISHI

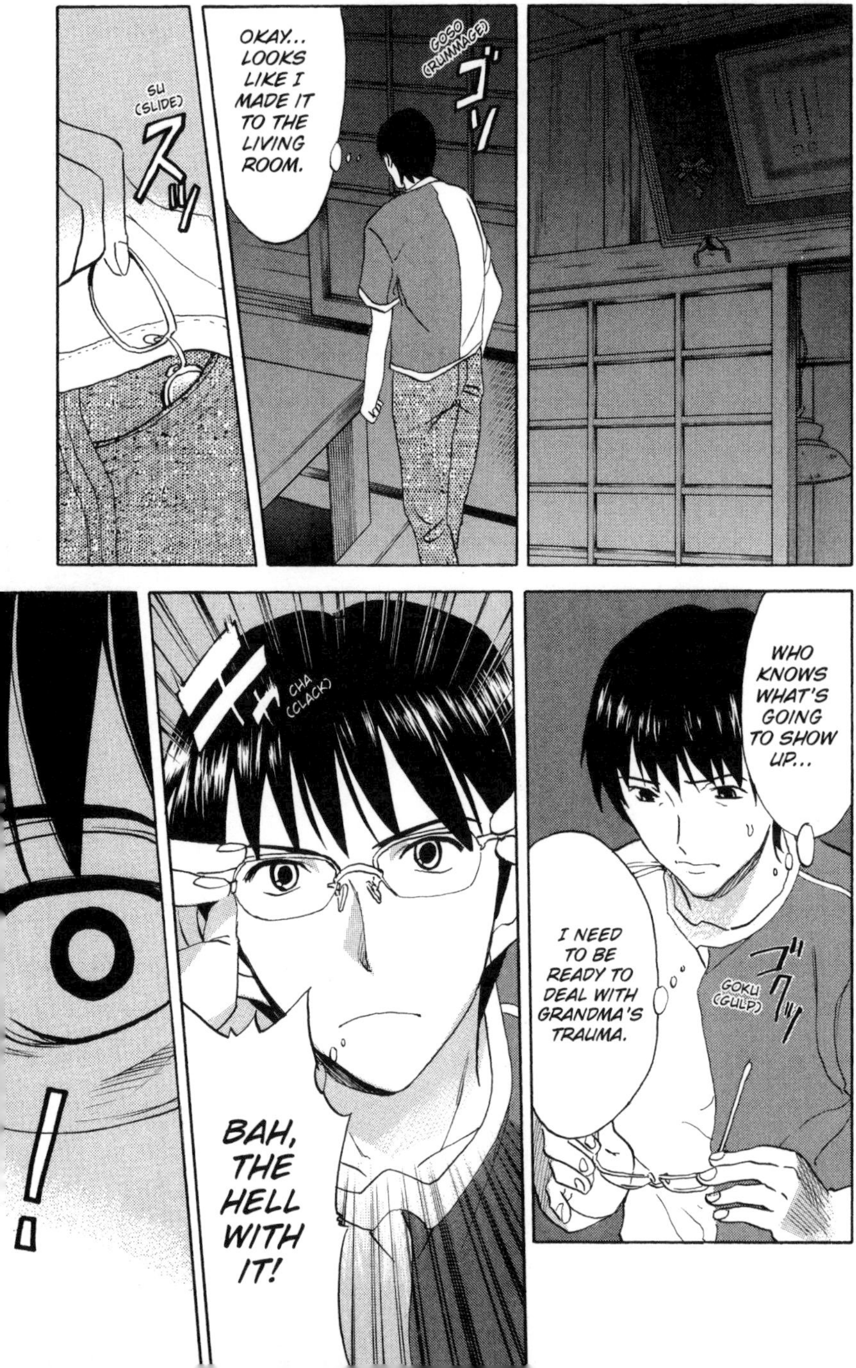
GOSO (RUMMAGE)
OKAY... LOOKS LIKE I MADE IT TO THE LIVING ROOM.
SU (SLIDE)
WHO KNOWS WHAT'S GOING TO SHOW UP...
I NEED TO BE READY TO DEAL WITH GRANDMA'S TRAUMA.
GOKU (GULP)
CHA (CLACK)
BAH, THE HELL WITH IT!
!!

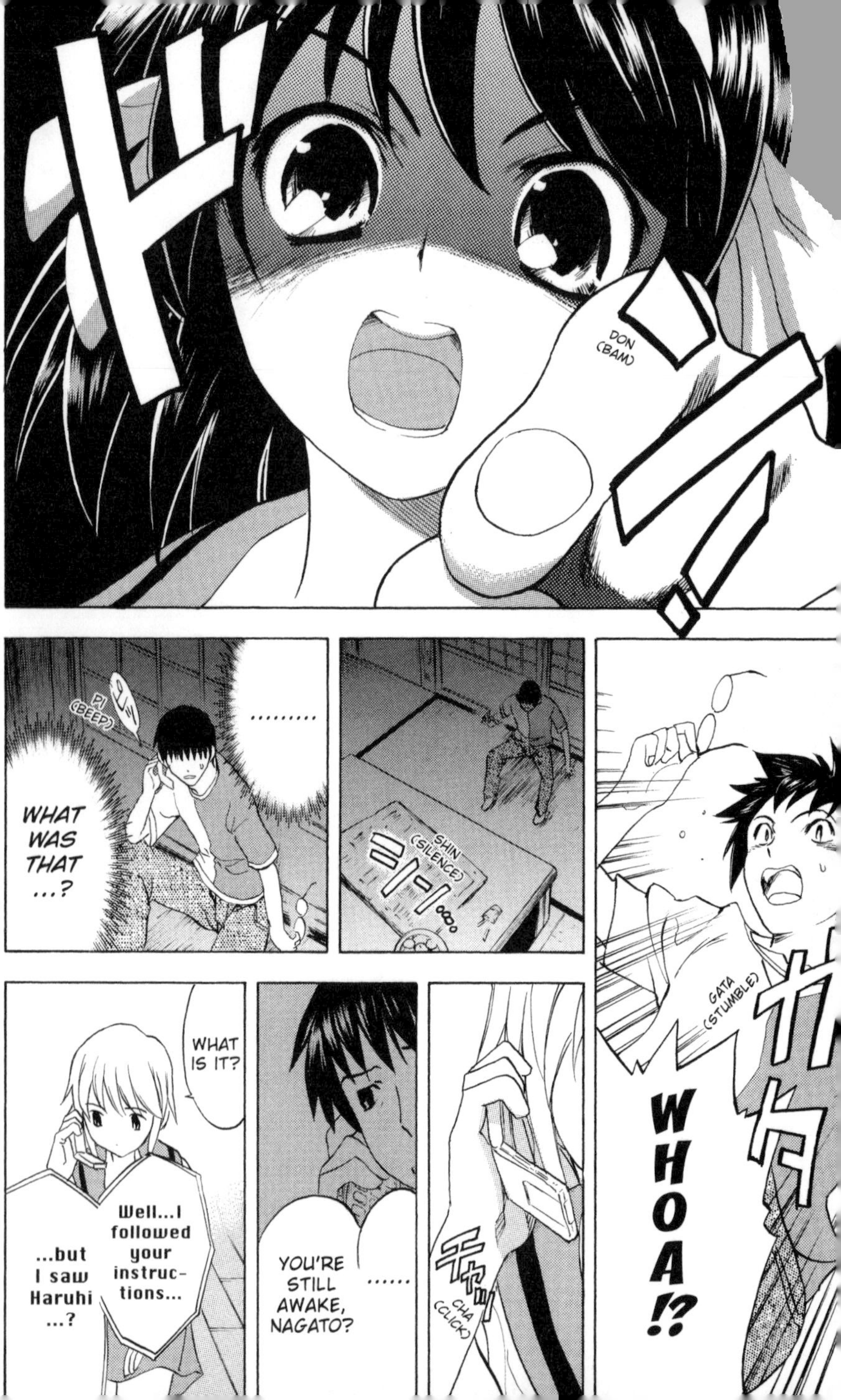

DON (BAM)
GATA (STUMBLE)
WHOA!?
SHIN (SILENCE)
PI (BEEP)
....
WHAT WAS THAT ...?
CHA (CLICK)
......
YOU'RE STILL AWAKE, NAGATO?
WHAT IS IT?
Well...I followed your instructions...
...but I saw Haruhi ...?

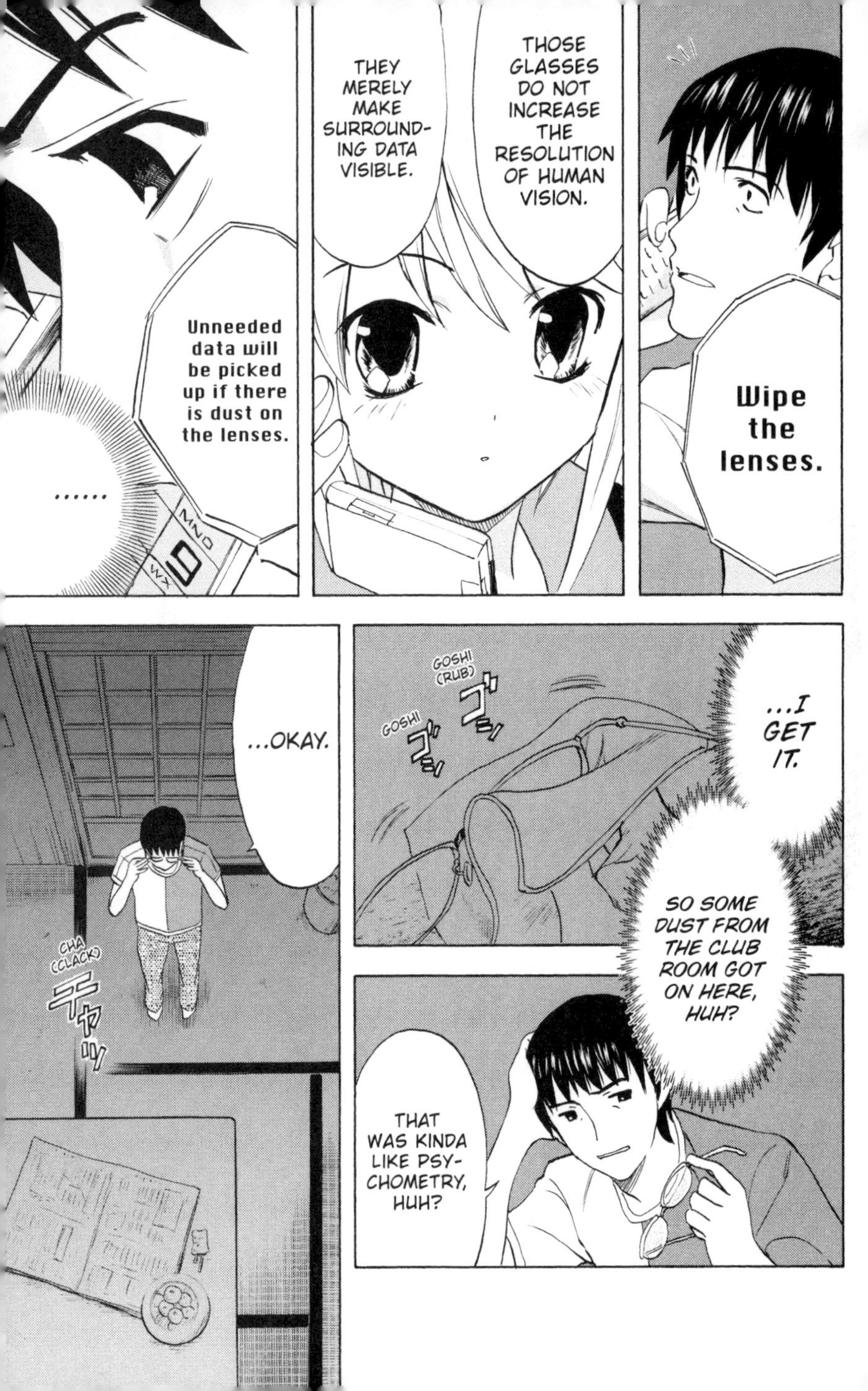
Wipe the lenses.
THOSE GLASSES DO NOT INCREASE THE RESOLUTION OF HUMAN VISION.
THEY MERELY MAKE SURROUNDING DATA VISIBLE.
Unneeded data will be picked up if there is dust on the lenses.
......
...I GET IT.
GOSHI (RUB)
GOSHI
SO SOME DUST FROM THE CLUB ROOM GOT ON HERE, HUH?
THAT WAS KINDA LIKE PSY-CHOMETRY, HUH?
...OKAY.
CHA (CLACK)

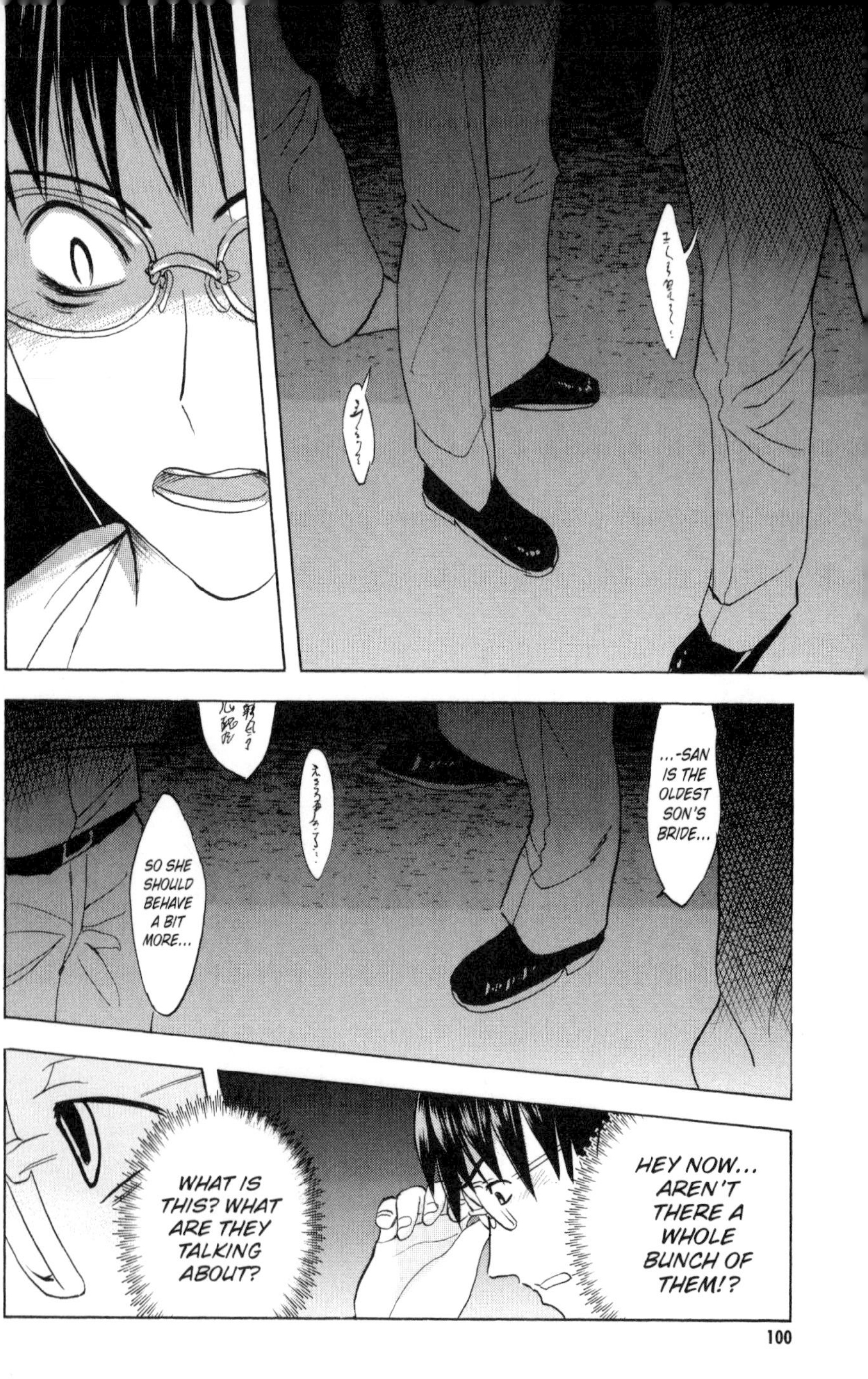
...-SAN IS THE OLDEST SON'S BRIDE...
SO SHE SHOULD BEHAVE A BIT MORE...
HEY NOW... AREN'T THERE A WHOLE BUNCH OF THEM!?
WHAT IS THIS? WHAT ARE THEY TALKING ABOUT?

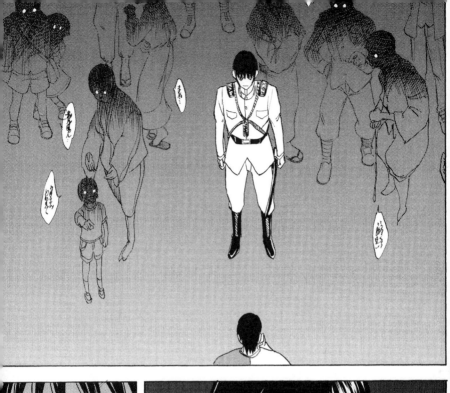

!!!?

CON-
SIDERING
THAT
CHEEKY
MOUTH OF
HERS...

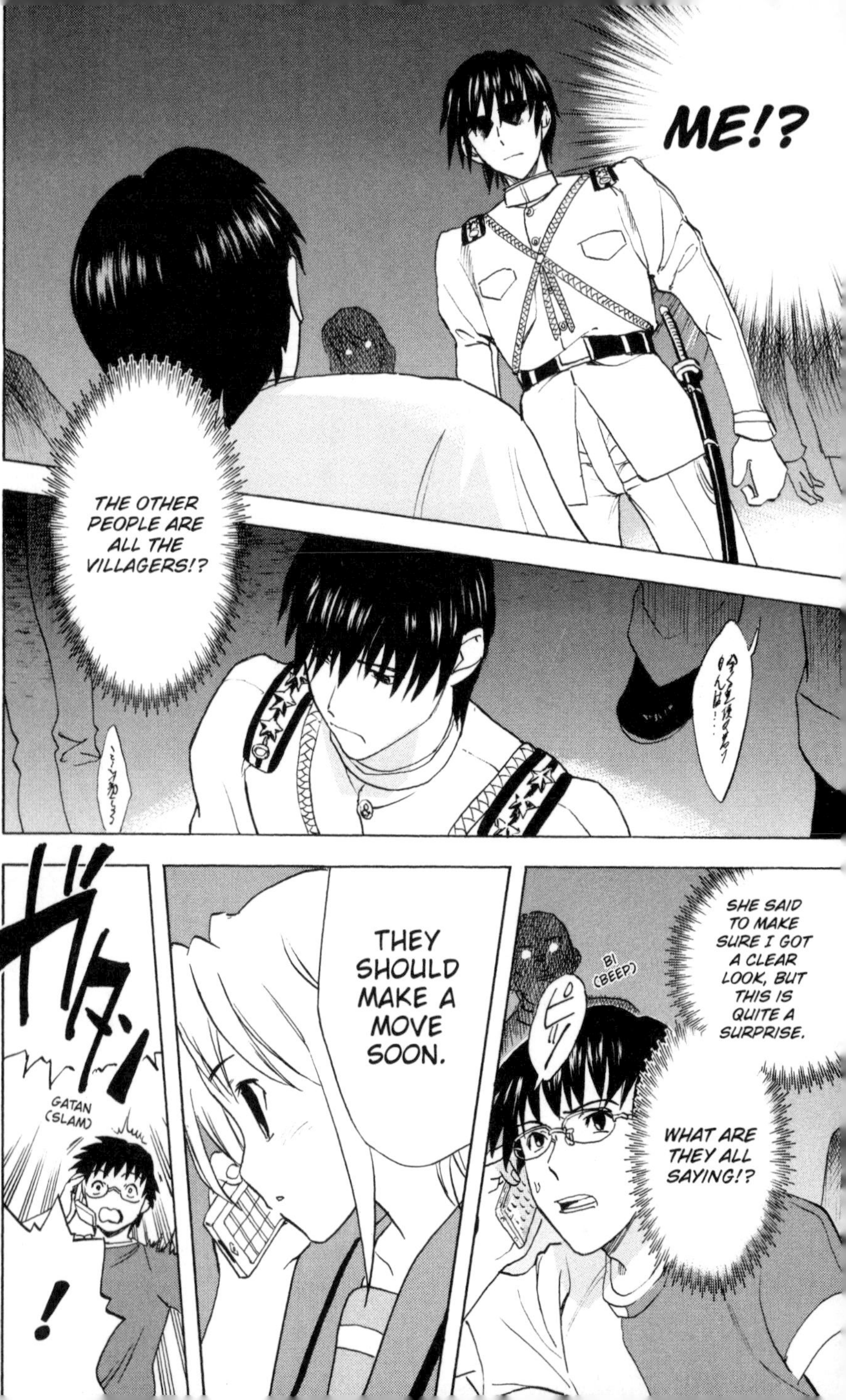
ME!?
THE OTHER PEOPLE ARE ALL THE VILLAGERS!?
SHE SAID TO MAKE SURE I GOT A CLEAR LOOK, BUT THIS IS QUITE A SURPRISE.
BI (BEEP)
WHAT ARE THEY ALL SAYING!?
THEY SHOULD MAKE A MOVE SOON.
GATAN (SLAM)

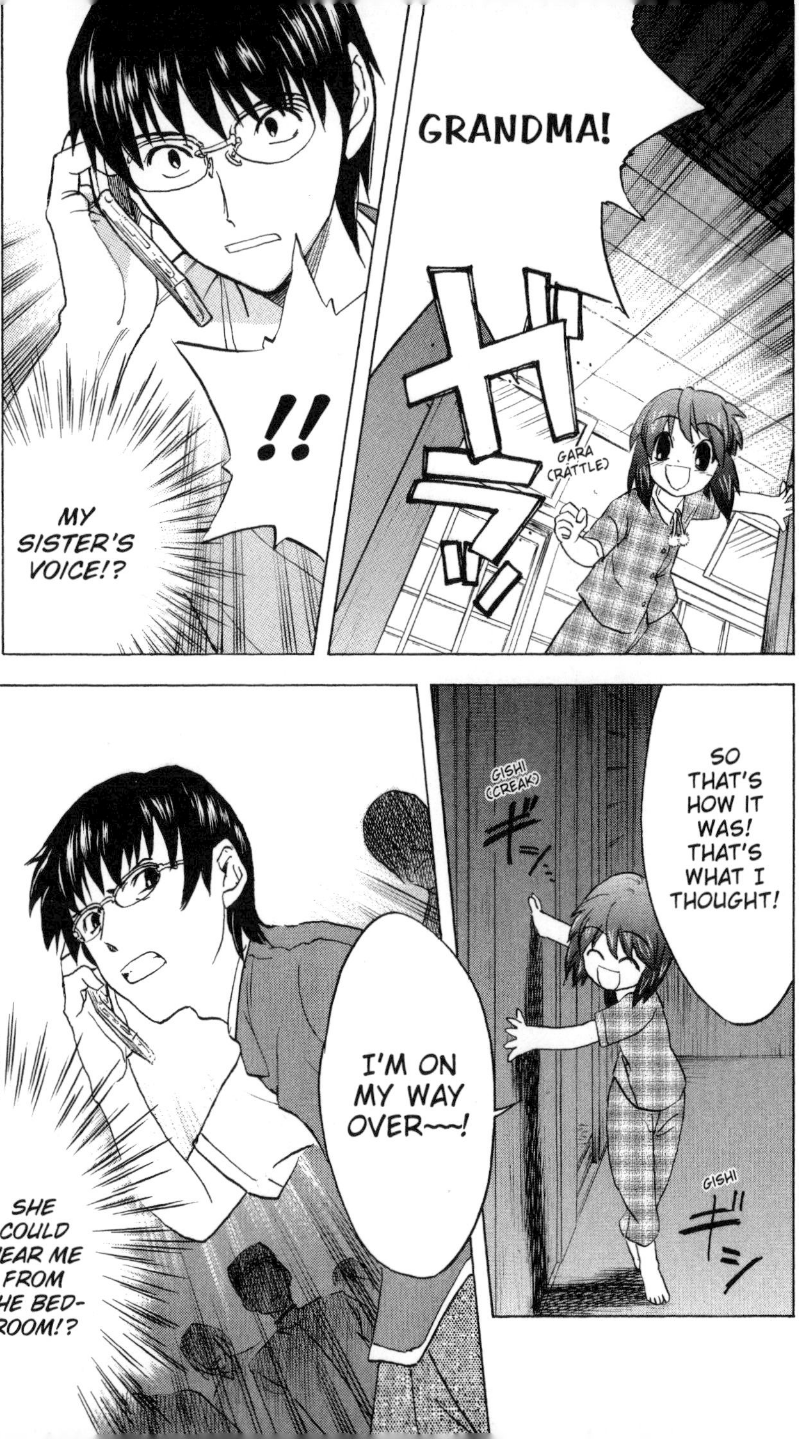
GRANDMA!
ガラッ
GARA (RATTLE)
!!
MY SISTER'S VOICE!?
SO THAT'S HOW IT WAS! THAT'S WHAT I THOUGHT!
GISHI (CREAK)
ギシッ
GISHI
ギシッ
I'M ON MY WAY OVER~~~!
SHE COULD HEAR ME FROM THE BED-ROOM!?

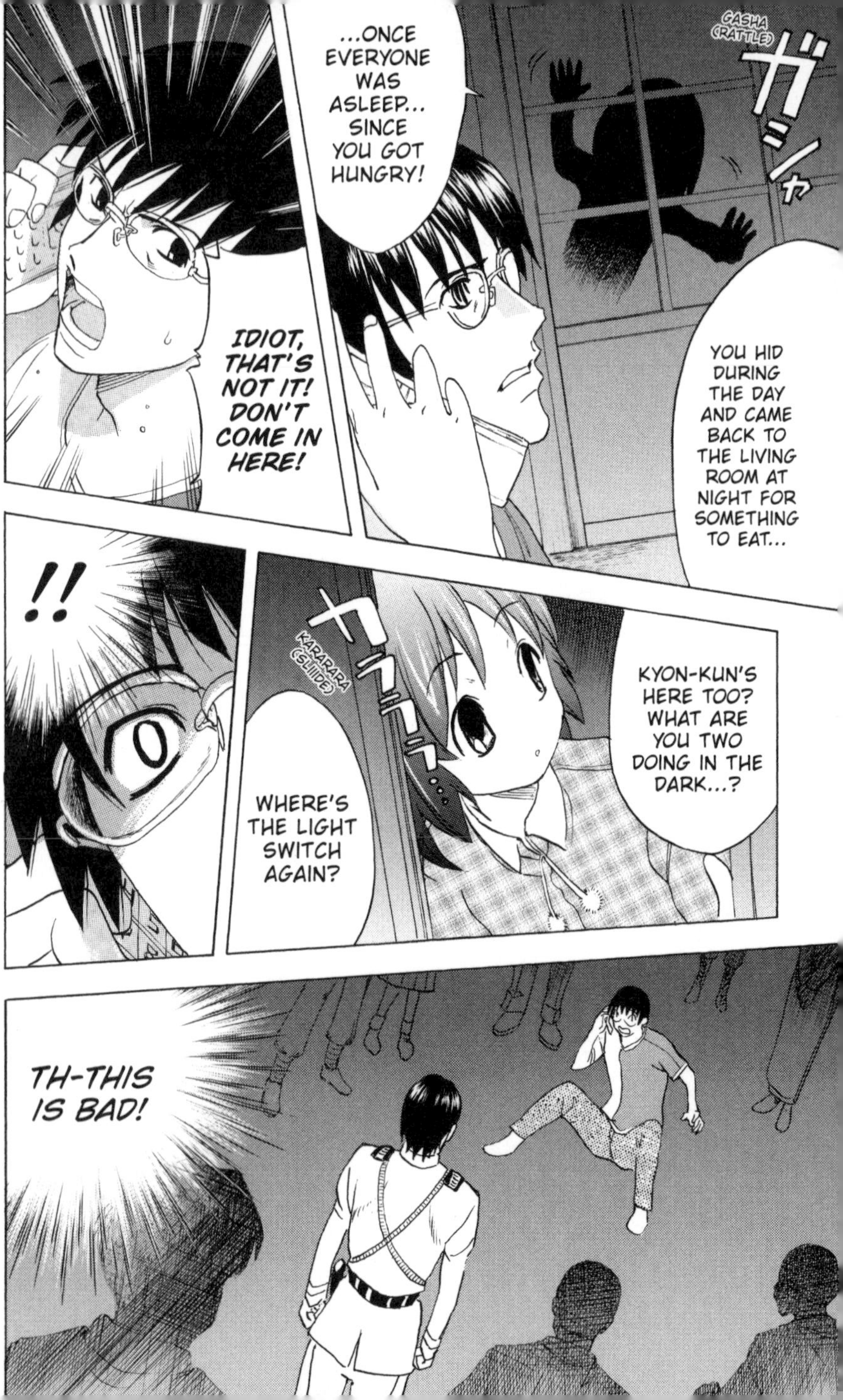

GASHA (RATTLE)
ガシャ
YOU HID DURING THE DAY AND CAME BACK TO THE LIVING ROOM AT NIGHT FOR SOMETHING TO EAT...
...ONCE EVERYONE WAS ASLEEP... SINCE YOU GOT HUNGRY!
IDIOT, THAT'S NOT IT! DON'T COME IN HERE!
KARARARA (SLIIIDE)
KYON-KUN'S HERE TOO? WHAT ARE YOU TWO DOING IN THE DARK...?
WHERE'S THE LIGHT SWITCH AGAIN?
!!
TH-THIS IS BAD!

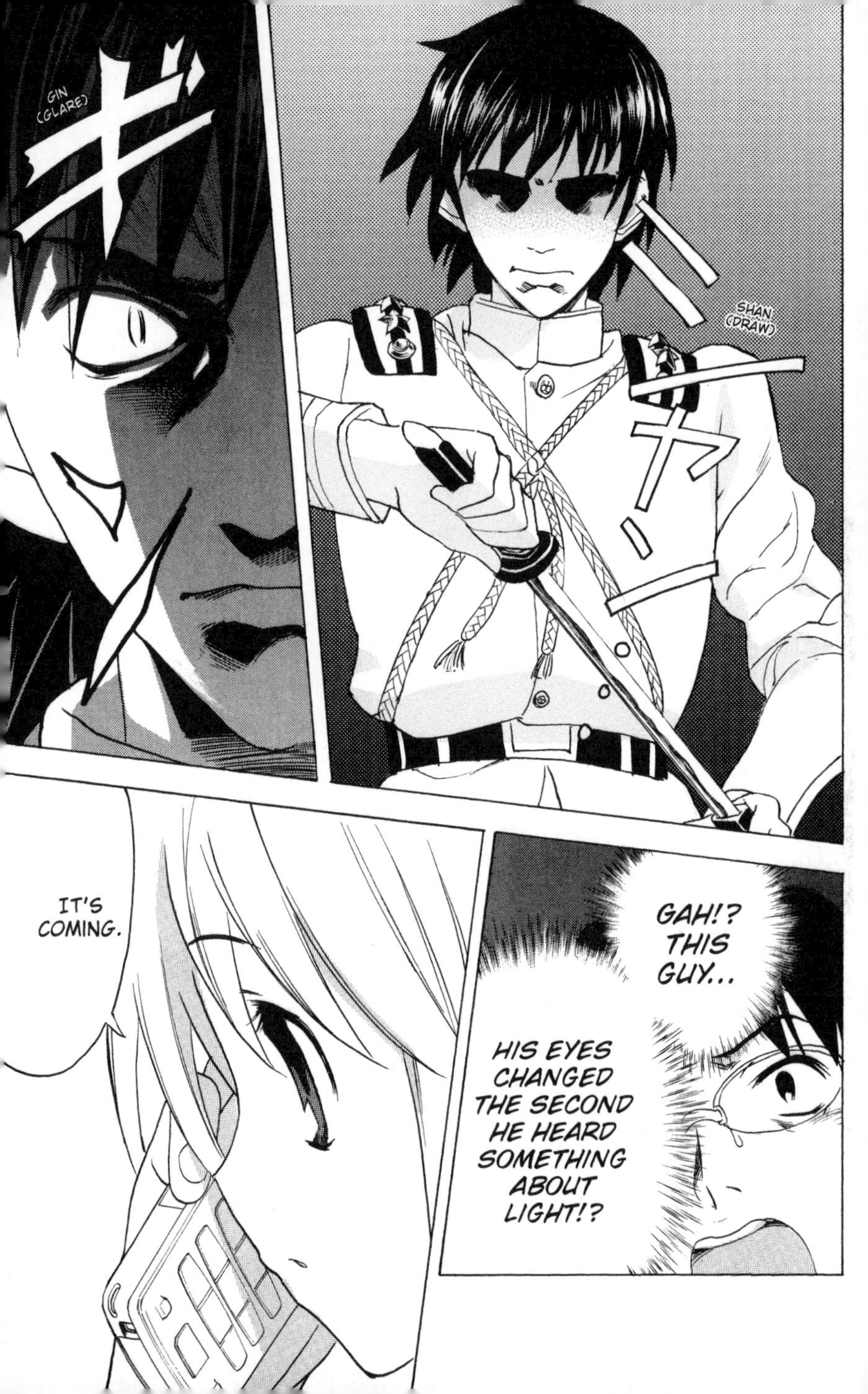
SHAN (DRAW)
GIN (GLARE)
GAH!? THIS GUY...
HIS EYES CHANGED THE SECOND HE HEARD SOMETHING ABOUT LIGHT!?
IT'S COMING.

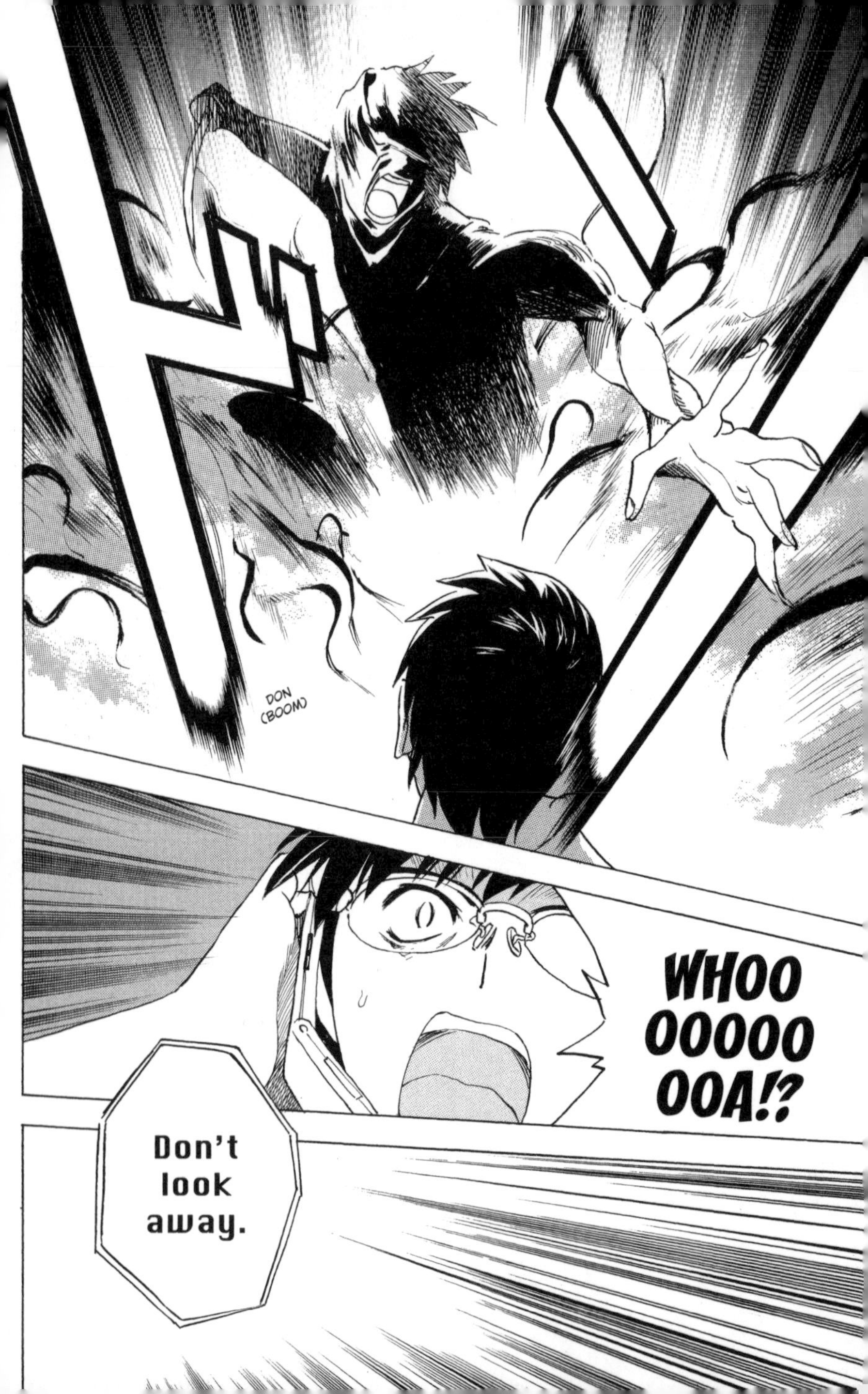
DON
(BOOM)
WHOO
OOOOO
OOA!?
Don't look away.

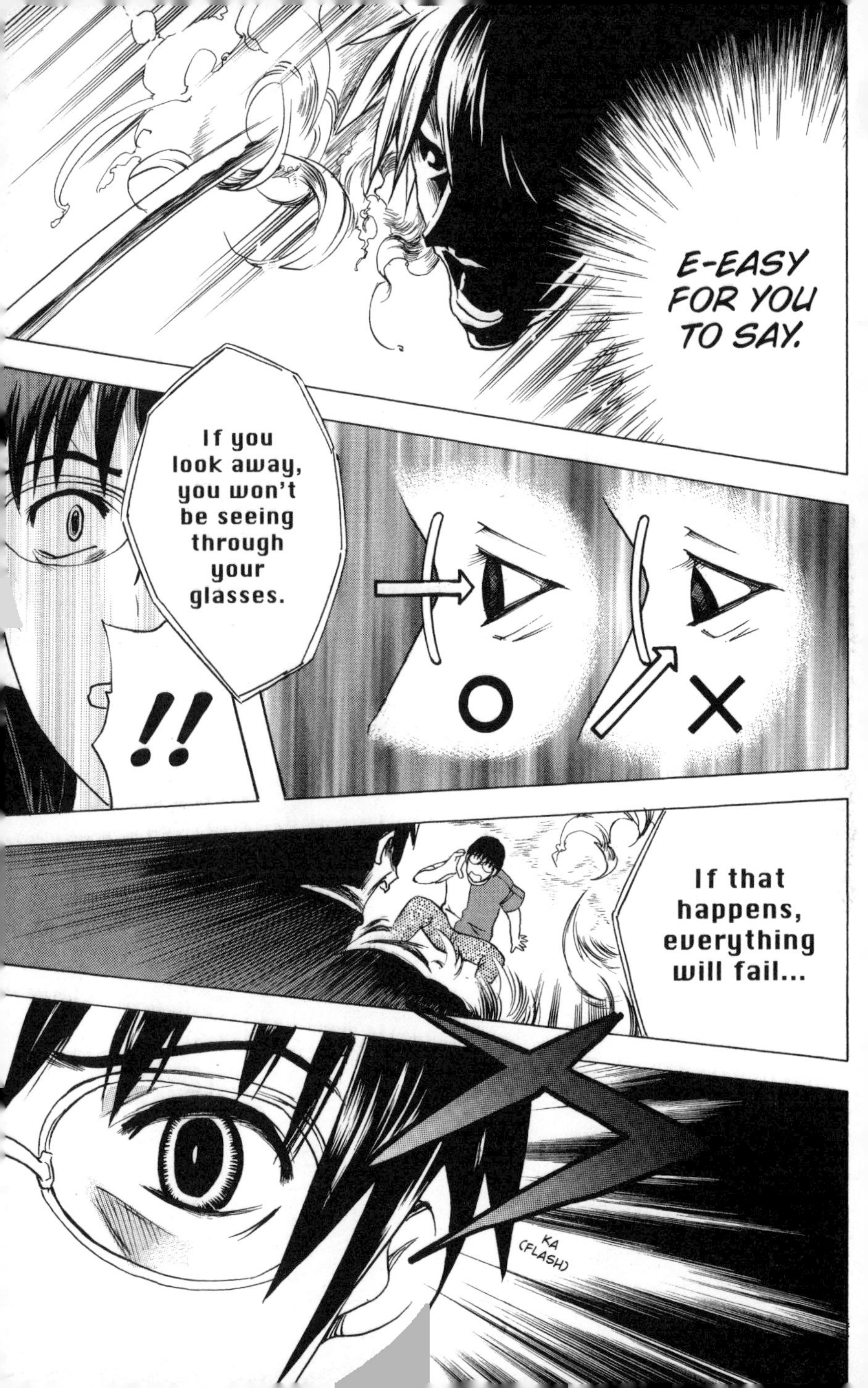
E-EASY FOR YOU TO SAY.
If you look away, you won't be seeing through your glasses.
!!
If that happens, everything will fail...
KA (FLASH)

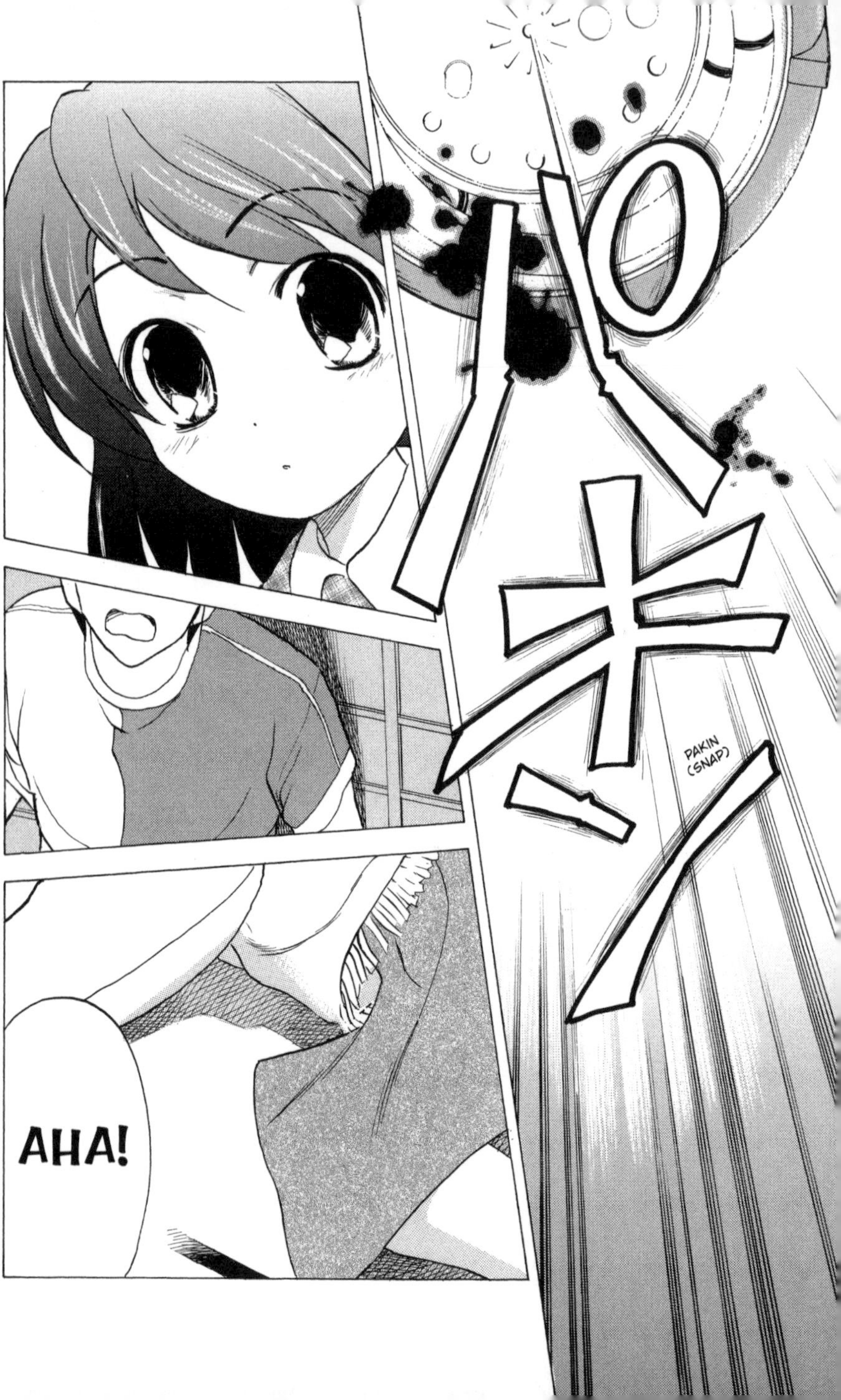
PAKIN
(SNAP)
AHA!

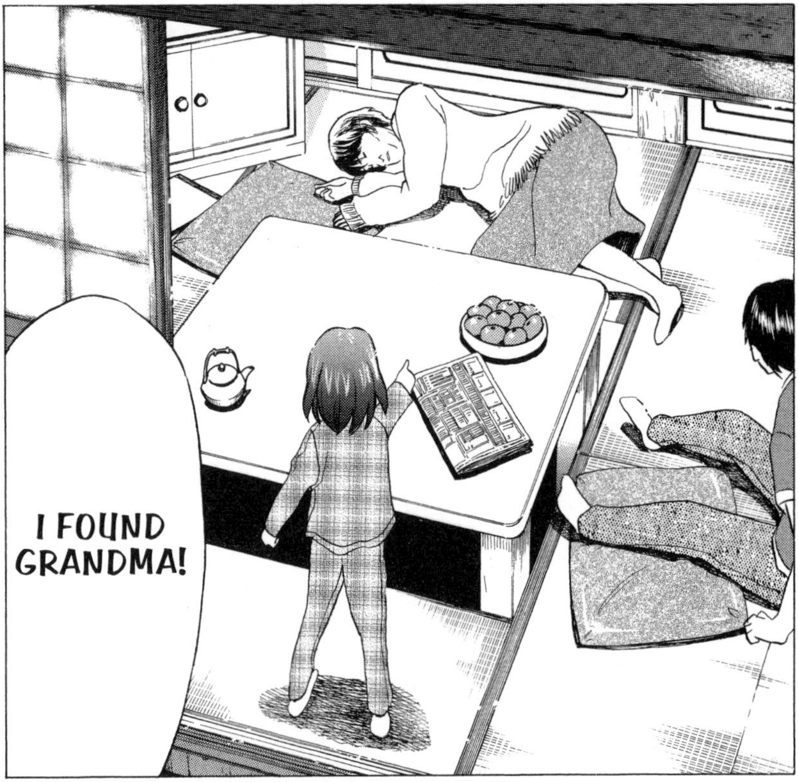
I FOUND GRANDMA!
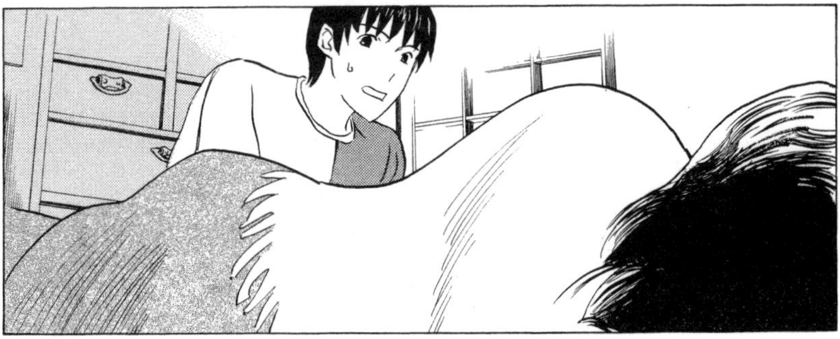

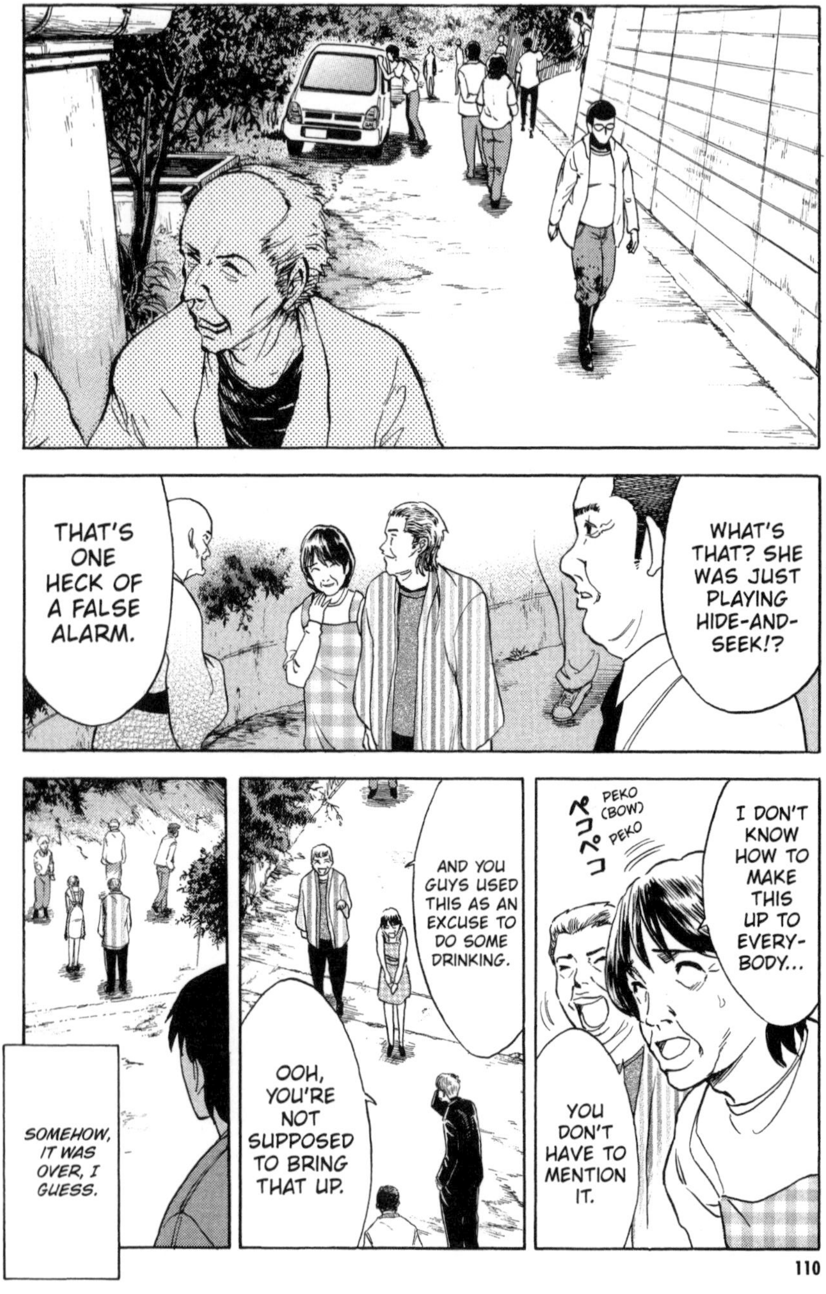
WHAT'S THAT? SHE WAS JUST PLAYING HIDE-AND-SEEK!?
THAT'S ONE HECK OF A FALSE ALARM.
ペコペコ
PEKO (BOW) PEKO
I DON'T KNOW HOW TO MAKE THIS UP TO EVERY-BODY...
YOU DON'T HAVE TO MENTION IT.
AND YOU GUYS USED THIS AS AN EXCUSE TO DO SOME DRINKING.
OOH, YOU'RE NOT SUPPOSED TO BRING THAT UP.
SOMEHOW, IT WAS OVER, I GUESS.

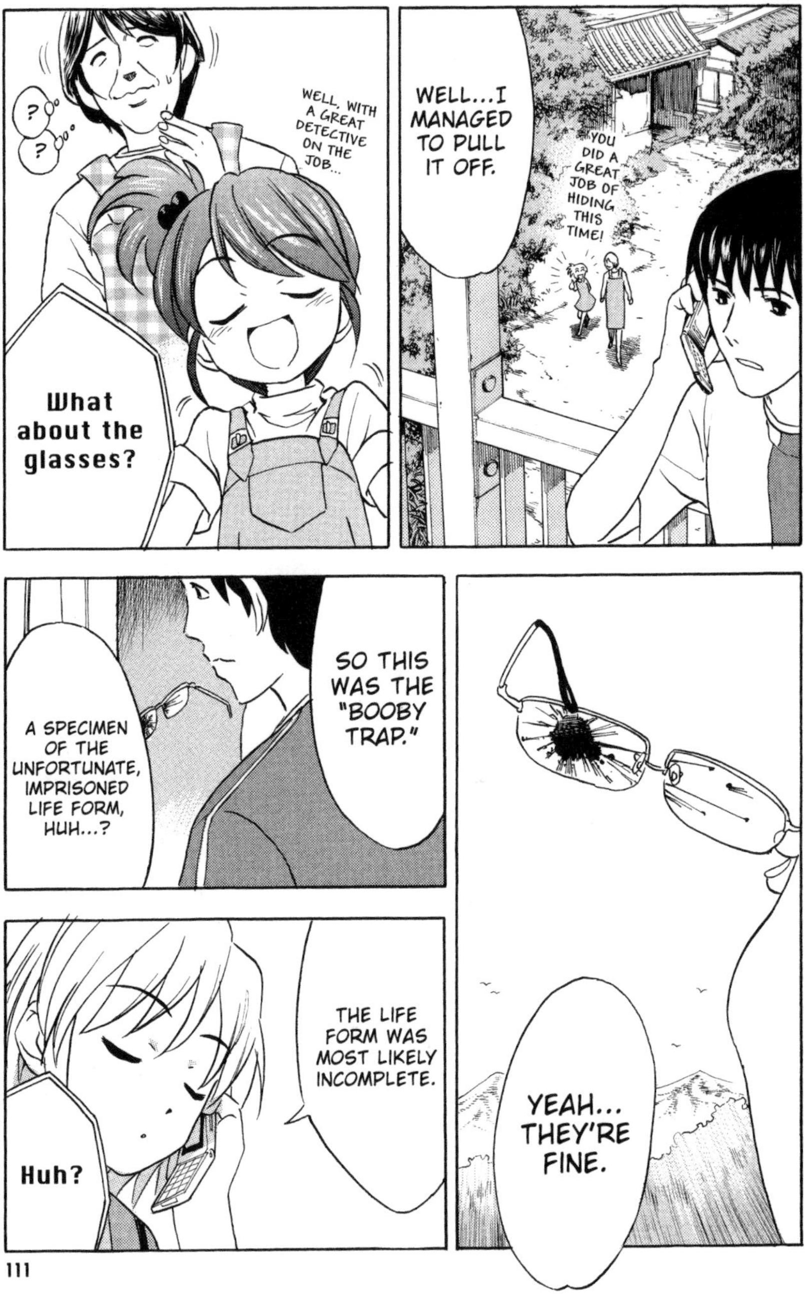
YOU DID A GREAT JOB OF HIDING THIS TIME!
WELL...I MANAGED TO PULL IT OFF.
WELL, WITH A GREAT DETECTIVE ON THE JOB...
What about the glasses?
YEAH... THEY'RE FINE.
SO THIS WAS THE "BOOBY TRAP."
A SPECIMEN OF THE UNFORTUNATE, IMPRISONED LIFE FORM, HUH...?
THE LIFE FORM WAS MOST LIKELY INCOMPLETE.
Huh?

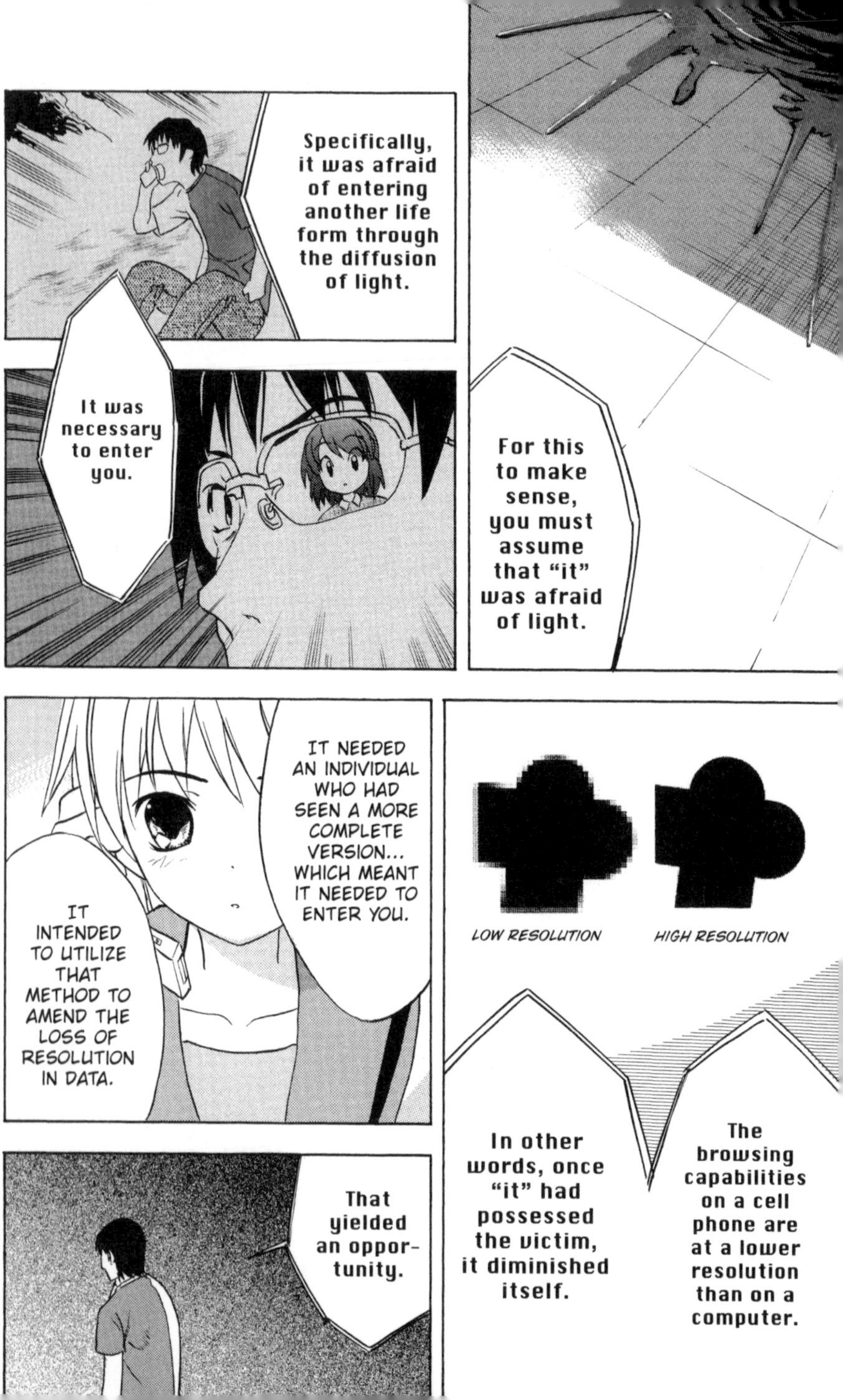
For this to make sense, you must assume that "it" was afraid of light.
Specifically, it was afraid of entering another life form through the diffusion of light.
It was necessary to enter you.
HIGH RESOLUTION
LOW RESOLUTION
The browsing capabilities on a cell phone are at a lower resolution than on a computer.
In other words, once "it" had possessed the victim, it diminished itself.
IT NEEDED AN INDIVIDUAL WHO HAD SEEN A MORE COMPLETE VERSION... WHICH MEANT IT NEEDED TO ENTER YOU.
IT INTENDED TO UTILIZE THAT METHOD TO AMEND THE LOSS OF RESOLUTION IN DATA.
That yielded an oppor-tunity.

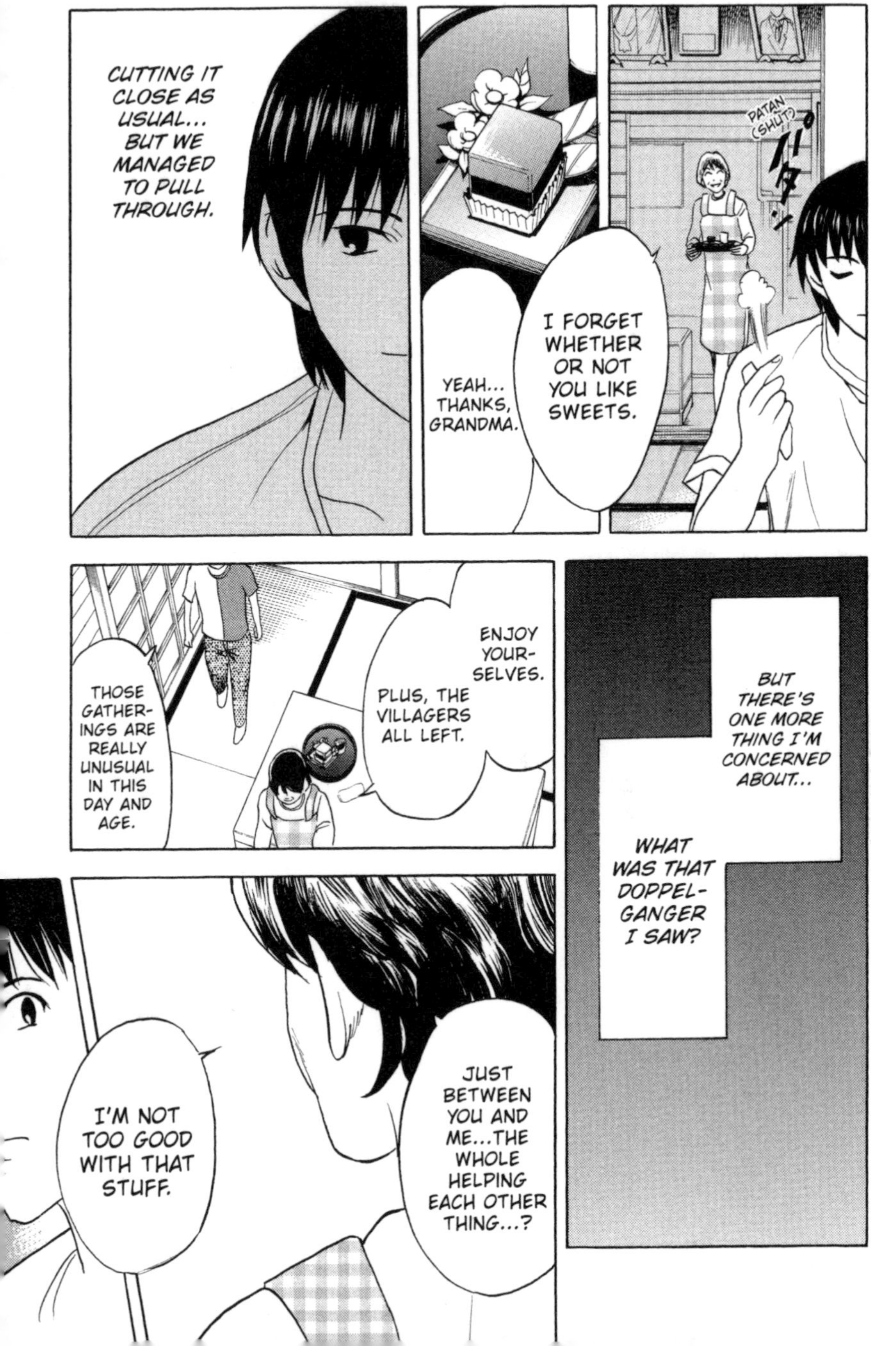
PATAN (SHUT)
I FORGET WHETHER OR NOT YOU LIKE SWEETS.
YEAH... THANKS, GRANDMA.
CUTTING IT CLOSE AS USUAL... BUT WE MANAGED TO PULL THROUGH.
BUT THERE'S ONE MORE THING I'M CONCERNED ABOUT...
WHAT WAS THAT DOPPEL-GANGER I SAW?
ENJOY YOUR-SELVES.
PLUS, THE VILLAGERS ALL LEFT.
THOSE GATHER-INGS ARE REALLY UNUSUAL IN THIS DAY AND AGE.
JUST BETWEEN YOU AND ME...THE WHOLE HELPING EACH OTHER THING...?
I'M NOT TOO GOOD WITH THAT STUFF.

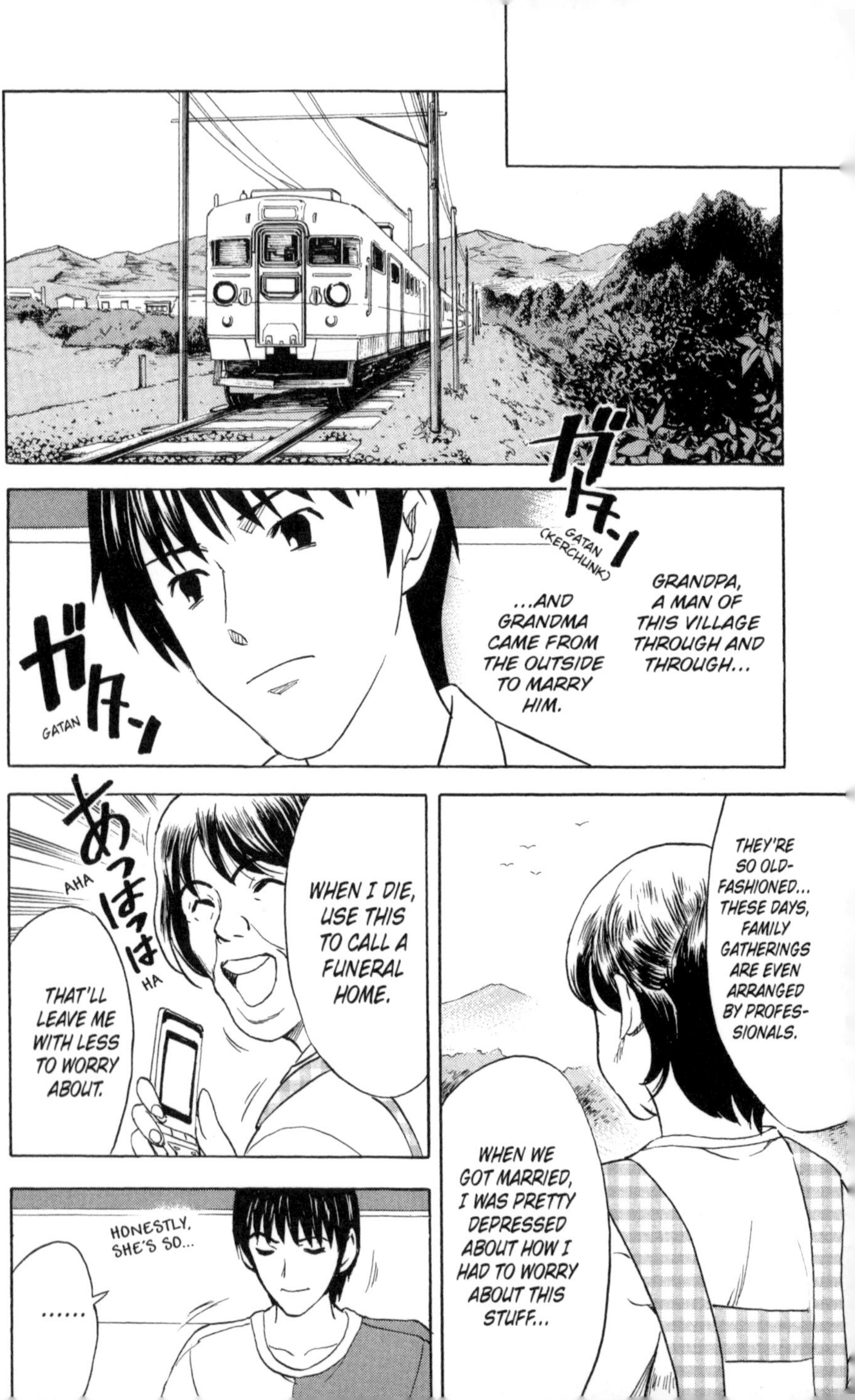
ガタン
GATAN (KERCHUNK)
GRANDPA, A MAN OF THIS VILLAGE THROUGH AND THROUGH...
...AND GRANDMA CAME FROM THE OUTSIDE TO MARRY HIM.
ガタン
GATAN
THEY'RE SO OLD-FASHIONED... THESE DAYS, FAMILY GATHERINGS ARE EVEN ARRANGED BY PROFES-SIONALS.
WHEN WE GOT MARRIED, I WAS PRETTY DEPRESSED ABOUT HOW I HAD TO WORRY ABOUT THIS STUFF...
WHEN I DIE, USE THIS TO CALL A FUNERAL HOME.
あっはっは
AHA HA
THAT'LL LEAVE ME WITH LESS TO WORRY ABOUT.
HONESTLY, SHE'S SO...
......

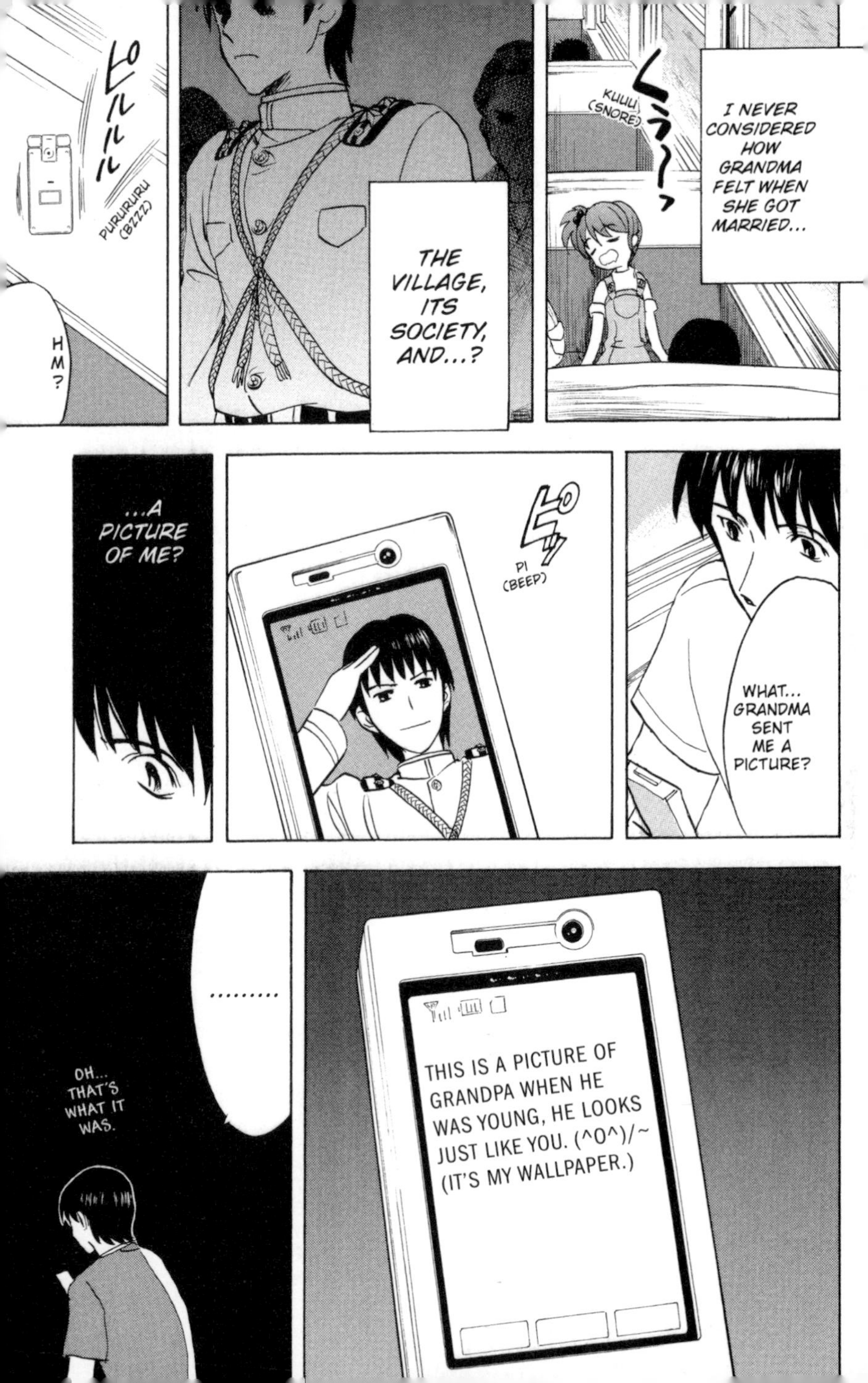
I NEVER CONSIDERED HOW GRANDMA FELT WHEN SHE GOT MARRIED...
KUUU (SNORE)
THE VILLAGE, ITS SOCIETY, AND...?
PURURURU (BZZZ)
HM?
WHAT... GRANDMA SENT ME A PICTURE?
PI (BEEP)
...A PICTURE OF ME?
THIS IS A PICTURE OF GRANDPA WHEN HE WAS YOUNG, HE LOOKS JUST LIKE YOU. (^O^)/~ (IT'S MY WALLPAPER.)
....
OH... THAT'S WHAT IT WAS.

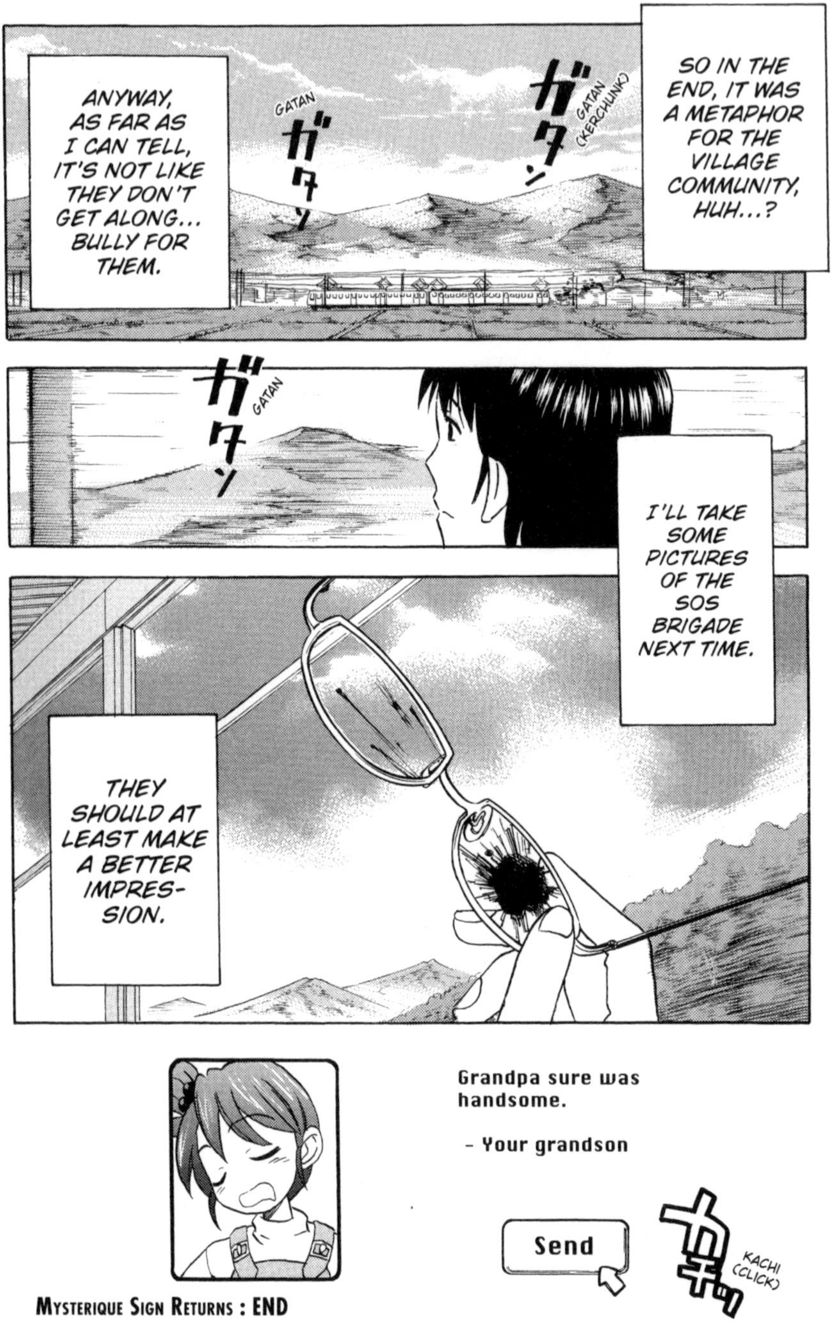
SO IN THE END, IT WAS A METAPHOR FOR THE VILLAGE COMMUNITY, HUH...?
GATAN (KERCHUNK)
GATAN
ANYWAY, AS FAR AS I CAN TELL, IT'S NOT LIKE THEY DON'T GET ALONG... BULLY FOR THEM.
GATAN
I'LL TAKE SOME PICTURES OF THE SOS BRIGADE NEXT TIME.
THEY SHOULD AT LEAST MAKE A BETTER IMPRES-SION.
Grandpa sure was handsome.
- Your grandson
Send
KACHI (CLICK)

MYSTERIQUE SIGN RETURNS : END

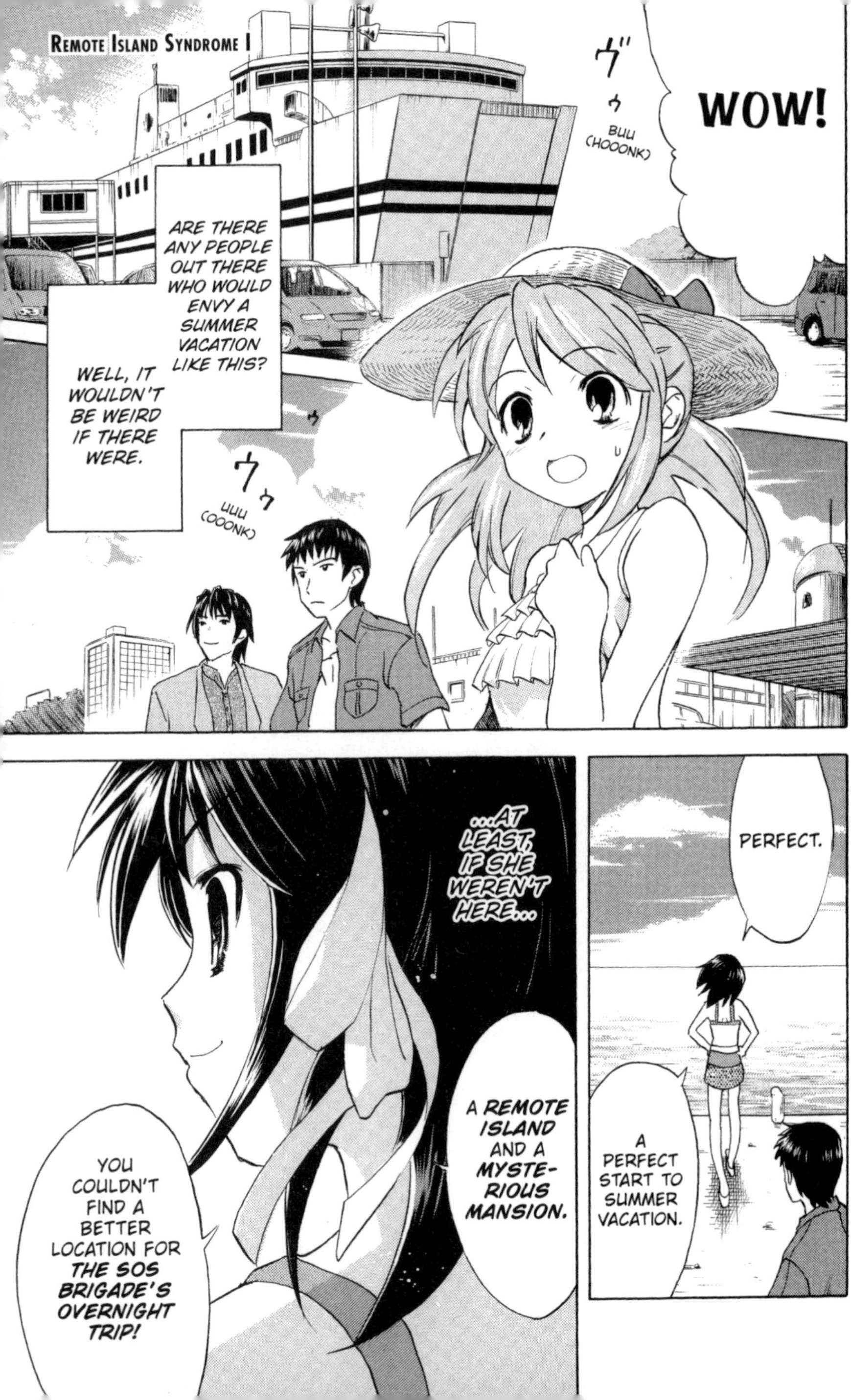
WOW!
ヴゥ
BUU (HOOONK)
ARE THERE ANY PEOPLE OUT THERE WHO WOULD ENVY A SUMMER VACATION LIKE THIS?
WELL, IT WOULDN'T BE WEIRD IF THERE WERE.
ウゥ
UUU (OOONK)
PERFECT.
A PERFECT START TO SUMMER VACATION.
...AT LEAST, IF SHE WEREN'T HERE...
A REMOTE ISLAND AND A MYSTE-RIOUS MANSION.
YOU COULDN'T FIND A BETTER LOCATION FOR THE SOS BRIGADE'S OVERNIGHT TRIP!

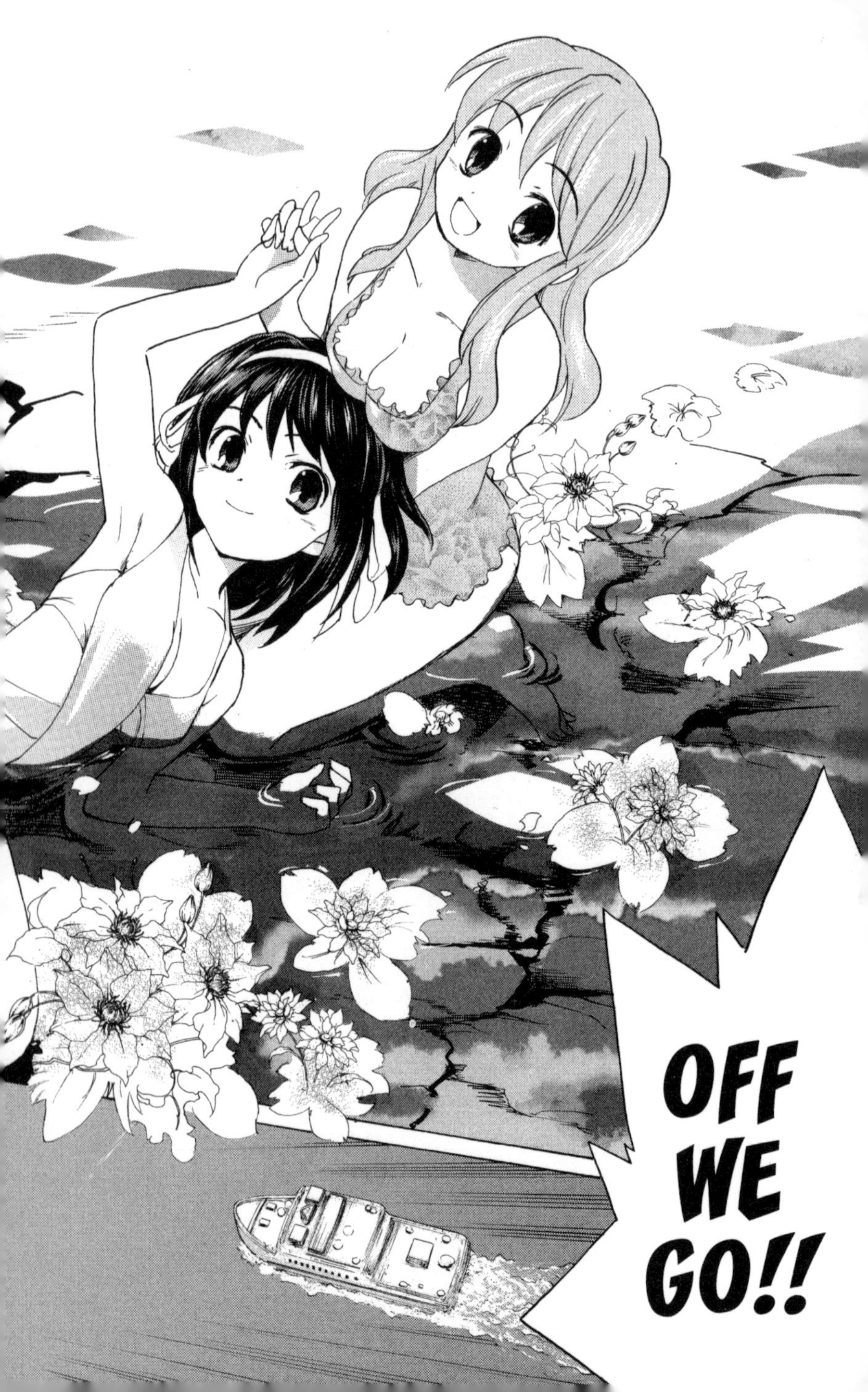
OFF WE GO!!

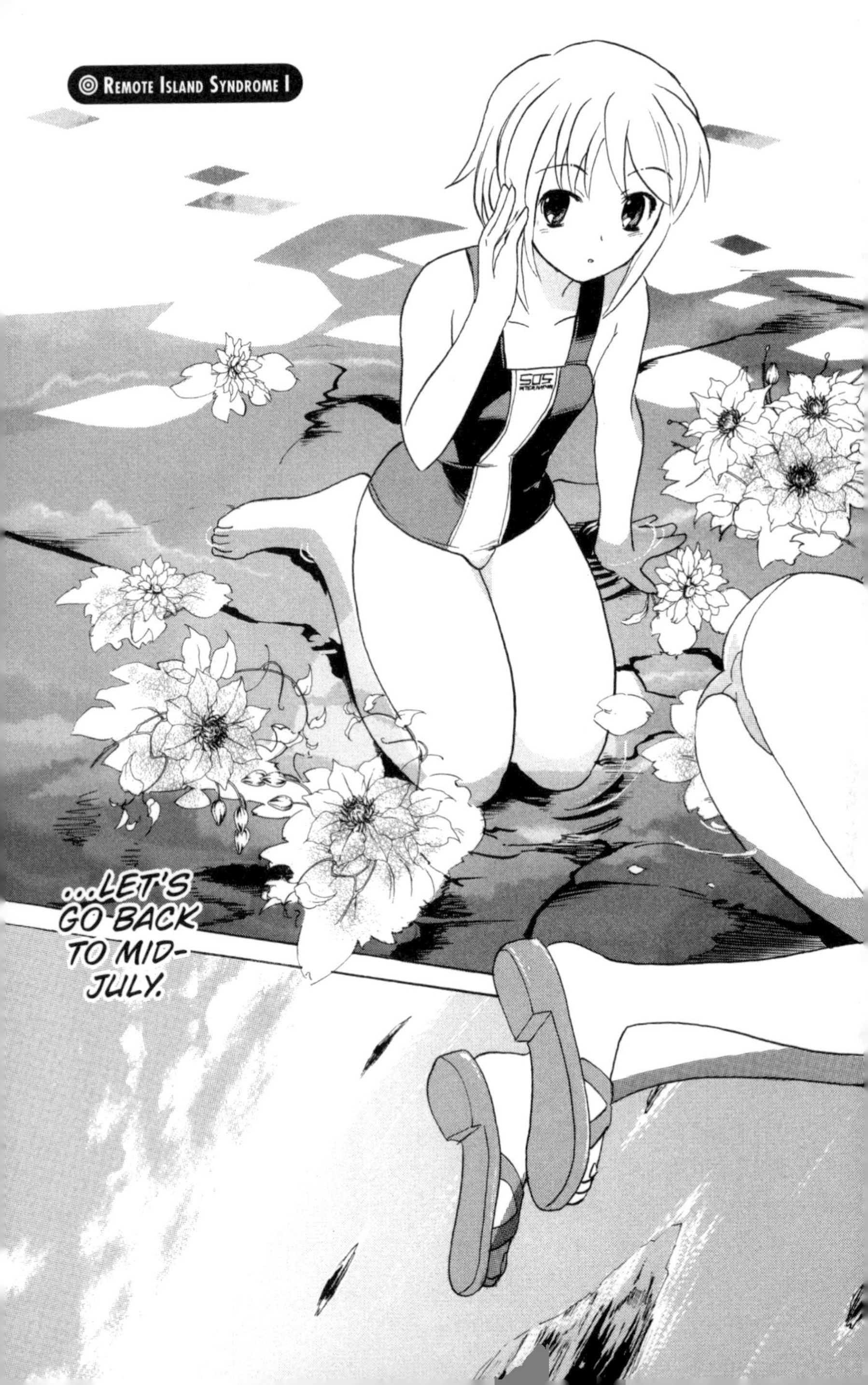
REMOTE ISLAND SYNDROME I
SOS
...LET'S GO BACK TO MID-JULY.

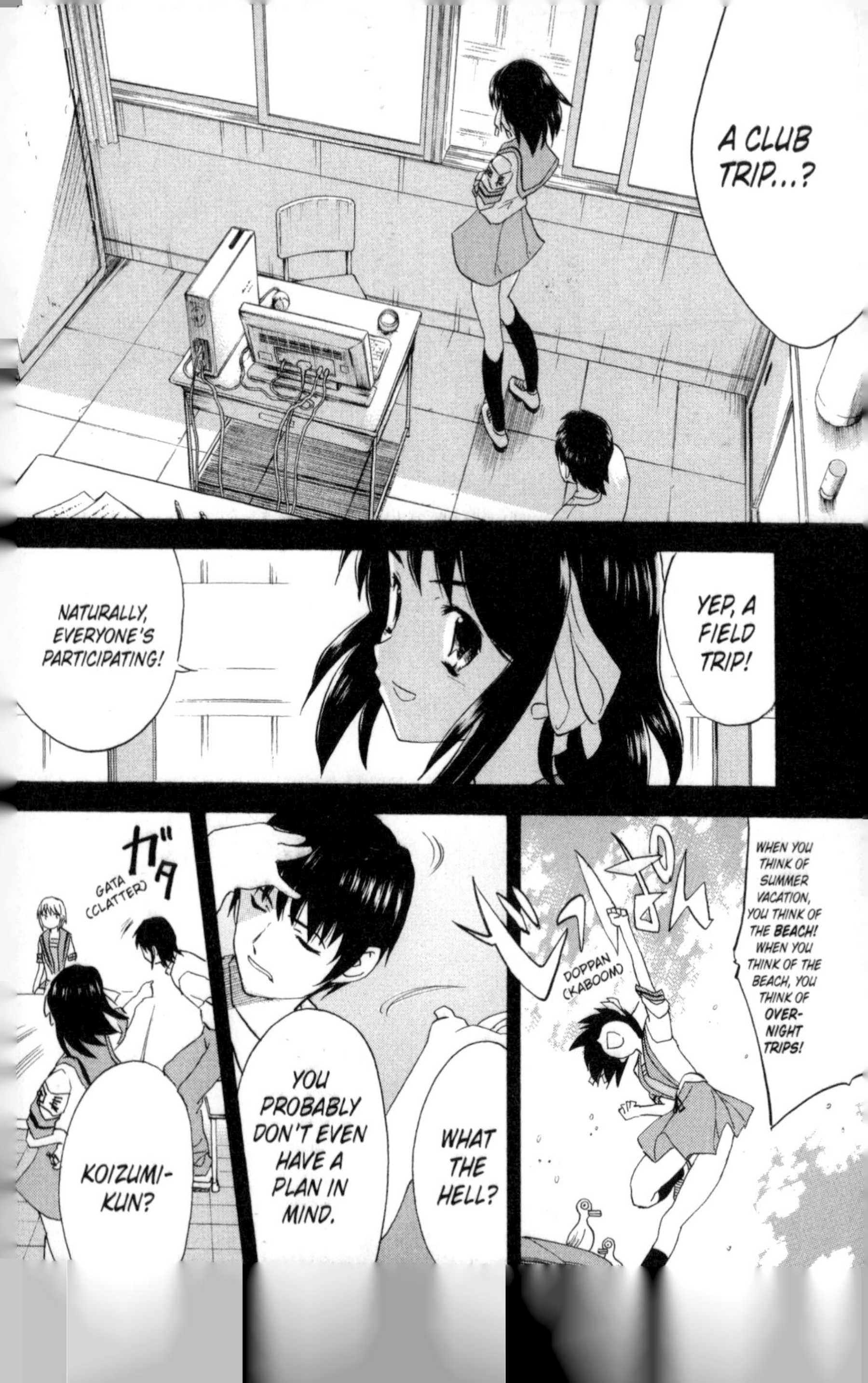
A CLUB TRIP...?
YEP, A FIELD TRIP!
NATURALLY, EVERYONE'S PARTICIPATING!
WHEN YOU THINK OF SUMMER VACATION, YOU THINK OF THE BEACH! WHEN YOU THINK OF THE BEACH, YOU THINK OF OVER-NIGHT TRIPS!
DOPPAN (KABOOM)
WHAT THE HELL?
YOU PROBABLY DON'T EVEN HAVE A PLAN IN MIND.
ガタ
GATA (CLATTER)
KOIZUMI-KUN?

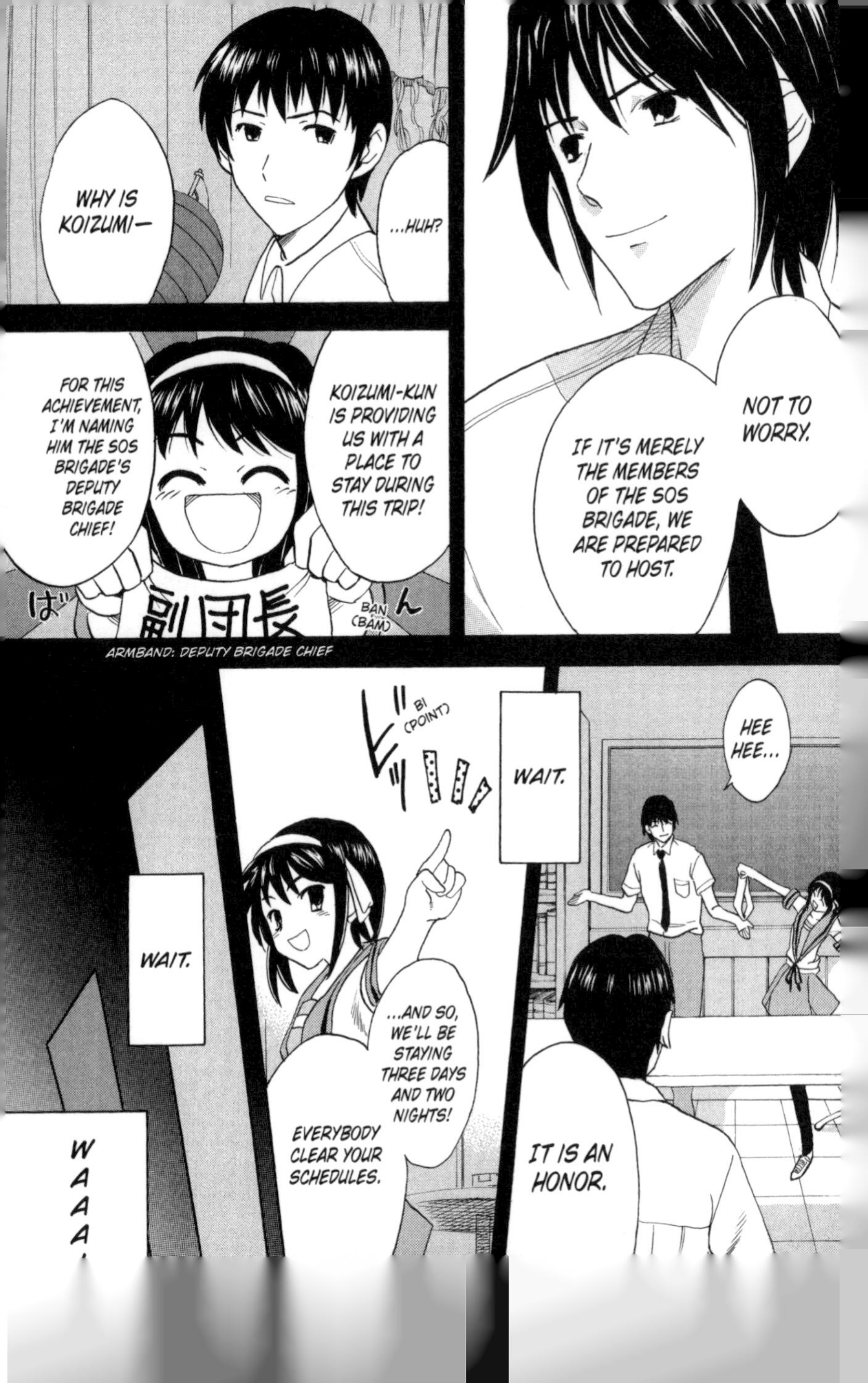
NOT TO WORRY.
IF IT'S MERELY THE MEMBERS OF THE SOS BRIGADE, WE ARE PREPARED TO HOST.
...HUH?
WHY IS KOIZUMI—
KOIZUMI-KUN IS PROVIDING US WITH A PLACE TO STAY DURING THIS TRIP!
FOR THIS ACHIEVEMENT, I'M NAMING HIM THE SOS BRIGADE'S DEPUTY BRIGADE CHIEF!
副団長
ばん
BAN (BAM)
ARMBAND: DEPUTY BRIGADE CHIEF
HEE HEE...
IT IS AN HONOR.
WAIT.
ビッ
BI (POINT)
...AND SO, WE'LL BE STAYING THREE DAYS AND TWO NIGHTS!
EVERYBODY CLEAR YOUR SCHEDULES.
WAIT.
WAAAA

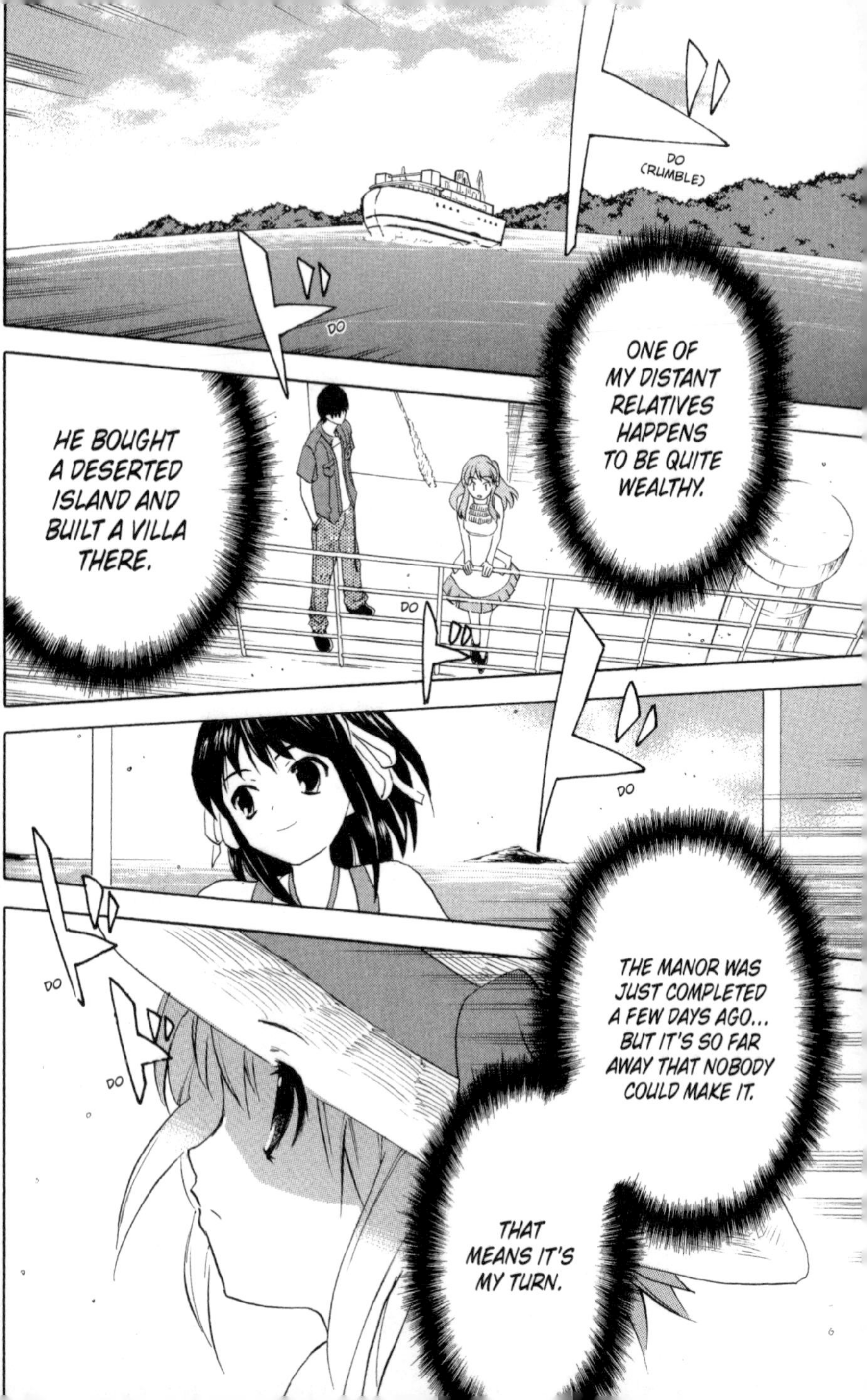
DO (RUMBLE)
DO
ONE OF MY DISTANT RELATIVES HAPPENS TO BE QUITE WEALTHY.
HE BOUGHT A DESERTED ISLAND AND BUILT A VILLA THERE.
DO
DO
THE MANOR WAS JUST COMPLETED A FEW DAYS AGO... BUT IT'S SO FAR AWAY THAT NOBODY COULD MAKE IT.
DO
DO
THAT MEANS IT'S MY TURN.

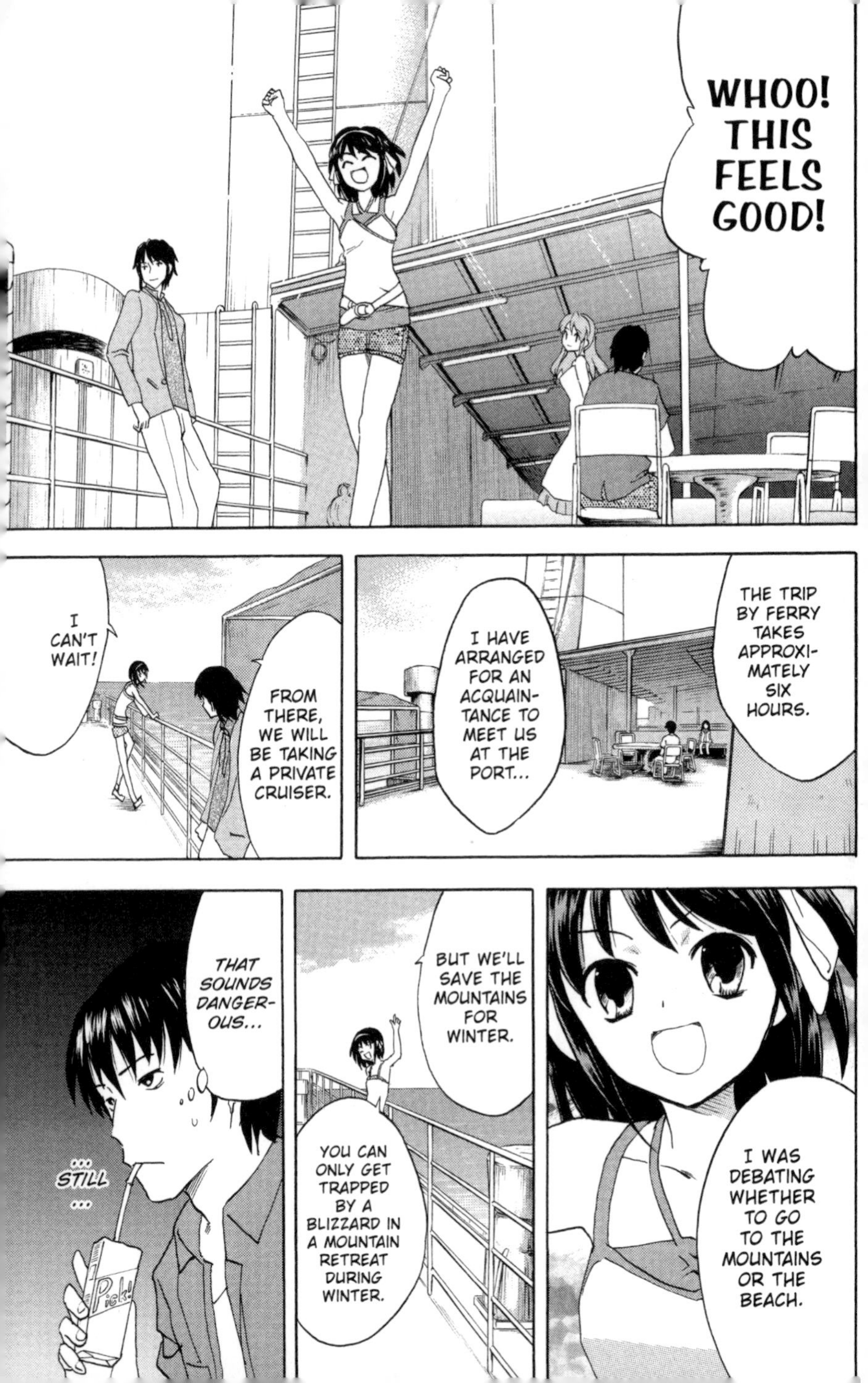
WHOO! THIS FEELS GOOD!
THE TRIP BY FERRY TAKES APPROXI-MATELY SIX HOURS.
I HAVE ARRANGED FOR AN ACQUAIN-TANCE TO MEET US AT THE PORT...
FROM THERE, WE WILL BE TAKING A PRIVATE CRUISER.
I CAN'T WAIT!
I WAS DEBATING WHETHER TO GO TO THE MOUNTAINS OR THE BEACH.
BUT WE'LL SAVE THE MOUNTAINS FOR WINTER.
YOU CAN ONLY GET TRAPPED BY A BLIZZARD IN A MOUNTAIN RETREAT DURING WINTER.
THAT SOUNDS DANGER-OUS...
...STILL...
Pick!

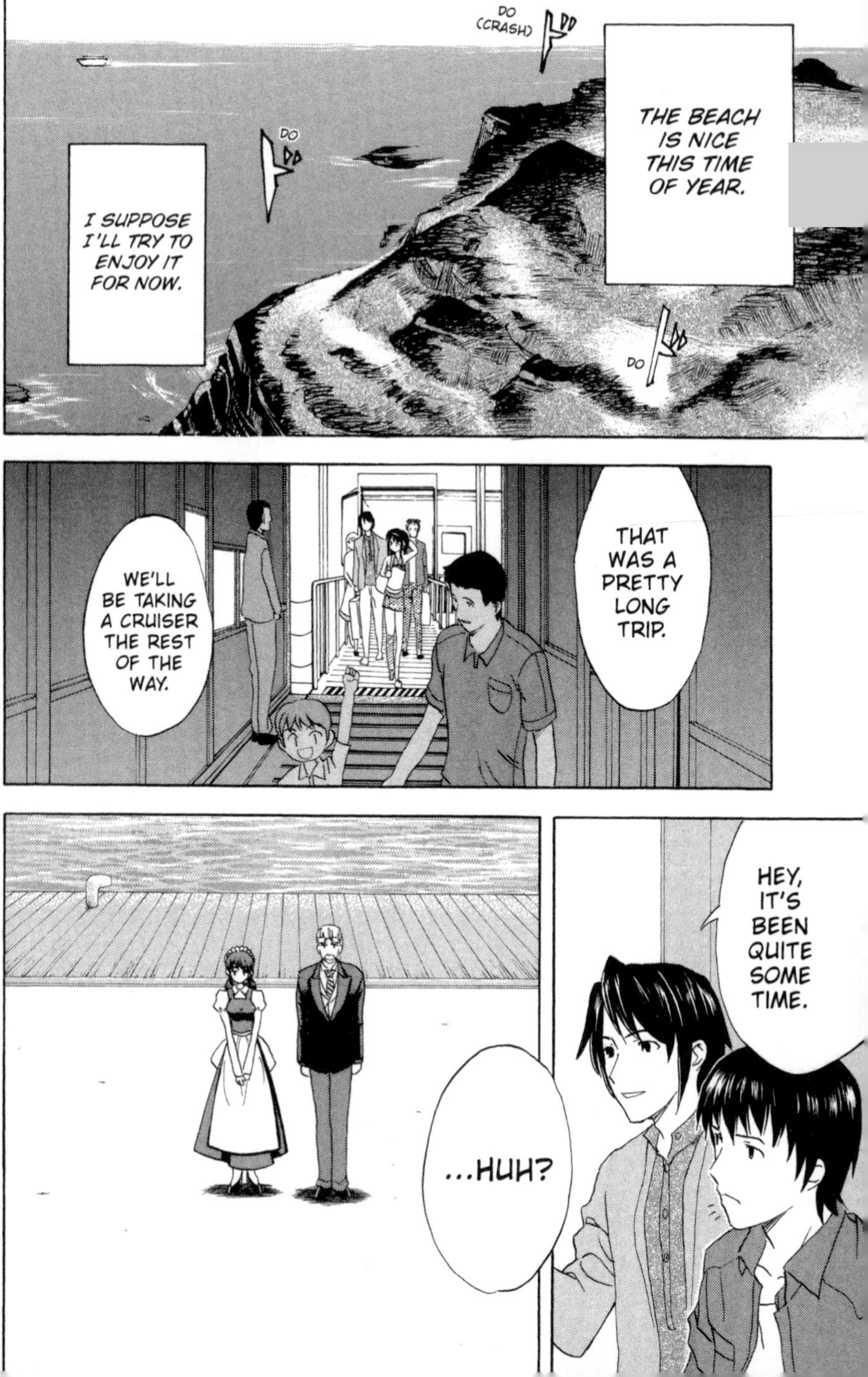
THE BEACH IS NICE THIS TIME OF YEAR.
DO (CRASH)
DO
DO
I SUPPOSE I'LL TRY TO ENJOY IT FOR NOW.
THAT WAS A PRETTY LONG TRIP.
WE'LL BE TAKING A CRUISER THE REST OF THE WAY.
HEY, IT'S BEEN QUITE SOME TIME.
...HUH?

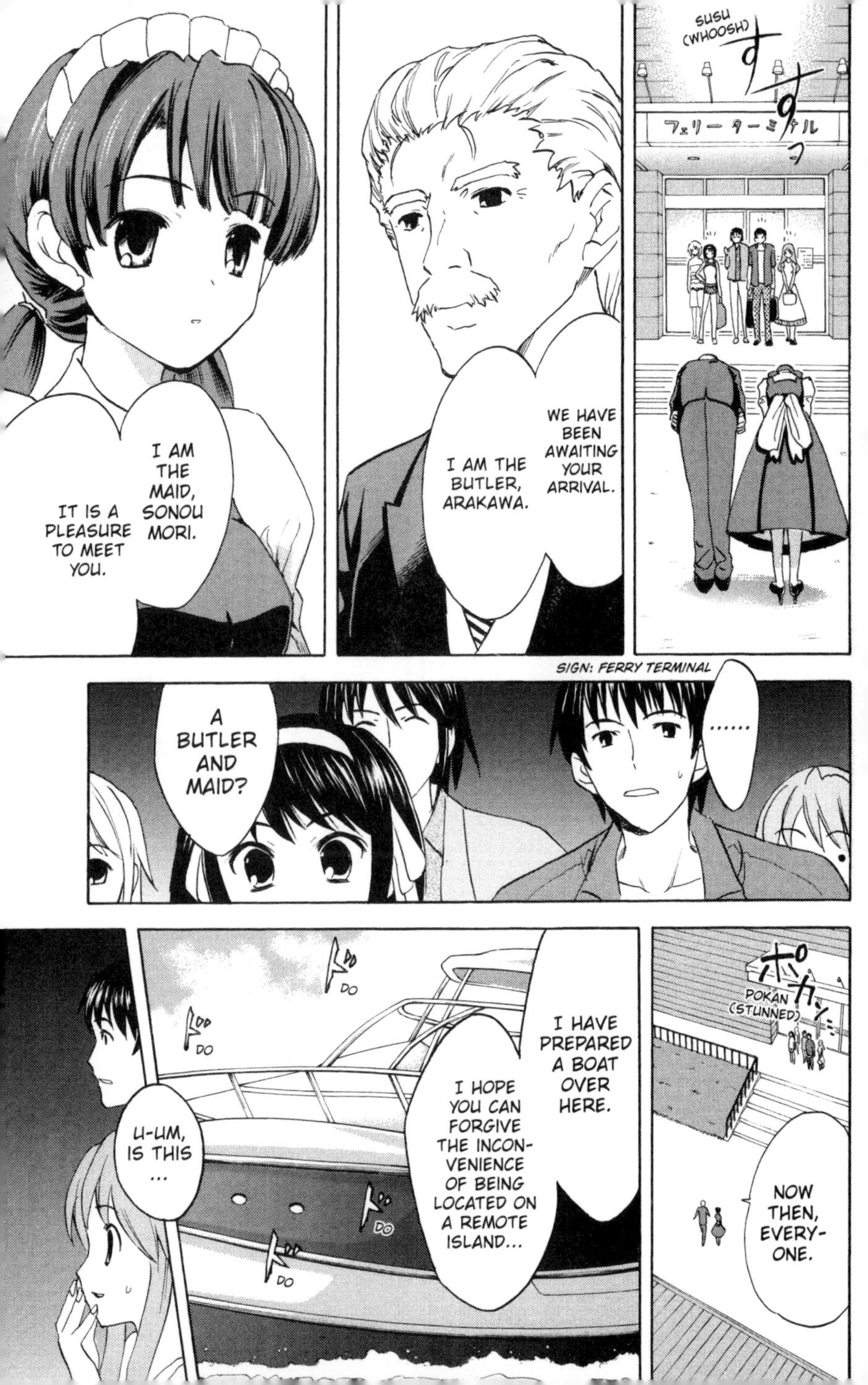

SUSU (WHOOSH)
フェリーターミナル
WE HAVE BEEN AWAITING YOUR ARRIVAL.
I AM THE BUTLER, ARAKAWA.
I AM THE MAID, SONOU MORI.
IT IS A PLEASURE TO MEET YOU.
SIGN: FERRY TERMINAL
......
A BUTLER AND MAID?
POKAN (STUNNED)
NOW THEN, EVERY-ONE.
I HAVE PREPARED A BOAT OVER HERE.
I HOPE YOU CAN FORGIVE THE INCON-VENIENCE OF BEING LOCATED ON A REMOTE ISLAND...
DO DO
DO DO
DO
DO
U-UM, IS THIS ...

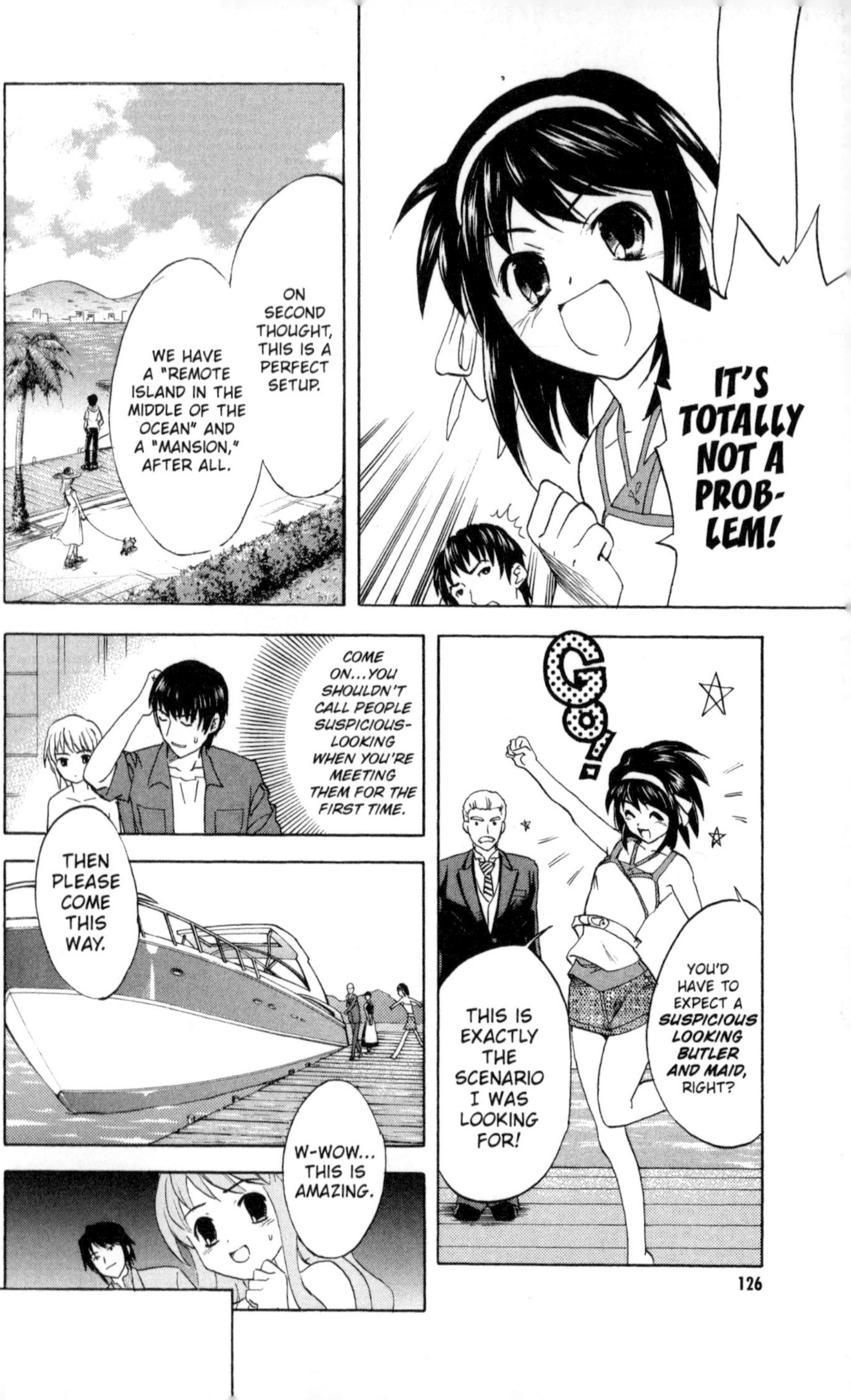
IT'S TOTALLY NOT A PROB-LEM!
ON SECOND THOUGHT, THIS IS A PERFECT SETUP.
WE HAVE A "REMOTE ISLAND IN THE MIDDLE OF THE OCEAN" AND A "MANSION," AFTER ALL.
GO!
YOU'D HAVE TO EXPECT A SUSPICIOUS LOOKING BUTLER AND MAID, RIGHT?
THIS IS EXACTLY THE SCENARIO I WAS LOOKING FOR!
COME ON...YOU SHOULDN'T CALL PEOPLE SUSPICIOUS-LOOKING WHEN YOU'RE MEETING THEM FOR THE FIRST TIME.
THEN PLEASE COME THIS WAY.
W-WOW... THIS IS AMAZING.

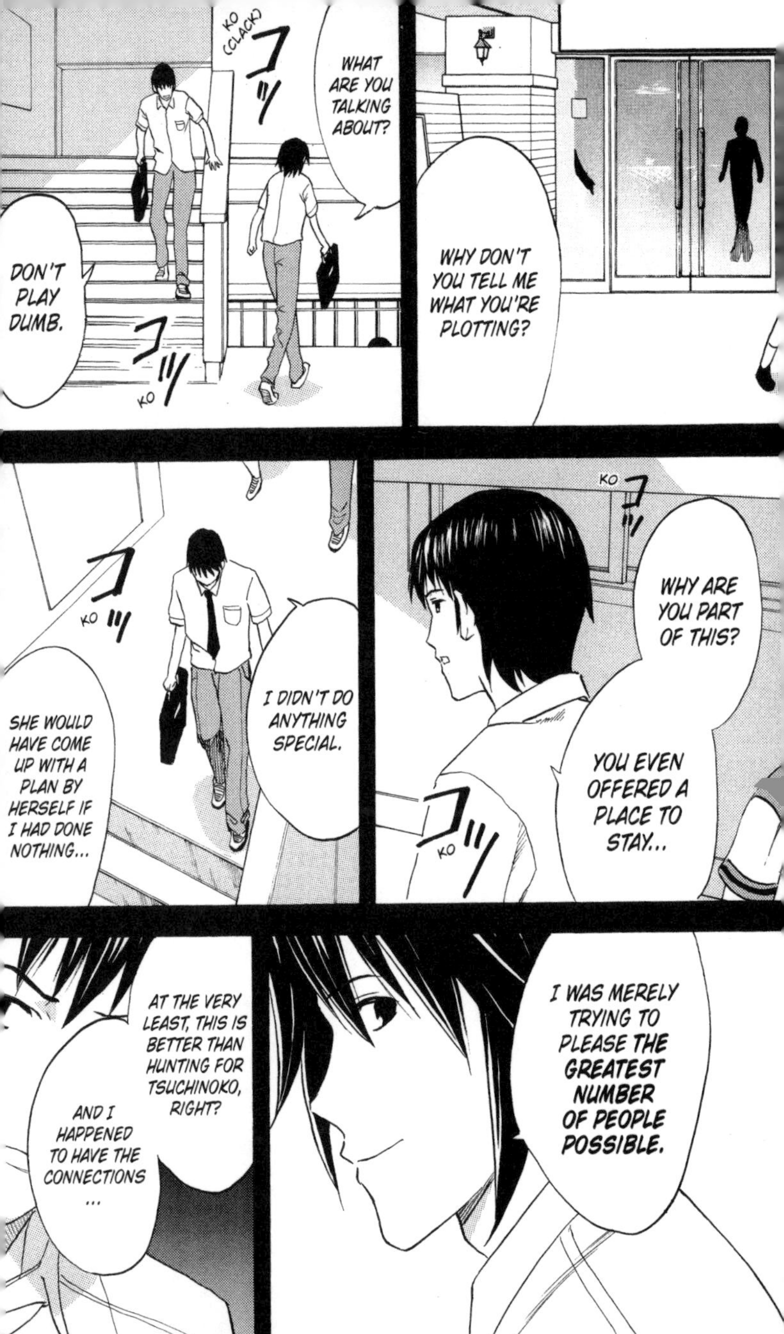
WHY DON'T YOU TELL ME WHAT YOU'RE PLOTTING?
KO (CLACK)
WHAT ARE YOU TALKING ABOUT?
DON'T PLAY DUMB.
KO
KO
WHY ARE YOU PART OF THIS?
YOU EVEN OFFERED A PLACE TO STAY...
KO
I DIDN'T DO ANYTHING SPECIAL.
KO
SHE WOULD HAVE COME UP WITH A PLAN BY HERSELF IF I HAD DONE NOTHING...
I WAS MERELY TRYING TO PLEASE THE GREATEST NUMBER OF PEOPLE POSSIBLE.
AT THE VERY LEAST, THIS IS BETTER THAN HUNTING FOR TSUCHINOKO, RIGHT?
AND I HAPPENED TO HAVE THE CONNECTIONS ...

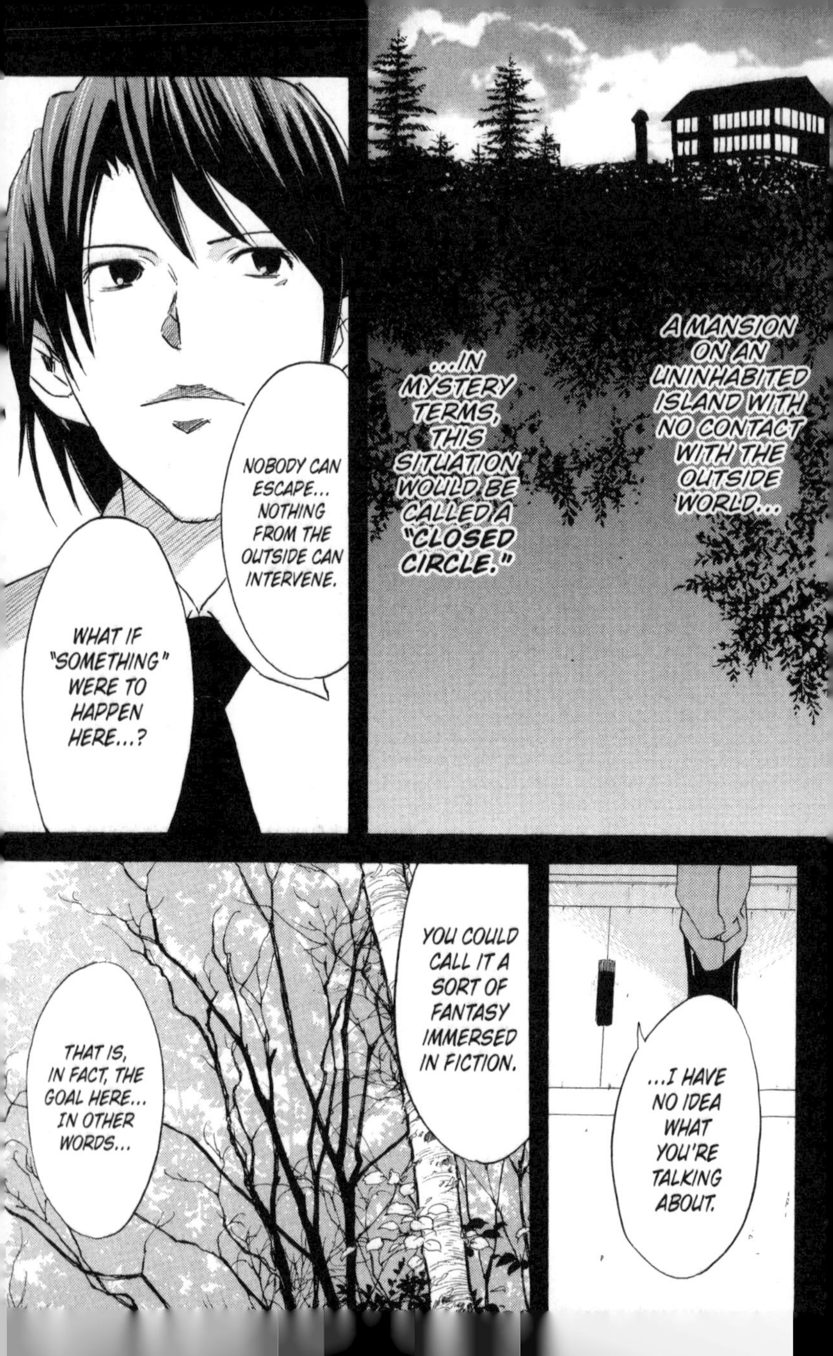
A MANSION ON AN UNINHABITED ISLAND WITH NO CONTACT WITH THE OUTSIDE WORLD...
...IN MYSTERY TERMS, THIS SITUATION WOULD BE CALLED A "CLOSED CIRCLE."
NOBODY CAN ESCAPE... NOTHING FROM THE OUTSIDE CAN INTERVENE.
WHAT IF "SOMETHING" WERE TO HAPPEN HERE...?
...I HAVE NO IDEA WHAT YOU'RE TALKING ABOUT.
YOU COULD CALL IT A SORT OF FANTASY IMMERSED IN FICTION.
THAT IS, IN FACT, THE GOAL HERE... IN OTHER WORDS...

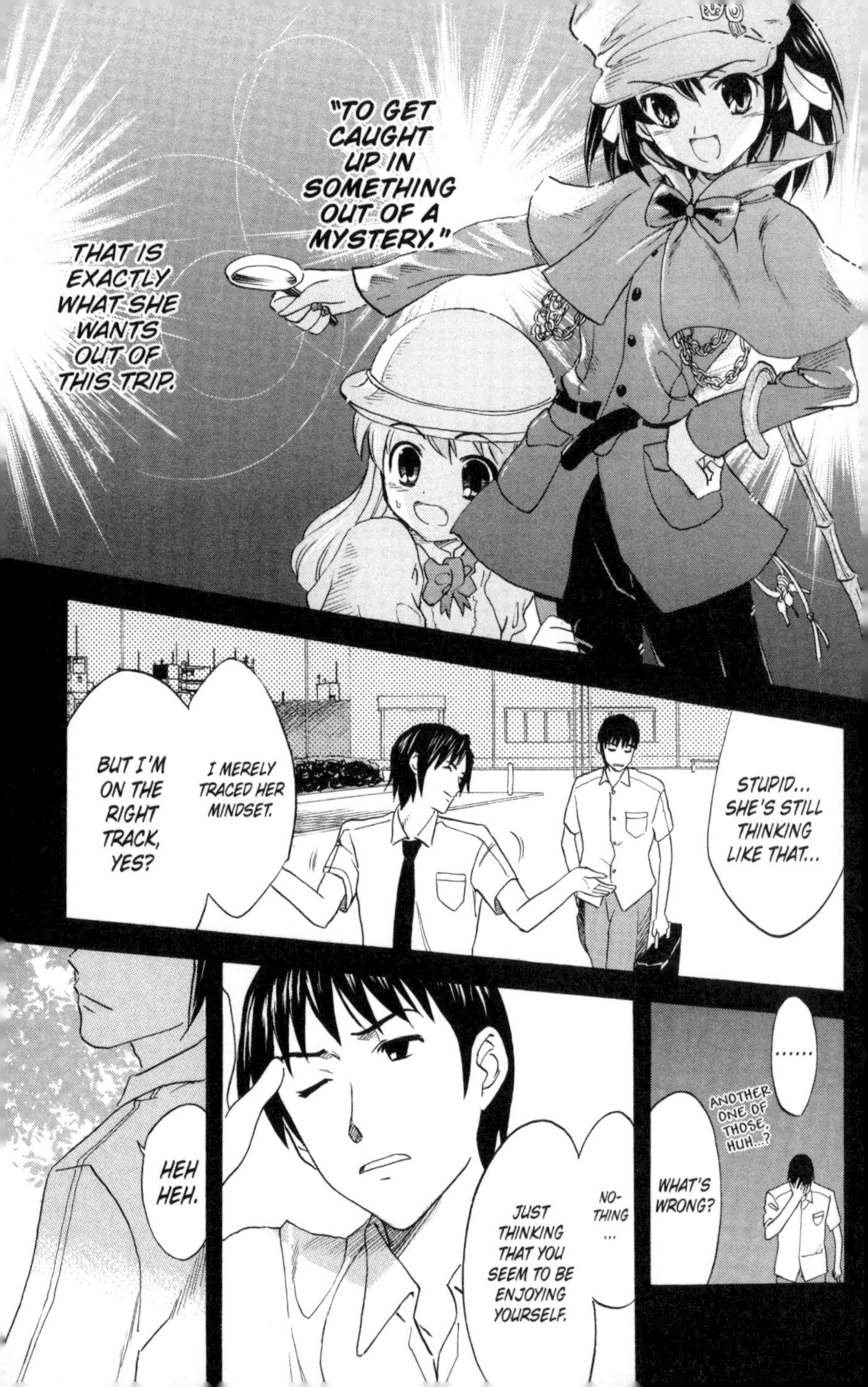
"TO GET CAUGHT UP IN SOMETHING OUT OF A MYSTERY."
THAT IS EXACTLY WHAT SHE WANTS OUT OF THIS TRIP.
STUPID... SHE'S STILL THINKING LIKE THAT...
I MERELY TRACED HER MINDSET.
BUT I'M ON THE RIGHT TRACK, YES?
......
ANOTHER ONE OF THOSE, HUH...?
WHAT'S WRONG?
NO-THING...
JUST THINKING THAT YOU SEEM TO BE ENJOYING YOURSELF.
HEH HEH.

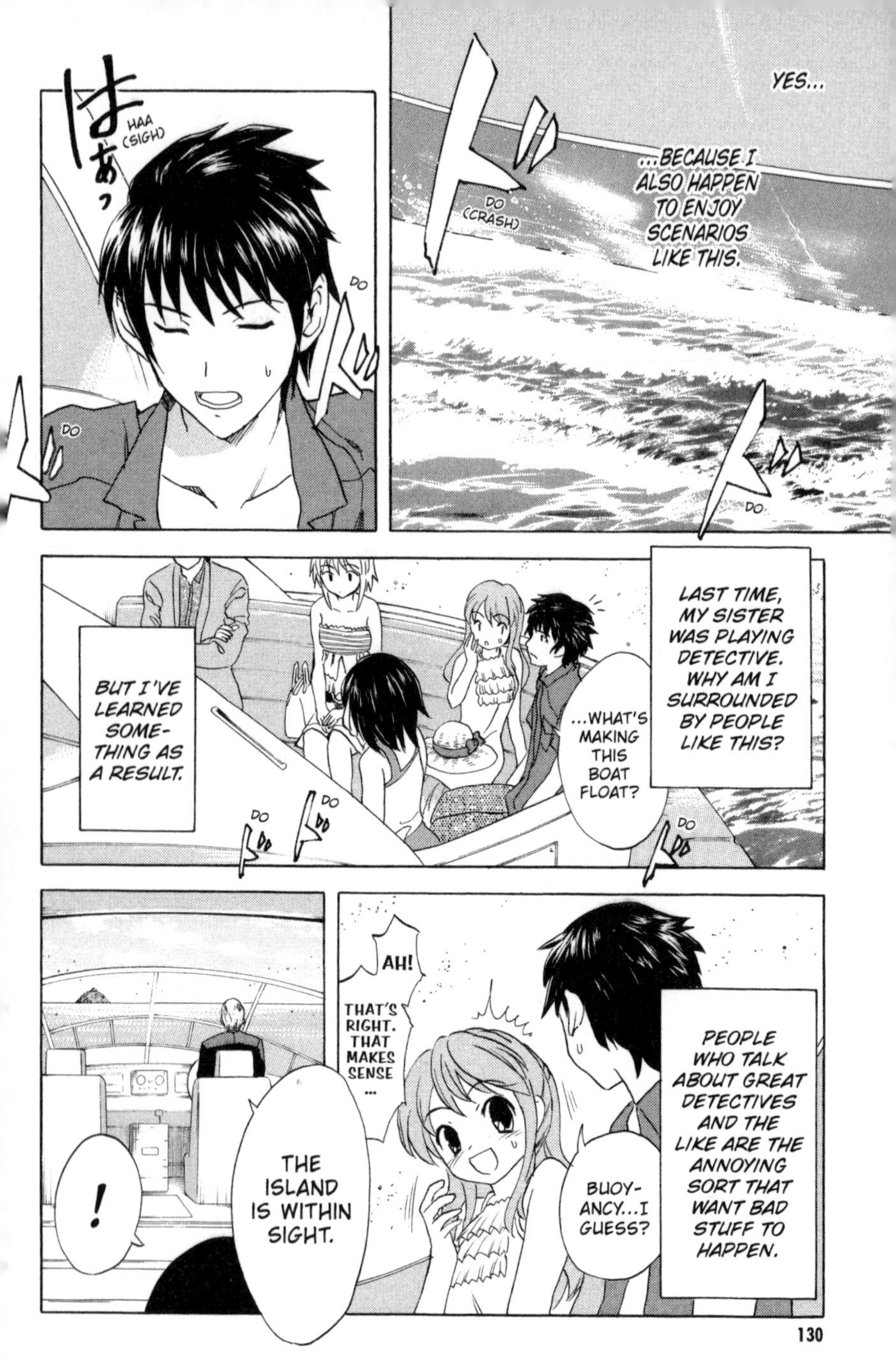
YES...
...BECAUSE I ALSO HAPPEN TO ENJOY SCENARIOS LIKE THIS.
DO (CRASH)
DO
はあっ
HAA (SIGH)
DO
DO
LAST TIME, MY SISTER WAS PLAYING DETECTIVE. WHY AM I SURROUNDED BY PEOPLE LIKE THIS?
...WHAT'S MAKING THIS BOAT FLOAT?
DO
BUT I'VE LEARNED SOME-THING AS A RESULT.
DO
DO
PEOPLE WHO TALK ABOUT GREAT DETECTIVES AND THE LIKE ARE THE ANNOYING SORT THAT WANT BAD STUFF TO HAPPEN.
BUOY-ANCY...I GUESS?
AH!
THAT'S RIGHT. THAT MAKES SENSE ...
THE ISLAND IS WITHIN SIGHT.
!

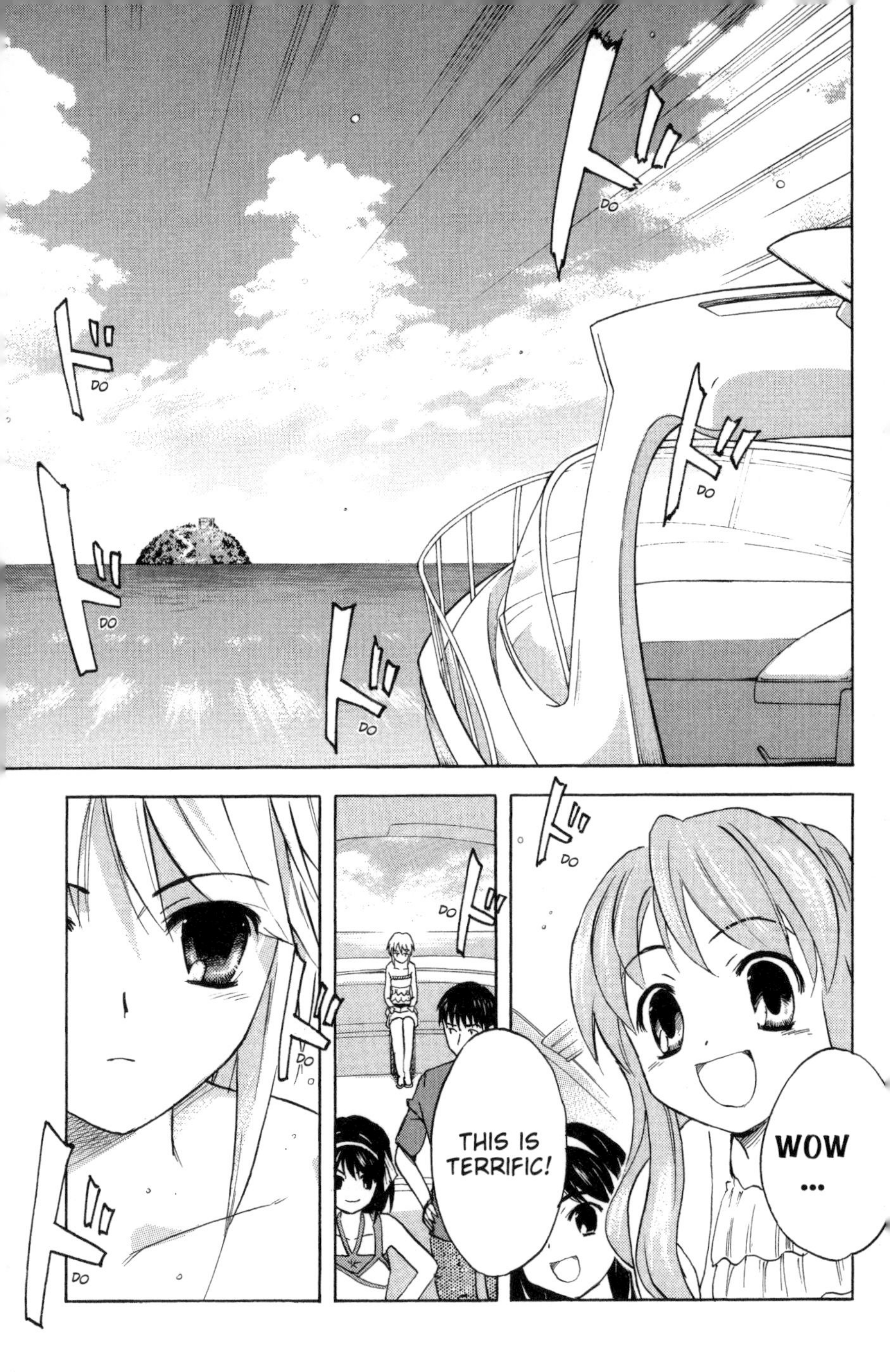
DO
DO
DO
DO
DO
DO
WOW ...
DO
THIS IS TERRIFIC!
DO
DO

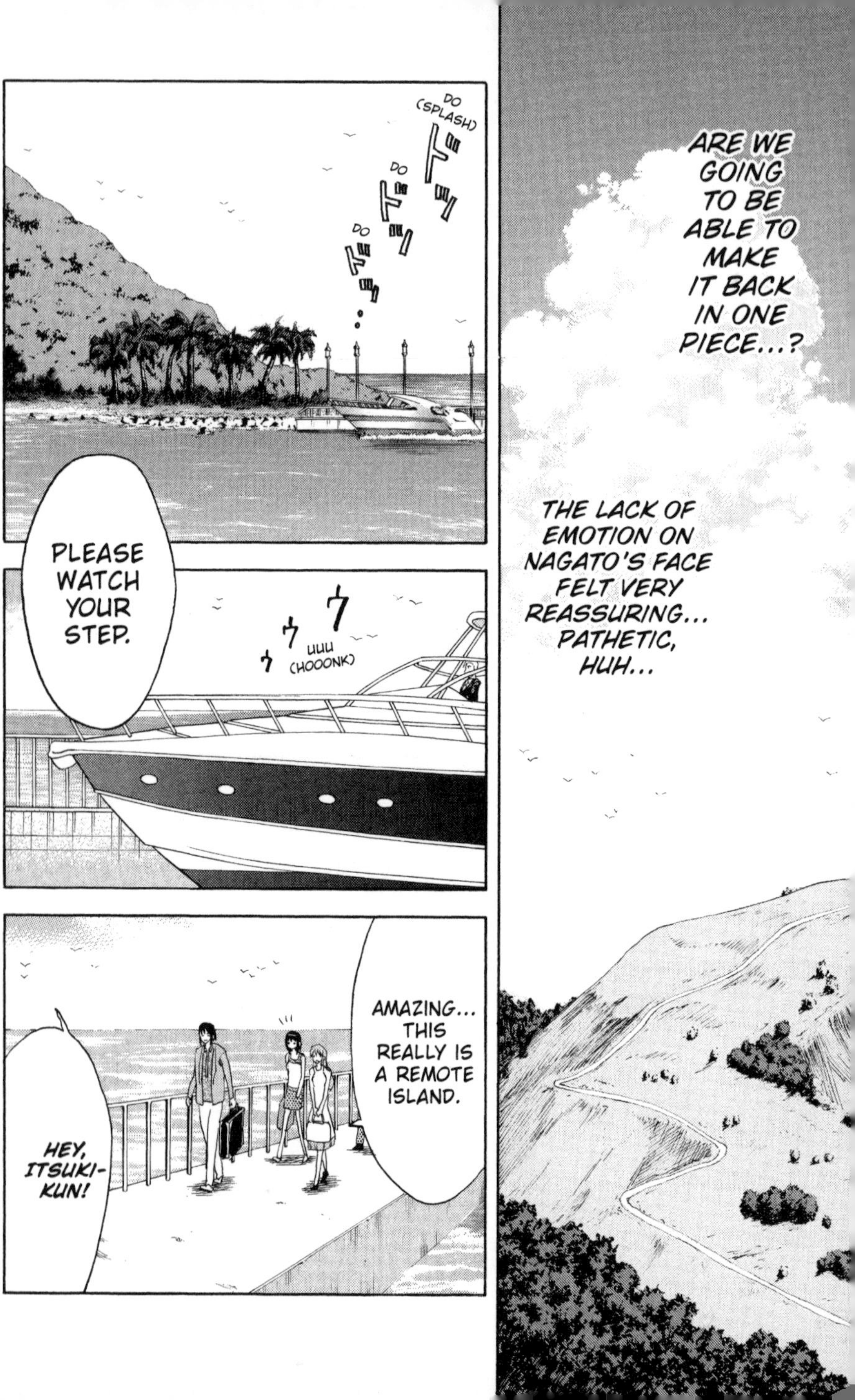
ARE WE GOING TO BE ABLE TO MAKE IT BACK IN ONE PIECE...?
THE LACK OF EMOTION ON NAGATO'S FACE FELT VERY REASSURING... PATHETIC, HUH...
DO (SPLASH)
DO
DO
UUU (HOOONK)
PLEASE WATCH YOUR STEP.
AMAZING... THIS REALLY IS A REMOTE ISLAND.
HEY, ITSUKI-KUN!

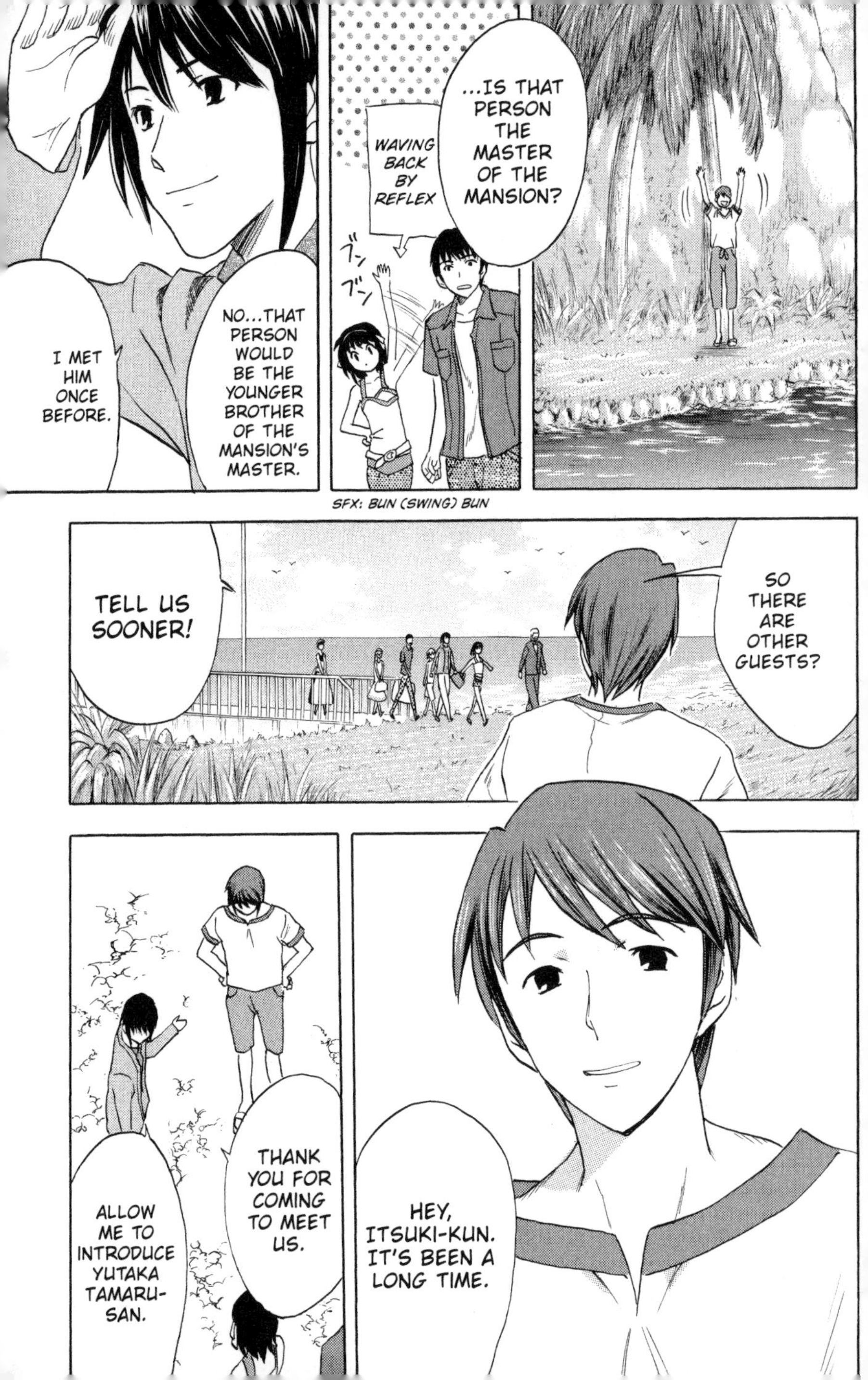
...IS THAT PERSON THE MASTER OF THE MANSION?
WAVING BACK BY REFLEX
ブン ブン
NO...THAT PERSON WOULD BE THE YOUNGER BROTHER OF THE MANSION'S MASTER.
I MET HIM ONCE BEFORE.
SFX: BUN (SWING) BUN
SO THERE ARE OTHER GUESTS?
TELL US SOONER!
HEY, ITSUKI-KUN. IT'S BEEN A LONG TIME.
THANK YOU FOR COMING TO MEET US.
ALLOW ME TO INTRODUCE YUTAKA TAMARU-SAN.

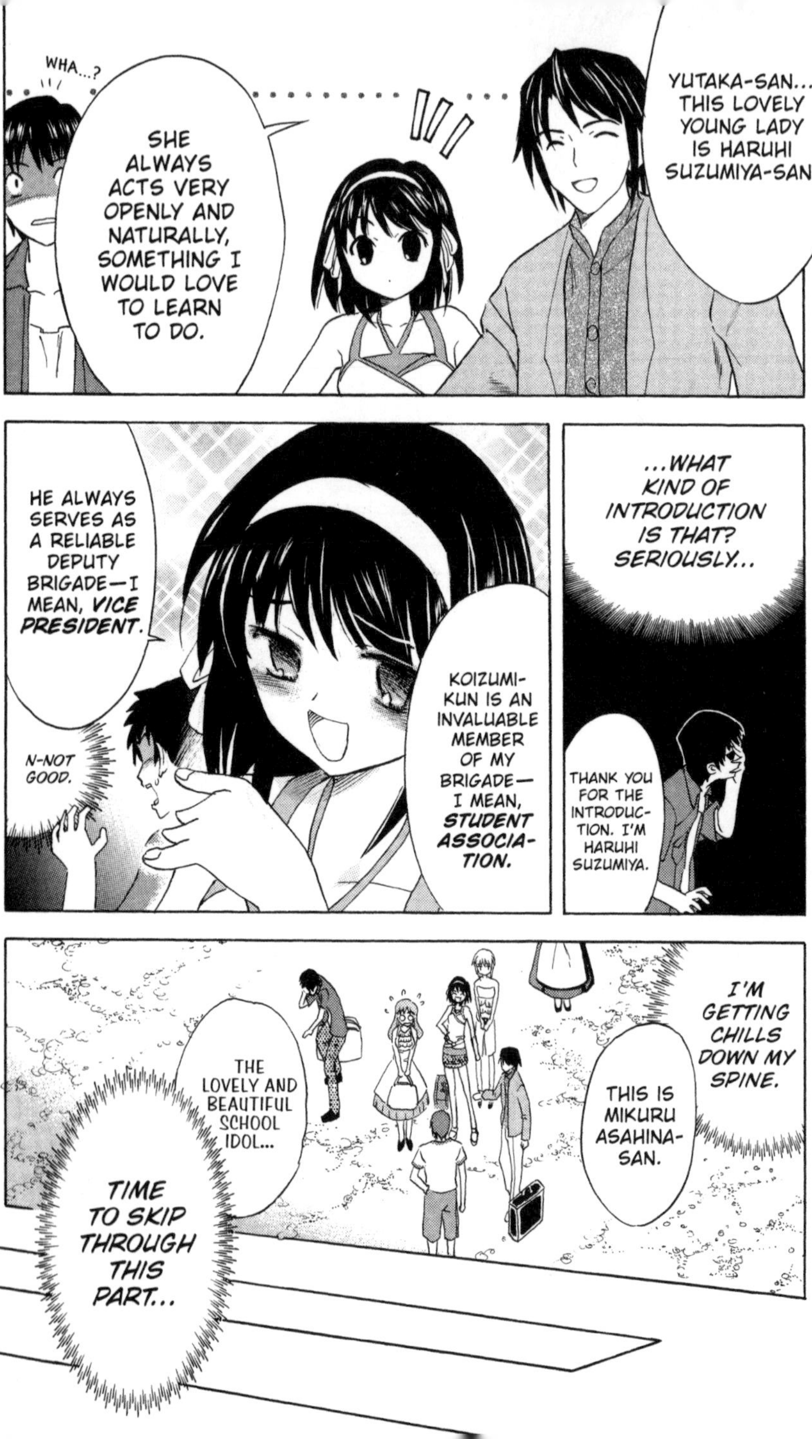
YUTAKA-SAN... THIS LOVELY YOUNG LADY IS HARUHI SUZUMIYA-SAN.
SHE ALWAYS ACTS VERY OPENLY AND NATURALLY, SOMETHING I WOULD LOVE TO LEARN TO DO.
WHA...?
...WHAT KIND OF INTRODUCTION IS THAT? SERIOUSLY...
THANK YOU FOR THE INTRODUCTION. I'M HARUHI SUZUMIYA.
KOIZUMI-KUN IS AN INVALUABLE MEMBER OF MY BRIGADE— I MEAN, STUDENT ASSOCIATION.
HE ALWAYS SERVES AS A RELIABLE DEPUTY BRIGADE—I MEAN, VICE PRESIDENT.
N-NOT GOOD.
I'M GETTING CHILLS DOWN MY SPINE.
THIS IS MIKURU ASAHINA-SAN.
THE LOVELY AND BEAUTIFUL SCHOOL IDOL...
TIME TO SKIP THROUGH THIS PART...

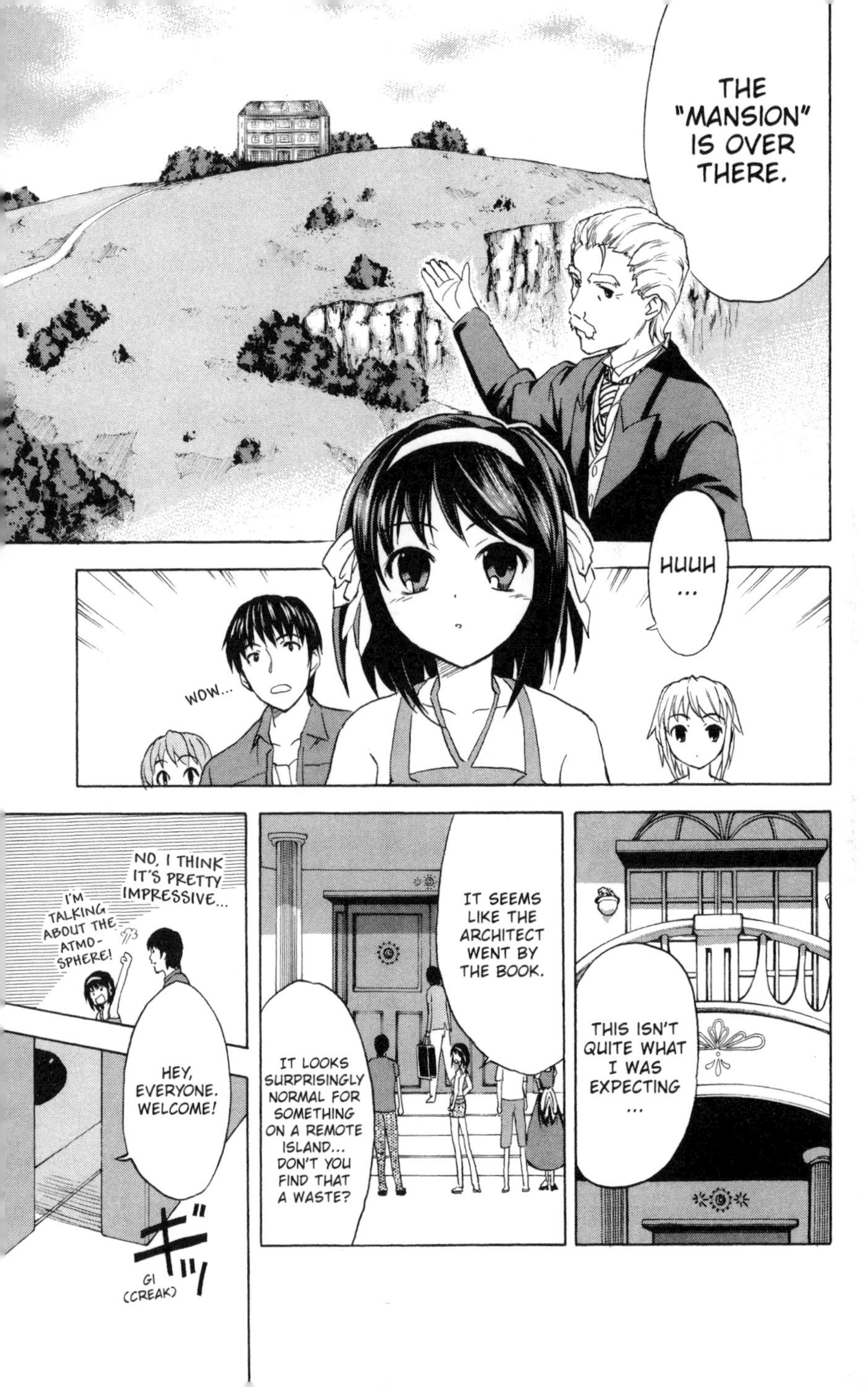
THE "MANSION" IS OVER THERE.
HUUH ...
WOW...
THIS ISN'T QUITE WHAT I WAS EXPECTING ...
IT SEEMS LIKE THE ARCHITECT WENT BY THE BOOK.
IT LOOKS SURPRISINGLY NORMAL FOR SOMETHING ON A REMOTE ISLAND... DON'T YOU FIND THAT A WASTE?
NO, I THINK IT'S PRETTY IMPRESSIVE...
I'M TALKING ABOUT THE ATMO-SPHERE!
HEY, EVERYONE. WELCOME!
ギッ
GI (CREAK)

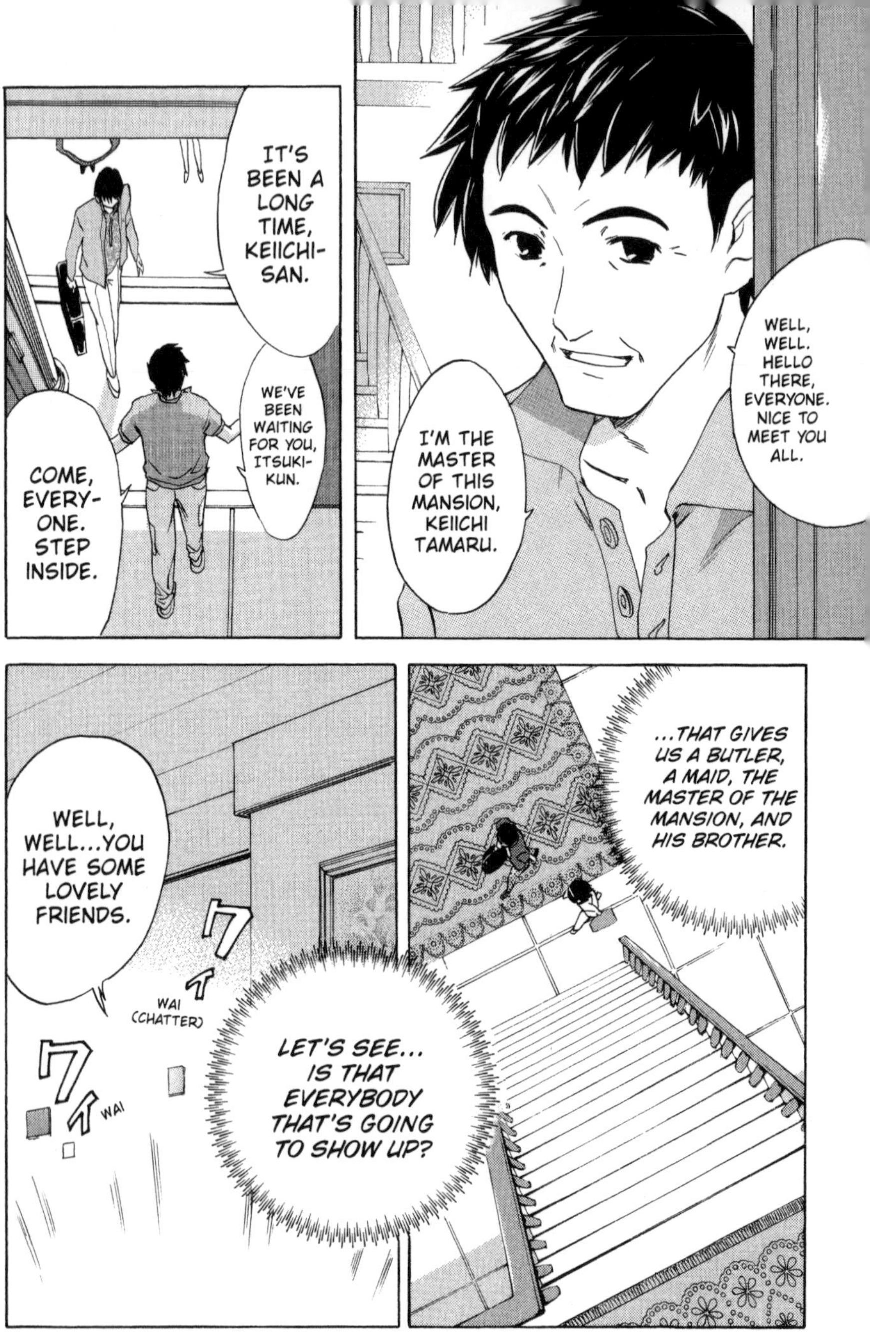
WELL, WELL. HELLO THERE, EVERYONE. NICE TO MEET YOU ALL.
I'M THE MASTER OF THIS MANSION, KEIICHI TAMARU.
IT'S BEEN A LONG TIME, KEIICHI-SAN.
WE'VE BEEN WAITING FOR YOU, ITSUKI-KUN.
COME, EVERY-ONE. STEP INSIDE.
...THAT GIVES US A BUTLER, A MAID, THE MASTER OF THE MANSION, AND HIS BROTHER.
LET'S SEE... IS THAT EVERYBODY THAT'S GOING TO SHOW UP?
WELL, WELL...YOU HAVE SOME LOVELY FRIENDS.
WAI (CHATTER)
WAI

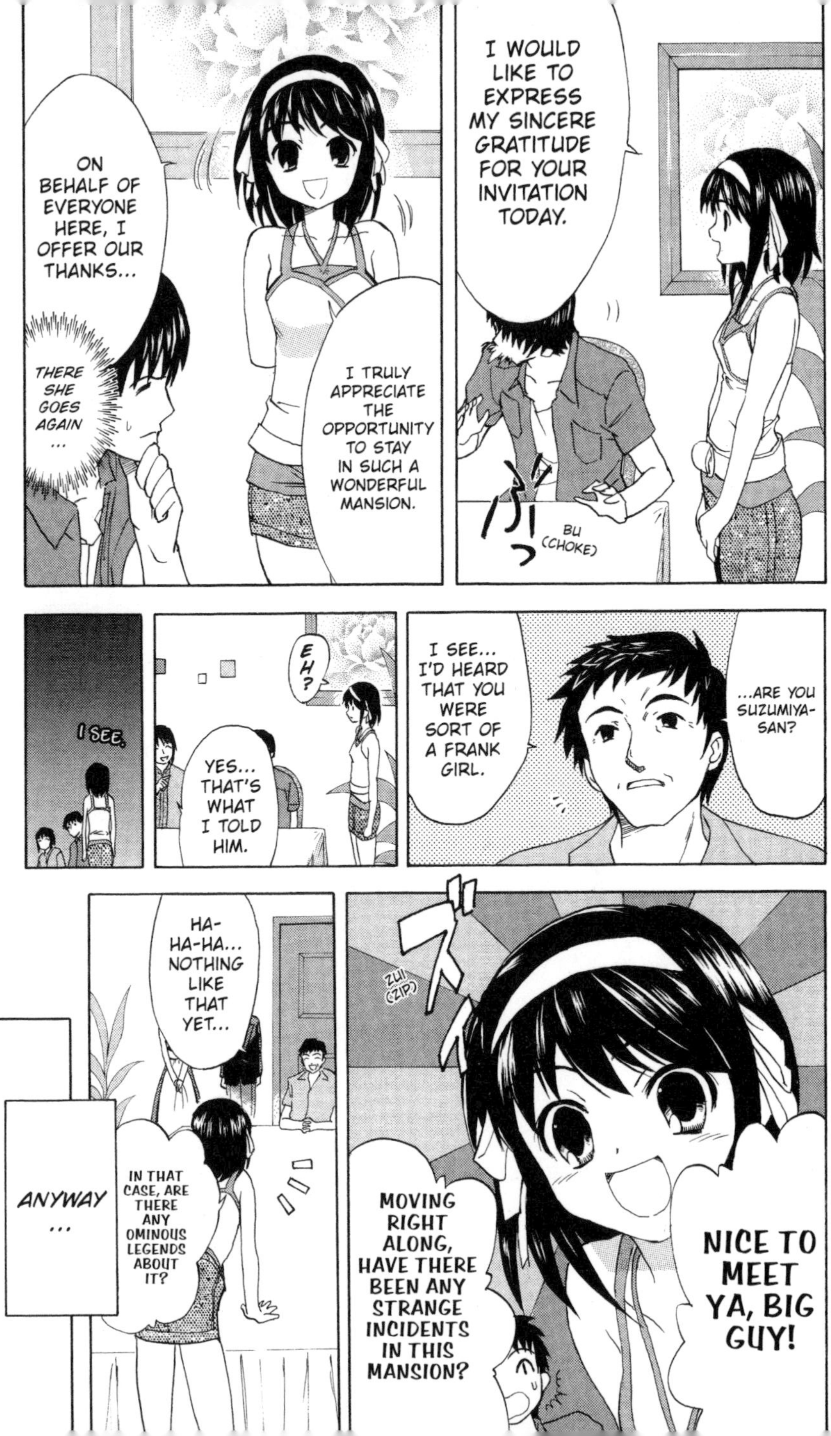
I WOULD LIKE TO EXPRESS MY SINCERE GRATITUDE FOR YOUR INVITATION TODAY.
BU (CHOKE)
ON BEHALF OF EVERYONE HERE, I OFFER OUR THANKS...
I TRULY APPRECIATE THE OPPORTUNITY TO STAY IN SUCH A WONDERFUL MANSION.
THERE SHE GOES AGAIN ...
...ARE YOU SUZUMIYA-SAN?
I SEE... I'D HEARD THAT YOU WERE SORT OF A FRANK GIRL.
EH?
YES... THAT'S WHAT I TOLD HIM.
I SEE.
ZUI (ZIP)
NICE TO MEET YA, BIG GUY!
MOVING RIGHT ALONG, HAVE THERE BEEN ANY STRANGE INCIDENTS IN THIS MANSION?
HA-HA-HA... NOTHING LIKE THAT YET...
IN THAT CASE, ARE THERE ANY OMINOUS LEGENDS ABOUT IT?
ANYWAY ...

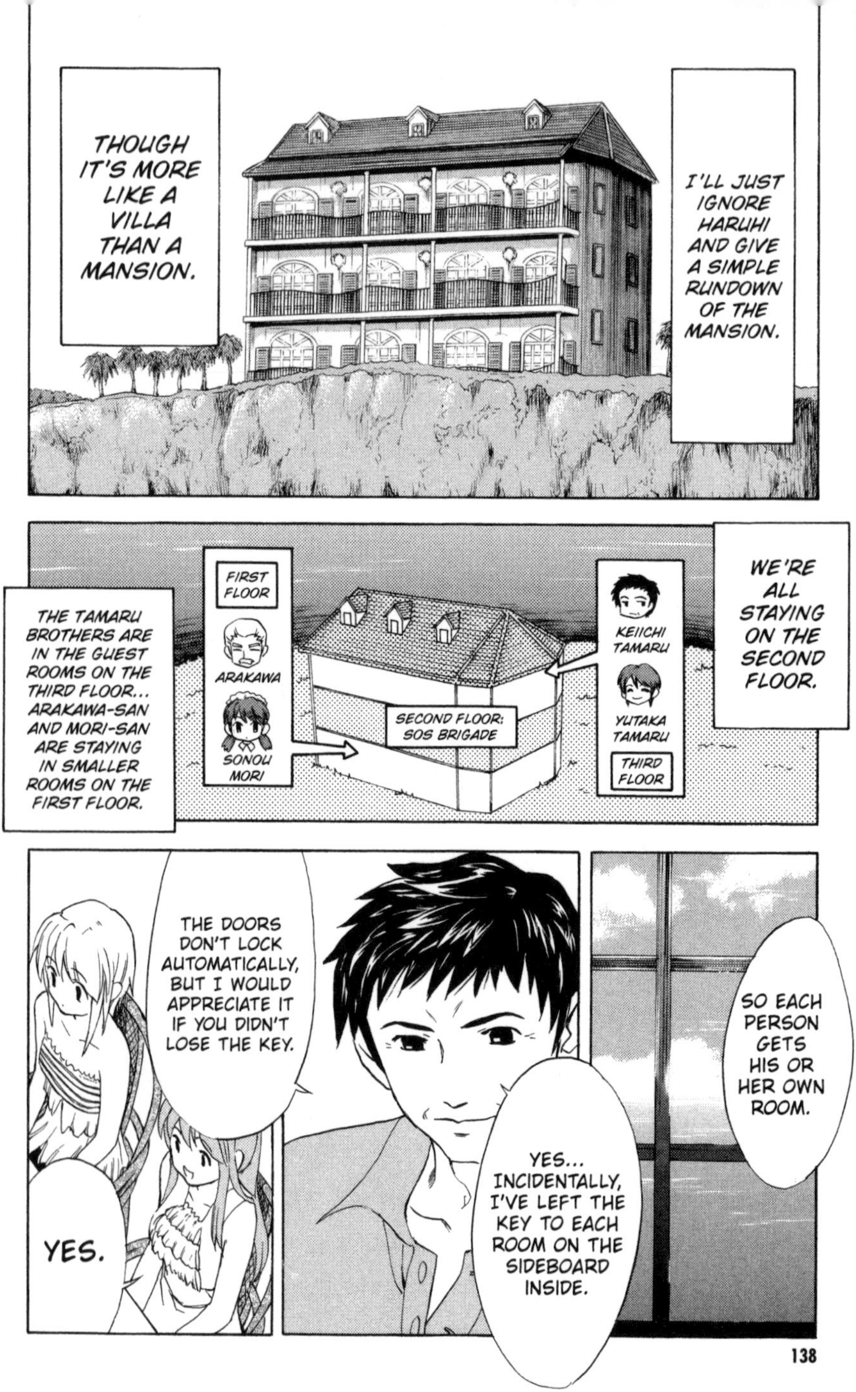
I'LL JUST IGNORE HARUHI AND GIVE A SIMPLE RUNDOWN OF THE MANSION.
THOUGH IT'S MORE LIKE A VILLA THAN A MANSION.
WE'RE ALL STAYING ON THE SECOND FLOOR.
THIRD FLOOR
KEIICHI TAMARU
YUTAKA TAMARU
SECOND FLOOR: SOS BRIGADE
FIRST FLOOR
ARAKAWA
SONOU MORI
THE TAMARU BROTHERS ARE IN THE GUEST ROOMS ON THE THIRD FLOOR... ARAKAWA-SAN AND MORI-SAN ARE STAYING IN SMALLER ROOMS ON THE FIRST FLOOR.
SO EACH PERSON GETS HIS OR HER OWN ROOM.
YES... INCIDENTALLY, I'VE LEFT THE KEY TO EACH ROOM ON THE SIDEBOARD INSIDE.
THE DOORS DON'T LOCK AUTOMATICALLY, BUT I WOULD APPRECIATE IT IF YOU DIDN'T LOSE THE KEY.
YES.

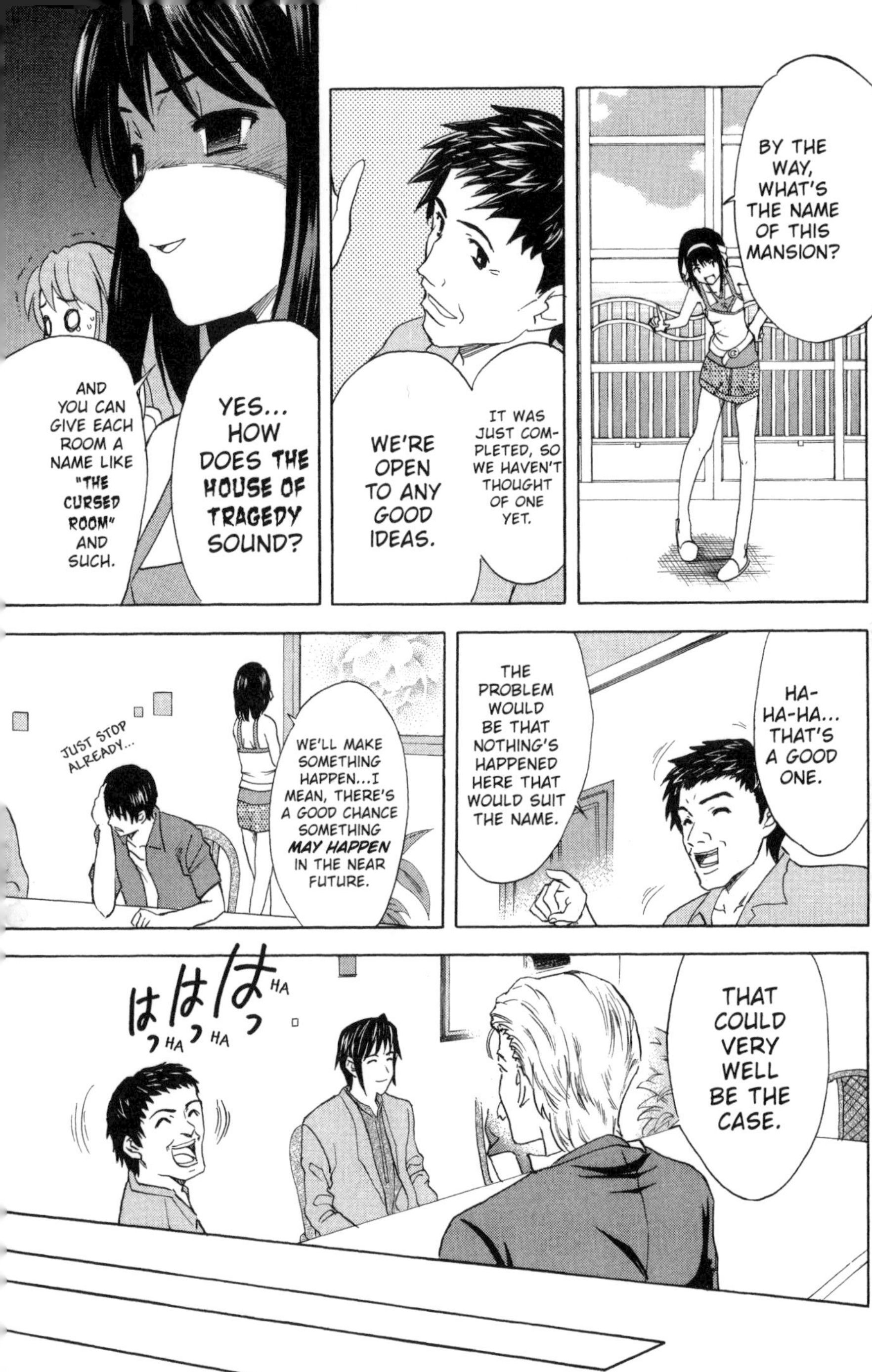
BY THE WAY, WHAT'S THE NAME OF THIS MANSION?
IT WAS JUST COM-PLETED, SO WE HAVEN'T THOUGHT OF ONE YET.
WE'RE OPEN TO ANY GOOD IDEAS.
YES... HOW DOES THE HOUSE OF TRAGEDY SOUND?
AND YOU CAN GIVE EACH ROOM A NAME LIKE "THE CURSED ROOM" AND SUCH.
HA-HA-HA... THAT'S A GOOD ONE.
THE PROBLEM WOULD BE THAT NOTHING'S HAPPENED HERE THAT WOULD SUIT THE NAME.
WE'LL MAKE SOMETHING HAPPEN...I MEAN, THERE'S A GOOD CHANCE SOMETHING *MAY HAPPEN* IN THE NEAR FUTURE.
JUST STOP ALREADY...
THAT COULD VERY WELL BE THE CASE.
はっはっはっ
HA HA HA

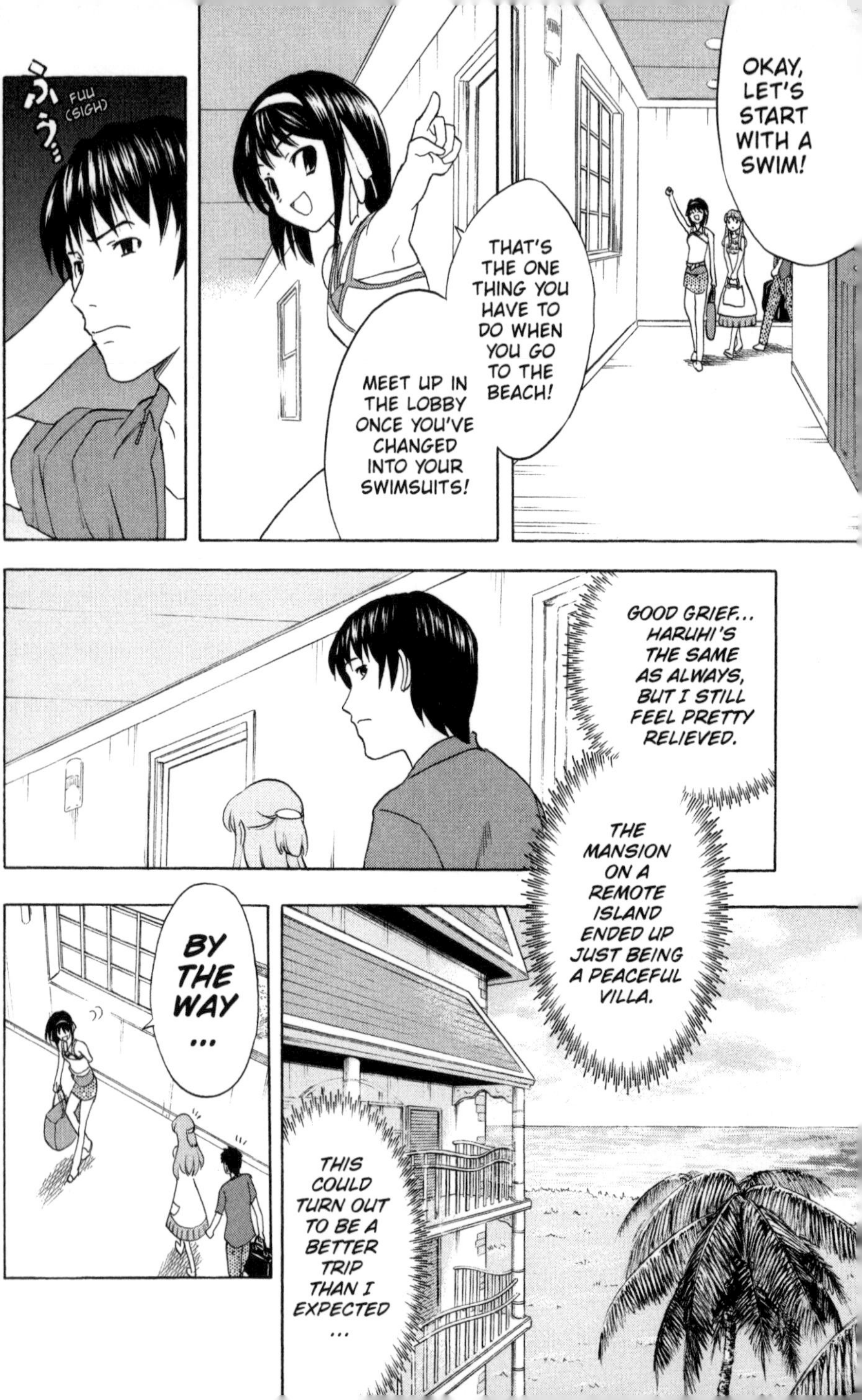
OKAY, LET'S START WITH A SWIM!
THAT'S THE ONE THING YOU HAVE TO DO WHEN YOU GO TO THE BEACH!
MEET UP IN THE LOBBY ONCE YOU'VE CHANGED INTO YOUR SWIMSUITS!
ふう...
FUU (SIGH)
GOOD GRIEF... HARUHI'S THE SAME AS ALWAYS, BUT I STILL FEEL PRETTY RELIEVED.
THE MANSION ON A REMOTE ISLAND ENDED UP JUST BEING A PEACEFUL VILLA.
THIS COULD TURN OUT TO BE A BETTER TRIP THAN I EXPECTED...
BY THE WAY...

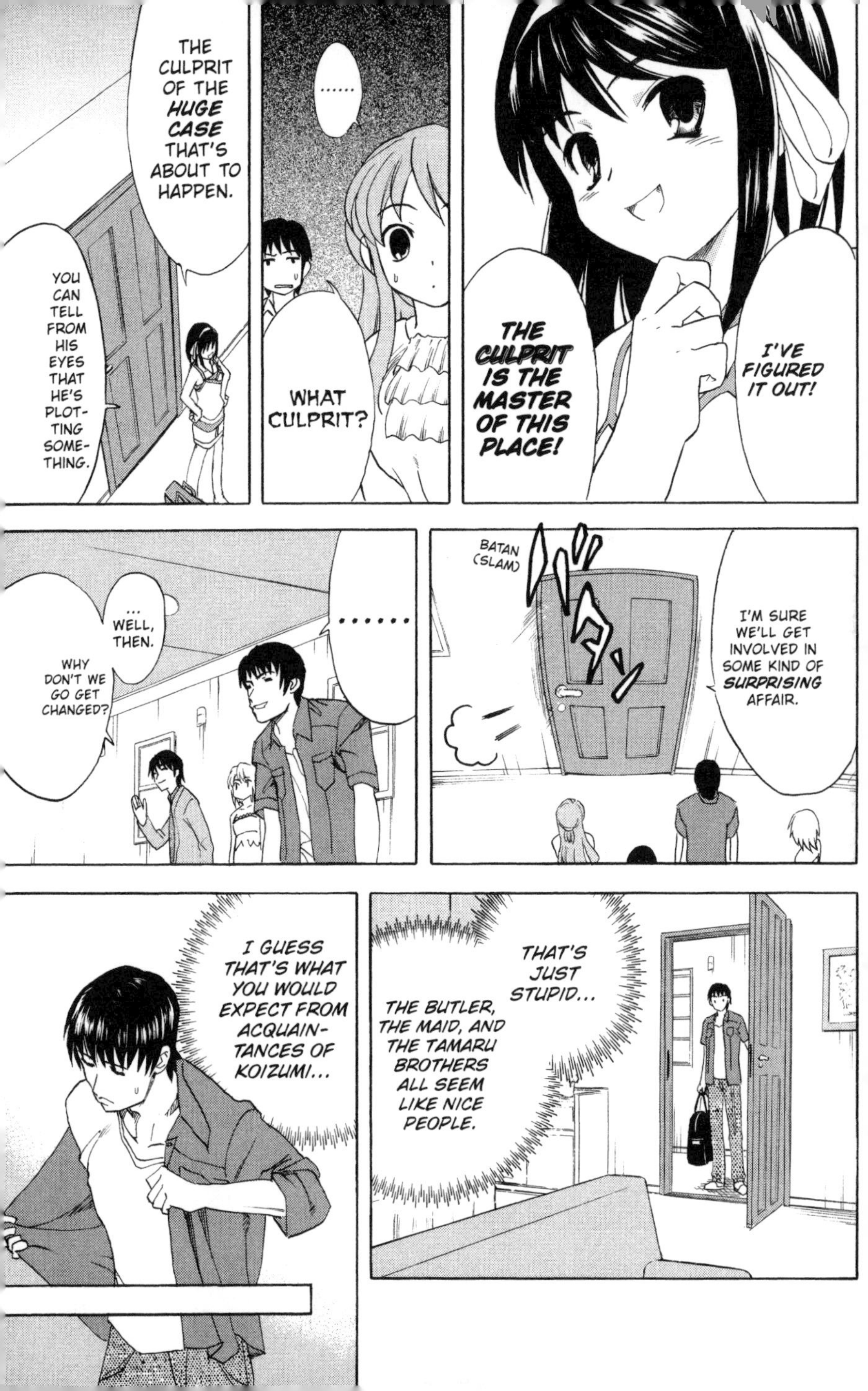
I'VE FIGURED IT OUT!
THE CULPRIT IS THE MASTER OF THIS PLACE!
....
WHAT CULPRIT?
THE CULPRIT OF THE HUGE CASE THAT'S ABOUT TO HAPPEN.
YOU CAN TELL FROM HIS EYES THAT HE'S PLOTTING SOMETHING.
I'M SURE WE'LL GET INVOLVED IN SOME KIND OF SURPRISING AFFAIR.
BATAN (SLAM)
......
... WELL, THEN.
WHY DON'T WE GO GET CHANGED?
THAT'S JUST STUPID...
THE BUTLER, THE MAID, AND THE TAMARU BROTHERS ALL SEEM LIKE NICE PEOPLE.
I GUESS THAT'S WHAT YOU WOULD EXPECT FROM ACQUAINTANCES OF KOIZUMI...

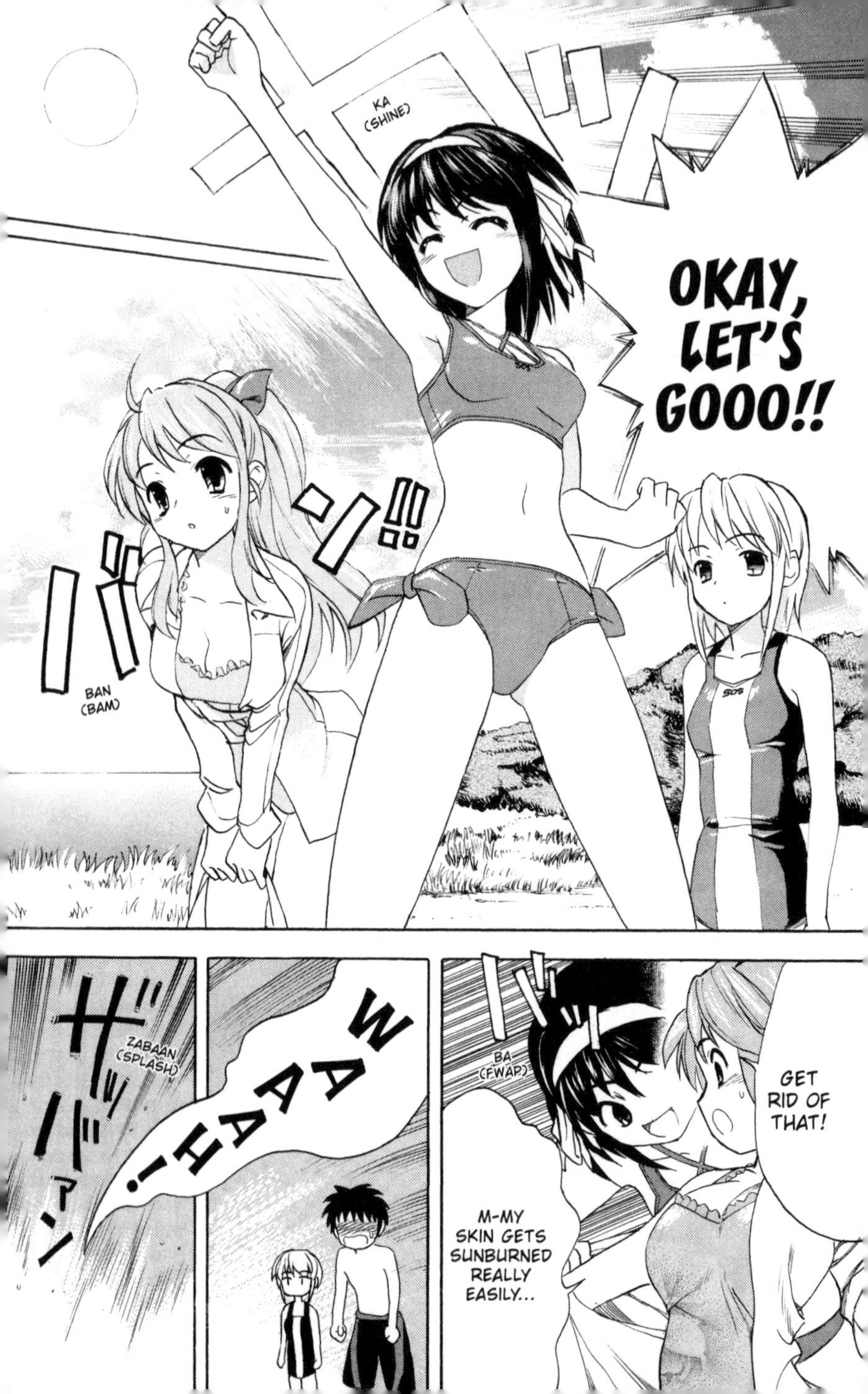
KA
(SHINE)
OKAY, LET'S GOOO!!
BAN
(BAM)
GET RID OF THAT!
BA
(FWAP)
M-MY SKIN GETS SUNBURNED REALLY EASILY...
WAAAHA!
ZABAAN
(SPLASH)

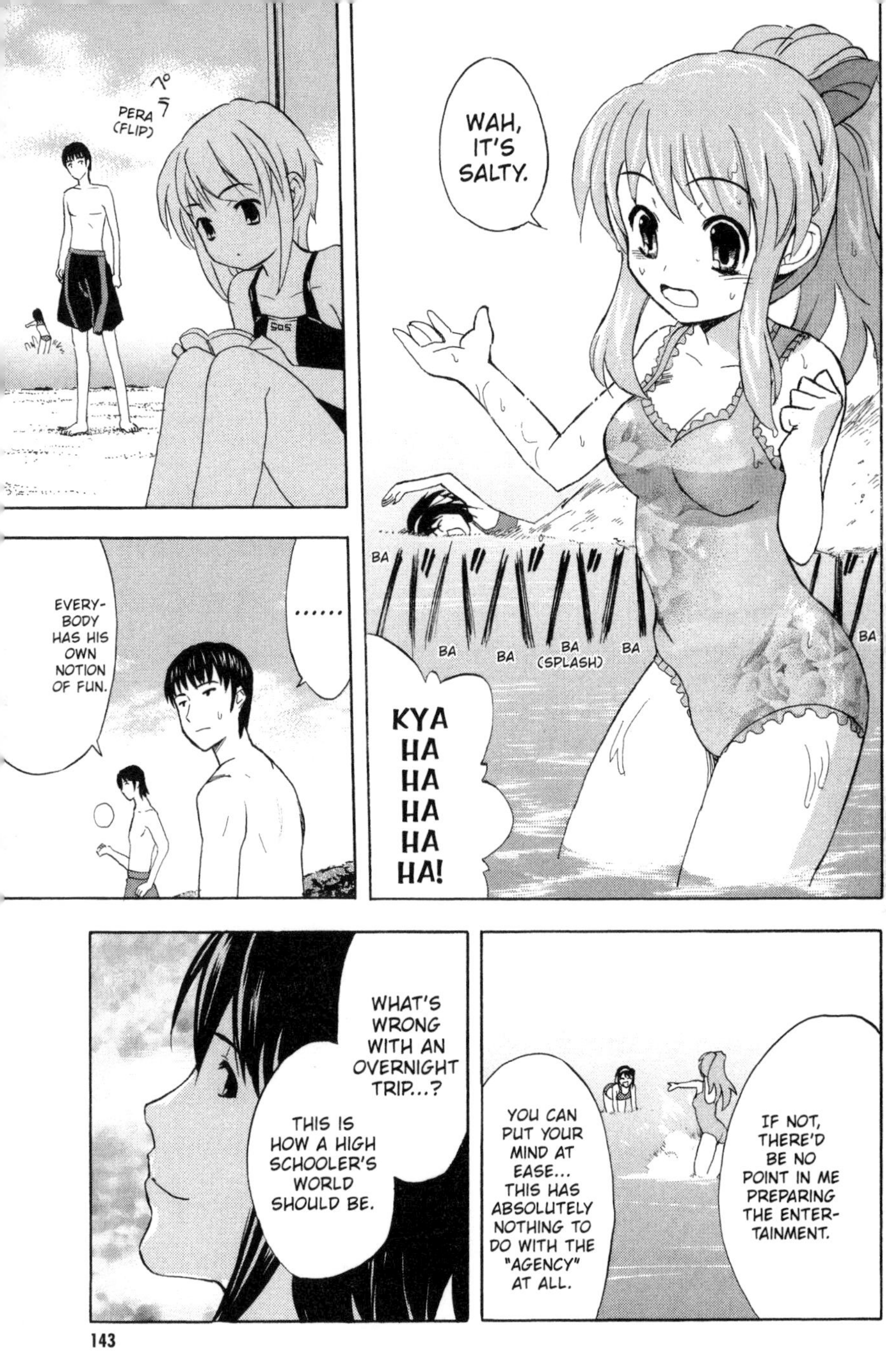
WAH, IT'S SALTY.
BA BA BA BA BA (SPLASH) BA BA
KYA HA HA HA HA HA!
ペラ
PERA (FLIP)
......
EVERY-BODY HAS HIS OWN NOTION OF FUN.
IF NOT, THERE'D BE NO POINT IN ME PREPARING THE ENTER-TAINMENT.
YOU CAN PUT YOUR MIND AT EASE... THIS HAS ABSOLUTELY NOTHING TO DO WITH THE "AGENCY" AT ALL.
WHAT'S WRONG WITH AN OVERNIGHT TRIP...?
THIS IS HOW A HIGH SCHOOLER'S WORLD SHOULD BE.

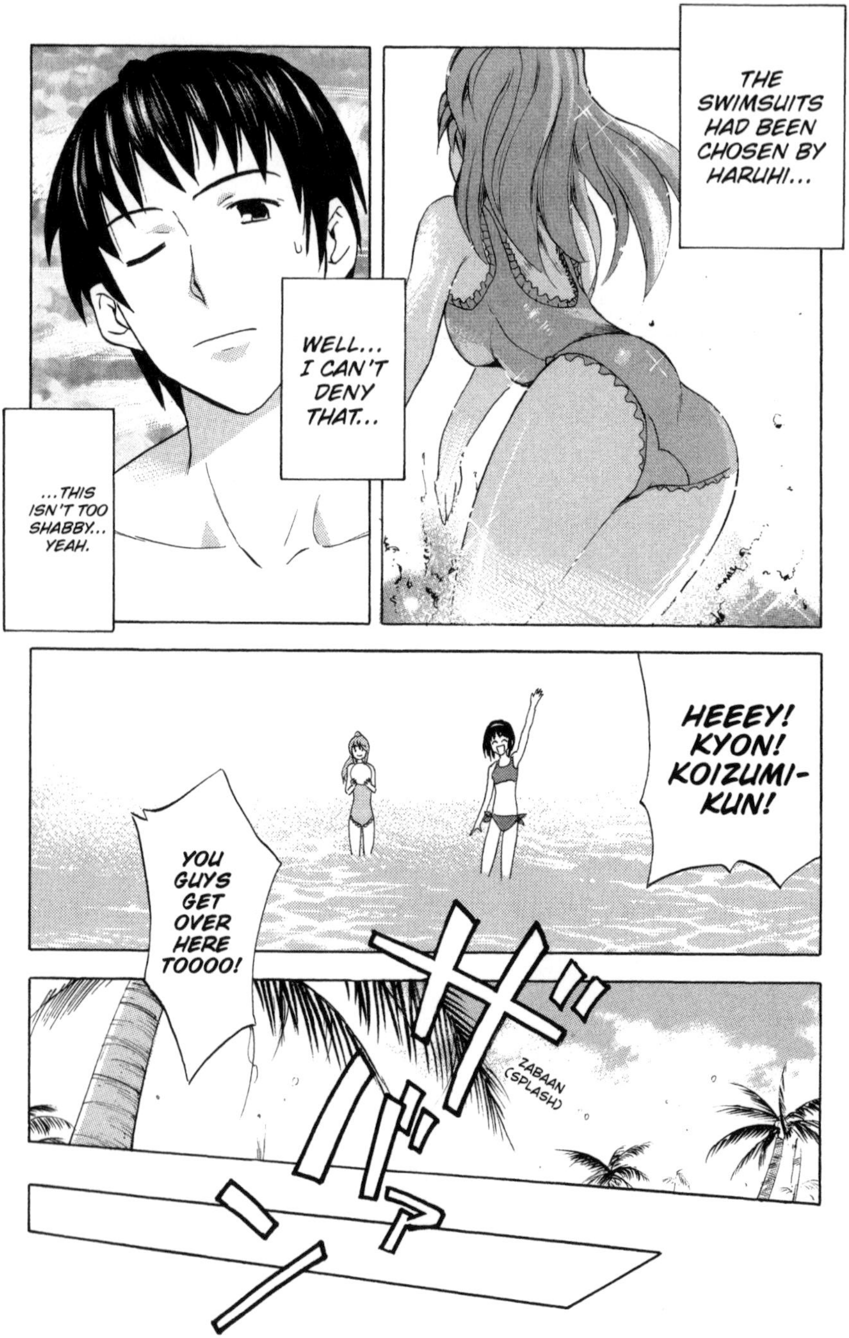
THE SWIMSUITS HAD BEEN CHOSEN BY HARUHI...
WELL... I CAN'T DENY THAT...
...THIS ISN'T TOO SHABBY... YEAH.
HEEEY! KYON! KOIZUMI-KUN!
YOU GUYS GET OVER HERE TOOOO!
ZABAAN (SPLASH)

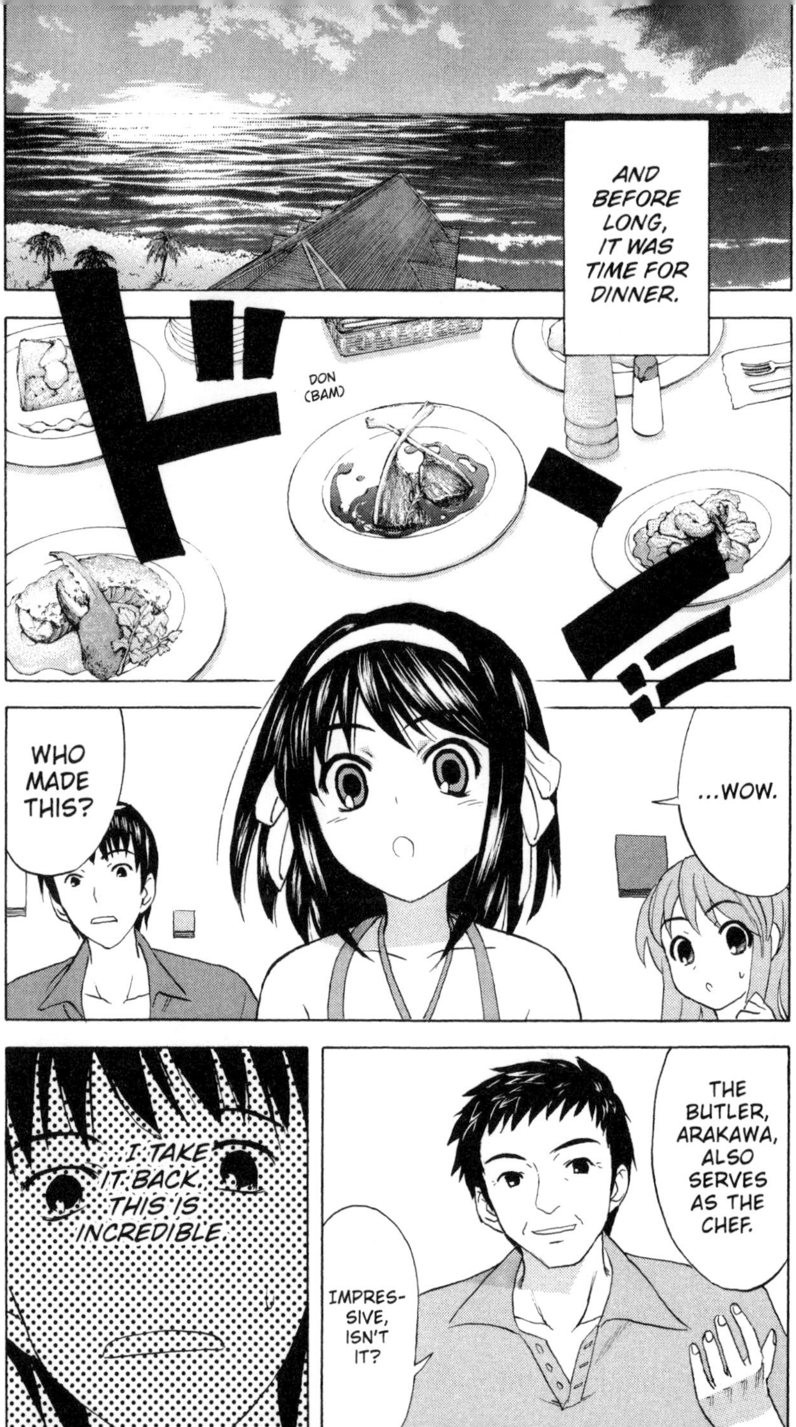
AND BEFORE LONG, IT WAS TIME FOR DINNER.
DON (BAM)
...WOW.
WHO MADE THIS?
THE BUTLER, ARAKAWA, ALSO SERVES AS THE CHEF.
IMPRESSIVE, ISN'T IT?
I TAKE IT BACK. THIS IS INCREDIBLE.

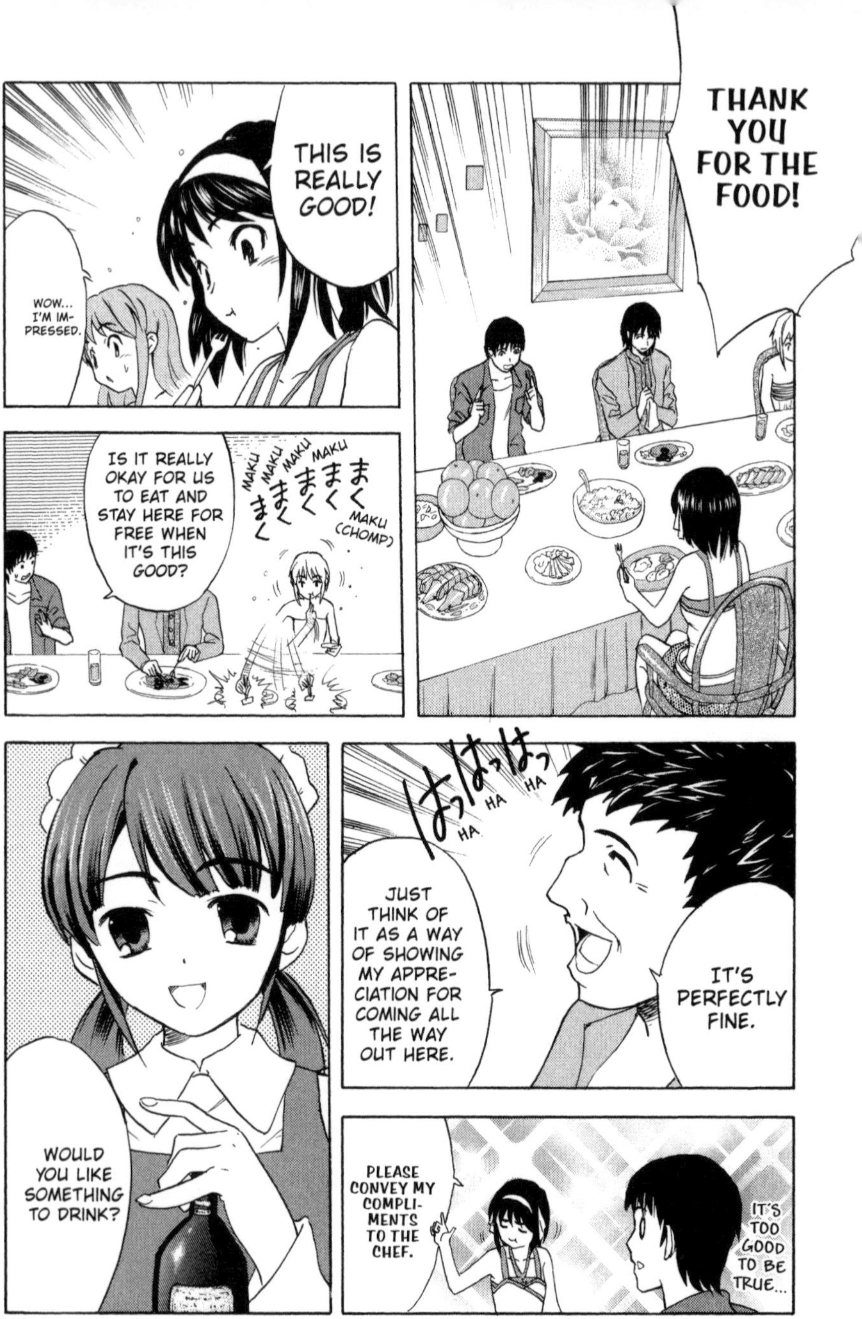
THANK YOU FOR THE FOOD!
THIS IS REALLY GOOD!
WOW... I'M IMPRESSED.
まくまくまくまく
MAKU MAKU MAKU MAKU
MAKU (CHOMP)
IS IT REALLY OKAY FOR US TO EAT AND STAY HERE FOR FREE WHEN IT'S THIS GOOD?
はっはっはっ
HA HA HA
IT'S PERFECTLY FINE.
JUST THINK OF IT AS A WAY OF SHOWING MY APPRECIATION FOR COMING ALL THE WAY OUT HERE.
IT'S TOO GOOD TO BE TRUE...
PLEASE CONVEY MY COMPLIMENTS TO THE CHEF.
WOULD YOU LIKE SOMETHING TO DRINK?

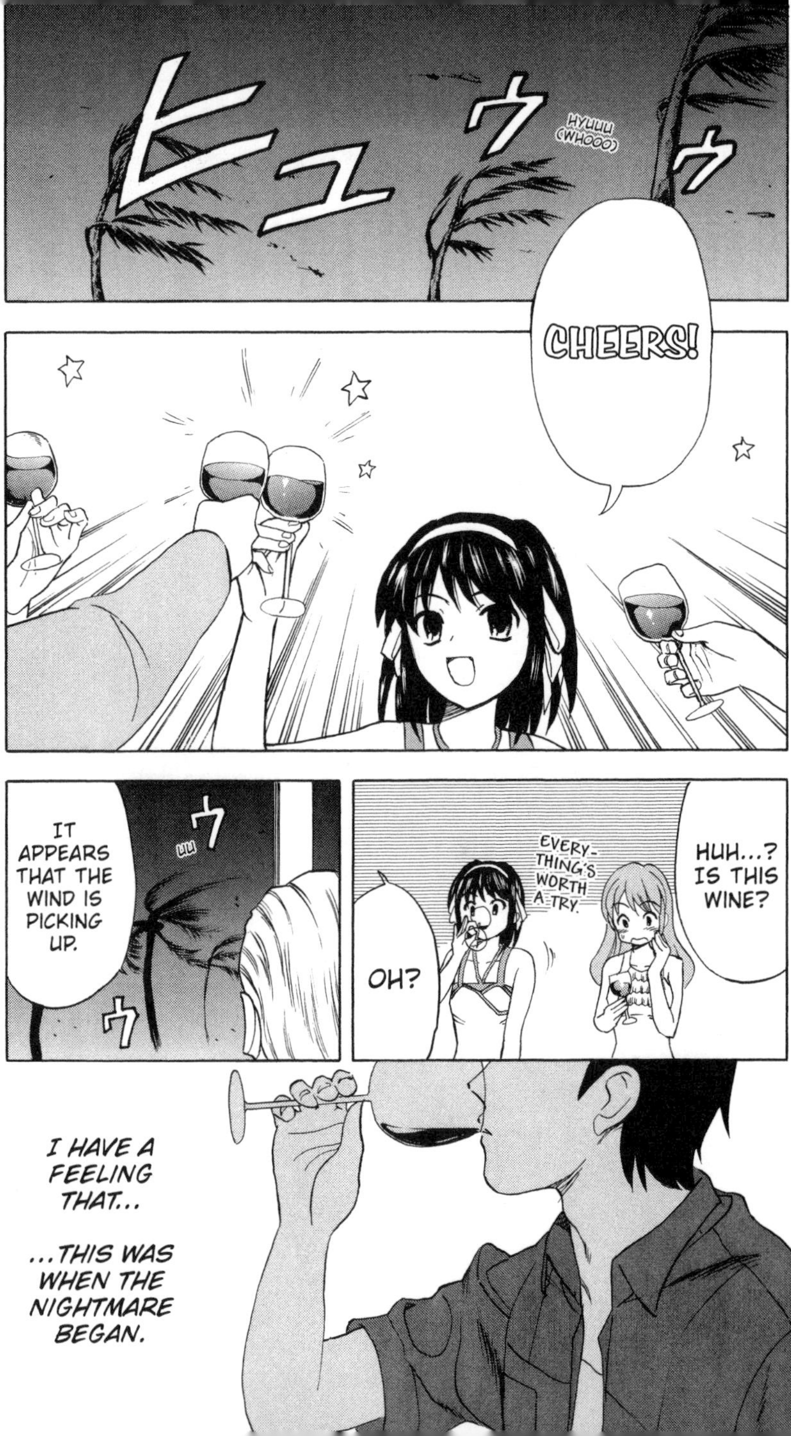
ヒュウゥゥ
HYUUU (WHOOO)
CHEERS!
HUH...? IS THIS WINE?
EVERY-THING'S WORTH A TRY.
OH?
ウ
UU
IT APPEARS THAT THE WIND IS PICKING UP.
ウ
I HAVE A FEELING THAT...
...THIS WAS WHEN THE NIGHTMARE BEGAN.

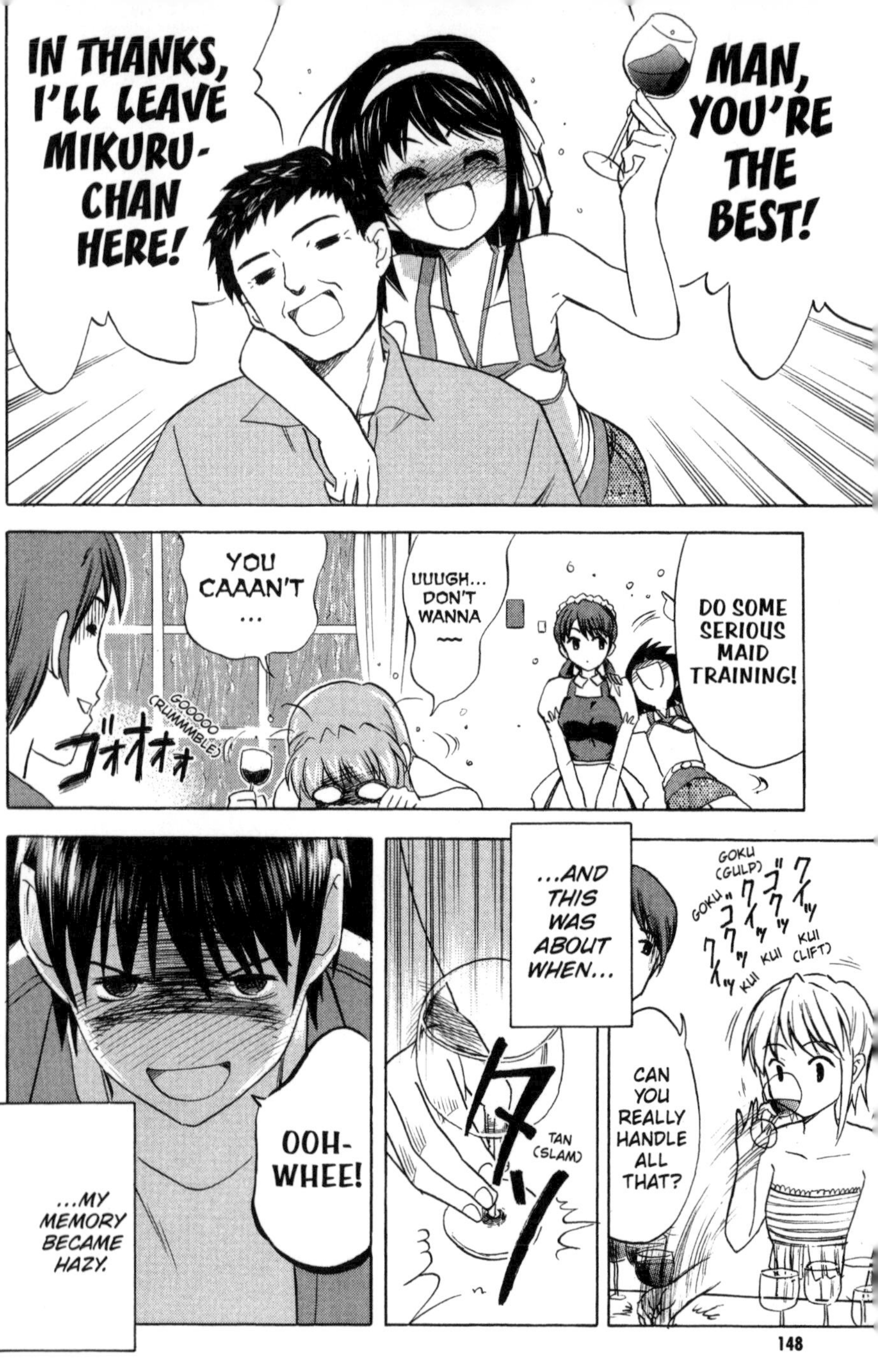
MAN, YOU'RE THE BEST!
IN THANKS, I'LL LEAVE MIKURU-CHAN HERE!
DO SOME SERIOUS MAID TRAINING!
UUUGH... DON'T WANNA ~~~
YOU CAAAN'T ...
GOOOOO (RUMMMBLE)
GOKU (GULP) GOKU
KUI (LIFT) KUI KUI
CAN YOU REALLY HANDLE ALL THAT?
...AND THIS WAS ABOUT WHEN...
TAN (SLAM)
OOH-WHEE!
...MY MEMORY BECAME HAZY.

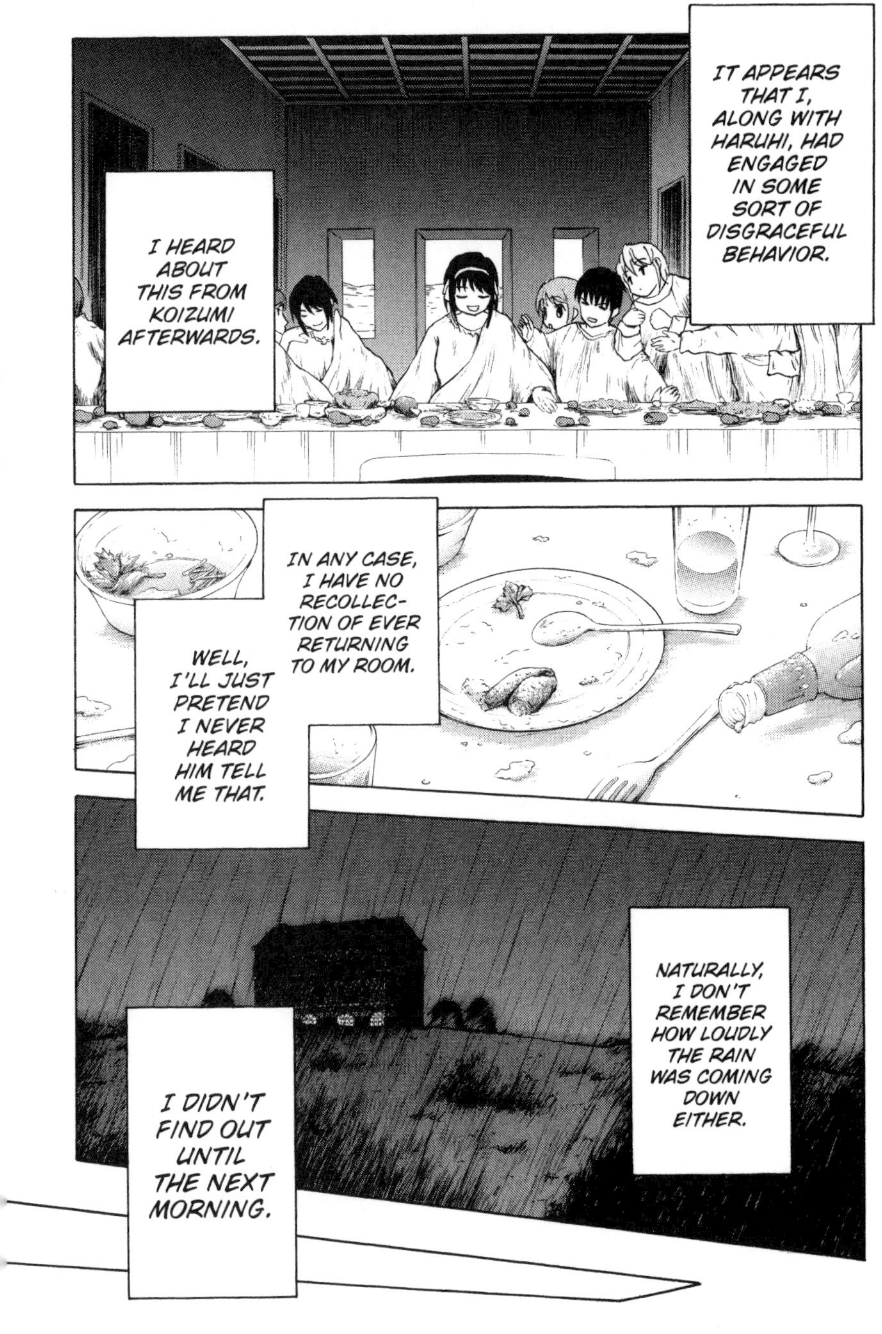

IT APPEARS THAT I, ALONG WITH HARUHI, HAD ENGAGED IN SOME SORT OF DISGRACEFUL BEHAVIOR.
I HEARD ABOUT THIS FROM KOIZUMI AFTERWARDS.
IN ANY CASE, I HAVE NO RECOLLECTION OF EVER RETURNING TO MY ROOM.
WELL, I'LL JUST PRETEND I NEVER HEARD HIM TELL ME THAT.
NATURALLY, I DON'T REMEMBER HOW LOUDLY THE RAIN WAS COMING DOWN EITHER.
I DIDN'T FIND OUT UNTIL THE NEXT MORNING.

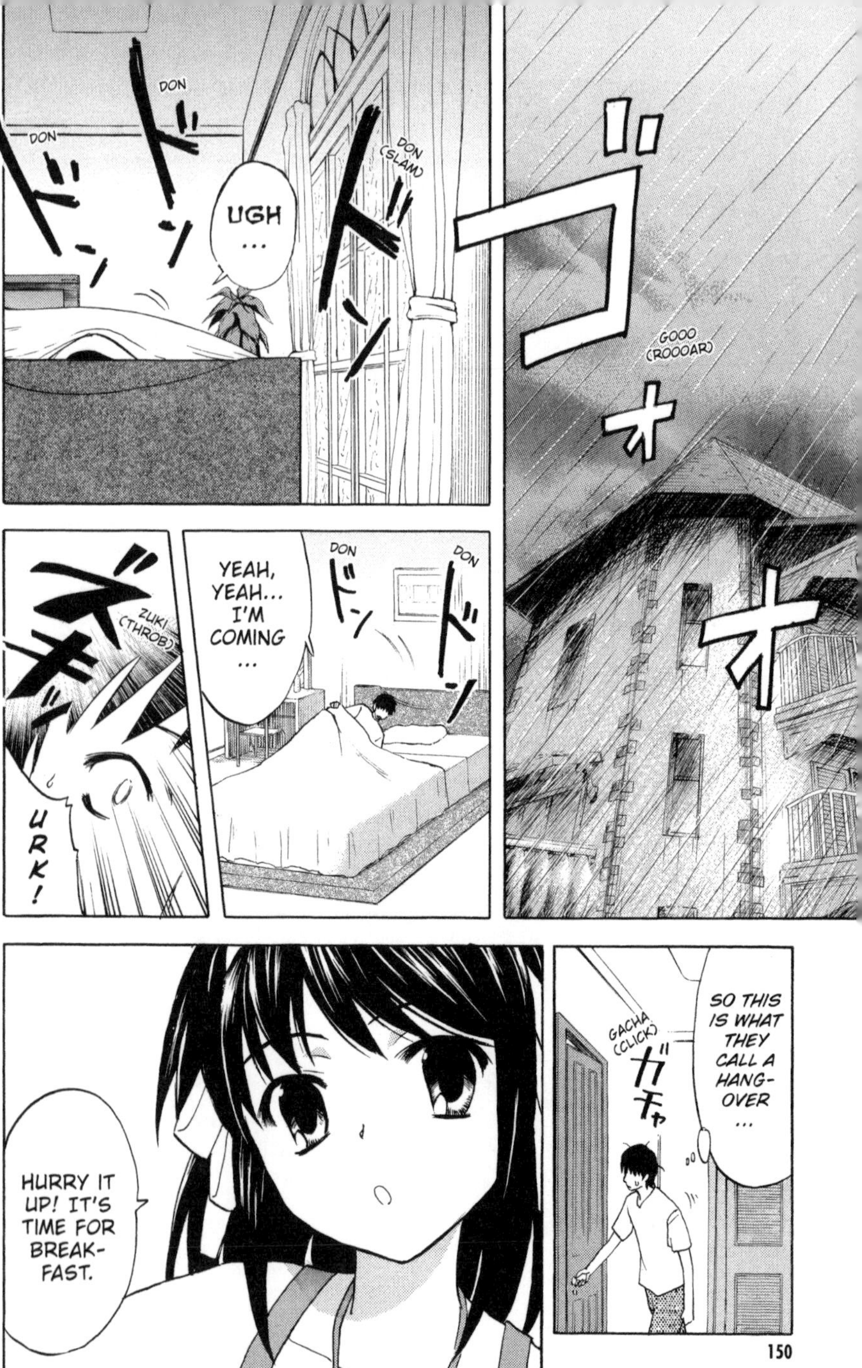
GOOO (ROOOAR)
DON (SLAM)
DON
UGH ...
DON
DON
DON
YEAH, YEAH... I'M COMING ...
ZUKI (THROB)
URK!
SO THIS IS WHAT THEY CALL A HANG-OVER ...
GACHA (CLICK)
HURRY IT UP! IT'S TIME FOR BREAK-FAST.

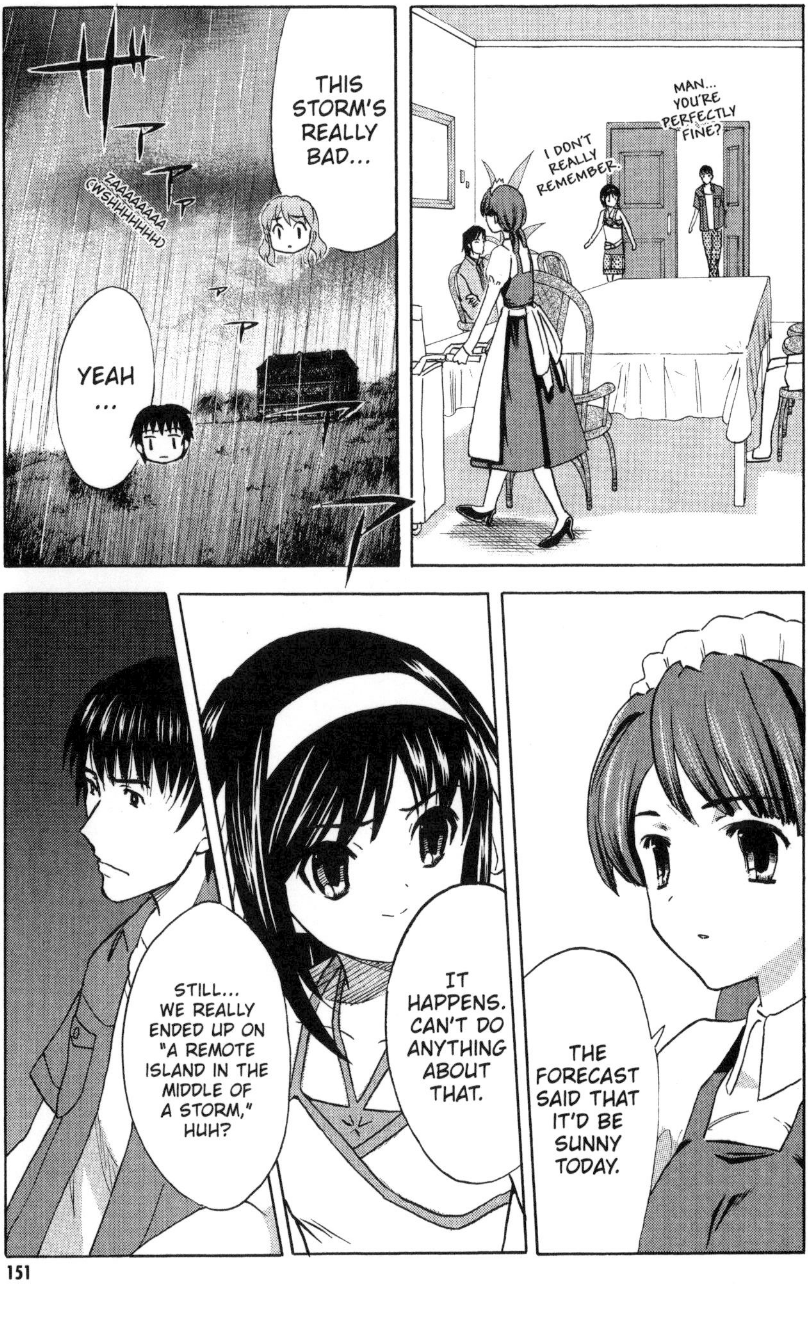
MAN... YOU'RE PERFECTLY FINE?
I DON'T REALLY REMEMBER.
THIS STORM'S REALLY BAD...
ZAAAAAAAA (WSHHHHHHH)
YEAH ...
THE FORECAST SAID THAT IT'D BE SUNNY TODAY.
IT HAPPENS. CAN'T DO ANYTHING ABOUT THAT.
STILL... WE REALLY ENDED UP ON "A REMOTE ISLAND IN THE MIDDLE OF A STORM," HUH?

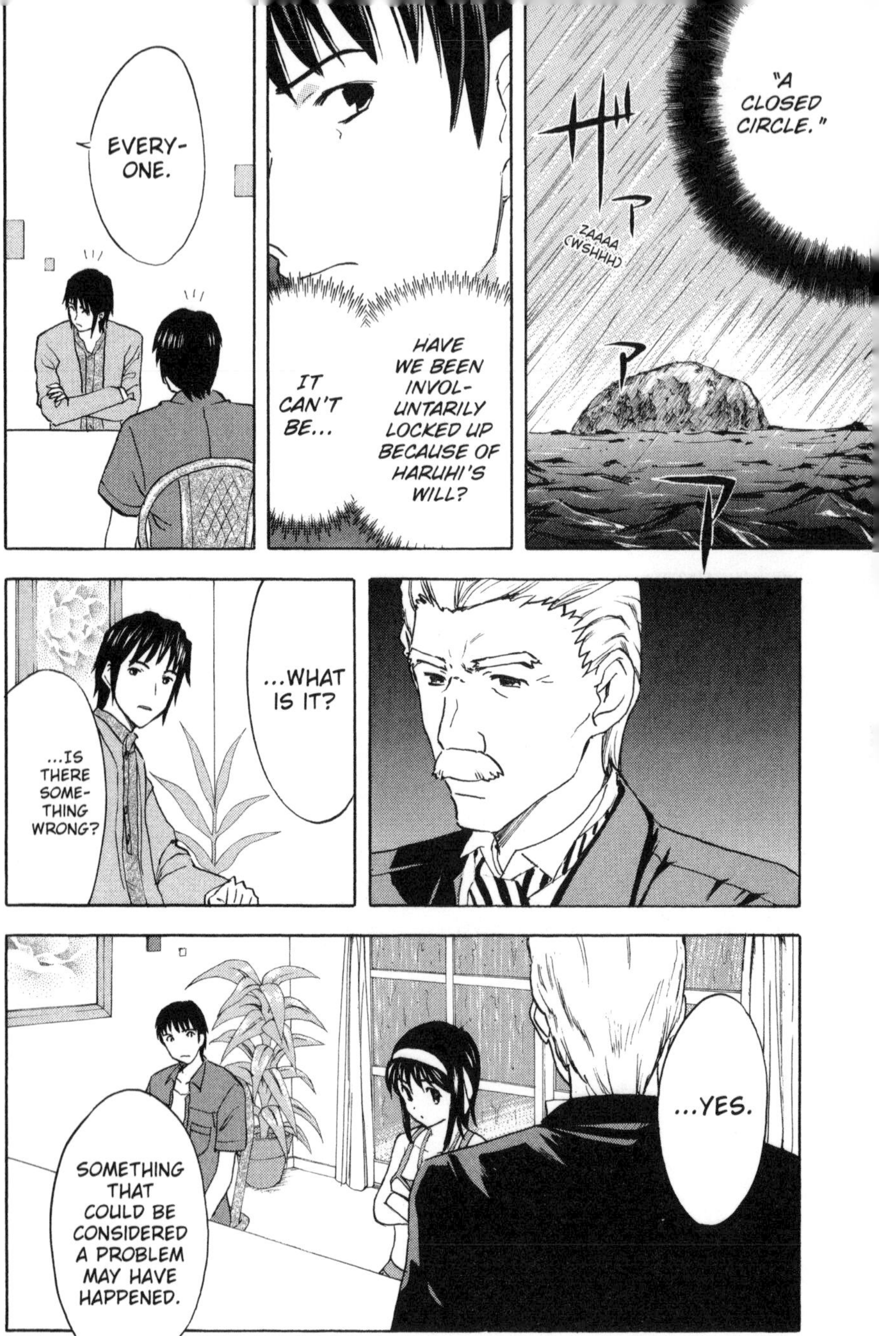
"A CLOSED CIRCLE."
ZAAAA (WSHHH)
HAVE WE BEEN INVOLUNTARILY LOCKED UP BECAUSE OF HARUHI'S WILL?
IT CAN'T BE...
EVERYONE.
...WHAT IS IT?
...IS THERE SOMETHING WRONG?
...YES.
SOMETHING THAT COULD BE CONSIDERED A PROBLEM MAY HAVE HAPPENED.

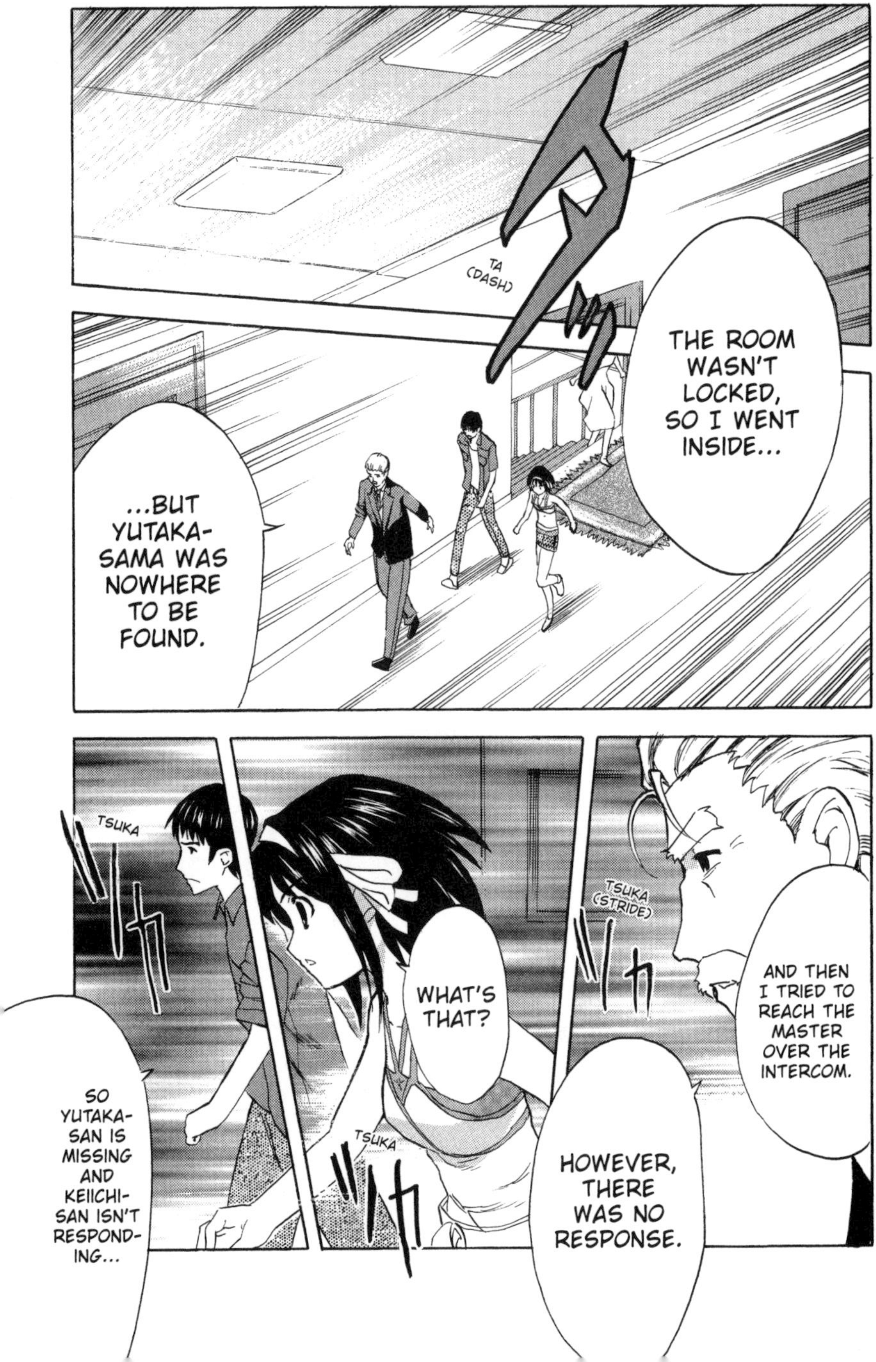
TA (DASH)
THE ROOM WASN'T LOCKED, SO I WENT INSIDE...
...BUT YUTAKA-SAMA WAS NOWHERE TO BE FOUND.
TSUKA (STRIDE)
AND THEN I TRIED TO REACH THE MASTER OVER THE INTERCOM.
HOWEVER, THERE WAS NO RESPONSE.
WHAT'S THAT?
TSUKA
TSUKA
SO YUTAKA-SAN IS MISSING AND KEIICHI-SAN ISN'T RESPOND-ING...

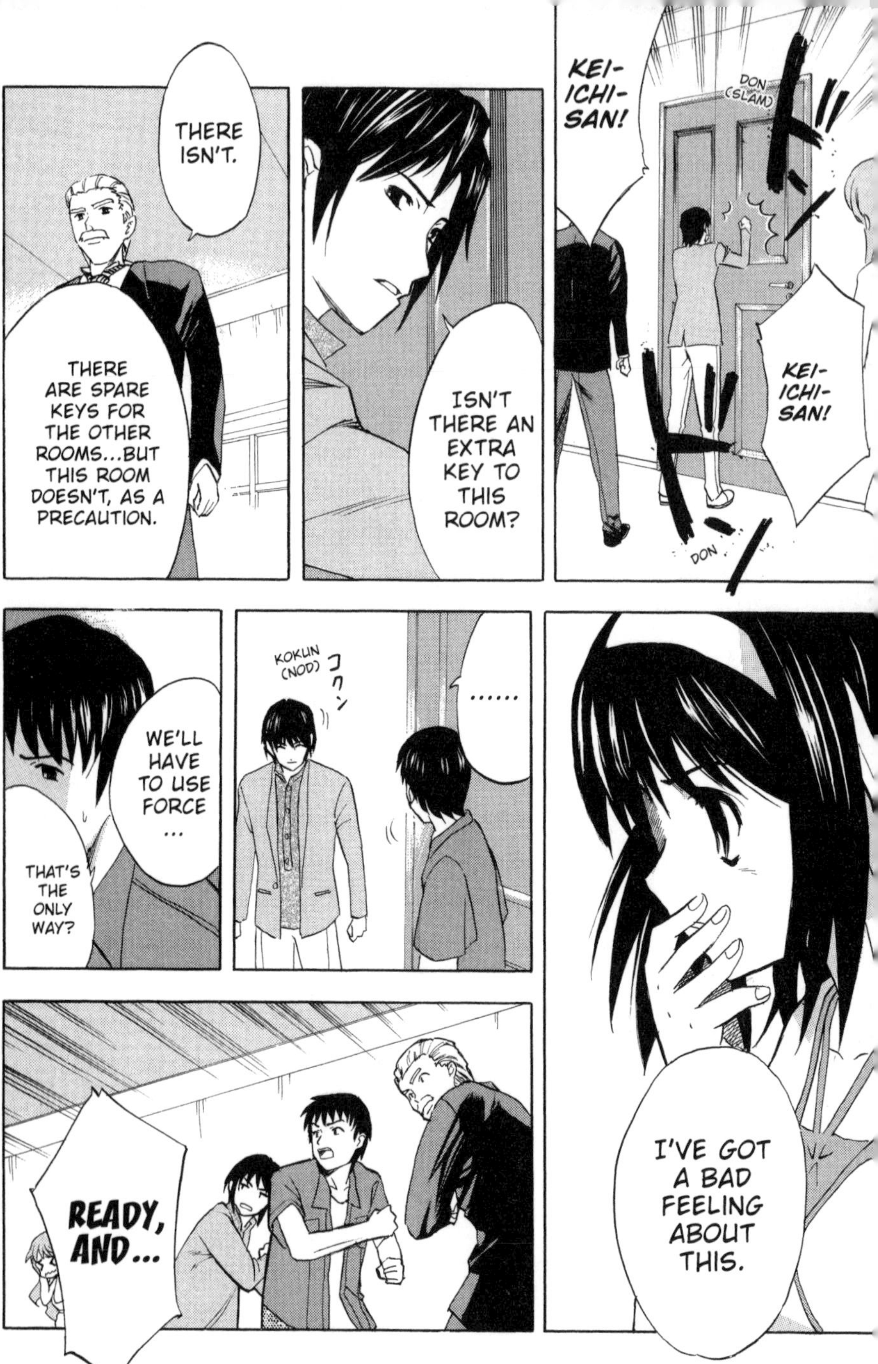
KEI-ICHI-SAN!
DON (SLAM)
KEI-ICHI-SAN!
DON
ISN'T THERE AN EXTRA KEY TO THIS ROOM?
THERE ISN'T.
THERE ARE SPARE KEYS FOR THE OTHER ROOMS...BUT THIS ROOM DOESN'T, AS A PRECAUTION.
I'VE GOT A BAD FEELING ABOUT THIS.
......
KOKUN (NOD)
コクン
WE'LL HAVE TO USE FORCE...
THAT'S THE ONLY WAY?
READY, AND...

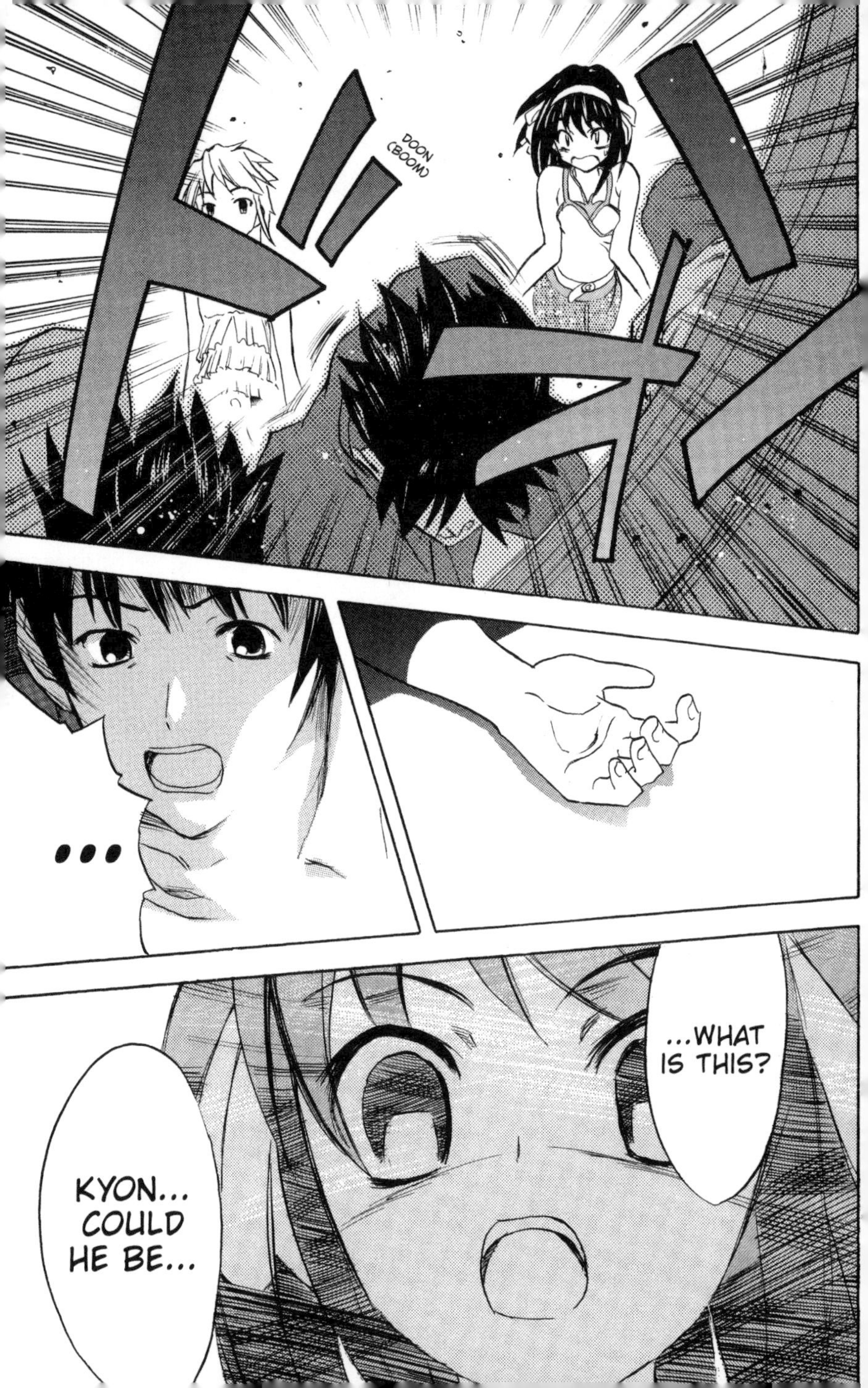
DOON (BOOM)
...
...WHAT IS THIS?
KYON... COULD HE BE...

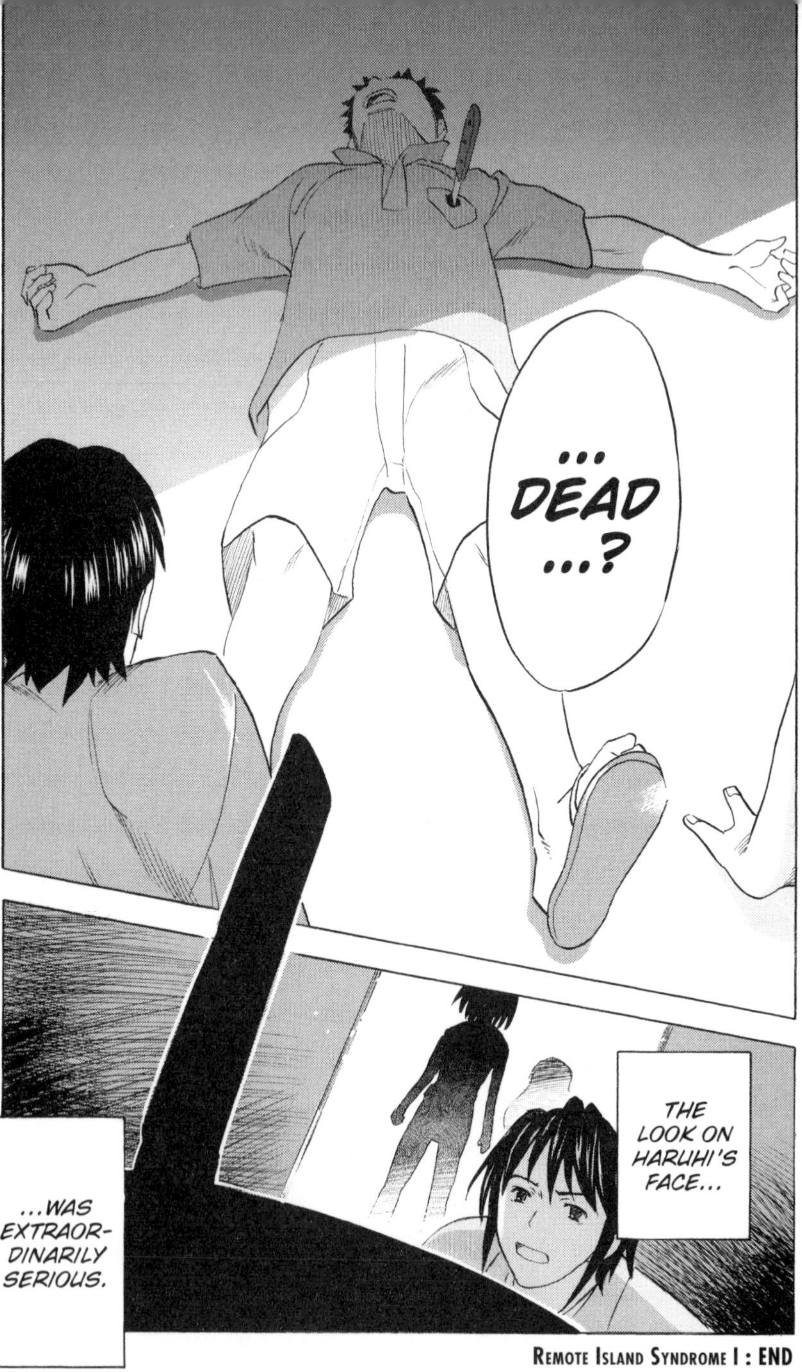
...DEAD ...?
THE LOOK ON HARUHI'S FACE...
...WAS EXTRAORDINARILY SERIOUS.

Remote Island Syndrome I : END

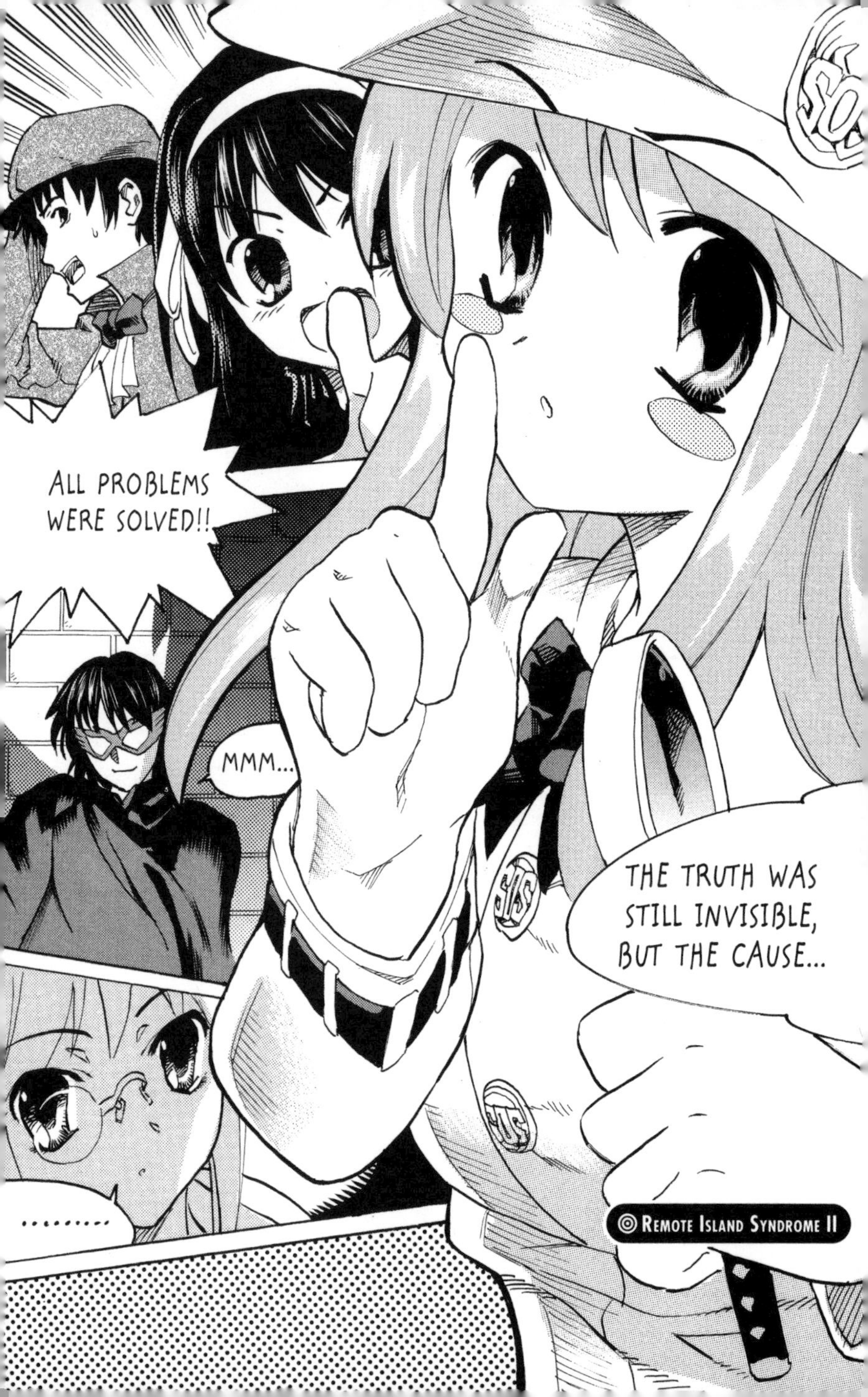
THE TRUTH WAS STILL INVISIBLE, BUT THE CAUSE...
◎ REMOTE ISLAND SYNDROME II
ALL PROBLEMS WERE SOLVED!!
MMM...
....

COULD
HE BE...

...
DEAD?

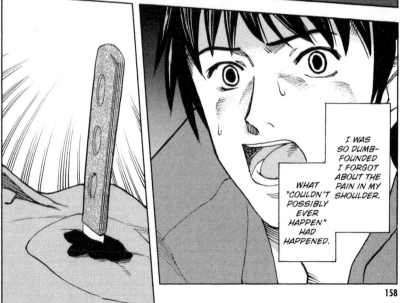

I WAS
SO DUMB-
FOUNDED
I FORGOT
ABOUT THE
PAIN IN MY
SHOULDER.

WHAT
"COULDN'T
POSSIBLY
EVER
HAPPEN"
HAD
HAPPENED.

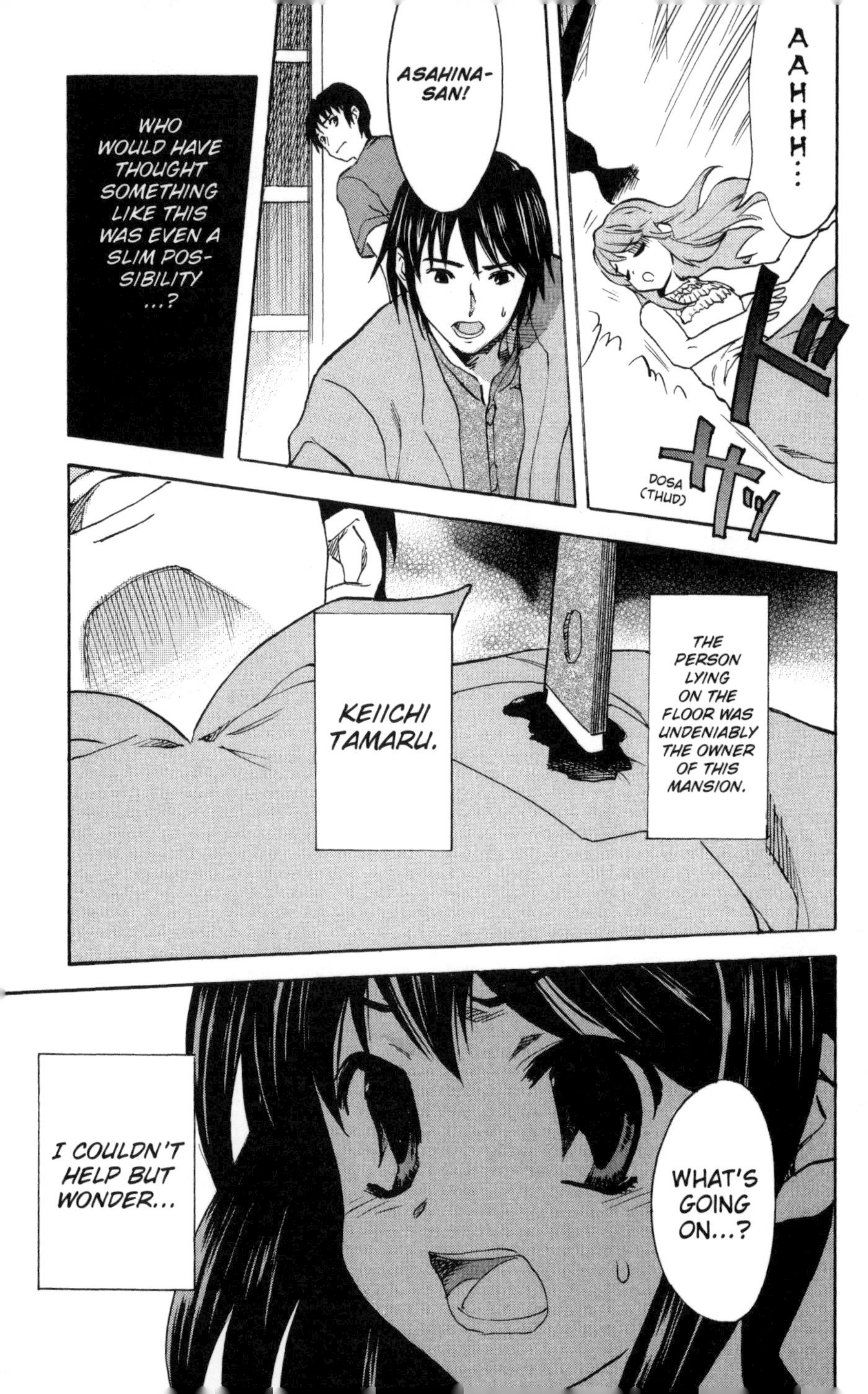
AAHHH...
DOSA (THUD)
ASAHINA-SAN!
WHO WOULD HAVE THOUGHT SOMETHING LIKE THIS WAS EVEN A SLIM POSSIBILITY ...?
THE PERSON LYING ON THE FLOOR WAS UNDENIABLY THE OWNER OF THIS MANSION.
KEIICHI TAMARU.
WHAT'S GOING ON...?
I COULDN'T HELP BUT WONDER...

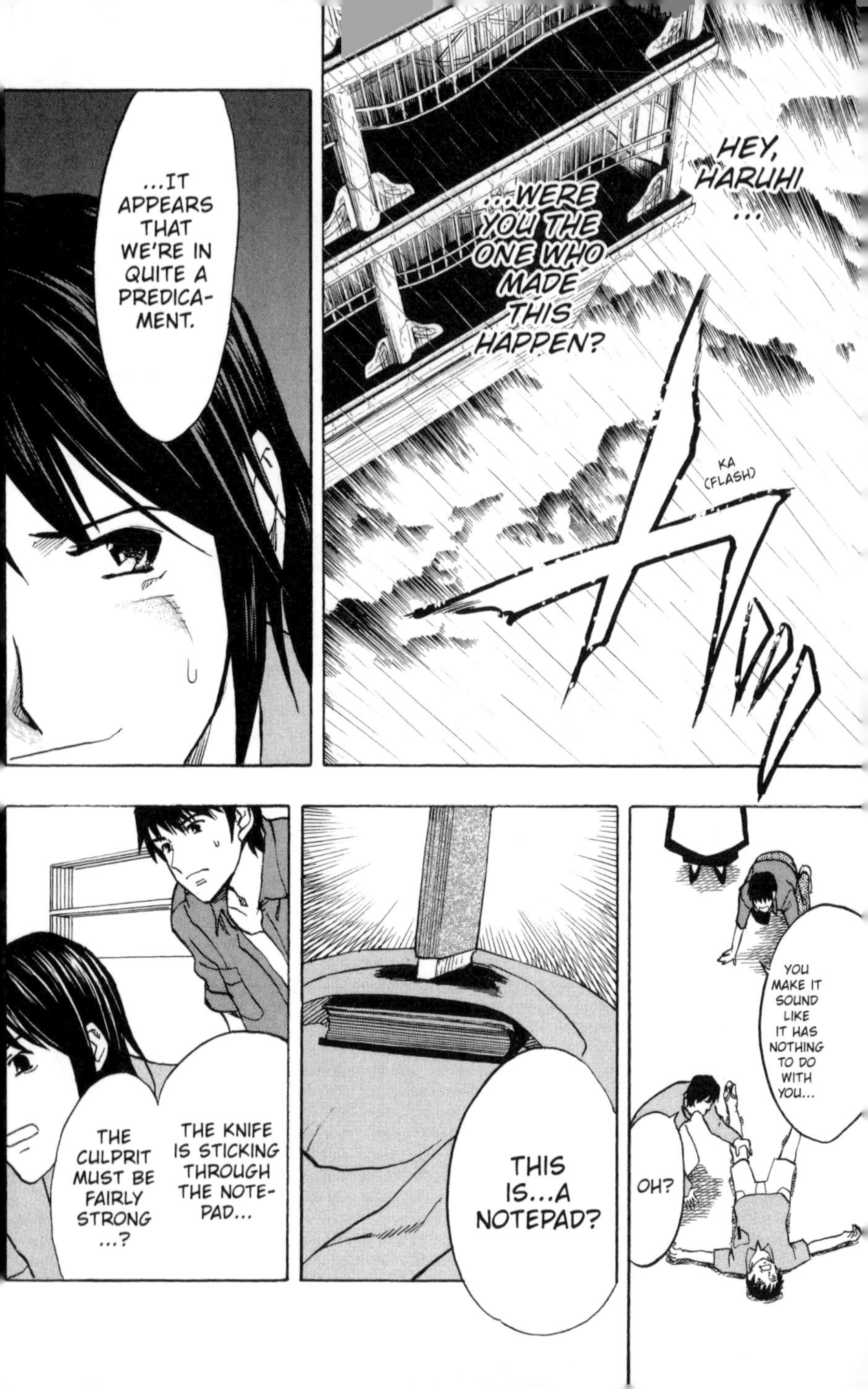
HEY, HARUHI ...
...WERE YOU THE ONE WHO MADE THIS HAPPEN?
KA (FLASH)
...IT APPEARS THAT WE'RE IN QUITE A PREDICA-MENT.
YOU MAKE IT SOUND LIKE IT HAS NOTHING TO DO WITH YOU...
OH?
THIS IS...A NOTEPAD?
THE KNIFE IS STICKING THROUGH THE NOTE-PAD...
THE CULPRIT MUST BE FAIRLY STRONG ...?

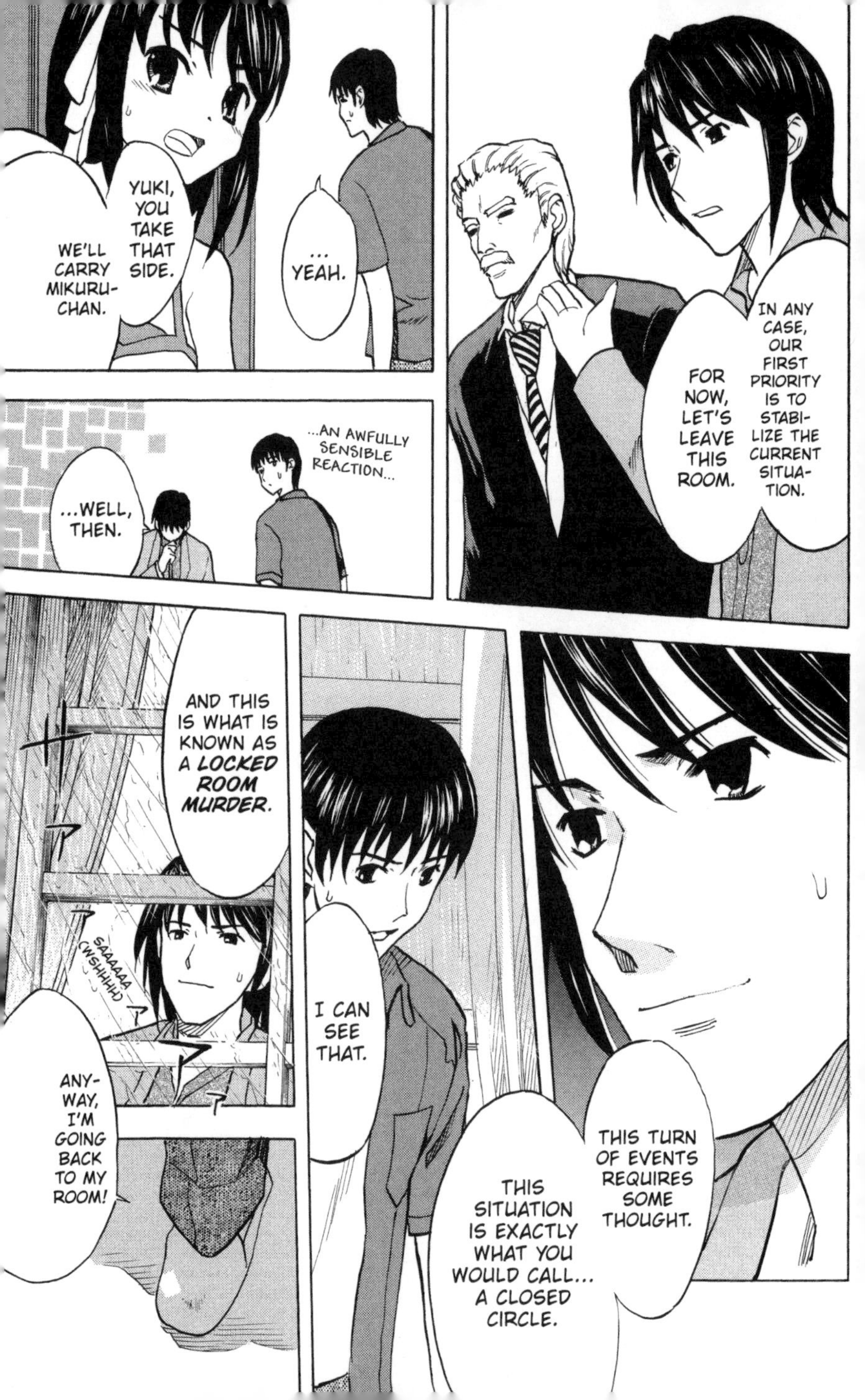
IN ANY CASE, OUR FIRST PRIORITY IS TO STABILIZE THE CURRENT SITUATION.
FOR NOW, LET'S LEAVE THIS ROOM.
... YEAH.
YUKI, YOU TAKE THAT SIDE.
WE'LL CARRY MIKURU-CHAN.
...AN AWFULLY SENSIBLE REACTION...
...WELL, THEN.
THIS TURN OF EVENTS REQUIRES SOME THOUGHT.
THIS SITUATION IS EXACTLY WHAT YOU WOULD CALL... A CLOSED CIRCLE.
I CAN SEE THAT.
AND THIS IS WHAT IS KNOWN AS A *LOCKED ROOM MURDER*.
SAAAAAA (WSHHHH)
ANY-WAY, I'M GOING BACK TO MY ROOM!

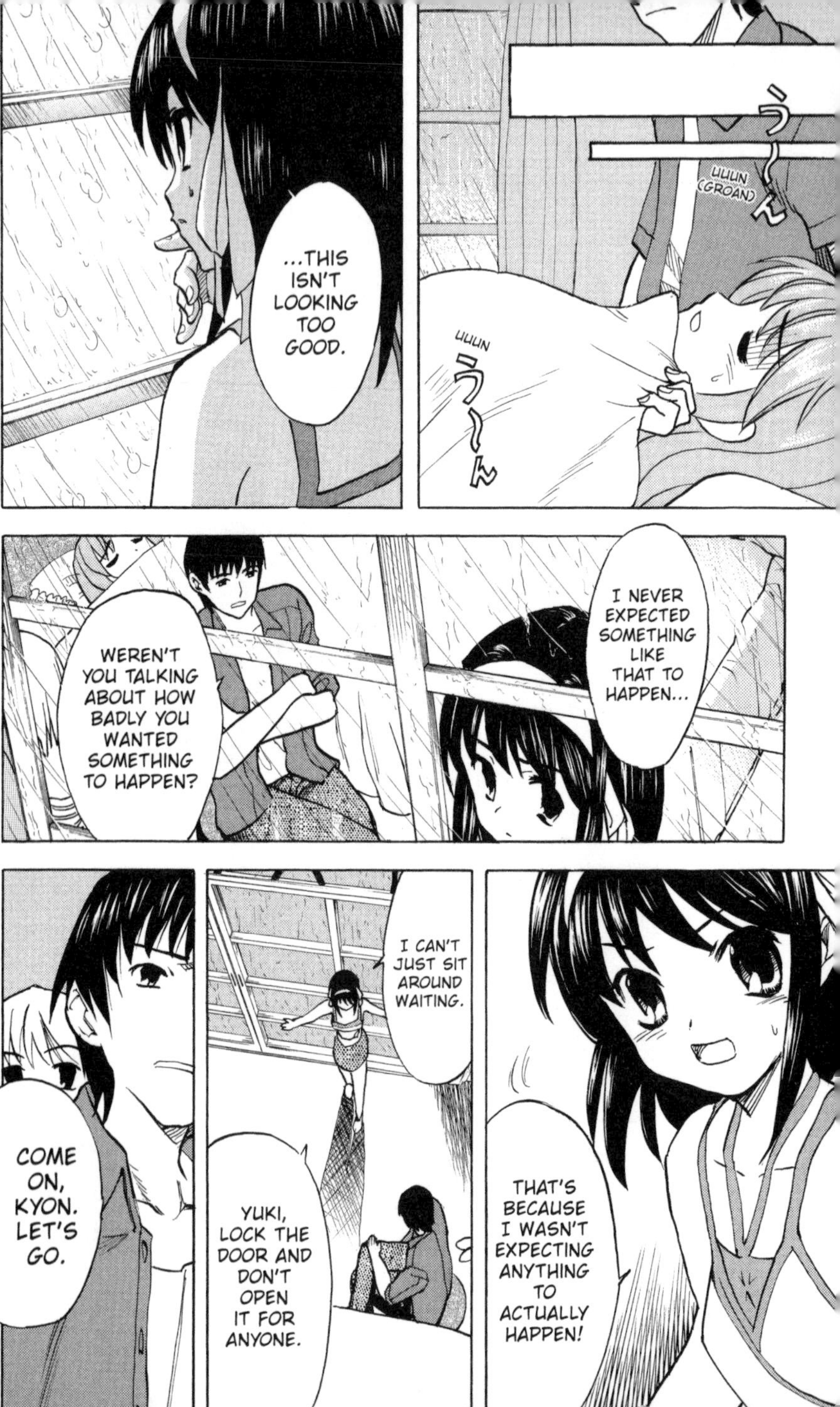
うーん
UUUN (GROAN)
UUUN
うーん
...THIS ISN'T LOOKING TOO GOOD.
I NEVER EXPECTED SOMETHING LIKE THAT TO HAPPEN...
WEREN'T YOU TALKING ABOUT HOW BADLY YOU WANTED SOMETHING TO HAPPEN?
THAT'S BECAUSE I WASN'T EXPECTING ANYTHING TO ACTUALLY HAPPEN!
I CAN'T JUST SIT AROUND WAITING.
YUKI, LOCK THE DOOR AND DON'T OPEN IT FOR ANYONE.
COME ON, KYON. LET'S GO.

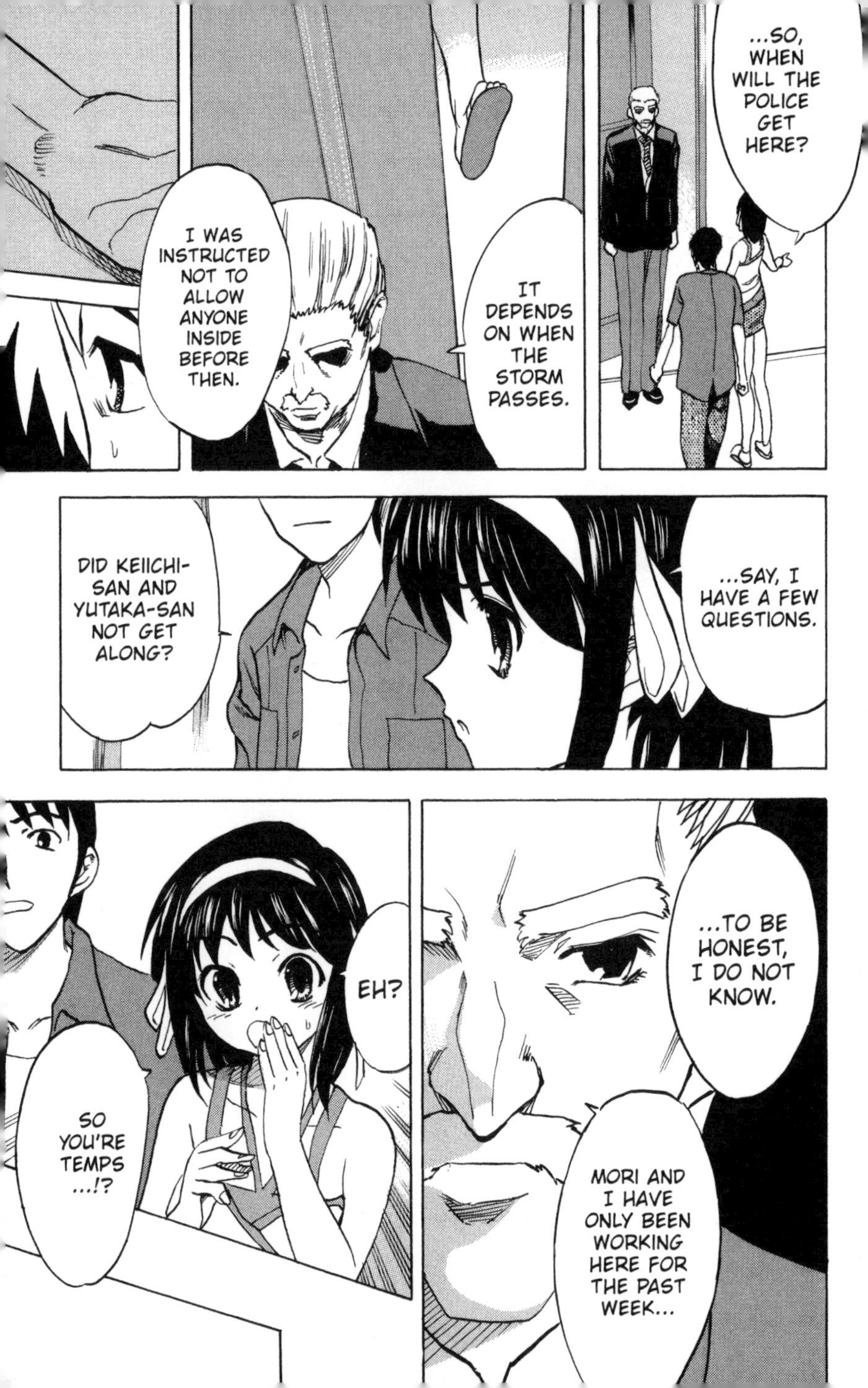
...SO, WHEN WILL THE POLICE GET HERE?
IT DEPENDS ON WHEN THE STORM PASSES.
I WAS INSTRUCTED NOT TO ALLOW ANYONE INSIDE BEFORE THEN.
...SAY, I HAVE A FEW QUESTIONS.
DID KEIICHI-SAN AND YUTAKA-SAN NOT GET ALONG?
...TO BE HONEST, I DO NOT KNOW.
MORI AND I HAVE ONLY BEEN WORKING HERE FOR THE PAST WEEK...
EH?
SO YOU'RE TEMPS ...!?

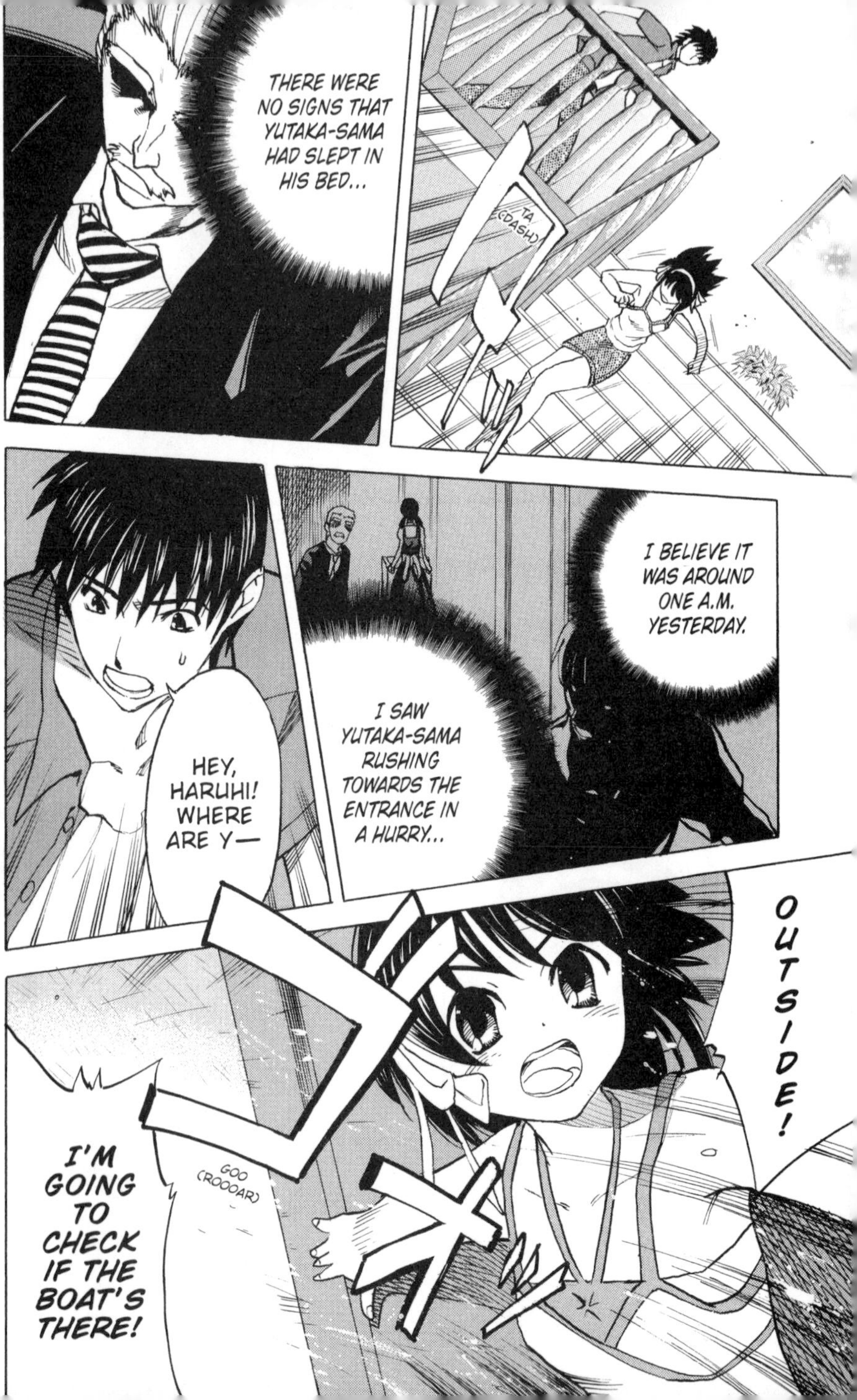
TA (DASH)
THERE WERE NO SIGNS THAT YUTAKA-SAMA HAD SLEPT IN HIS BED...
I BELIEVE IT WAS AROUND ONE A.M. YESTERDAY.
I SAW YUTAKA-SAMA RUSHING TOWARDS THE ENTRANCE IN A HURRY...
HEY, HARUHI! WHERE ARE Y—
OUTSIDE!
GOO (ROOOAR)
I'M GOING TO CHECK IF THE BOAT'S THERE!

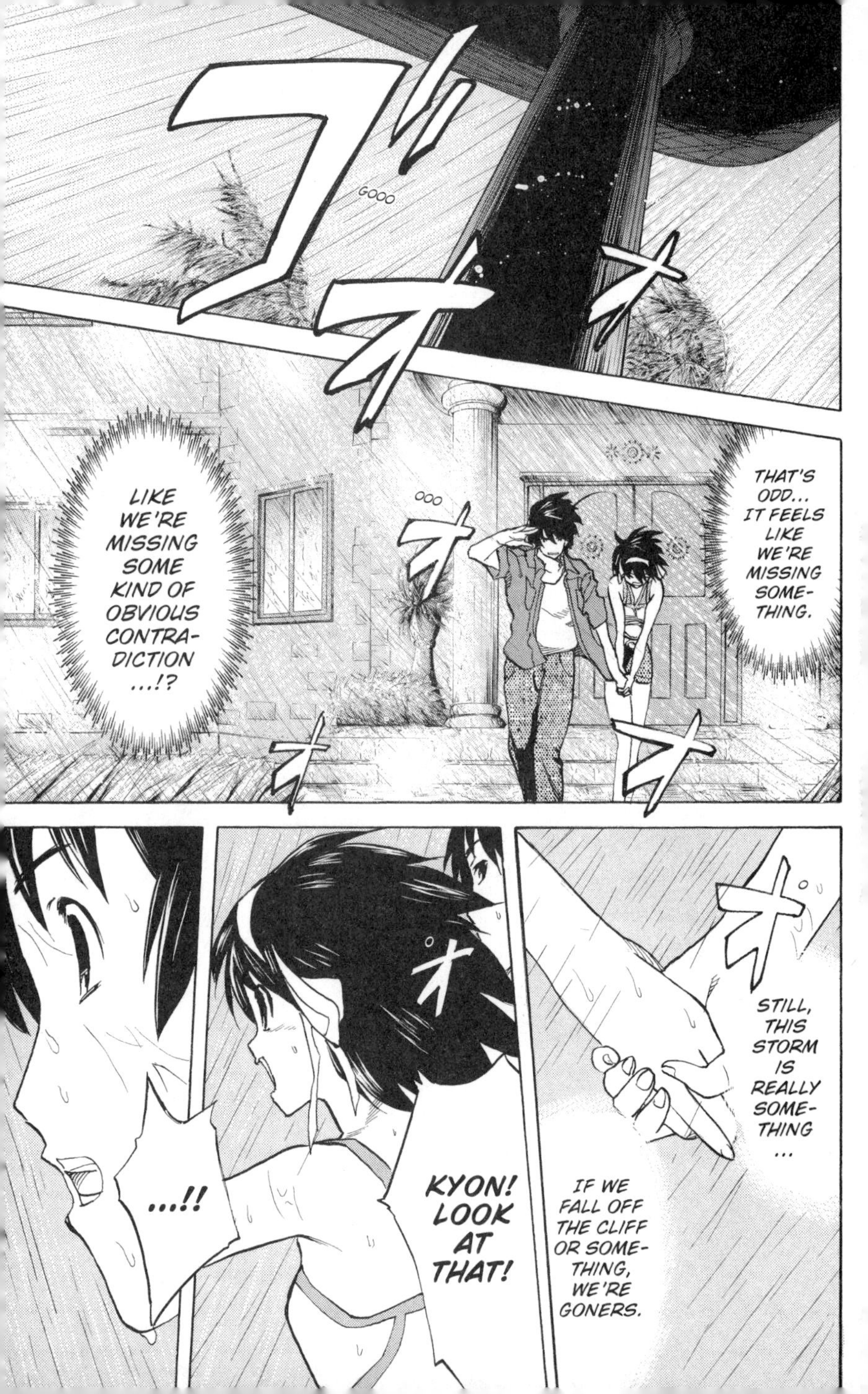
GOOO
THAT'S ODD... IT FEELS LIKE WE'RE MISSING SOME-THING.
OOO
LIKE WE'RE MISSING SOME KIND OF OBVIOUS CONTRA-DICTION ...!?
STILL, THIS STORM IS REALLY SOME-THING ...
IF WE FALL OFF THE CLIFF OR SOME-THING, WE'RE GONERS.
KYON! LOOK AT THAT!
...!!

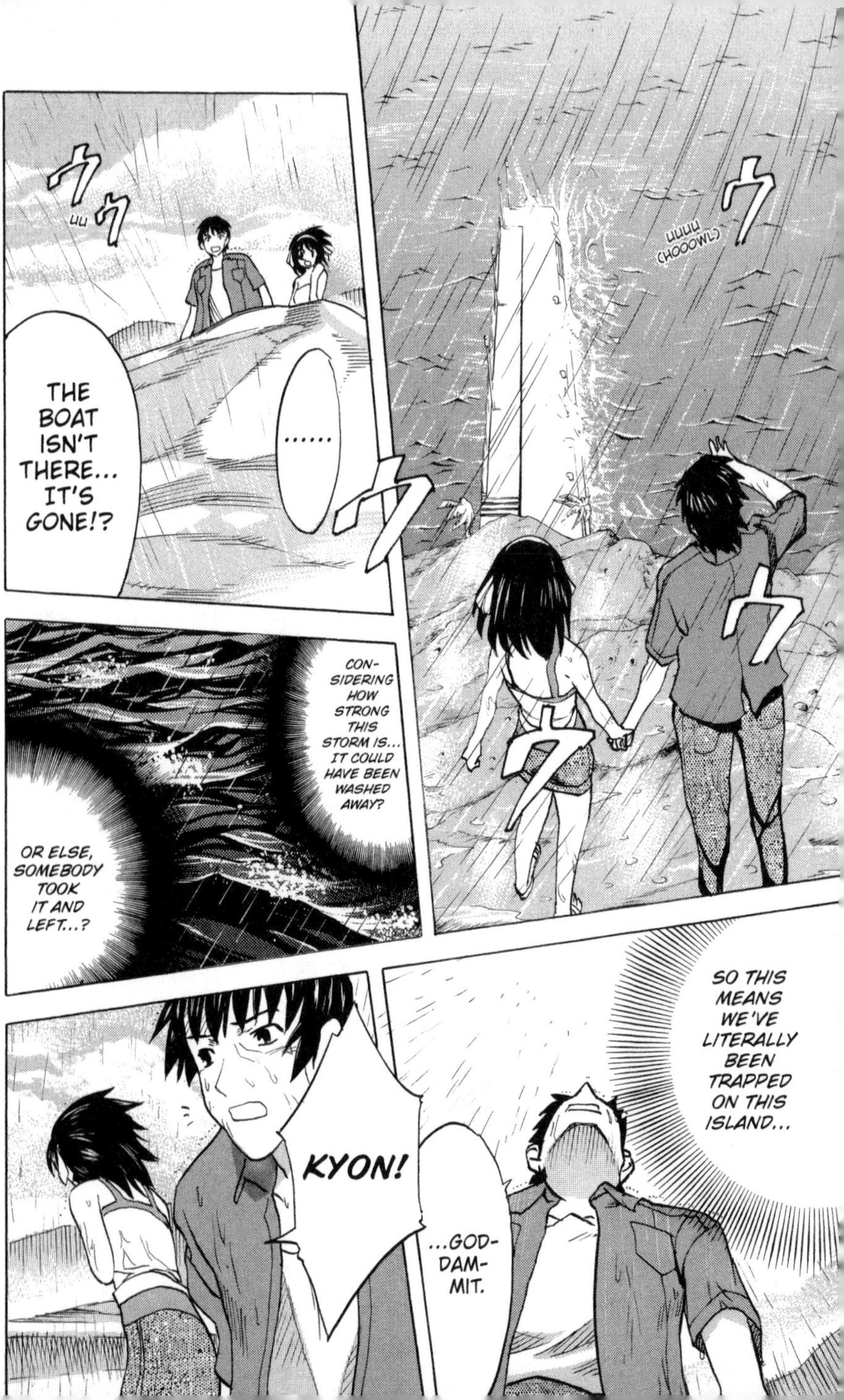
ウ
UUUU (HOOOWL)
ウ
ウ
ウ
ウ
ウ
UU
......
THE BOAT ISN'T THERE... IT'S GONE!?
CONSIDERING HOW STRONG THIS STORM IS... IT COULD HAVE BEEN WASHED AWAY?
OR ELSE, SOMEBODY TOOK IT AND LEFT...?
SO THIS MEANS WE'VE LITERALLY BEEN TRAPPED ON THIS ISLAND...
...GOD-DAM-MIT.
KYON!

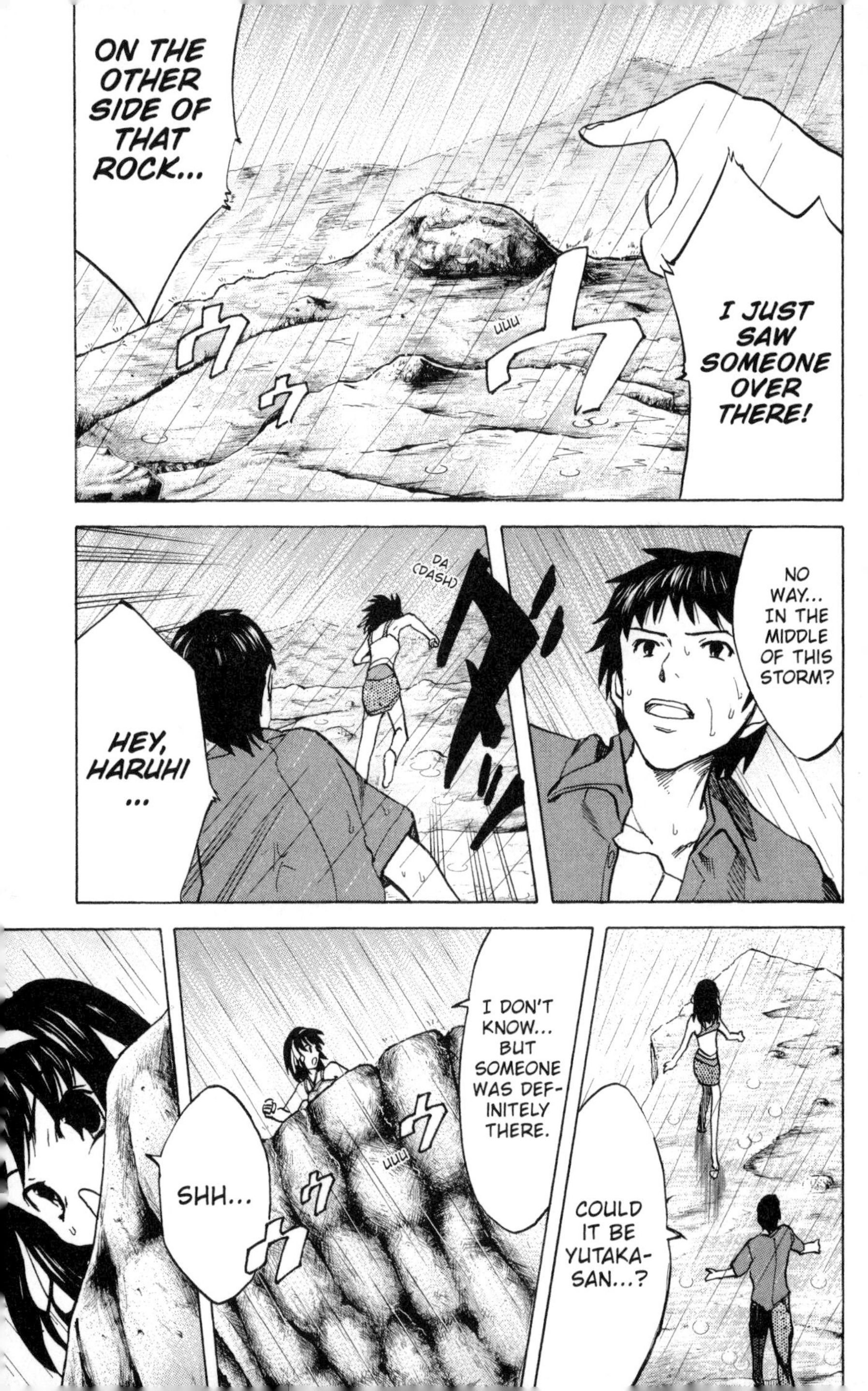
I JUST SAW SOMEONE OVER THERE!
ON THE OTHER SIDE OF THAT ROCK...
UUU
NO WAY... IN THE MIDDLE OF THIS STORM?
DA (DASH)
HEY, HARUHI ...
COULD IT BE YUTAKA-SAN...?
I DON'T KNOW... BUT SOMEONE WAS DEF-INITELY THERE.
UUU
SHH...

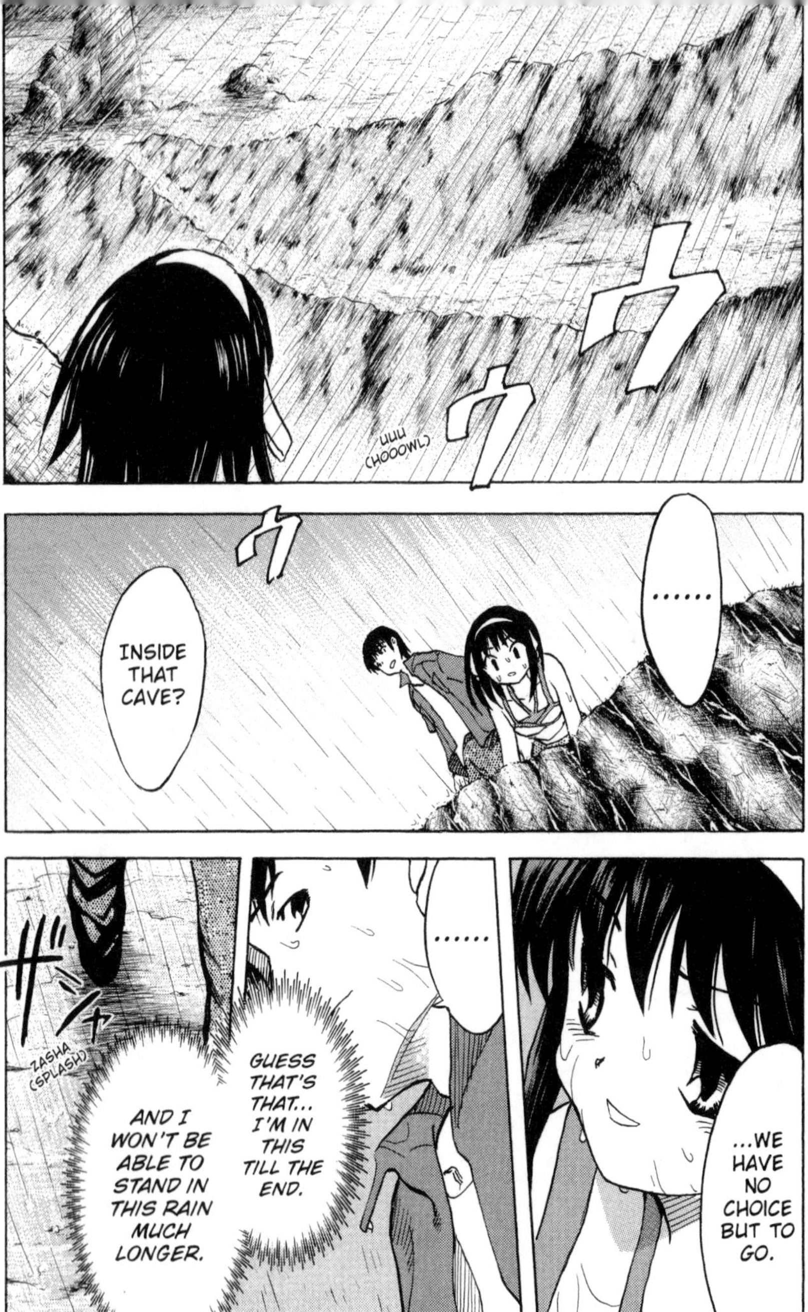
ウ
ウ
UUU (HOOOWL)
......
ウ
INSIDE THAT CAVE?
...WE HAVE NO CHOICE BUT TO GO.
......
GUESS THAT'S THAT... I'M IN THIS TILL THE END.
AND I WON'T BE ABLE TO STAND IN THIS RAIN MUCH LONGER.
ザシャ
ZASHA (SPLASH)

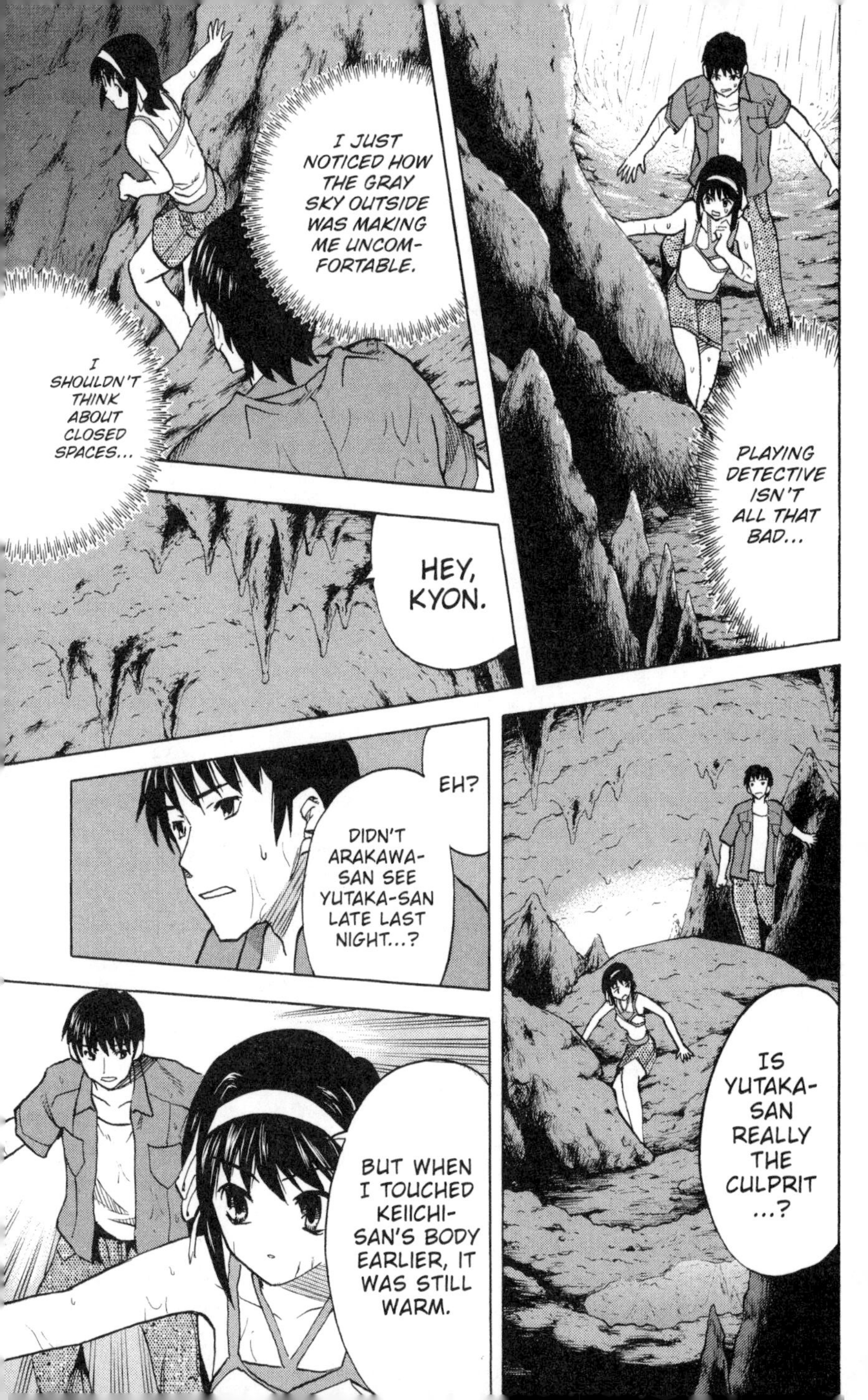
PLAYING DETECTIVE ISN'T ALL THAT BAD...
I JUST NOTICED HOW THE GRAY SKY OUTSIDE WAS MAKING ME UNCOMFORTABLE.
I SHOULDN'T THINK ABOUT CLOSED SPACES...
HEY, KYON.
IS YUTAKA-SAN REALLY THE CULPRIT ...?
EH?
DIDN'T ARAKAWA-SAN SEE YUTAKA-SAN LATE LAST NIGHT...?
BUT WHEN I TOUCHED KEIICHI-SAN'S BODY EARLIER, IT WAS STILL WARM.

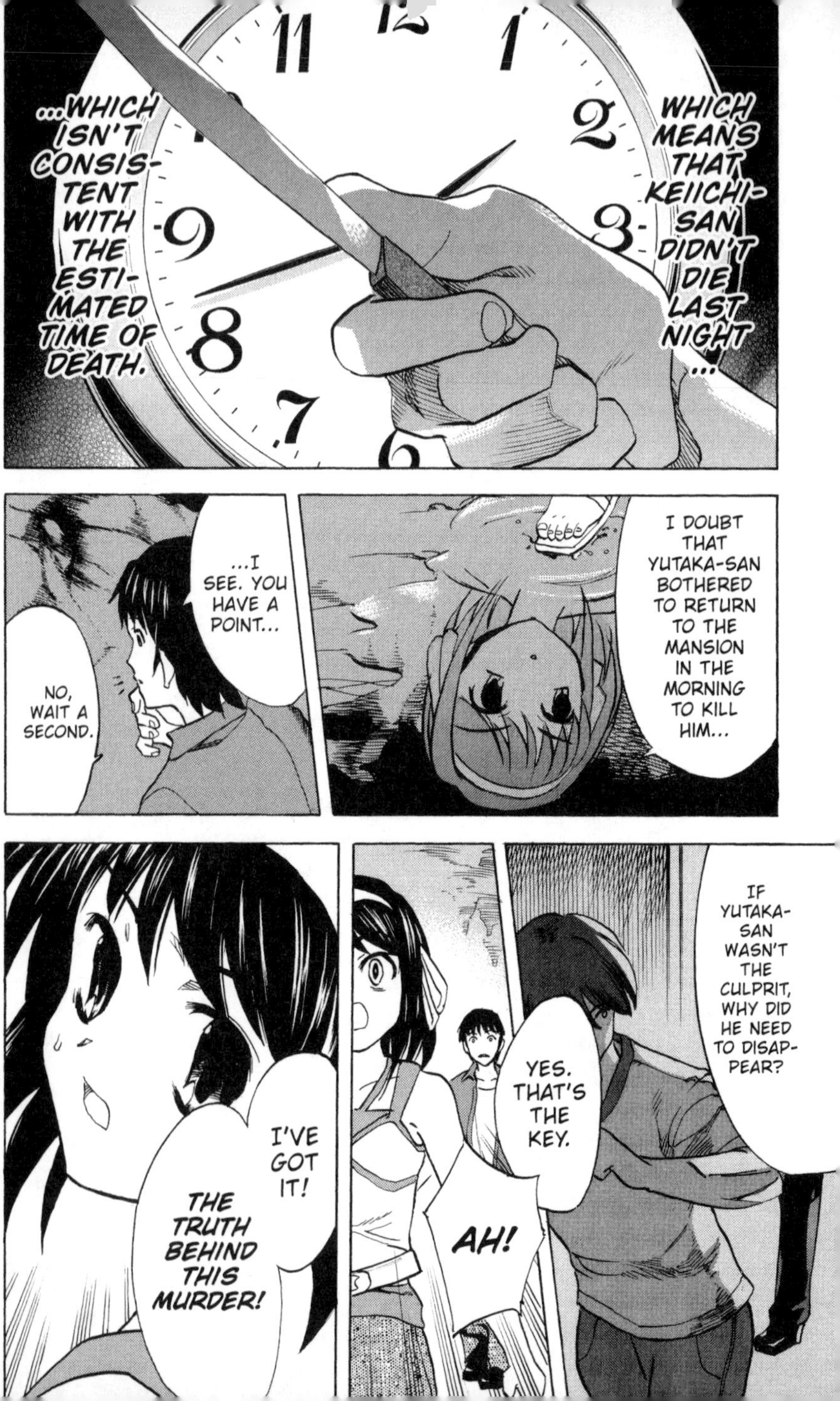
WHICH MEANS THAT KEIICHI-SAN DIDN'T DIE LAST NIGHT...
...WHICH ISN'T CONSISTENT WITH THE ESTIMATED TIME OF DEATH.
I DOUBT THAT YUTAKA-SAN BOTHERED TO RETURN TO THE MANSION IN THE MORNING TO KILL HIM...
...I SEE. YOU HAVE A POINT...
NO, WAIT A SECOND.
IF YUTAKA-SAN WASN'T THE CULPRIT, WHY DID HE NEED TO DISAPPEAR?
YES. THAT'S THE KEY.
AH!
I'VE GOT IT!
THE TRUTH BEHIND THIS MURDER!

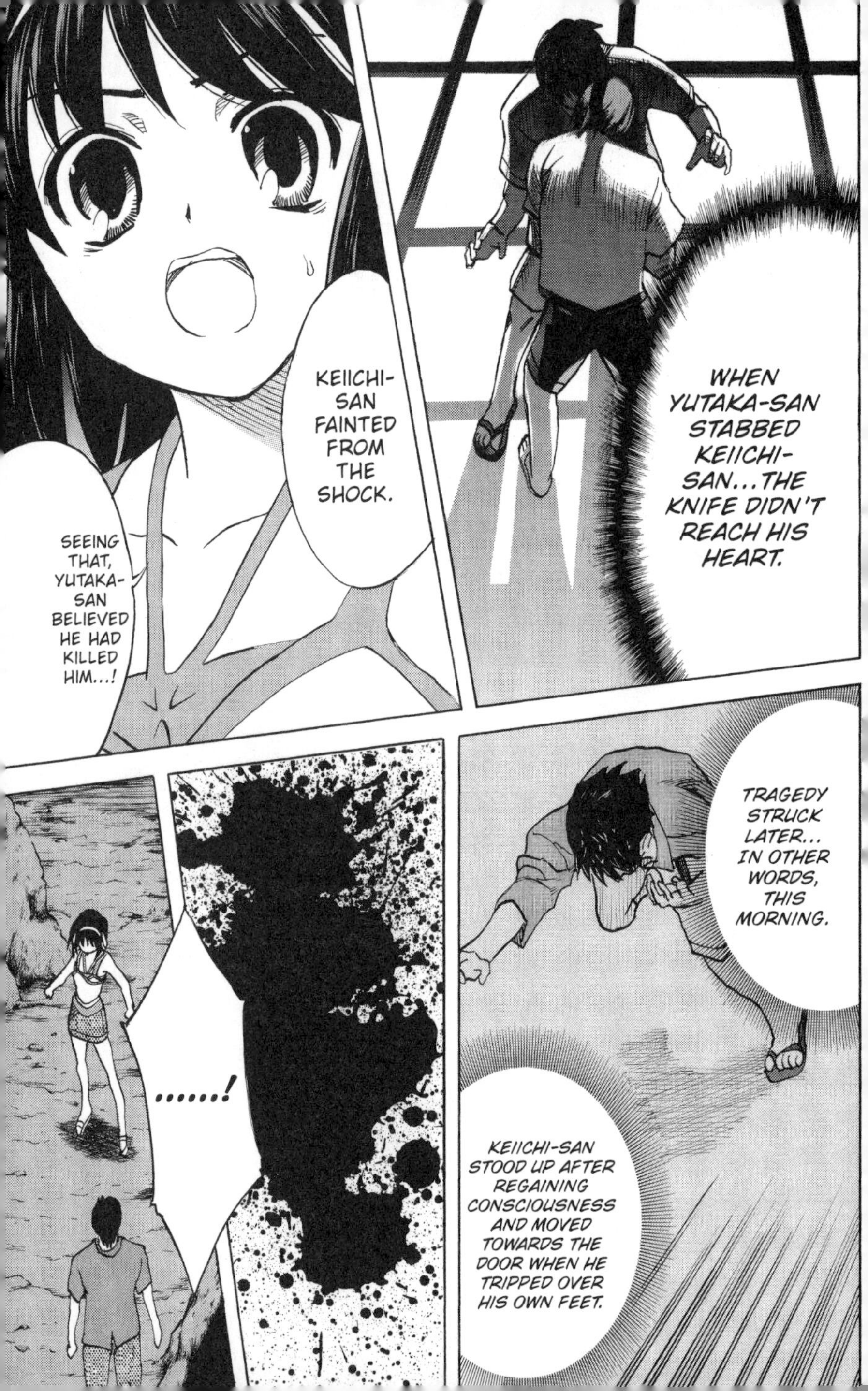
WHEN YUTAKA-SAN STABBED KEIICHI-SAN...THE KNIFE DIDN'T REACH HIS HEART.
KEIICHI-SAN FAINTED FROM THE SHOCK.
SEEING THAT, YUTAKA-SAN BELIEVED HE HAD KILLED HIM...!
TRAGEDY STRUCK LATER... IN OTHER WORDS, THIS MORNING.
KEIICHI-SAN STOOD UP AFTER REGAINING CONSCIOUSNESS AND MOVED TOWARDS THE DOOR WHEN HE TRIPPED OVER HIS OWN FEET.
......!

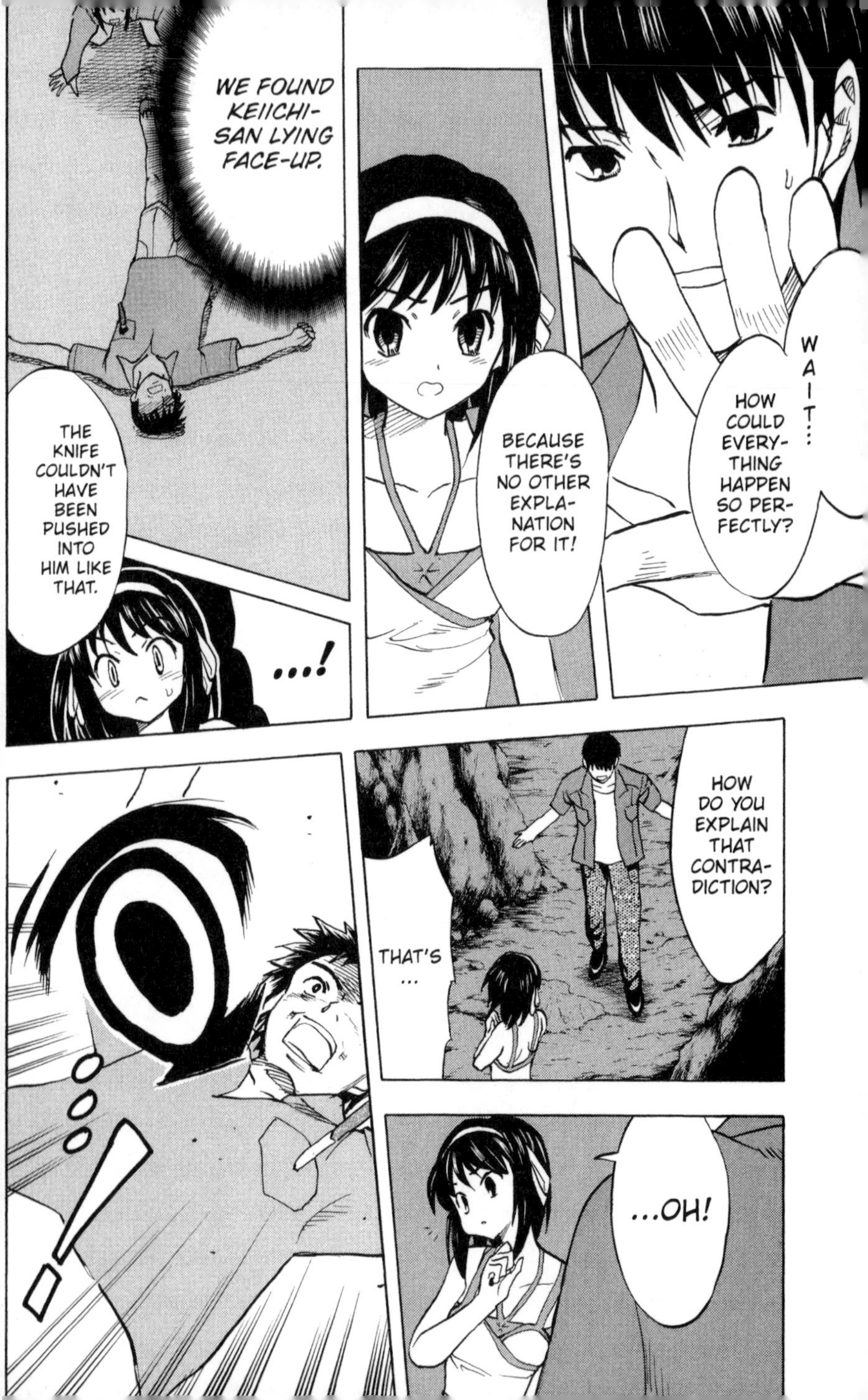
WAIT...
HOW COULD EVERYTHING HAPPEN SO PERFECTLY?
BECAUSE THERE'S NO OTHER EXPLANATION FOR IT!
WE FOUND KEIICHI-SAN LYING FACE-UP.
THE KNIFE COULDN'T HAVE BEEN PUSHED INTO HIM LIKE THAT.
...!
HOW DO YOU EXPLAIN THAT CONTRADICTION?
THAT'S ...
...OH!

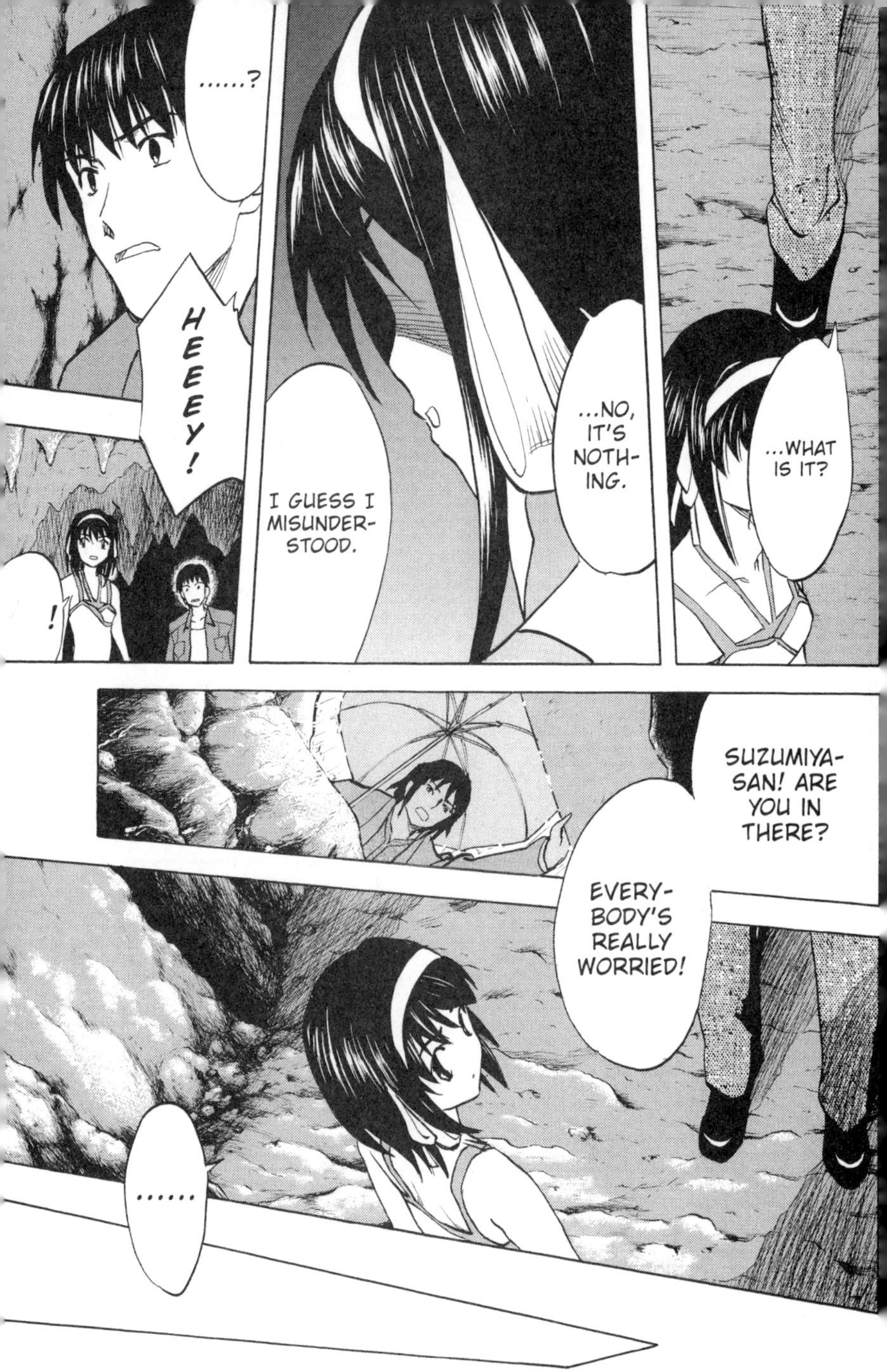
...WHAT IS IT?
...NO, IT'S NOTHING.
I GUESS I MISUNDERSTOOD.
......?
HEEEY!
!
SUZUMIYA-SAN! ARE YOU IN THERE?
EVERYBODY'S REALLY WORRIED!
......

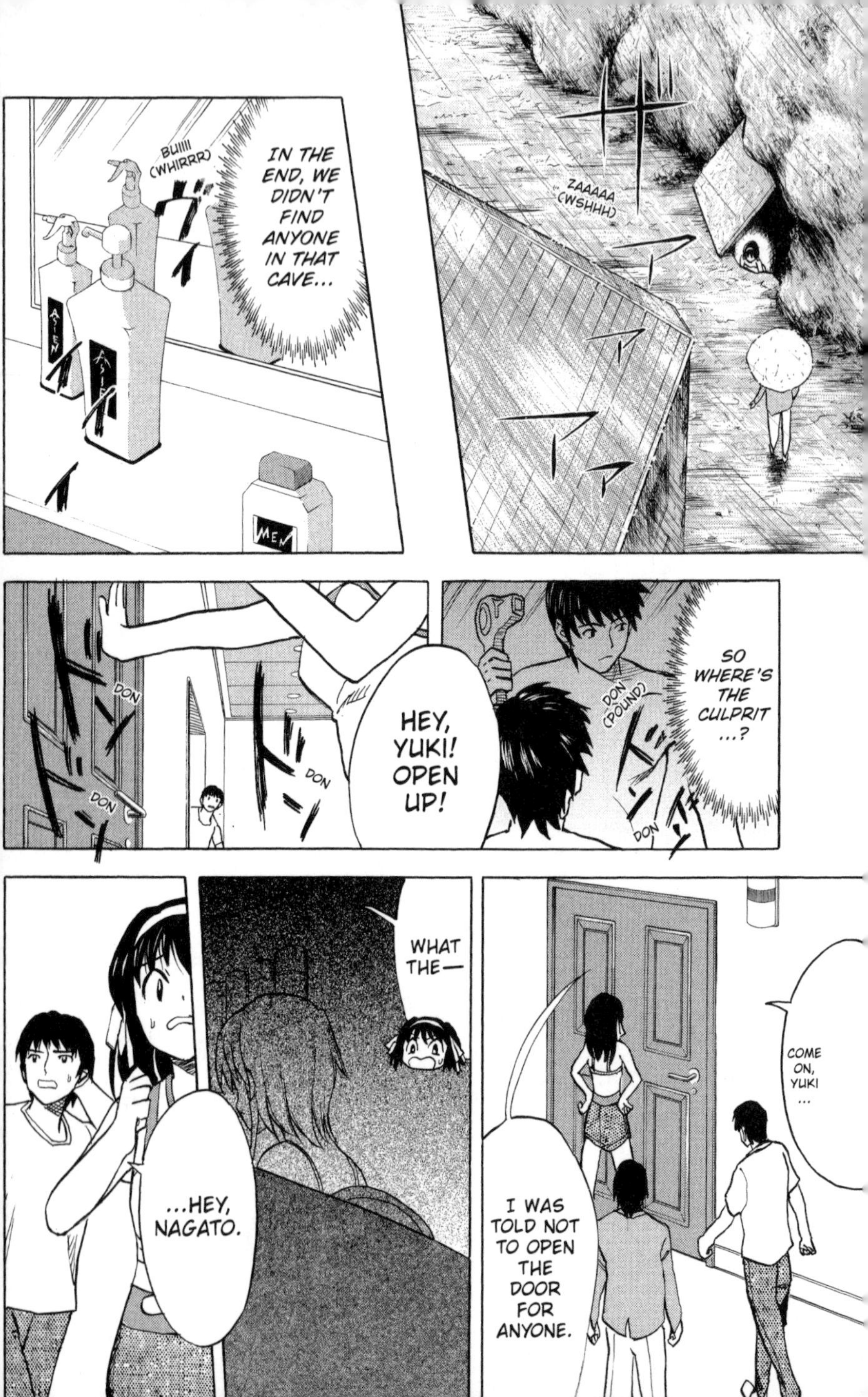
ZAAAAA (WSHHH)
BUIIII (WHIRRR)
IN THE END, WE DIDN'T FIND ANYONE IN THAT CAVE...
SO WHERE'S THE CULPRIT ...?
DON (POUND)
DON
HEY, YUKI! OPEN UP!
DON
DON
DON
COME ON, YUKI ...
I WAS TOLD NOT TO OPEN THE DOOR FOR ANYONE.
WHAT THE—
...HEY, NAGATO.

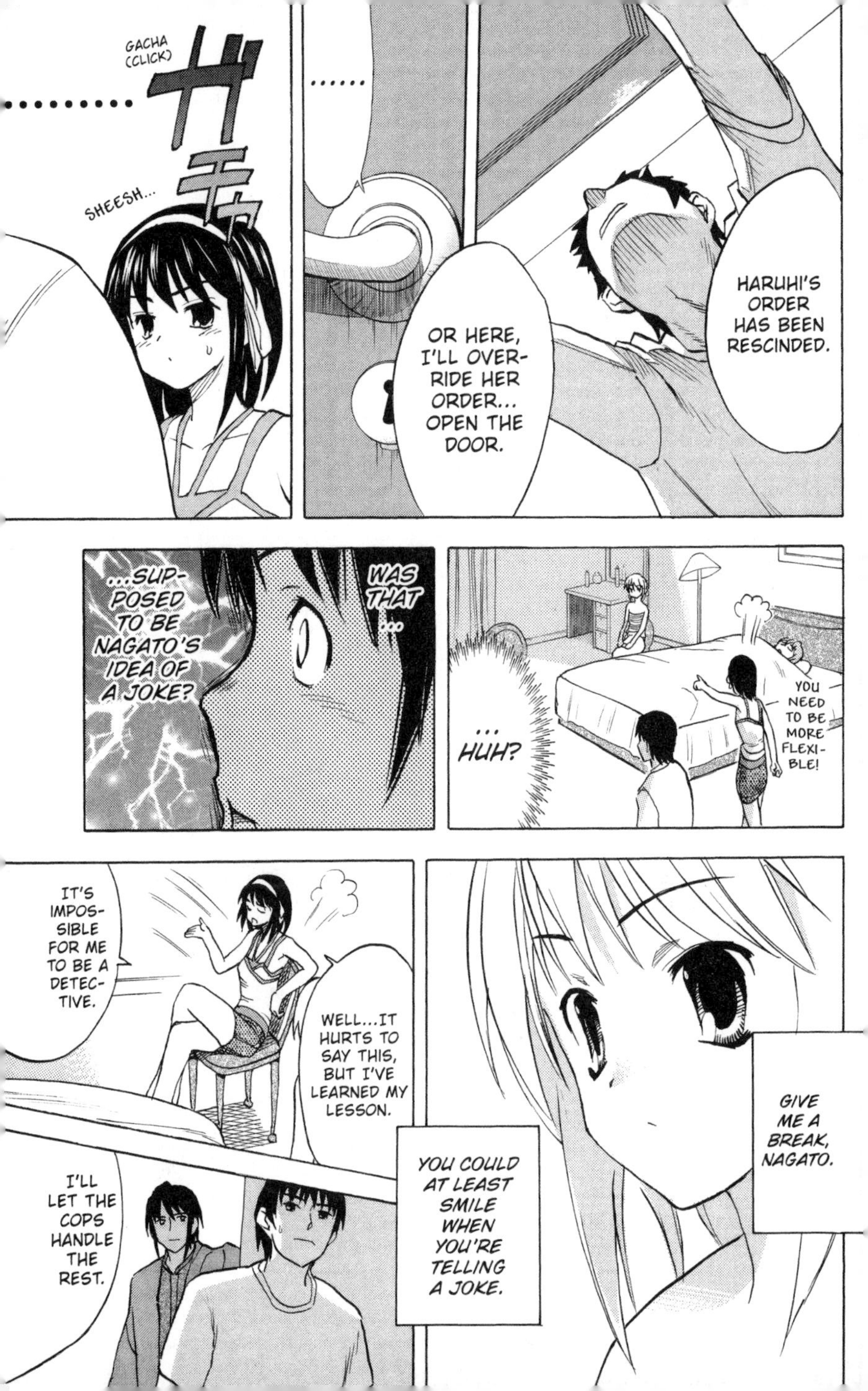
HARUHI'S ORDER HAS BEEN RESCINDED.
OR HERE, I'LL OVER-RIDE HER ORDER... OPEN THE DOOR.
......
GACHA (CLICK)
....
SHEESH...
YOU NEED TO BE MORE FLEXI-BLE!
...HUH?
WAS THAT...
...SUP-POSED TO BE NAGATO'S IDEA OF A JOKE?
GIVE ME A BREAK, NAGATO.
YOU COULD AT LEAST SMILE WHEN YOU'RE TELLING A JOKE.
IT'S IMPOS-SIBLE FOR ME TO BE A DETEC-TIVE.
WELL...IT HURTS TO SAY THIS, BUT I'VE LEARNED MY LESSON.
I'LL LET THE COPS HANDLE THE REST.

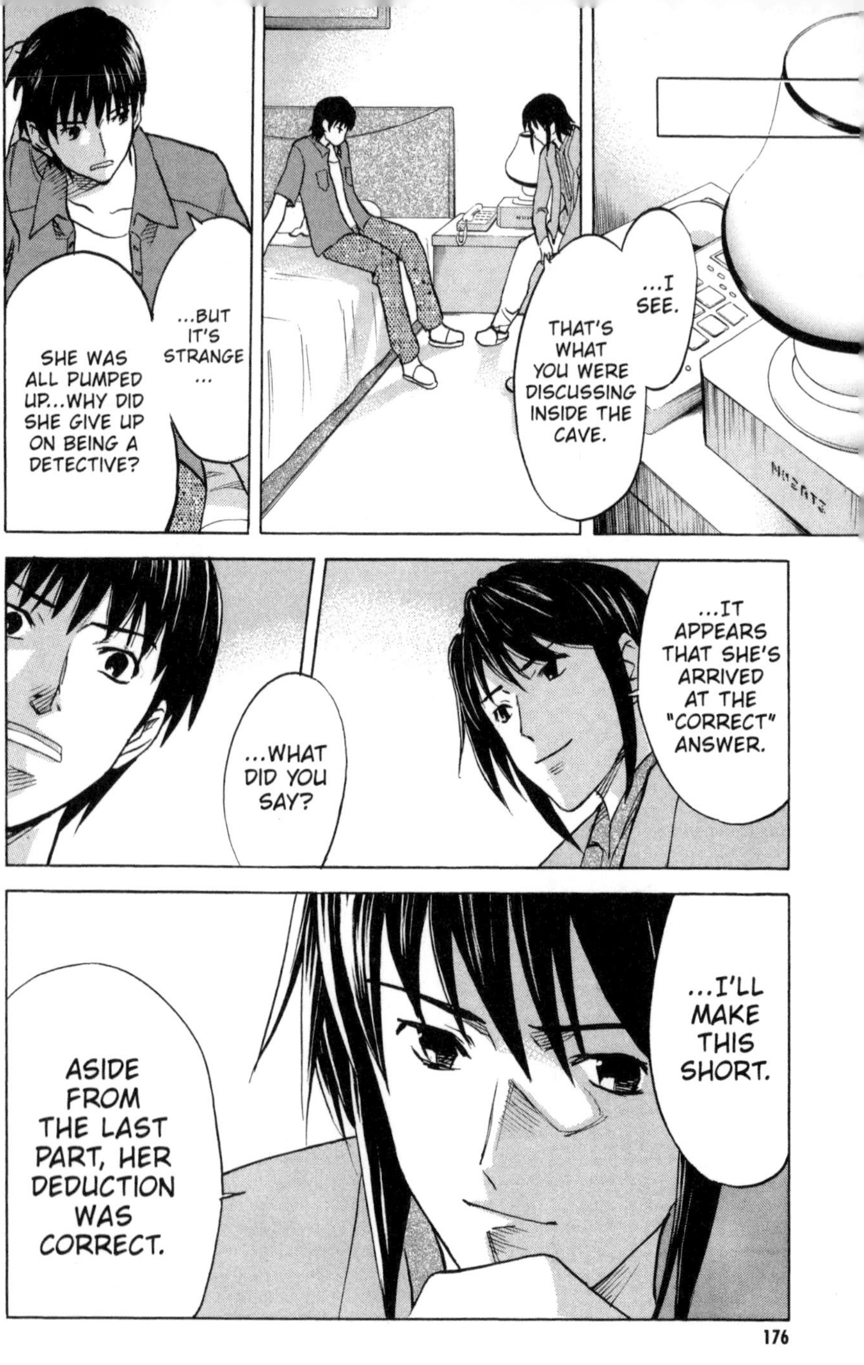
...I SEE.
THAT'S WHAT YOU WERE DISCUSSING INSIDE THE CAVE.
...BUT IT'S STRANGE ...
SHE WAS ALL PUMPED UP...WHY DID SHE GIVE UP ON BEING A DETECTIVE?
...IT APPEARS THAT SHE'S ARRIVED AT THE "CORRECT" ANSWER.
...WHAT DID YOU SAY?
...I'LL MAKE THIS SHORT.
ASIDE FROM THE LAST PART, HER DEDUCTION WAS CORRECT.

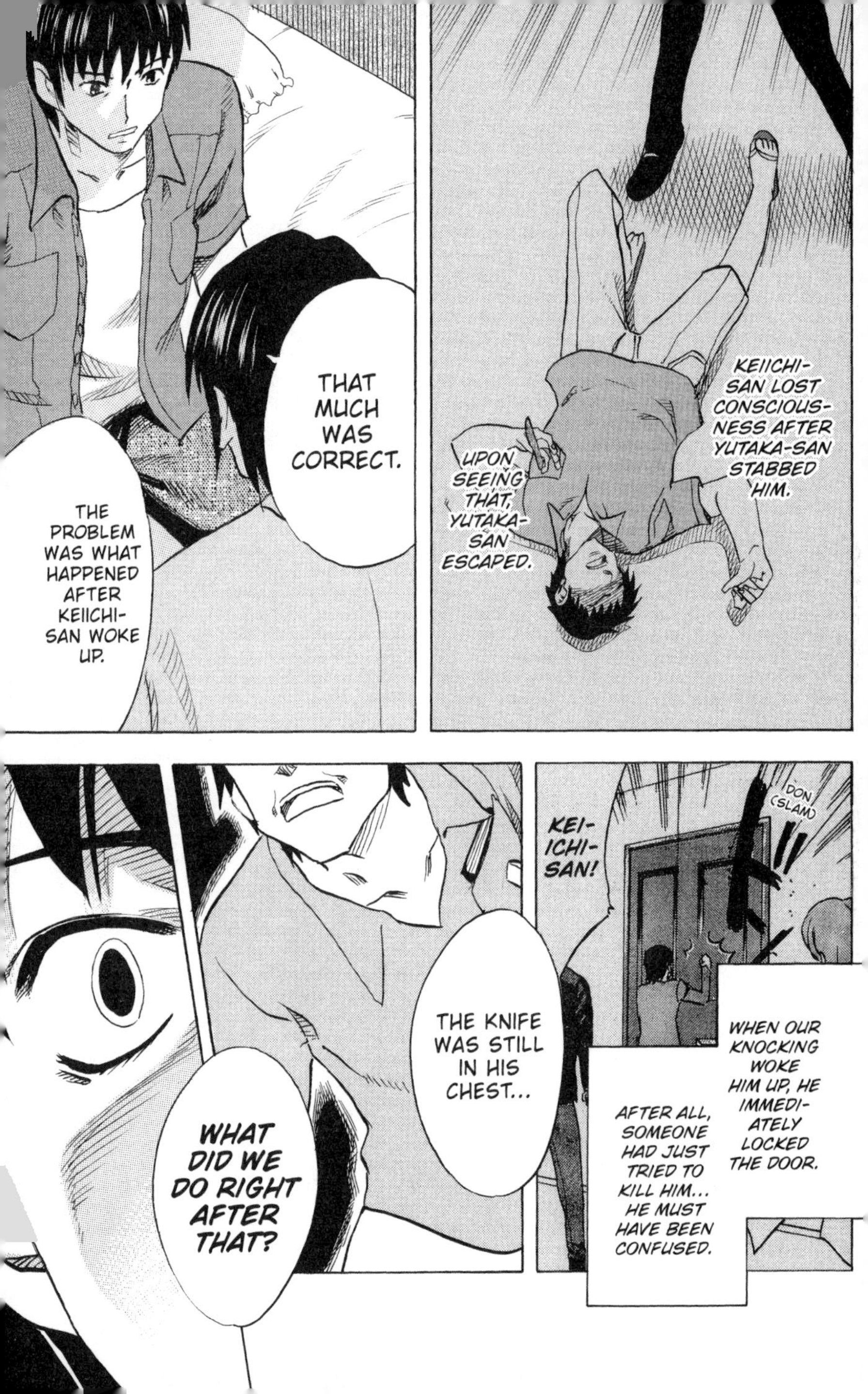
KEIICHI-SAN LOST CONSCIOUSNESS AFTER YUTAKA-SAN STABBED HIM.
UPON SEEING THAT, YUTAKA-SAN ESCAPED.
THAT MUCH WAS CORRECT.
THE PROBLEM WAS WHAT HAPPENED AFTER KEIICHI-SAN WOKE UP.
DON (SLAM)
KEI-ICHI-SAN!
WHEN OUR KNOCKING WOKE HIM UP, HE IMMEDIATELY LOCKED THE DOOR.
AFTER ALL, SOMEONE HAD JUST TRIED TO KILL HIM... HE MUST HAVE BEEN CONFUSED.
THE KNIFE WAS STILL IN HIS CHEST...
WHAT DID WE DO RIGHT AFTER THAT?

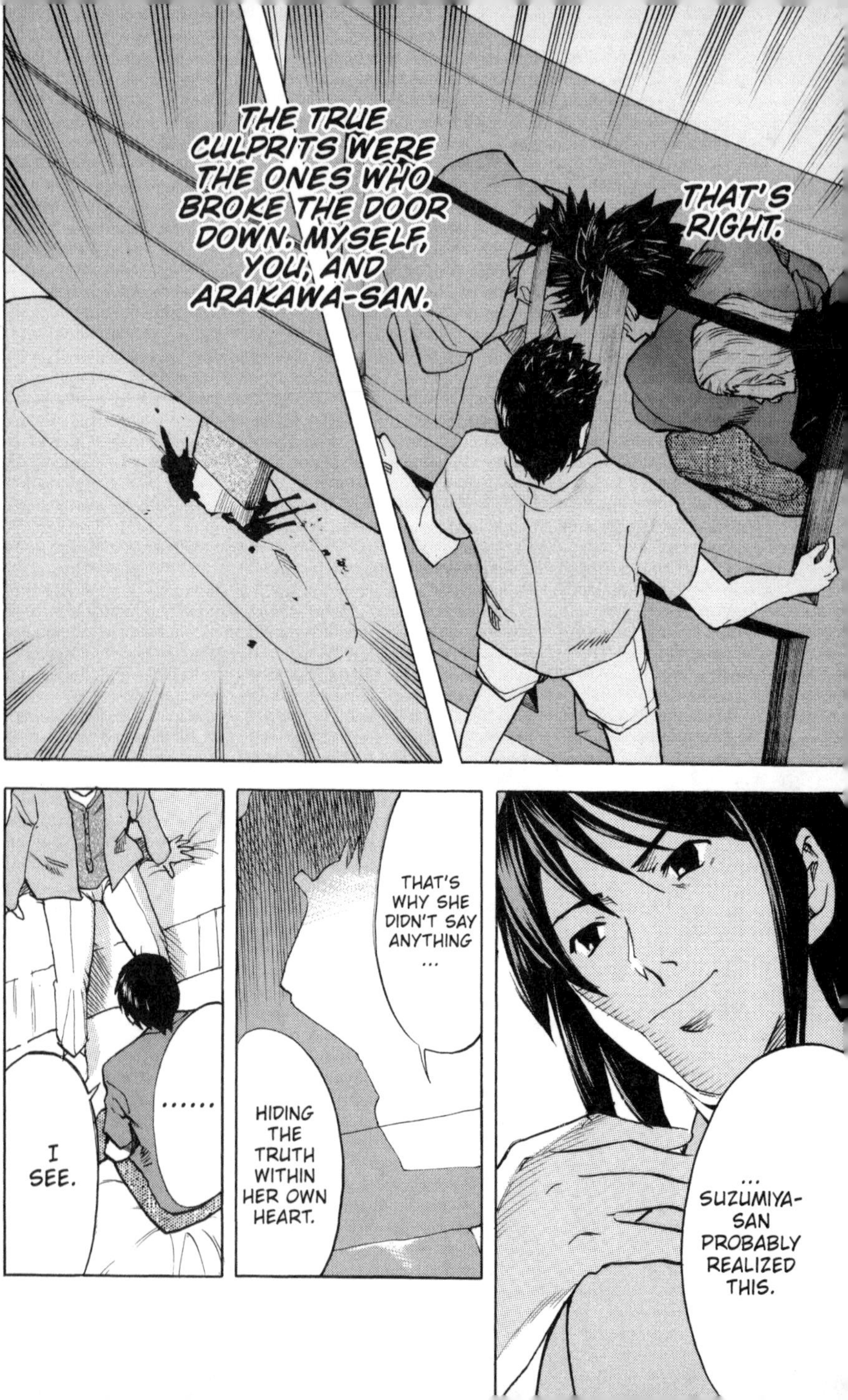
THAT'S RIGHT.
THE TRUE CULPRITS WERE THE ONES WHO BROKE THE DOOR DOWN. MYSELF, YOU, AND ARAKAWA-SAN.
... SUZUMIYA-SAN PROBABLY REALIZED THIS.
THAT'S WHY SHE DIDN'T SAY ANYTHING ...
HIDING THE TRUTH WITHIN HER OWN HEART.
......
I SEE.

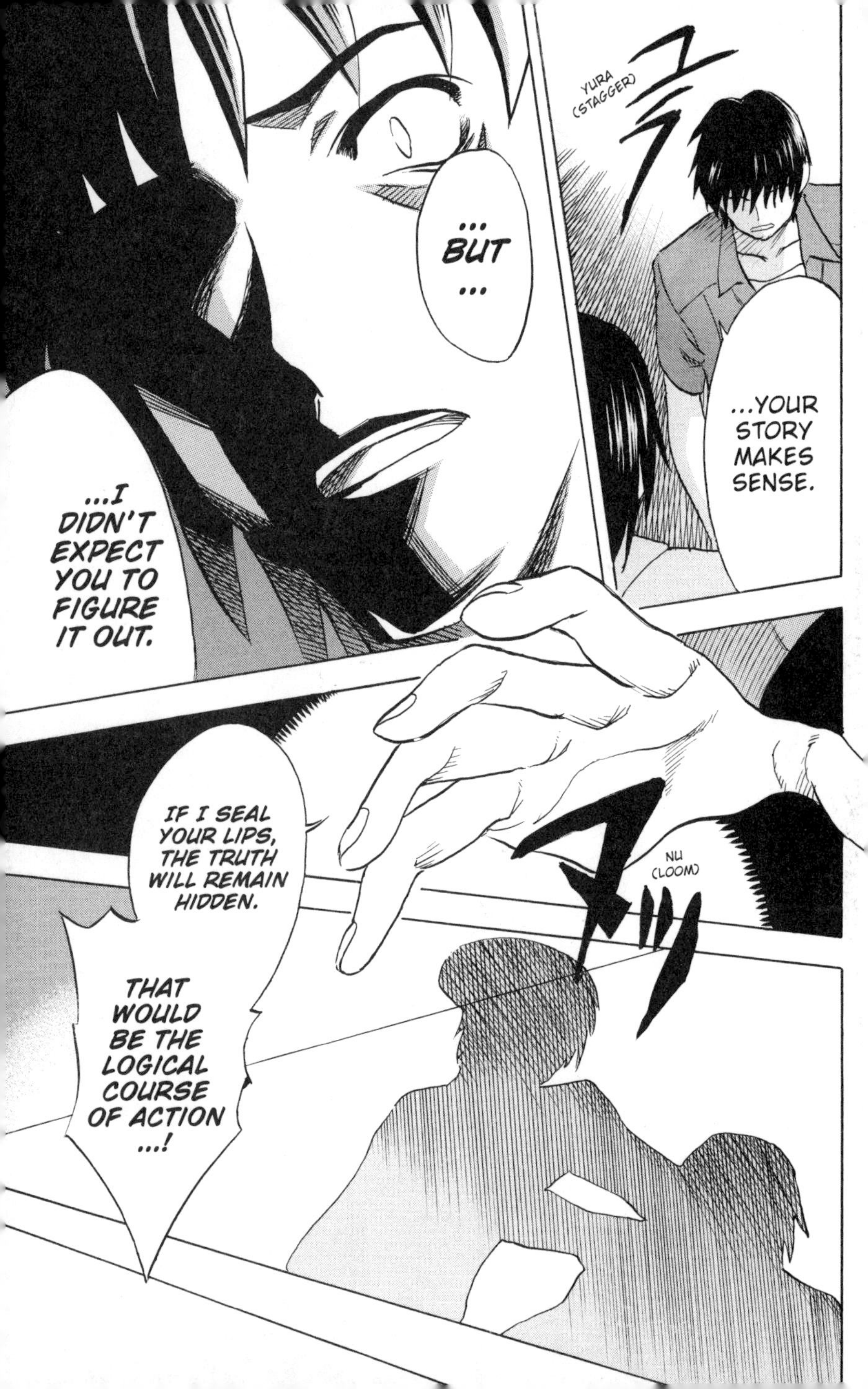
YURA (STAGGER)
...YOUR STORY MAKES SENSE.
...BUT...
...I DIDN'T EXPECT YOU TO FIGURE IT OUT.
NU (LOOM)
IF I SEAL YOUR LIPS, THE TRUTH WILL REMAIN HIDDEN.
THAT WOULD BE THE LOGICAL COURSE OF ACTION ...!

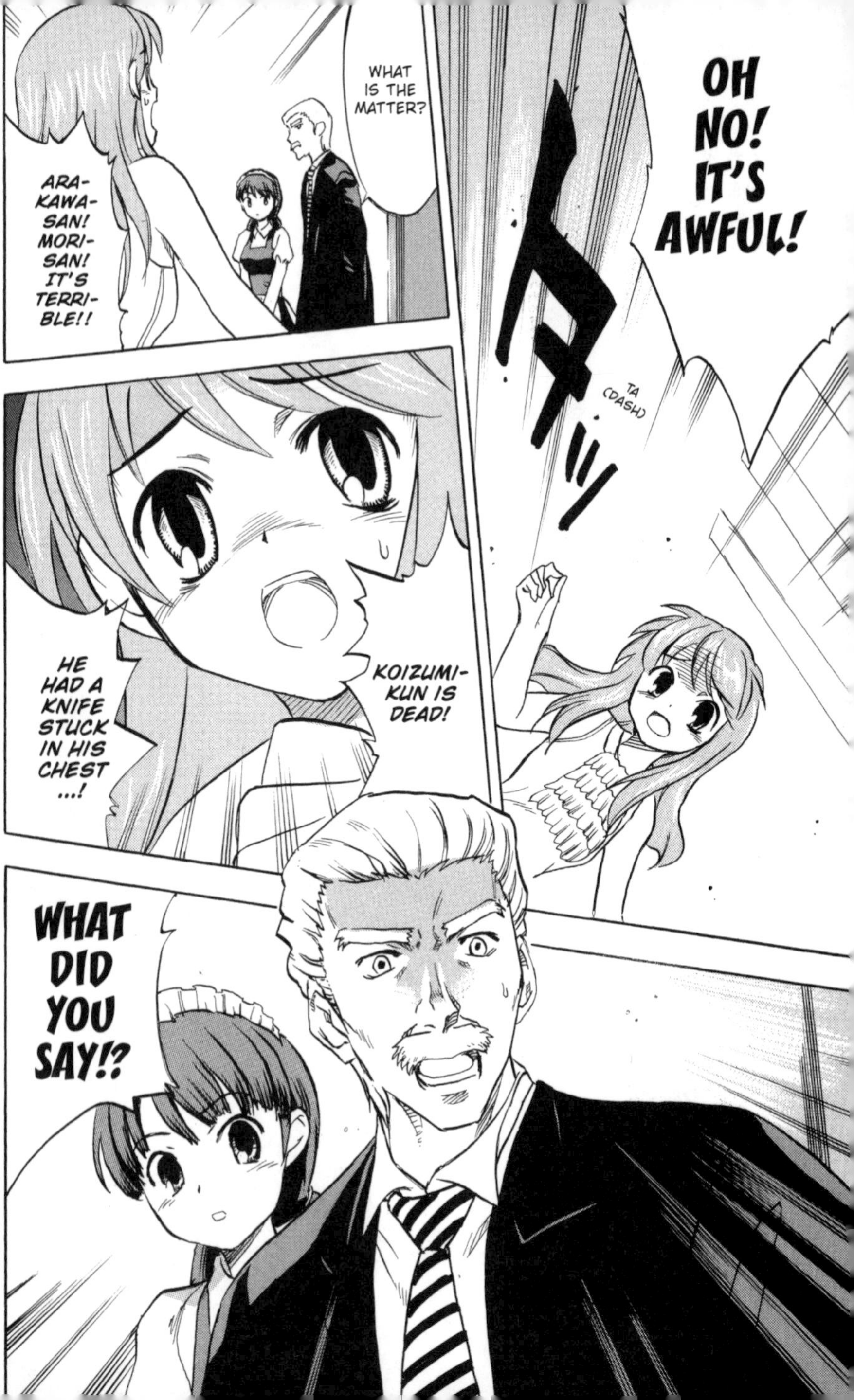

OH NO! IT'S AWFUL!
TA (DASH)
WHAT IS THE MATTER?
ARAKAWA-SAN! MORI-SAN! IT'S TERRIBLE!!
KOIZUMI-KUN IS DEAD!
HE HAD A KNIFE STUCK IN HIS CHEST ...!
WHAT DID YOU SAY!?

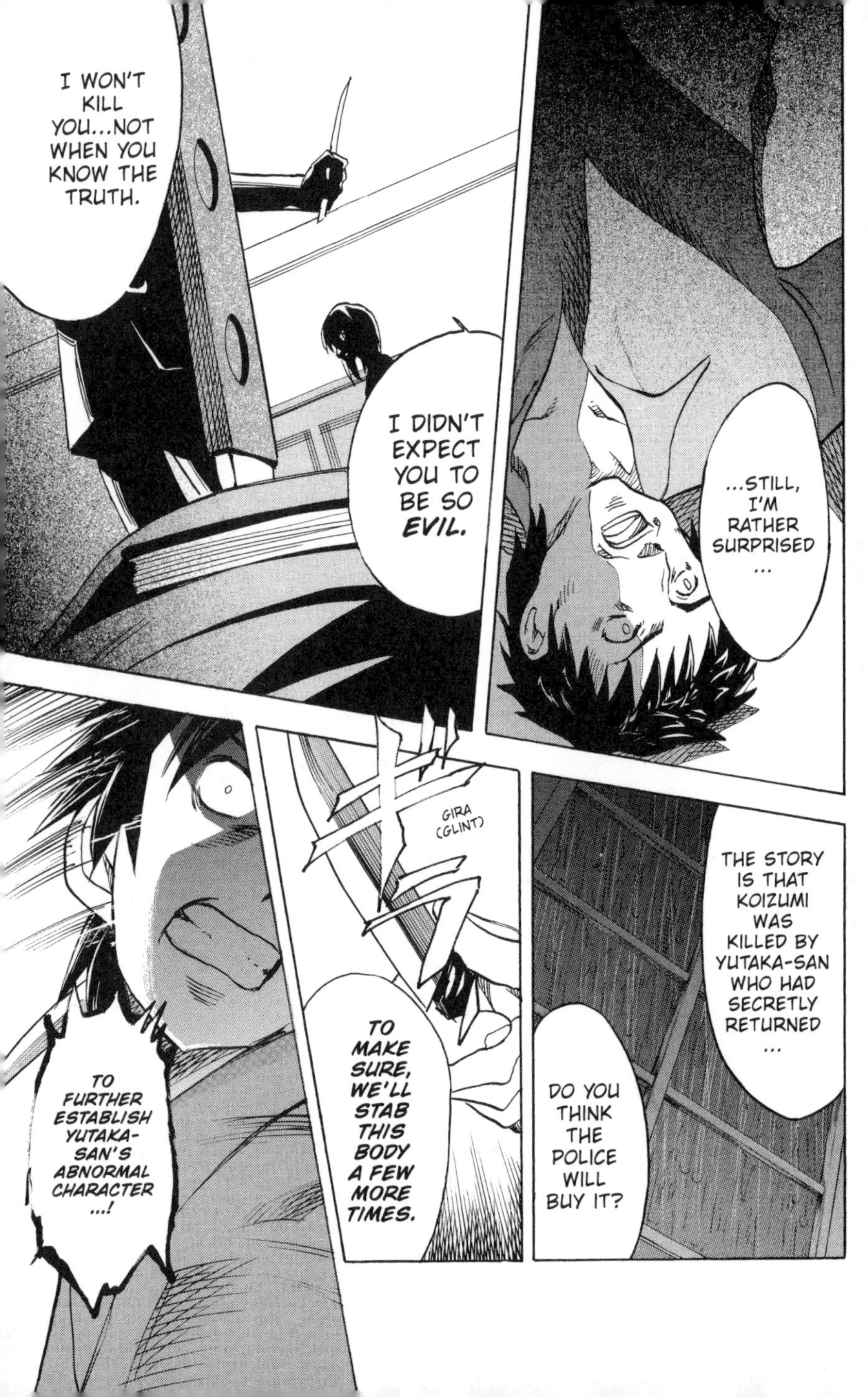
...STILL, I'M RATHER SURPRISED ...
I DIDN'T EXPECT YOU TO BE SO EVIL.
I WON'T KILL YOU...NOT WHEN YOU KNOW THE TRUTH.
THE STORY IS THAT KOIZUMI WAS KILLED BY YUTAKA-SAN WHO HAD SECRETLY RETURNED ...
DO YOU THINK THE POLICE WILL BUY IT?
GIRA (GLINT)
TO MAKE SURE, WE'LL STAB THIS BODY A FEW MORE TIMES.
TO FURTHER ESTABLISH YUTAKA-SAN'S ABNORMAL CHARACTER ...!

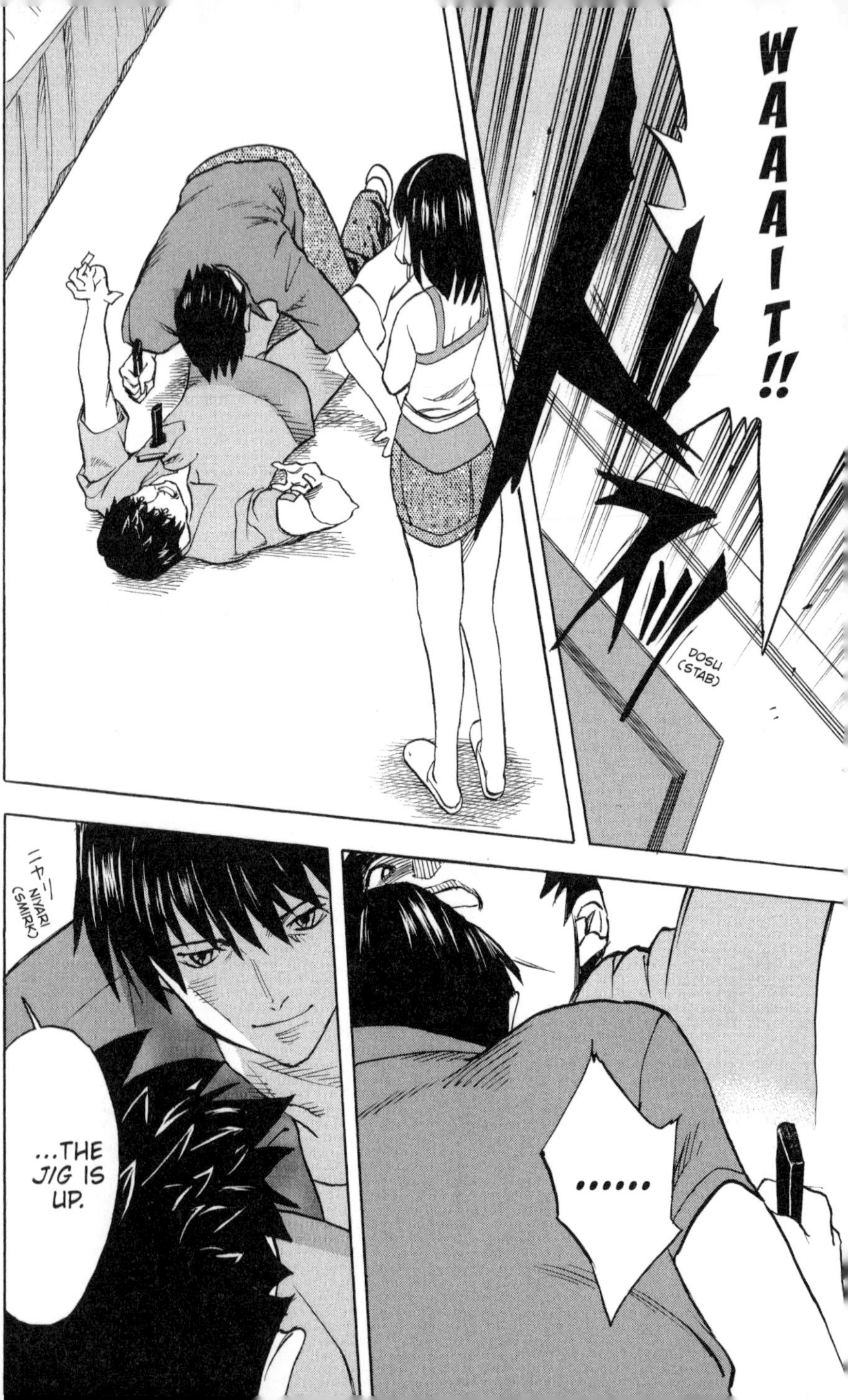
WAAAAIT!!
DOSU (STAB)
......
NIYARI (SMIRK)
...THE JIG IS UP.

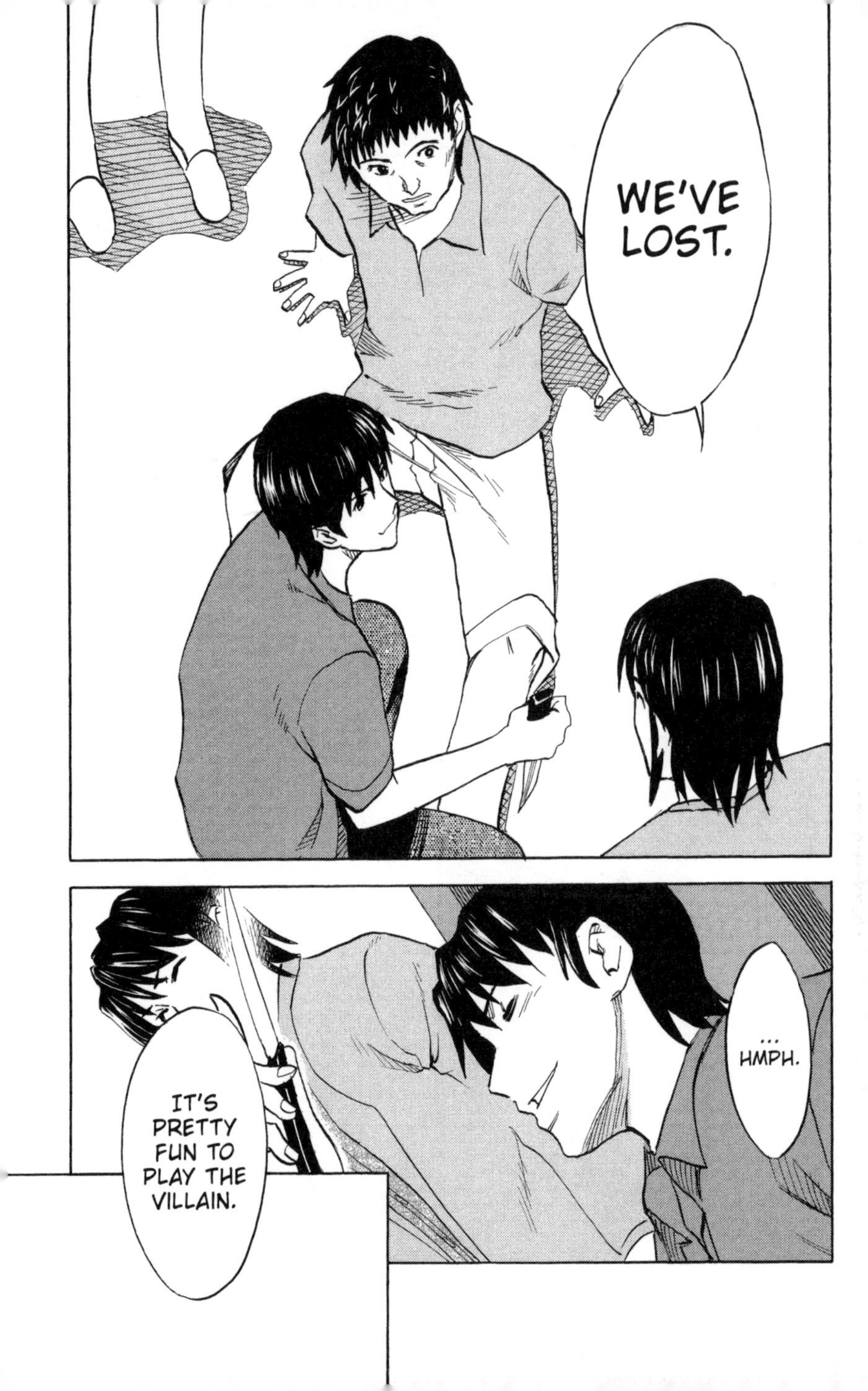
WE'VE LOST.
...HMPH.
IT'S PRETTY FUN TO PLAY THE VILLAIN.

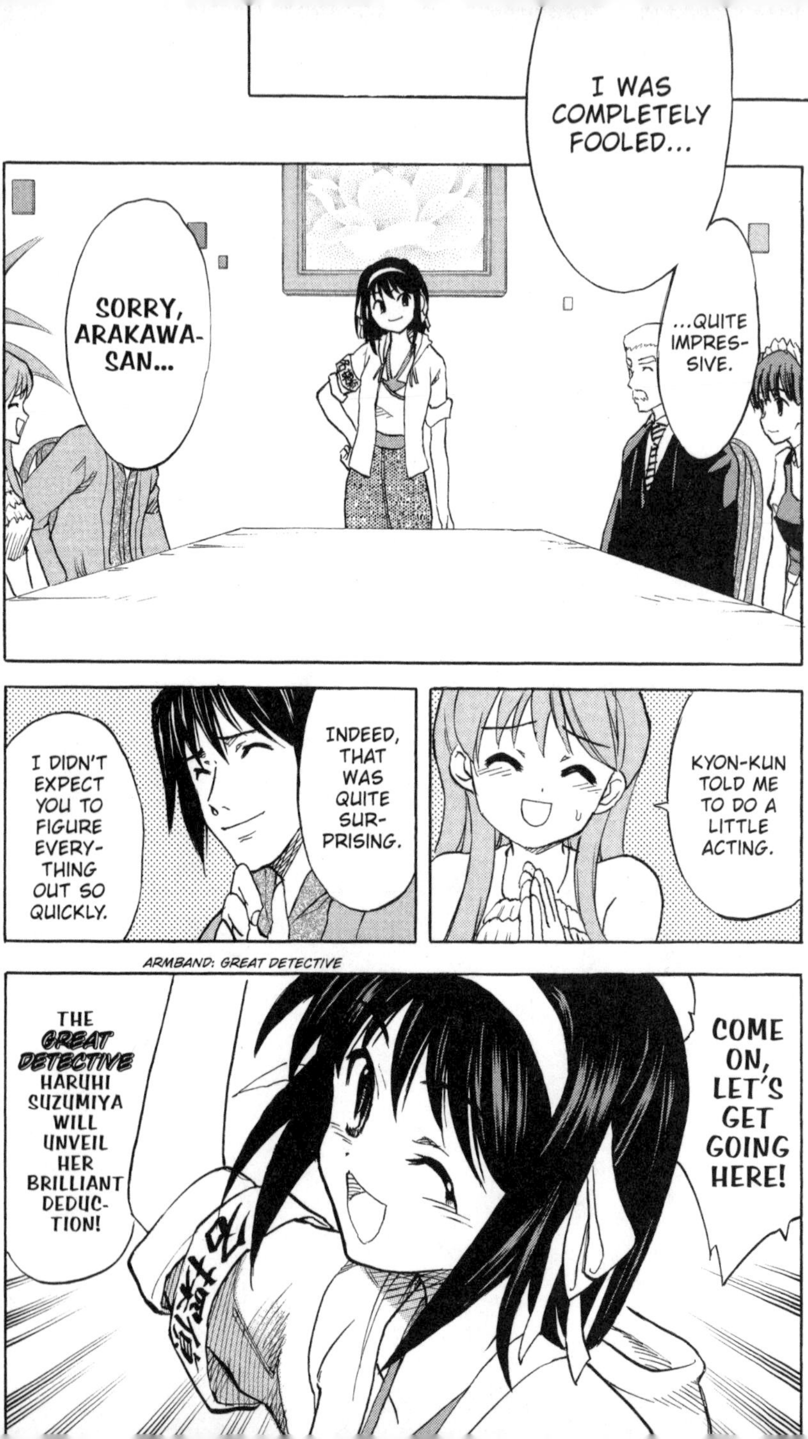
I WAS COMPLETELY FOOLED...
...QUITE IMPRESSIVE.
SORRY, ARAKAWA-SAN...
KYON-KUN TOLD ME TO DO A LITTLE ACTING.
INDEED, THAT WAS QUITE SURPRISING.
I DIDN'T EXPECT YOU TO FIGURE EVERYTHING OUT SO QUICKLY.
ARMBAND: GREAT DETECTIVE
COME ON, LET'S GET GOING HERE!
THE *GREAT DETECTIVE* HARUHI SUZUMIYA WILL UNVEIL HER BRILLIANT DEDUCTION!

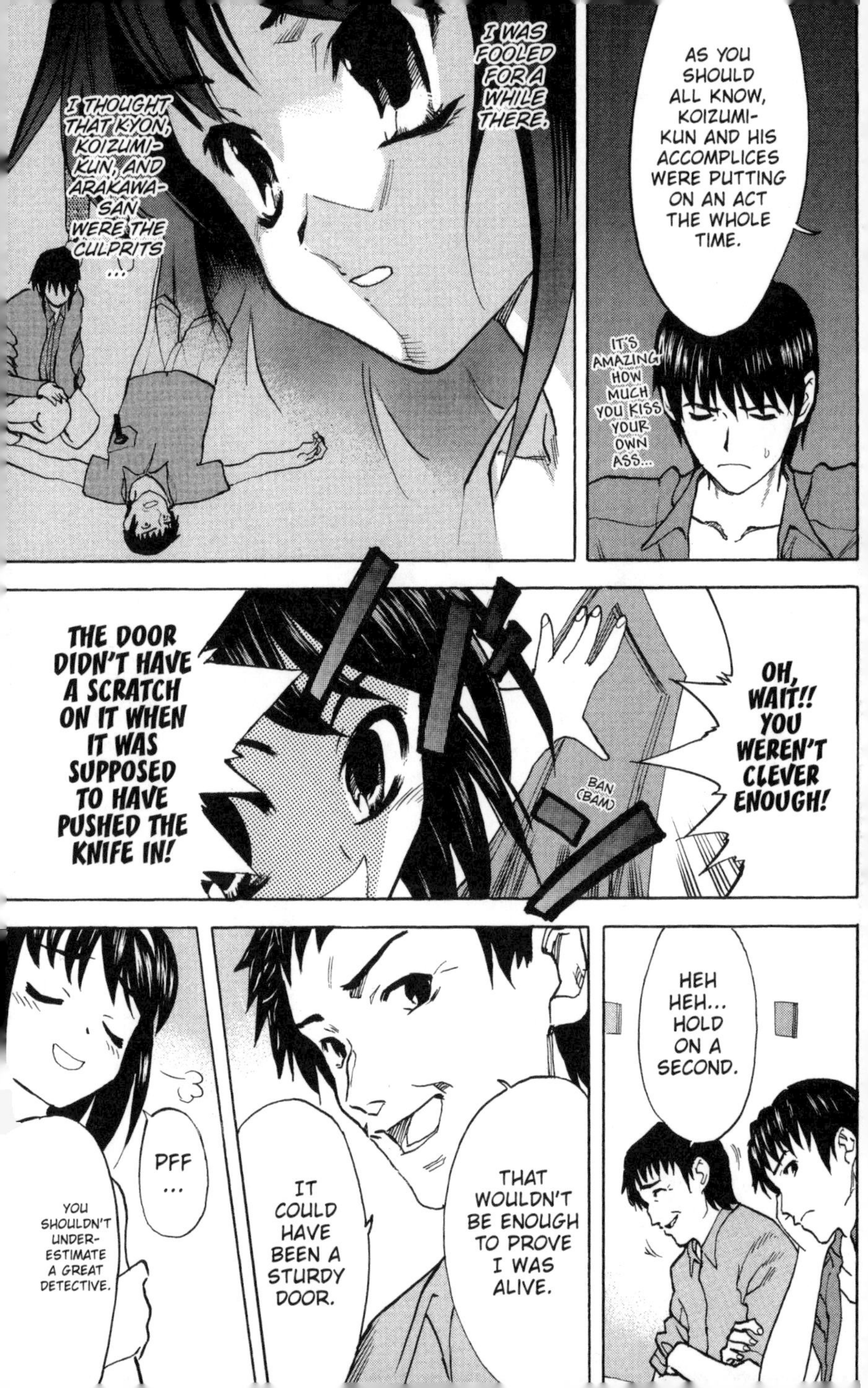
AS YOU SHOULD ALL KNOW, KOIZUMI-KUN AND HIS ACCOMPLICES WERE PUTTING ON AN ACT THE WHOLE TIME.
IT'S AMAZING HOW MUCH YOU KISS YOUR OWN ASS...
I WAS FOOLED FOR A WHILE THERE.
I THOUGHT THAT KYON, KOIZUMI-KUN, AND ARAKAWA-SAN WERE THE CULPRITS ...
OH, WAIT!! YOU WEREN'T CLEVER ENOUGH!
BAN (BAM)
THE DOOR DIDN'T HAVE A SCRATCH ON IT WHEN IT WAS SUPPOSED TO HAVE PUSHED THE KNIFE IN!
HEH HEH... HOLD ON A SECOND.
THAT WOULDN'T BE ENOUGH TO PROVE I WAS ALIVE.
IT COULD HAVE BEEN A STURDY DOOR.
PFF ...
YOU SHOULDN'T UNDER-ESTIMATE A GREAT DETECTIVE.

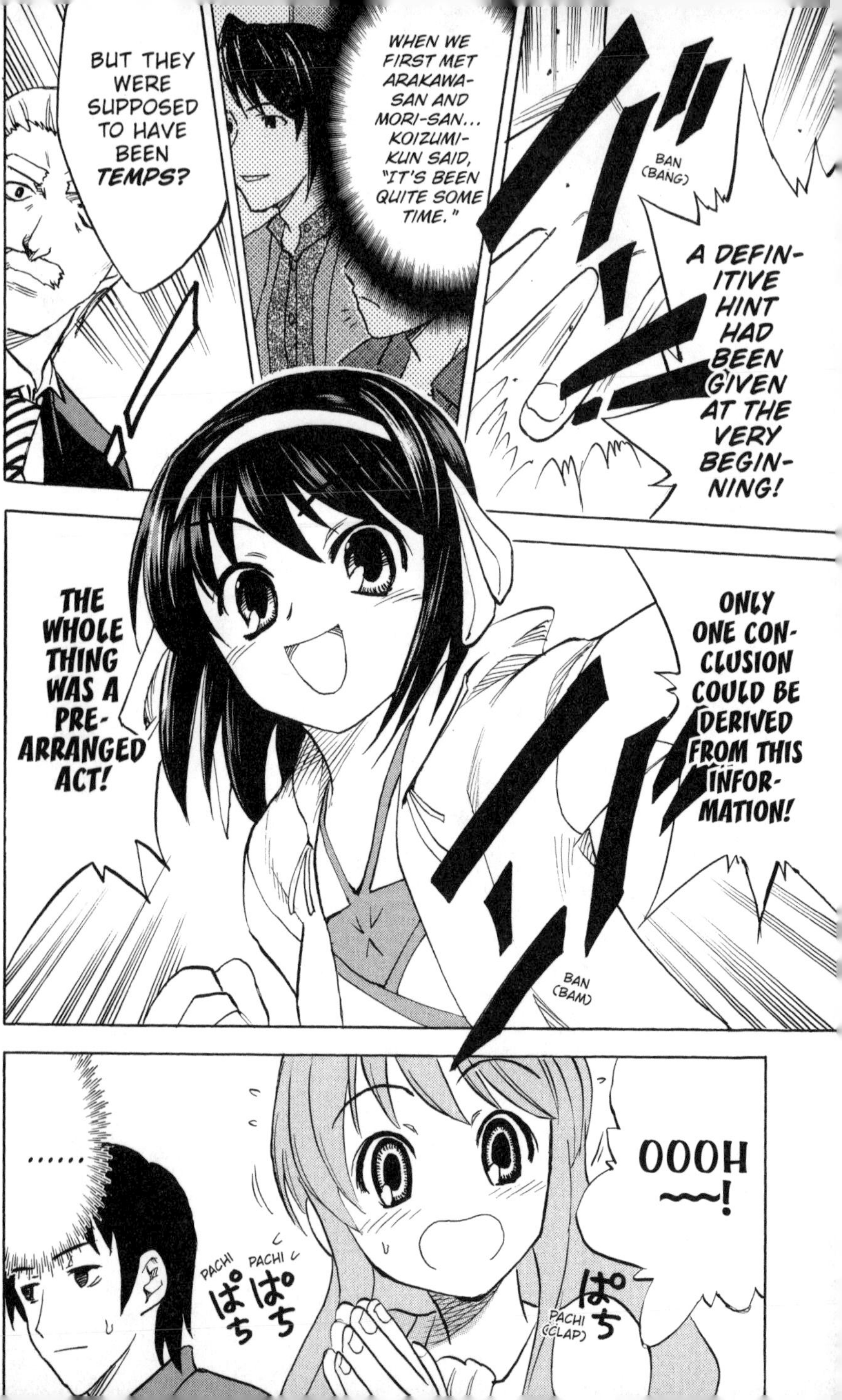
BAN (BANG)
A DEFINITIVE HINT HAD BEEN GIVEN AT THE VERY BEGINNING!
WHEN WE FIRST MET ARAKAWA-SAN AND MORI-SAN... KOIZUMI-KUN SAID, "IT'S BEEN QUITE SOME TIME."
BUT THEY WERE SUPPOSED TO HAVE BEEN TEMPS?
ONLY ONE CONCLUSION COULD BE DERIVED FROM THIS INFORMATION!
BAN (BAM)
THE WHOLE THING WAS A PRE-ARRANGED ACT!
OOOH~~~!
ぱち
PACHI (CLAP)
ぱち ぱち
PACHI PACHI
......

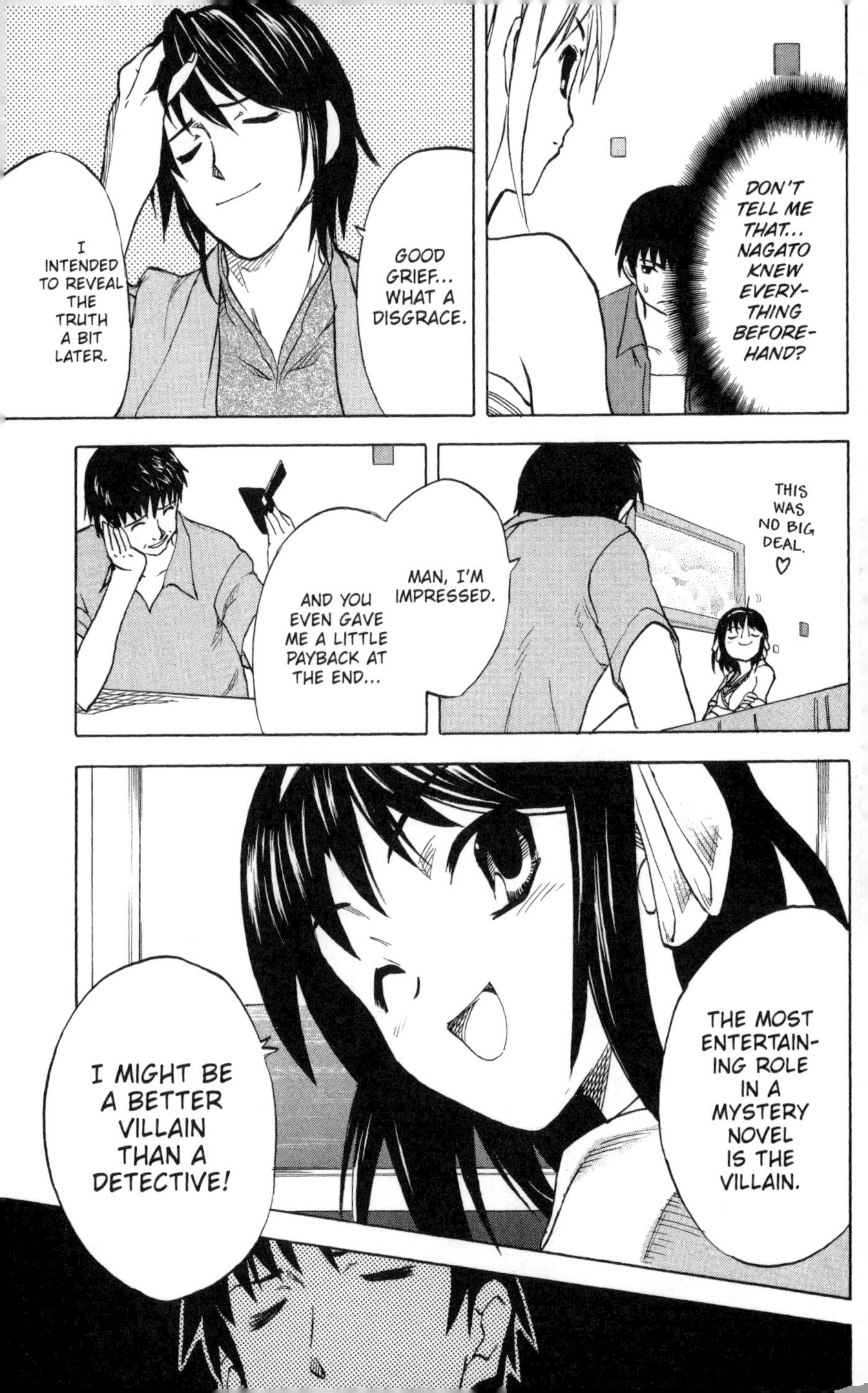
DON'T TELL ME THAT... NAGATO KNEW EVERYTHING BEFOREHAND?
GOOD GRIEF... WHAT A DISGRACE.
I INTENDED TO REVEAL THE TRUTH A BIT LATER.
THIS WAS NO BIG DEAL. ♡
MAN, I'M IMPRESSED.
AND YOU EVEN GAVE ME A LITTLE PAYBACK AT THE END...
THE MOST ENTERTAINING ROLE IN A MYSTERY NOVEL IS THE VILLAIN.
I MIGHT BE A BETTER VILLAIN THAN A DETECTIVE!

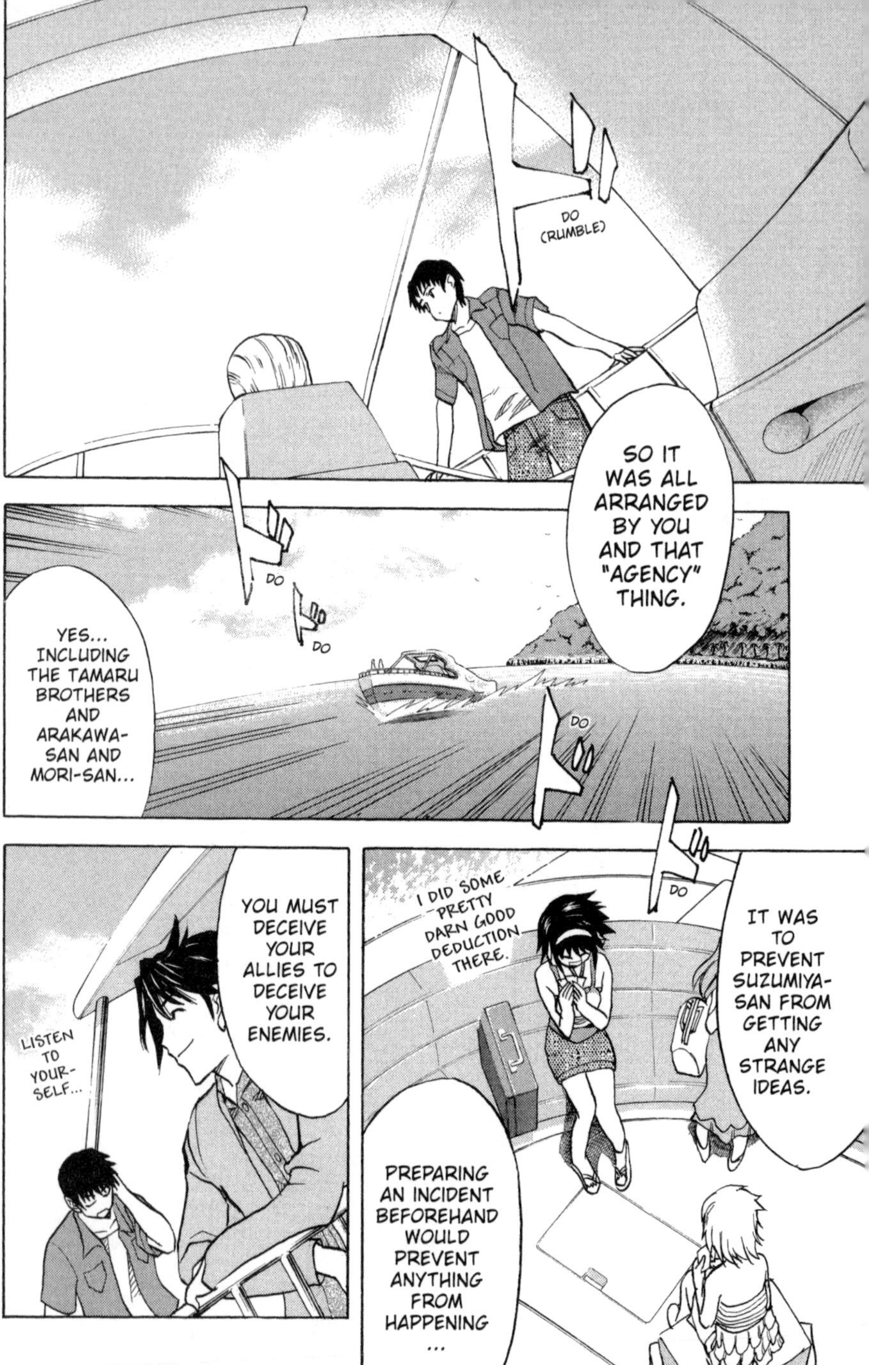
DO (RUMBLE)
SO IT WAS ALL ARRANGED BY YOU AND THAT "AGENCY" THING.
DO
DO
DO
YES... INCLUDING THE TAMARU BROTHERS AND ARAKAWA-SAN AND MORI-SAN...
DO
IT WAS TO PREVENT SUZUMIYA-SAN FROM GETTING ANY STRANGE IDEAS.
I DID SOME PRETTY DARN GOOD DEDUCTION THERE.
PREPARING AN INCIDENT BEFOREHAND WOULD PREVENT ANYTHING FROM HAPPENING...
YOU MUST DECEIVE YOUR ALLIES TO DECEIVE YOUR ENEMIES.
LISTEN TO YOUR-SELF...

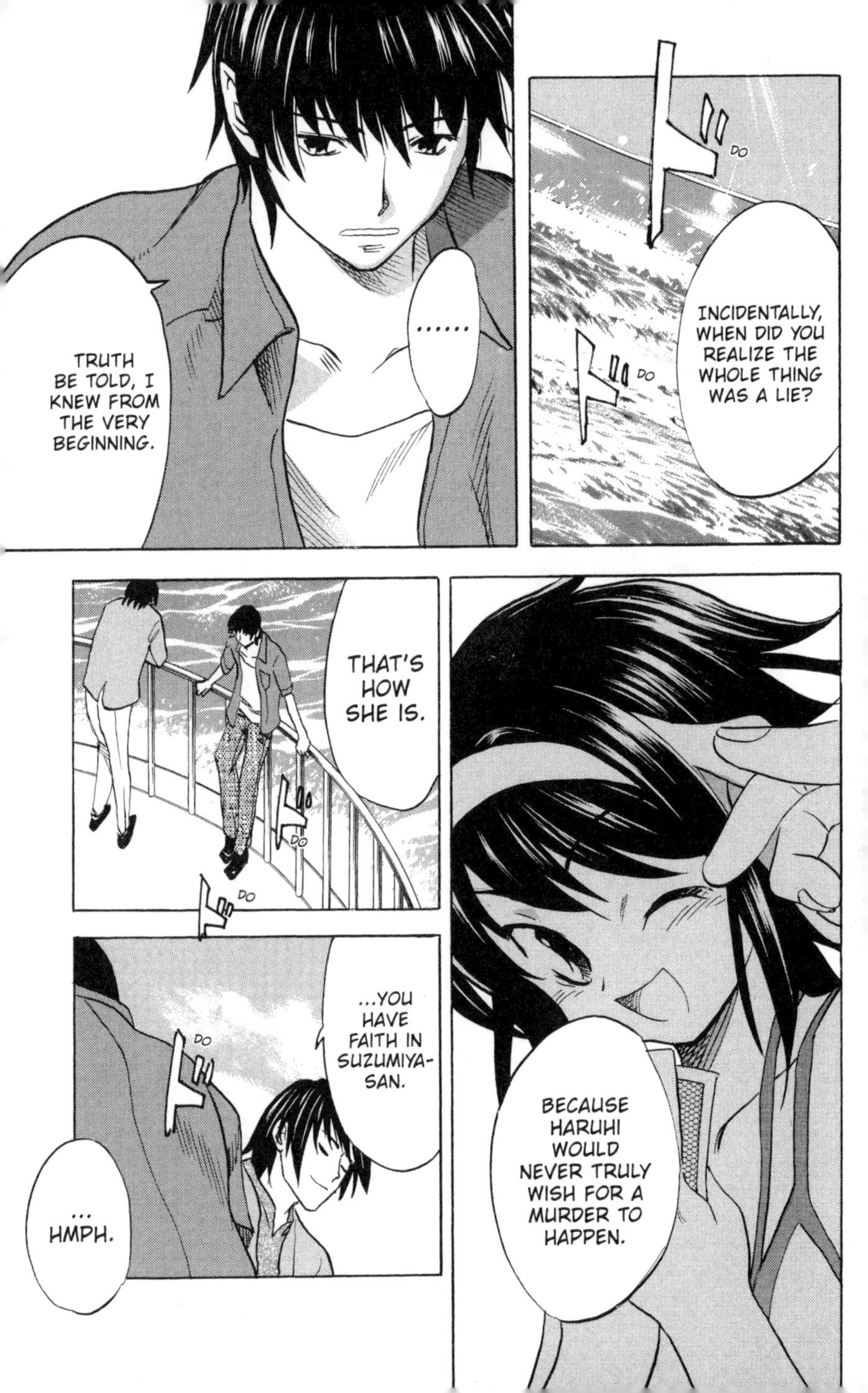
DO
DO
INCIDENTALLY, WHEN DID YOU REALIZE THE WHOLE THING WAS A LIE?
......
TRUTH BE TOLD, I KNEW FROM THE VERY BEGINNING.
BECAUSE HARUHI WOULD NEVER TRULY WISH FOR A MURDER TO HAPPEN.
THAT'S HOW SHE IS.
DO
DO
...YOU HAVE FAITH IN SUZUMIYA-SAN.
DO
... HMPH.

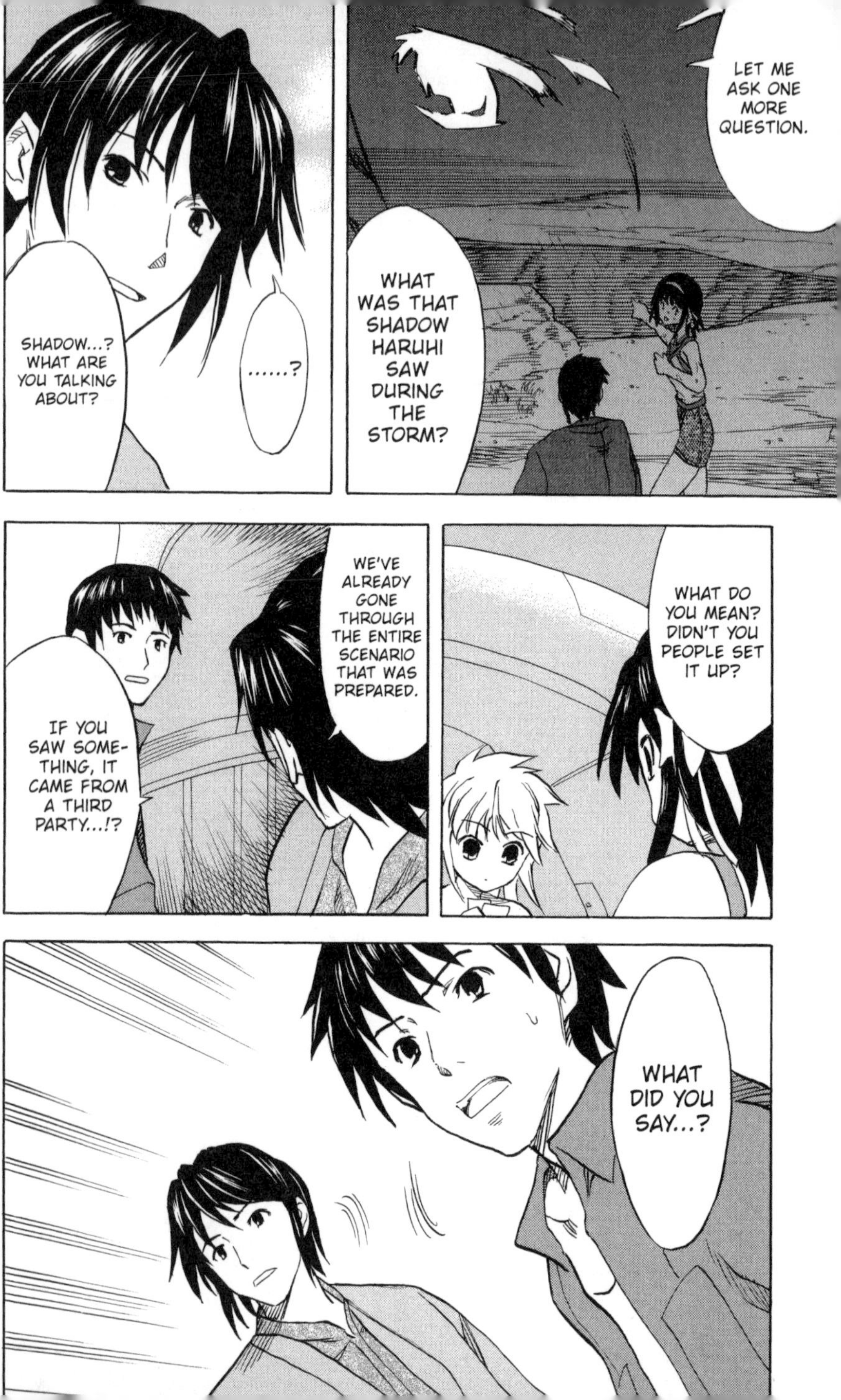
LET ME ASK ONE MORE QUESTION.
WHAT WAS THAT SHADOW HARUHI SAW DURING THE STORM?
......?
SHADOW...? WHAT ARE YOU TALKING ABOUT?
WHAT DO YOU MEAN? DIDN'T YOU PEOPLE SET IT UP?
WE'VE ALREADY GONE THROUGH THE ENTIRE SCENARIO THAT WAS PREPARED.
IF YOU SAW SOME-THING, IT CAME FROM A THIRD PARTY...!?
WHAT DID YOU SAY...?

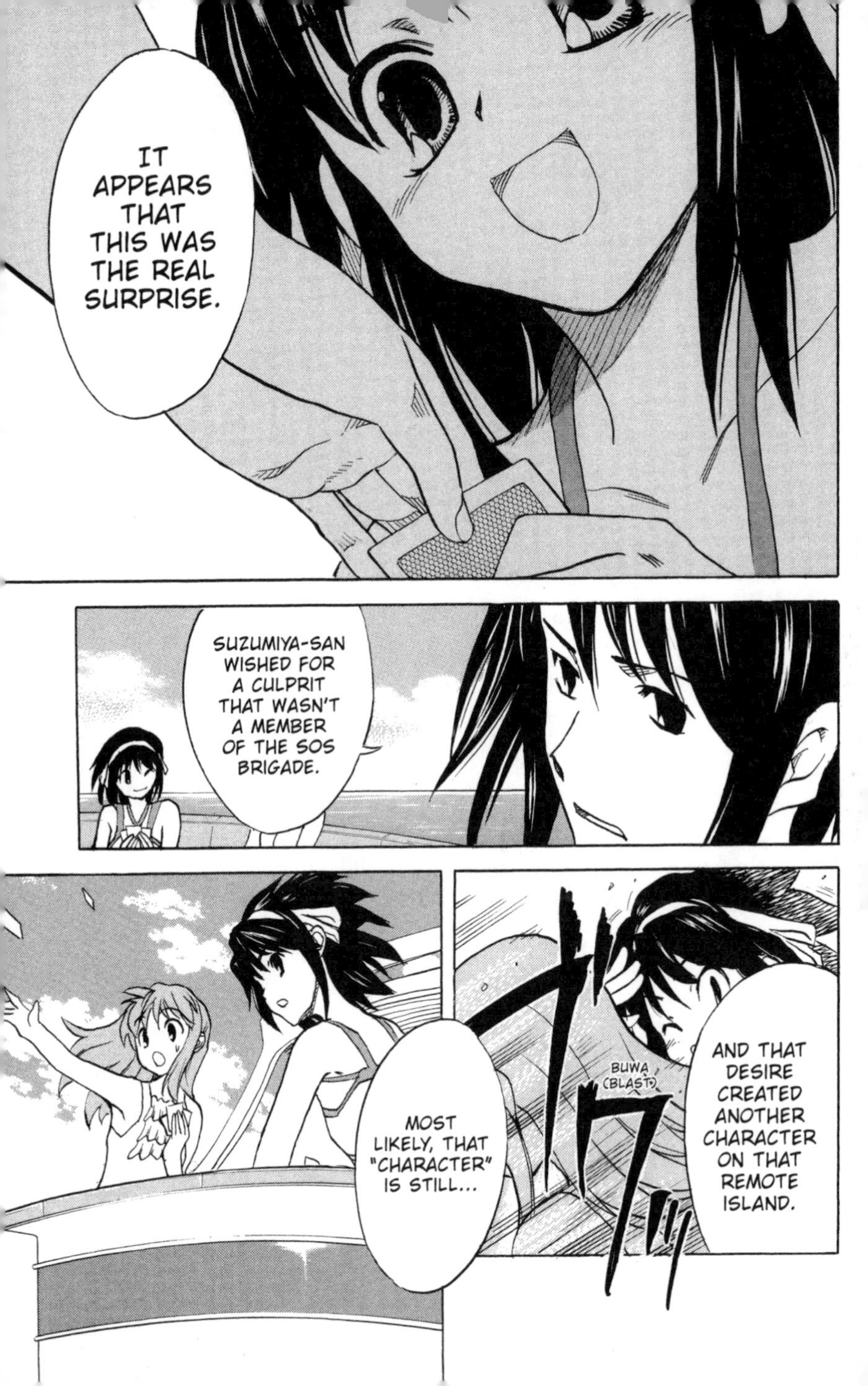
IT APPEARS THAT THIS WAS THE REAL SURPRISE.
SUZUMIYA-SAN WISHED FOR A CULPRIT THAT WASN'T A MEMBER OF THE SOS BRIGADE.
AND THAT DESIRE CREATED ANOTHER CHARACTER ON THAT REMOTE ISLAND.
BUWA (BLAST)
MOST LIKELY, THAT "CHARACTER" IS STILL...

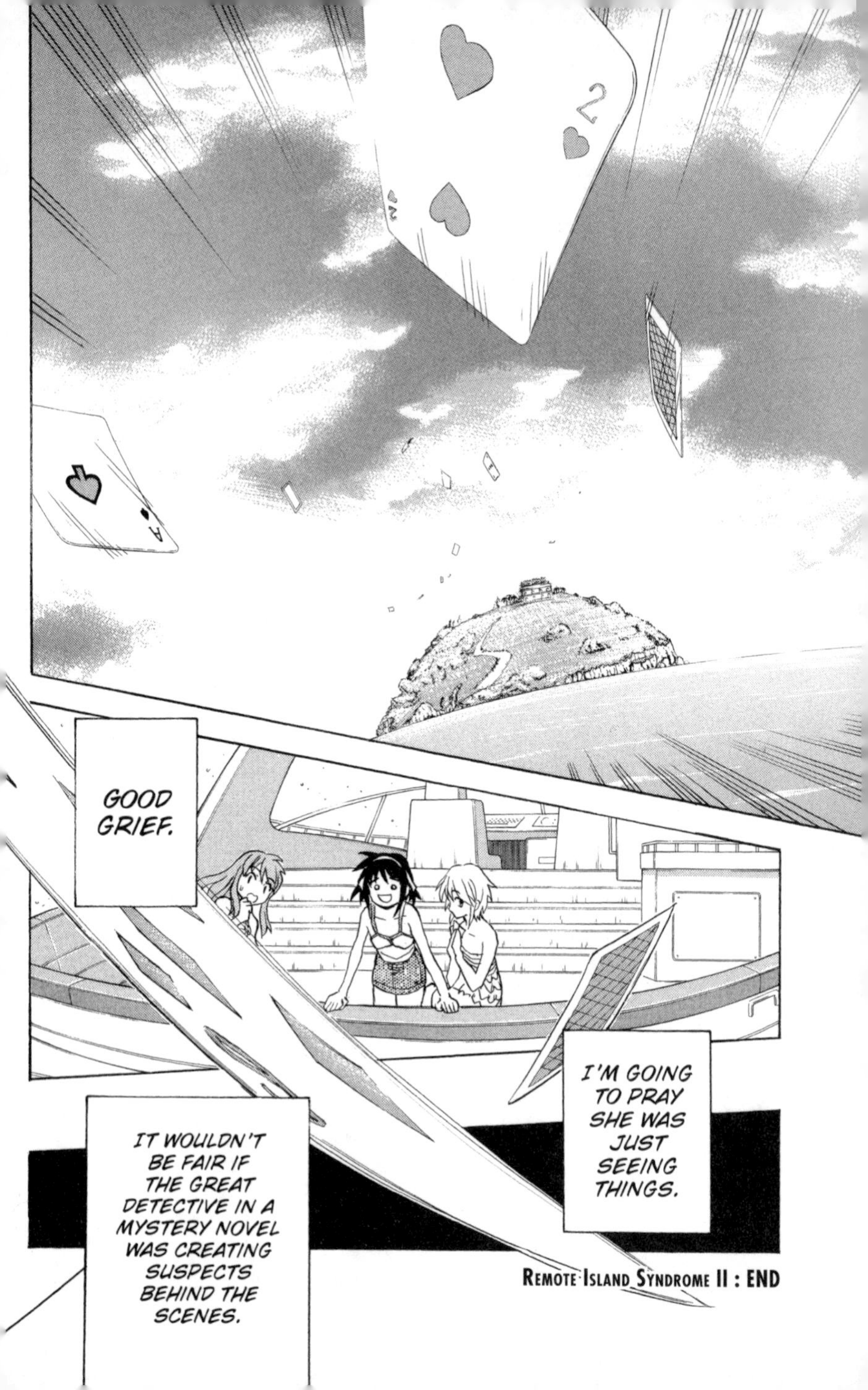
GOOD GRIEF.
I'M GOING TO PRAY SHE WAS JUST SEEING THINGS.
IT WOULDN'T BE FAIR IF THE GREAT DETECTIVE IN A MYSTERY NOVEL WAS CREATING SUSPECTS BEHIND THE SCENES.

REMOTE ISLAND SYNDROME II : END

TRANSLATION NOTES

Page 25
A *hikikomori* is an individual who has shut himself off from society for a period of six months or more, usually sequestering themselves at home and venturing outdoors only to obtain sustenance on occasion; a shut-in.

Page 27
Warabimochi is a summer confection of bracken starch and sweet toasted soybean flour.

Page 127
Tsuchinoko is a creature from Japanese legend that resembles a venomous snake.

TO BE CONTINUED

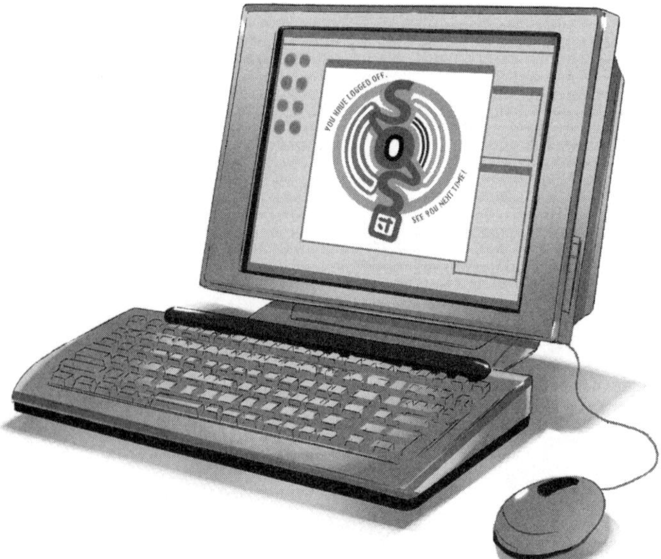
YOU HAVE LOGGED OFF.
SEE YOU NEXT TIME!

THE MELANCHOLY OF HARUHI SUZUMIYA

4

Original Story: Nagaru Tanigawa
Manga: Gaku Tsugano
Character Design: Noizi Ito

Translation: Chris Pai for MX Media LLC
Lettering: Alexis Eckerman

SUZUMIYA HARUHI NO YUUTSU Volume 4 © Nagaru TANIGAWA • Noizi ITO 2007 © Gaku TSUGANO 2007. First published in Japan in 2007 by KADOKAWA SHOTEN PUBLISHING CO., LTD., Tokyo. English translation rights arranged with KADOKAWA SHOTEN PUBLISHING CO., LTD., Tokyo through TUTTLE-MORI AGENCY, INC., Tokyo.

English translation © 2009 by Hachette Book Group, Inc.

Yen Press
Hachette Book Group
237 Park Avenue, New York, NY 10017

Visit our websites at www.HachetteBookGroup.com and www.YenPress.com.

Yen Press is an imprint of Hachette Book Group, Inc. The Yen Press name and logo are trademarks of Hachette Book Group, Inc.

First Yen Press Edition: October 2009

ISBN: 978-0-7595-2947-2

10 9 8 7 6 5 4 3 2 1

BVG

Printed in the United States of America